INTERNATIONAL DEVELOPMENT IN FOCUS

Strategic Investment Funds

Establishment and Operations

SHANTHI DIVAKARAN, HÅVARD HALLAND, GIANNI LORENZATO,
PAUL ROSE, AND SEBASTIAN SARMIENTO-SAHER

Contents

Acknowledgments   *xi*
About the Authors   *xv*
Executive Summary   *xvii*
Abbreviations   *xxii*

CHAPTER 1   **Introduction**   **1**

Context   1
Objective and methodology   5
Structure   8
Notes   9
References   10

PART 1   **DESIGN OF STRATEGIC INVESTMENT FUNDS**

CHAPTER 2   **Overview of Strategic Investment Funds**   **15**

Introduction   15
What is a strategic investment fund?   15
SIF ownership and management models   16
SIF operational models   17
Double bottom line mandate   19
Rationale for SIFs   22
Concessionality for a SIF   29
Macrofiscal implications of a SIF   31
Limitations of a SIF   33
Challenges to establishing a SIF   34
Issues to consider before establishing a SIF   36
Preparatory studies to establish a SIF   37
Key takeaways   39
Notes   40
References   42

CHAPTER 3   **Legal Framework**   **45**

Introduction   45
Legal framework for SIFs   47
Private agreements in setting up a SIF   64
Applicability of other domestic, supranational, and
     international laws to SIFs   66
Key takeaways   72

Notes   73
References   75

CHAPTER 4   **Governance   79**

Introduction   79
The SIF's governance challenges   80
Key decision-making bodies and their functions   82
Key takeaways   109
Notes   109
References   112

CHAPTER 5   **Investment and Risk Management   115**

Introduction   115
Investment management framework: Key concepts   115
Key actors in the investment management framework   118
Components of the investment policy   119
Components of the investment strategy   123
Risk management framework: Key concepts   131
Components of the risk management framework
    and key actors   134
Key takeaways   137
Notes   138
References   141

CHAPTER 6   **Investment Process   143**

Introduction   143
Investment origination   145
Investment evaluation   148
Investment execution   150
Investment ownership and supervision   151
Investment exit   153
Key takeaways   155
Notes   155
References   156

CHAPTER 7   **Transparency and Disclosure   159**

Introduction   159
Global transparency and disclosure requirements   160
Legal and regulatory context   166
Target audience   167
Core components of disclosure framework and
    mechanisms of disclosure   169
Unique features of the transparency and disclosure
    framework for SIFs   172
Key takeaways   174
Notes   175
References   176

PART 2   **CASE STUDIES**

CHAPTER 8   **Case Study—Asia Climate Partners: Targeting
              Demonstration Effects for Foreign Investors   181**

Background and mission   181
Fund structure   183
Mandate for investment   184
Investment strategy   185
Portfolio and track record   185
Additionality and multiplier considerations   186

Governance   187
Staffing and recruitment   188
Economic impact and ESG reporting   189
Financial disclosure   190
Notes   190
Reference   190

CHAPTER 9   **Case Study—FONSIS: Pursuing a Triple Bottom Line of Economic Impact, Financial Returns, and Private Capital Mobilization   191**

Background and mission   191
Fund structure   193
Mandate for investment   195
Investment strategy   195
Investment process   198
Portfolio and track record   199
Additionality and multiplier considerations   201
Governance   202
Staffing and recruitment   205
Economic impact and ESG reporting   205
Financial disclosure and risk policies   206
Notes   206
References   206

CHAPTER 10   **Case Study—The Ireland Strategic Investment Fund: A Strategic Investor in a High-Performance Economy   207**

Background and mission   207
Fund structure   209
Mandate for investment   209
Investment strategy   213
Portfolio and track record   214
Additionality and multiplier considerations   215
Governance   217
Staffing and recruitment   219
Economic impact and ESG reporting   220
Financial disclosure and risk policies   221
Notes   223
References   224

CHAPTER 11   **Case Study—The Marguerite Fund: An Infrastructure Fund Sponsored by Development Banks   225**

Background and mission   225
Mandate for investment   229
Investment strategy   230
Portfolio and track record   232
Additionality and multiplier considerations   233
Governance   236
Staffing and recruitment   238
Economic impact and ESG reporting   239
Financial disclosure   239
Notes   240
References   240

CHAPTER 12   **Case Study—National Investment and Infrastructure Fund: A Collaborative Model to Mobilize Foreign Investment   241**

Background and mission   241
Fund structure   242
Investment strategy   245
Investment process   248

Additionality and multiplier considerations   248
Governance   249
Staffing and recruitment   252
Economic impact and ESG reporting   252
Financial disclosure   253
Notes   253
References   253

CHAPTER 13 **Case Study—Nigeria Sovereign Investment
Authority-Nigeria Infrastructure Fund   255**

Background and mission   255
Legal structure   256
Mandate for investment   257
Investment strategy   258
Portfolio and track record   259
Additionality and multiplier considerations   262
Governance   262
Staffing and recruitment   266
Economic impact and ESG reporting   267
Financial disclosure and risk policies   267
Notes   269
References   270

Appendix A **Thematic Reviews   271**

Appendix B **Illustrative List of Global Strategic Investment Funds   284**

Appendix C **List of Interviewees   302**

Bibliography   306

Boxes

2.1   ISIF's approach to managing the double bottom line requirement   22
2.2   Palestine Investment Fund   26
2.3   Concessional finance and strategic investment funds   29
2.4   Santiago Principles and macroeconomic implications of SWFs   32
2.5   Complex authorizing environment for China government guidance funds   35
2.6   Preliminary study for the Green Investment Bank, United Kingdom   38
2.7   Key features of a feasibility study to establish a SIF   39
3.1   Santiago Principles: Key legal principles for SWFs   46
3.2   Establishment laws that rely on commercial legislation: The case of FONSIS   50
3.3   Specifying the transfer of state assets into a SIF with the SIF law   52
3.4   Core features of the GP/LP structure   61
3.5   Most popular domiciles   63
3.6   The significance of arbitration clauses for SIFs   67
3.7   National security legislation: The US example   71
3.8   Factors determining selection of legal counsel   72
4.1   Santiago Principles: Key governance principles for SWFs   80
4.2   Governing council: The example of the Nigeria Sovereign Investment Authority   85
4.3   Definition of an independent board member   90
4.4   Safeguards for government representatives on SIF boards   91
4.5   Limitations to aligning financial interests in a limited partnership model or equivalent structure   98
4.6   Staffing the NIIF   102
4.7   Recruiting an external manager for a SIF: PINAI   103
4.8   The four Ps of external manager due diligence   106

5.1   Investment policy–related guidance within the Santiago Principles   116
5.2   Investment strategy: Snapshot on defining investment scope for infrastructure SIFs   124
5.3   Definitions of capital instruments investible by strategic investment funds   127
5.4   Investor protection provisions in shareholder agreements   128
5.5   EU AIFMD key requirements on risk management   133
5.6   Santiago Principles: Key risk principles for SWFs   133
6.1   Formalizing the process for investment proposals by the public sponsor: The NSIA-NIF example   146
6.2   FONSIS: Originating investment opportunities as a project developer   147
6.3   Africa50's multifaceted investment origination strategy   148
6.4   ISIF's adherence to double bottom line mandate through investment evaluation process   150
6.5   Commercial terms to be negotiated in transaction documents   151
6.6   Exercising active ownership   152
6.7   Investment exit: The case of Marguerite   154
7.1   Santiago Principles: Key transparency and accountability principles for SWFs   161
7.2   Transparency requirements of the European Union's Directive on Alternative Investment Fund Managers   163
7.3   Invest Europe Handbook of Professional Standards 2018: Investor reporting guidelines   164
7.4   Truman Scoreboard for SWFs (Transparency and Accountability) and Linaburg-Maduell Transparency Index for SWFs   165
7.5   Legally required reporting obligations of the Ireland Strategic Investment Fund   167
7.6   Core components of disclosure for a strategic investment fund   170
7.7   ISIF approach to monitoring and reporting on economic impact   173
9.1   FONSIS's solar investments   197
11.1   Key features of the Luxembourg SCSp   238
A.1   Key components of the AIMM score   278

Figures

ES.1   Establishment of national-level strategic investment funds   xviii
1.1   Establishment of national-level strategic investment funds   2
B3.4.1 Commonly used private equity fund organizational model: The GP/LP structure   61
6.1   Phases of the SIF's investment process   144
6.2   NSIA-NIF investment evaluation process and responsibilities   149
8.1   Breakdown of ACP's committed capital, by source   182
8.2   ACP's structure   183
9.1   Investment decision process, FONSIS   198
9.2   Investments approved by FONSIS since inception in 2013   199
9.3   Portfolio breakdown by sector, FONSIS   200
9.4   FONSIS organizational structure   204
10.1   Structure of NTMA and ISIF   210
10.2   ISIF's capital committed to Irish investments by sector, as of December 31, 2018   212
10.3   Breakdown of ISIF's Irish Portfolio commitments as of December 31, 2018   216
10.4   ISIF investment decision process   219
11.1   Simplified Marguerite I structure at closing   227
11.2   Simplified Marguerite II structure   228
11.3   Simplified Marguerite Pantheon structure   228
12.1   NIIF structure   242
12.2   NIIF's Master Fund structure   246
12.3   NIIF's governance structure   250
13.1   NIF investment decision responsibilities   265

13.2   NIF investment process   265
BA.1.1   AIMM rating methodology   278

Tables

1.1   Classification of case study SIFs   7
2.1   Ownership and management models for select SIFs   17
2.2   Management model for SIFs   17
2.3   Operating models of SIFs   18
2.4   SIF mandates, examples from case studies   20
2.5   Managing the DBL   21
2.6   The additional value of SIFs: Case study examples   24
2.7   Illustrative list of strategic alliances between global SIFs and SWFs   27
2.8   Estimated multiplier effect of SIFs   28
2.9   Mechanisms for embedding financial incentives for SIF co-investors and managers   30
3.1   SIF-specific law and legal structure for a variety of public capital SIFs   47
3.2   Common features of primary SIF legislation: Foundational elements   53
3.3   Common features of primary SIF legislation: Operational elements   55
3.4   SIFs formed entirely under commercial law   58
3.5   Examples of legal structures used by global SIFs   60
3.6   Legal structure and domicile for a variety of SIFs   62
3.7   Factors affecting the choice of legal structure and domicile   65
3.8   Commonly used fund documents for SIFs set up under private equity norms   66
B3.6.1   Popular arbitral seats and institutions   67
3.9   Other laws affecting SIF cross-border activities   70
4.1   Ownership structures for public capital and mixed capital SIFs   84
4.2   Public sponsor ownership functions in a SIF   87
4.3   Board composition of select case study SIFs   92
4.4   SIF board functions   94
4.5   Indicative RFP content for external manager selection   105
4.6   Indicative timeline for external manager selection   106
4.7   Typical terms of a limited partnership agreement   107
5.1   Key elements of a SIF's investment policy and strategy   123
5.2   Majority vs. minority stakes as targeted by case study SIFs   127
7.1   Financial reporting standards of select SIFs   171
B7.7.1   Comprehensive sample of metrics disclosed in ISIF's economic impact report   173
8.1   ACP's target sectors and subsectors   184
8.2   ACP's portfolio companies as of November 2018   186
8.3   Summary of ACP's governance bodies   188
8.4   Metrics contained in ACP's impact report   189
9.1   FONSIS projects approved from inception in 2013 to the time of writing   201
9.2   Summary of FONSIS governance bodies   203
10.1   Summary of ISIF's portfolio as of December 31, 2018   215
10.2   Breakdown of capital committed to ISIF's Irish Portfolio as of December 31, 2018   215
10.3   ISIF's infrastructure investment in the Irish Portfolio as of December 31, 2018   216
10.4   Summary of ISIF's governance bodies   218
10.5   Comprehensive sample of metrics disclosed in ISIF's economic impact report   220
10.6   ISIF Irish Portfolio risk categories   222
11.1   Marguerite II's eligible sectors   231
11.2   Marguerite portfolio companies   234
11.3   Summary of Marguerite II's core bodies and functions   237
11.4   Marguerite's ESG assessment throughout the investment process   239
12.1   NIIF's anticipated fund size and investors at time of writing   244

12.2   Summary of NIIF Limited's governance bodies   251
13.1   NIF current and expected future capital commitments   260
13.2   NSIA-NIF core governance bodies   263
13.3   NIF Investment Policy Statement: Impact and financial KPIs   268
A.1   Twelve risk factors assessed in CDP Equity's equity risk model   281
B.1   National strategic investment funds   285
B.2   Multinational strategic investment funds   294

Acknowledgments

This publication is an initiative funded by the Public-Private Infrastructure Advisory Facility administered by the World Bank. It was authored by a team consisting of Shanthi Divakaran (team leader and senior financial sector specialist); senior consultants Håvard Halland, Gianni Lorenzato, and Paul Rose; and Sebastian Sarmiento-Saher (researcher). The case studies were written by Gianni Lorenzato, with research assistance from Sebastian Sarmiento-Saher. Thematic reviews were written by Gianni Lorenzato and Sebastian Sarmiento-Saher. In addition, the team received technical input and support from Professor Steve Kyle (Cornell University), Tim Hu (researcher), and Saba Sadri (researcher). Anderson Caputo Silva (practice manager, Long-Term Finance, Finance, Competitiveness, and Innovation Global Practice [FCI GP] of the World Bank Group) provided overall guidance and support.

The publication is based on a concept developed by Håvard Halland (former senior economist, FCI GP) and Michel Noël (former head of investment funds, FCI GP) following publication of their 2016 World Bank Policy Research Working Paper 7851, "Strategic Investment Funds: Opportunities and Challenges," co-authored with Silvana Tordo (lead energy economist, World Bank) and Jacob J. Kloper-Owens (former consultant, World Bank).

The authors are particularly grateful to Professor Patrick Schena, Tufts University and co-head of SovereigNet, for his immense support that extended from the conceptualization of this project until its finalization. The authors are indebted also to the project's External Advisory Committee, chaired by Professor Schena and comprising Daniel Adamson (senior managing director, Wafra Investment Advisory Group, Inc.), Peter Mixon (partner, Nossaman LLP, and former general counsel at CalPERS), Eugene O'Callaghan (former director, Ireland Strategic Investment Fund), Stella Ojekwe-Onyejeli (former executive director and chief operating officer, Nigeria Sovereign Investment Authority), and Ahmad Zulqarnain Onn (former executive director, investments, Khazanah Nasional Berhad) for their feedback and input.

The authors also acknowledge the insights, support, and feedback of peer reviewers Abed Al Abwah (chief audit executive of the Palestine Investment Fund), Kevin Carey (practice manager, Macroeconomics, Trade and Investment Global Practice, World Bank Group), Adam Dixon (associate professor,

Globalization and Development, Maastricht University), Catiana Garcia Kilroy (lead financial sector specialist, FCI GP), and Edwin Truman (nonresident senior fellow, Peterson Institute for International Economics). The review meeting was co-chaired by Caroline Freund (former global director, Trade, Investment and Competitiveness Global Practice), and William Maloney (chief economist, Equitable Growth, Finance, and Institutions Vice Presidency [EFI VP]) at the time. The team received detailed feedback and guidance from Jean Pesme (global director, FCI GP). The team is also thankful to Ayhan Kose (chief economist and director, EFI GP), for his guidance and support.

The authors received useful input and insights on successive drafts of the publication from consultations with Abed Al Abwah (chief audit executive, Palestine Investment Fund), Chinua Azubike (chief executive officer, InfraCredit), Barbara Boos (head of infrastructure funds and climate action division, European Investment Bank), Ana Cebreiro Gomez (senior economist, Fiscal Policy and Sustainable Growth Unit, World Bank), Richard Claudet (senior financial sector specialist, World Bank), James Comyn (partner, Hunton Andrews Kurth), Mona Dallal Tarpey (principal counsel, International Finance Corporation [IFC] Asset Management Company), Udaibir Das (assistant director, Monetary and Capital Markets Department, International Monetary Fund), Timothy Diggins (partner, Ropes & Gray, LLP), Henri Fortin (lead financial management specialist, World Bank), Ekaterina Gratcheva (lead financial officer, World Bank Treasury), Janette Hall (director of investment funds and special initiatives, Asian Development Bank), Sunita Kikeri (former lead financial sector specialist, World Bank), Johanna Klein (principal, IFC Asset Management Company Fund of Funds), Daniel Kolb (partner, Ropes & Gray LLP), Maria Kozloski (former senior manager, IFC Fund of Funds), François Lefebvre (former senior financial officer, World Bank), Patrick McGinnis (senior consultant, World Bank), Margaret Niles (partner, K&L Gates), Mathieu Peller (partner, chief operating officer Africa, Meridiam), Lasitha Perera (chief executive officer, GuarantCo), Charles Purcell (partner, K&L Gates), Donald Purka (principal investment officer, IFC), Solomon Quaynor (vice president, African Development Bank and former head of infrastructure, IFC—Sub-Saharan Africa), Emile J. M. Van Der Does De Willebois (lead financial sector specialist, World Bank), and Nicholas Vickery (senior manager, IFC Disruptive Technologies and Funds). The team also received input from Diego Lopez (managing director, Global SWF), Samuel Schneider (consultant), and Xuanhe Wang (consultant).

The team extends special thanks to Public-Private Infrastructure Advisory Facility colleagues Jemima Sy (program manager), Philippe Neves (senior infrastructure specialist), and Luciana Guimaraes Drummond e Silva (program officer) for their consistent and much appreciated support throughout the project.

The team also thanks the International Forum of Sovereign Wealth Funds Secretariat and Tufts University's SovereigNet for their leading role in co-organizing a June 2018 workshop on strategic investment funds hosted at the World Bank.

The authors thank Elizabeth Price (senior external affairs officer, EFI) for communications advice; Youjin Choi (senior financial sector specialist, EFI) for knowledge management advice; Baloko Makala (consultant, FCI GP) for production support; Noxi Nyathi (program assistant, FCI GP) for her administrative support; Caroline Polk for coordinating the editing, design, and production; Honora Mara for technical editing; Sherrie Brown for proofreading; and Datapage for design and layout.

Finally, the authors acknowledge the major data providers—Asia Climate Partners, the Asian Development Bank, CDP Equity, Fonds Souverain d'Investissements Stratégiques de Senegal, InfraCredit, the Ireland Strategic Investment Fund, GuarantCo, Marguerite Investment Management S.A., Meridiam, the National Investment and Infrastructure Fund of India, and the Nigeria Sovereign Investment Authority—for their cooperation and data in preparing the case studies and topical reviews.

About the Authors

Shanthi Divakaran is a senior financial sector specialist in the World Bank's Finance, Competitiveness, and Innovation Global Practice, where she focuses on advising governments in emerging markets and developing economies on investment funds, including mutual funds, private equity and venture capital funds, and sovereign wealth funds. Divakaran previously worked for four years in both investment banking and corporate banking for the Financial Institutions Group at JP Morgan Chase, New York. Divakaran holds an MBA from the Yale School of Management and a BA in physics from Mount Holyoke College.

Håvard Halland is a senior economist at the Organisation for Economic Co-operation and Development's Development Centre, where his work focuses on the effects of the clean-energy transition in fossil fuel–exporting countries. He also works on the role of sovereign wealth funds and strategic investment funds in the clean-energy transition. Halland previously worked as a senior economist at the World Bank and has also been a visiting scholar at Stanford University. His op-eds and essays have been covered by Bloomberg, Environmental Finance, the FT Sustainable Views, and S&P Global, among others. Prior to his work with the World Bank, Halland was a delegate of the International Committee of the Red Cross to the armed conflicts in Colombia and the Democratic Republic of Congo. He holds a PhD in economics from the University of Cambridge.

Gianni Lorenzato is an independent consultant specializing in blended and green finance. His clients include the World Bank, the United Nations Development Programme, the United Nations Capital Development Fund, and the Deutsche Gesellschaft für Internationale Zusammenarbeit. Lorenzato focuses on policies and financial instruments to attract private capital to sustainable development projects and on the design of blended commercial and concessional facilities. He was previously an investment director at Taconic Capital, a US$8 billion hedge fund, and an executive director at Goldman Sachs in London. He also spent two years in Silicon Valley developing a financial technology start-up. Lorenzato holds an MPA from Harvard Kennedy School and a BA in economics from Università Bocconi.

Paul Rose teaches courses in business associations, comparative corporate law, corporate finance, investment management law, and securities regulation at The Ohio State University (OSU) Moritz College of Law. He has written extensively on sovereign wealth funds, corporate governance, and securities regulation and has consulted with and provided testimony on these topics to numerous regulators and other agencies, including the US Senate Committee on Banking, Housing and Urban Affairs; the US Securities and Exchange Commission; the US Government Accountability Office; and the Congressional Research Service. He is an affiliate with the Sovereign Wealth Fund Initiative, a research project at The Fletcher School at Tufts University; a nonresident fellow of the Esade Center for Global Economy and Geopolitics; an affiliate with IE Business School; and an affiliate with the Sovereign Investment Lab, a research project at Università Bocconi. Before joining the faculty at the OSU Moritz College of Law, Rose was a visiting assistant professor in securities and finance at the Northwestern University School of Law. He previously practiced law in the corporate and securities practice group of Covington & Burling LLP's San Francisco office. Before attending law school, Rose worked as an assistant trader in equity and emerging market derivatives at Citibank in New York.

Sebastian Sarmiento-Saher is a business information developer at Anthem, Inc., focusing on health economics. He was previously at the World Bank Group, where he worked as a results measurement consultant modeling the development impact of projects across sectors. Sarmiento-Saher also undertook research roles for initiatives in infrastructure finance and coauthored publications on a range of topics, including flaring and methane emission reduction, strategic investment funds, and small and medium enterprises. He holds a BA from Boston College and an MSc from Georgetown University.

Executive Summary

Strategic investment funds (SIFs) are special-purpose investment vehicles backed by governments or public institutions that seek a double bottom line of financial and economic returns. They invest in, and mobilize commercial capital to, sectors and regions where private investors would not invest or would invest to a limited extent. SIFs may be set up to exclusively enact a SIF-specific mandate or may be part of a larger sovereign wealth fund or public policy purpose (see chapter 1 for a definition of sovereign wealth funds). SIFs that are fully capitalized by a government or other public entity are public capital SIFs; public capital SIFs wholly capitalized by a single government are sometimes referred to as sovereign development funds.[1] In contrast, SIFs initiated by a public entity but also invested in by commercial entities are mixed capital SIFs. Several regional SIFs backed by multilateral finance institutions are mixed capital funds (see appendix C for an overview of regional and multinational SIFs).

Since 2000, over 30 SIFs have been formed at the national level, typically to boost economic growth through infrastructure or small and medium enterprises investment.[2] Several SIFs already existed before the global financial crisis, and, in the years immediately following the crisis, about 15 SIFs were established in countries of all income levels, ranging from Nigeria and Senegal to India and Ireland (see figure ES.1). Similarly, SIFs have also attracted attention in the current economically strained COVID-19 (coronavirus) environment as governments globally have provided equity to companies of high economic relevance, often through sovereign investment vehicles,[3] or have used sovereign funds to proactively address the pandemic.

SIFs exhibit six characteristics.[4] They

1. Are initiated, and fully or partly capitalized, by one or more governments, or by government-owned global or regional development finance institutions (quasi-sovereign entities);
2. Invest primarily in unlisted assets[5] (either domestically or thematically)[6] to achieve financial returns and a policy objective[7] (double bottom line);
3. Aim to mobilize commercial co-investment at the fund or project level;

FIGURE ES.1

Establishment of national-level strategic investment funds

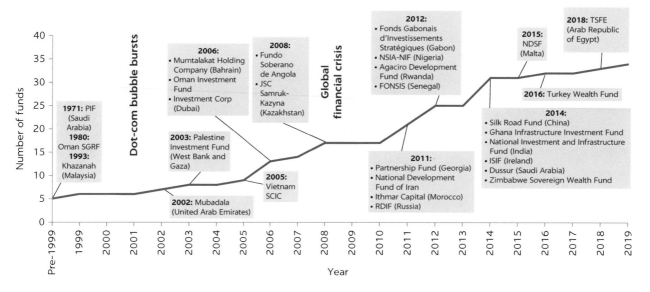

Source: World Bank.

Note: This figure is illustrative and is not a comprehensive list of national-level SIFs. Other strategic investment funds (SIFs) have emerged at the national level in countries like Indonesia and Morocco (in addition to Ithmar) since the pandemic. After the data collection period of this publication ended, the Oman SGRF merged with the Oman Investment Fund to establish the Oman Investment Authority in June 2020. Fundo Soberano de Angola has reduced its development-focused investment portfolio since 2017 to focus on savings and stabilization mandates. FONADIN = Fondo Nacional de Infraestructura (National Infrastructure Fund); FONSIS = Fonds Souverain d'Investissements Stratégiques (Sovereign Fund for Strategic Investments); ISIF = Ireland Strategic Investment Fund; NDSF = National Development and Social Fund; NSIA-NIF = Nigeria Sovereign Investment Authority – Nigeria Infrastructure Fund; PIF = Public Investment Fund; RDIF = Russian Direct Investment Fund; SCIC = State Capital Investment Corporation; SGRF = State General Reserve Fund (Local Initiatives Portfolio); TSFE = The Sovereign Fund of Egypt.

4. Provide long-term patient capital, primarily as equity, but also as quasi equity and debt;

5. Operate as professional fund managers on behalf of their investors; and

6. Are established as pools of assets (or funds) through a variety of legal structures.

As public sector–backed long-term investors, SIFs can counter market failures and bring stable capital to investment opportunities that would not be conventionally targeted by many private sector financial institutions for various reasons, such as the perception of excessive investment risk. A successful SIF (1) has deployed substantial capital additional to the capital already available in the private markets, (2) realizes its stated/expected financial returns, (3) fulfills its policy objective and has crowded in commercial capital, (4) has effectively and transparently navigated the complex network of public and private relations inherent in the SIF model, and (5) has done so with limited political interference.

Despite the important advantages they can bring, SIFs are not always the best policy solution to fill investment gaps in policy-relevant sectors. They cannot fix overall structural investment constraints or substitute for good fiscal management. Without a clear purpose, a SIF may instead complicate government oversight of public expenditure and fiscal risk. By injecting funds into the domestic economy, public capital SIFs can risk fragmenting government spending and budget procedure, making overall macroeconomic consistency between the SIF and the sovereign's budgetary process vital.[8] SIFs are also not a substitute for a strong regulatory framework, overall strong governance, and rule of law as relevant to investment and ease of doing business. The establishment and operations of such funds can be fraught with risks, particularly in country contexts of weaker governance, inadequate rule of law, and insufficient financial market regulation.

The legitimacy of a SIF thus hinges on many factors, chief among them being the governance, legal, and disclosure frameworks that discipline a SIF's investment activities. This book seeks to provide guidance on these important factors to the policy maker setting up a government-sponsored SIF.[9] It recognizes that creating a SIF is an exercise in complex decision-making and guides the policy maker through a series of key decision areas, including through the use of global case studies.

In summary, this book discusses the following key decision points for the policy maker setting up a SIF.[10]

- *Rationale.* The primary argument for setting up a SIF is the extent to which it can contribute additionality to both what exists in the market and what is provided by the government. The secondary, and interrelated, argument for setting up a SIF is to crowd in commercial capital. Among the policy maker's first responsibilities are to (1) articulate the additionality the proposed fund could bring to the market and to government infrastructure, (2) validate the fund's viability and its coherence with macroeconomic policies by submitting the proposed idea to the rigor of a feasibility study, and (3) define clear policy and economic criteria that justify the limited occasions within which a SIF may employ concessional financing, which must occur in a manner that restricts market distortion.[11]
- *Legal framework.* The SIF's legal framework must secure the fund's legitimacy and longevity, align the fund's mandate to national priorities, and transmit signals of commercial orientation to private co-investors. Key decision points are to choose (1) either a SIF-specific law or a commercial law as the establishing legal framework of the SIF, (2) a legal structure that has strong governance features and the life span needed to accommodate the fund's investment horizon, and (3) an optimal domicile for both the public sponsor and expected co-investors.[12]
- *Governance.* The SIF's governance framework must balance the manager's operational independence with accountability to the public sponsor. Key decision points include the following. First, identify the entity that will serve as the SIF's legal owner; for a government-sponsored public capital SIF this entity is typically the ministry of finance. Second, identify the fund's oversight mechanism. Public capital SIFs commonly employ a board of directors to closely monitor the SIF's adherence to the double bottom line mandate, while buffering the manager from too much interference by the owner. Third, select board members according to clearly outlined criteria, with emphasis on professional experience and fit and proper assessments. Fourth, ideally, the board should be chaired by an independent director and most board members should be independent (unaffiliated with the government sponsor or owners). Fifth, to protect the SIF's commercial orientation, government representatives must not be on the fund's investment committee. Finally, identify the SIF's management model. The public sponsor usually signals the SIF's commercial orientation either by employing a well-reputed manager selected by a competitive process or by ensuring that the SIF's chief executive officer and staff have strong private sector investment backgrounds.

- *Investment and risk management.* The SIF's investment and risk framework concretizes the fund's accountability framework, informs key organizational decisions, and converges stakeholder views on risk tolerance. Key decision points are to (1) define eligible investments, the fund's investment horizon, return expectations, responsible investment policy, and performance monitoring framework; (2) provide details on target sectors and geographies, the ability to take majority or minority stakes, the size of individual investments, co-investment strategy, and so on; (3) clarify risk appetite through investment limits and restrictions, and create a risk management system to monitor, mitigate, and report on investment- and portfolio-level risk; and (4) increase visibility and narrow information asymmetry between the SIF's manager and owner by defining the SIF's investment process.
- *Transparency and disclosure.* The SIF's transparency and disclosure framework helps mitigate and rectify asymmetries of information between the public sponsor and the fund manager, and between the SIF and its external stakeholders. Key decision points are to (1) embed the transparency and disclosure framework into the SIF's establishment law, regulations, and policies; (2) identify up front key information the SIF is expected to disclose, bearing in mind that—as an entity managing public capital—the SIF is held to higher standards of public disclosure; (3) identify the mechanisms for public disclosure, such as annual or quarterly reports and the SIF's website; (4) adopt accounting standards (often International Financial Reporting Standards); and (5) identify the SIF's auditor, typically an independent well-reputed firm.

NOTES

1. Santiso (2008) uses the term "sovereign development fund" when he highlights that SWFs could "grow to become major actors of development finance: Sovereign Development Funds."
2. Several more SIFs have been formed since research on this publication was completed, including after the pandemic.
3. In July 2020, International Monetary Fund chief economist, Gita Gopinath, endorsed governments' shifting focus to "equity-like" support in order to help companies recovering from the crisis avoid hyperindebtedness (Reuters 2020).
4. These characteristics are based on, but modified from, the definition in Halland et al. (2016).
5. That is, their strategic mandate does not include investing in publicly traded assets.
6. Thematically, such as making climate-friendly investments.
7. Typically, economic and social returns.
8. Clear-cut and publicly disclosed fiscal rules must ideally allow for contribution into the fund during times of surplus and withdrawal from the fund during times of deficit (see chapter 2 for more detail).
9. See the chapters of the publication for further operational details, examples of how these frameworks are used by different global SIFs, and a systematic outline of the menu of choices facing policy makers as they seek to balance these multiple objectives.
10. Although the book also examines SIFs sponsored by quasi-sovereign entities, its key messages target the policy maker setting up a government-sponsored SIF.
11. Note, this publication does not advocate for the use of concessional financing by SIFs but recognizes that some SIFs do employ such mechanisms to incentivize the mobilization of private capital.
12. For public capital SIFs, which do not need to consider whether the fund domicile is desirable to outside investors, the sponsor's home jurisdiction is typically found adequate as a domicile if the domestic legal framework provides a sufficiently robust structure (see discussion in chapter 3).

REFERENCES

Halland, Håvard, Michel Noël, Silvana Tordo, and Jacob J. Kloper-Owens. 2016. "Strategic Investment Funds: Opportunities and Challenges." Policy Research Working Paper 7851, World Bank, Washington, DC. https://openknowledge.worldbank.org/bitstream/handle /10986/25168/WPS7851.pdf?sequence=5&isAllowed=y.

Reuters. 2020. "IMF's Chief Economist Urges 'Equity-Like' Govt Support for Virus-Hit Firms." Reuters, July 9, 2020. https://www.reuters.com/article/imf-world-bank/imfs-chief -economist-urges-equity-like-govt-support-for-virus-hit-firms-idINT9N2DM008.

Santiso, Javier. 2008. "Sovereign Development Funds: Key Financial Actors of the Shifting Wealth of Nations." OECD Emerging Markets Network Paper, OECD Development Centre, Paris.

Abbreviations

ACP	Asia Climate Partners
ADB	Asian Development Bank
AfDB	African Development Bank
AIFM	alternative investment fund manager
AIIB	Asian Infrastructure Investment Bank
AIMM	Anticipated Impact Measurement and Monitoring
AuM	assets under management
BOA	Bank of Africa Senegal
CEO	chief executive officer
CP3	Climate Public Private Partnership Program
DFI	development finance institution
EIB	European Investment Bank
ESG	environmental, social, and governance
EU AIFMD	European Union Directive 2011/61/EU on Alternative Investment Fund Managers
FONADIN	Fondo Nacional de Infraestructura (National Infrastructure Fund [Mexico])
FONSIS	Fonds Souverain d'Investissements Stratégiques (Sovereign Fund for Strategic Investments [Senegal])
GAPPs	generally accepted principles and practices
GCF	Green Climate Fund
GDP	gross domestic product
GGF	government guidance fund
GIB	Green Investment Bank
GP	general partner
GSIS	Government Service Insurance System
GVA	gross value added
IFC	International Finance Corporation
IFRS	International Financial Reporting Standards
IPO	initial public offering
IRR	internal rate of return
ISIF	Ireland Strategic Investment Fund
KPI	key performance indicator

LP	limited partner
LPA	limited partnership agreement
MDB	multilateral development bank
MIRA	Macquarie Infrastructure and Real Assets
NDC	Nationally Determined Contribution
NIF	Nigeria Infrastructure Fund
NIIF	National Investment and Infrastructure Fund
NSIA	Nigeria Sovereign Investment Authority
NTMA	National Treasury Management Agency
OHADA	Organisation pour l'Harmonisation en Afrique du Droit des Affaires (Organization for the Harmonization of Corporate Law in Africa)
PCF	private capital fund
PIDF	Presidential Infrastructure Development Fund
PIF	Palestine Investment Fund
PINAI	Philippine Investment Alliance for Infrastructure
PPP	public-private partnership
PSE	Plan Sénégal Emergent
RFP	request for proposal
SCSp	societé en commandite spéciale
SEBI	Securities and Exchange Board of India
SICAV/SIF	société d'investissement à capital variable / specialized investment fund
SIF	strategic investment fund
SMEs	small and medium enterprises
SOE	state-owned enterprise
SWF	sovereign wealth fund
UNPRI	United Nations Principles of Responsible Investment
VCTF	Venture Capital Trust Fund

1 Introduction

CONTEXT

Strategic investment funds (SIFs) are special-purpose investment vehicles, backed by governments or other public institutions, that seek a double bottom line of financial and economic returns. They invest in, and mobilize commercial capital to, sectors and regions where private investors would otherwise not invest or would invest to a limited extent. Governments engage in a wide range of investment activities, from state-owned enterprises and public-private partnerships to managing international reserves and public pension funds. Within this range of government investment activities lie both traditional sovereign wealth funds and strategic investment funds. Traditional sovereign wealth funds (SWFs) are defined as "special-purpose investment funds or arrangements that are owned by the general government. . . . [and that] hold, manage, or administer assets to achieve financial objectives, and employ a set of investment strategies that include investing in foreign financial assets."[1] SWFs primarily invest abroad; SIFs primarily invest in strategic activities at home. Whereas SWFs emerged in contexts of abundance, frequently to manage excess fiscal revenues from natural resource exports or large foreign exchange reserves, SIFs have often been a response to scarcity. In fiscally constrained circumstances, governments and multilateral institutions alike have recognized the importance of mobilizing private capital, and SIFs have served as a policy instrument response to this need.

As long-term investors backed by the public sector, SIFs can counter market failures and bring stable capital to investment opportunities that would not be conventionally targeted by many private sector financial institutions for a variety of reasons, such as (1) the lack of a previous track record of private investment in certain sectors or themes that lead prospective investors to attribute excessive risk to such investments, (2) information asymmetries regarding the pipeline of potential investments,[2] or (3) inefficient or underdeveloped exit markets (such as initial public offerings). For instance, SIFs are often deployed to play a significant role in filling the funding gap for infrastructure investments, particularly in emerging market and developing economies,[3] where investment barriers prevent the full involvement of domestic and international infrastructure funds. Specifically, SIFs can help counter government and market failures in the infrastructure sector. Many governments of emerging market and developing economies lack the human capital to transform projects into bankable, fully documented projects that can be tendered to investors. With their in-house investment expertise, SIFs are able to complement and enhance the project preparation capacity of their host country. Senegal's SIF, FONSIS (Fonds Souverain d'Investissements Stratégiques, or Sovereign Fund for Strategic Investments), one of the case studies in this book, for instance, acts as project developer in the infrastructure sector, unlocking a pipeline of strategic assets for other investors to co-invest.

SIFs have gained increased prominence over the past few decades. Governments and other public sponsors globally have increasingly coopted the investment fund model to further a policy objective through the setup of SIFs. Since 2000, over 30 SIFs have been formed at the national level, typically to boost economic growth through investment in infrastructure or small and medium enterprises (see figure 1.1). Several SIFs already existed before the global financial crisis of 2008; they included Malaysia's Khazanah Nasional Berhad, Saudi Arabia's Public Investment Fund, and Mubadala Investment Company in Abu Dhabi, the United Arab Emirates. But, in the years immediately following the global financial crisis, about 15 SIFs were set up in countries of all income levels, ranging from Nigeria and Senegal to India and Ireland, indicating that postcrisis financing gaps for long-term investment may have driven

FIGURE 1.1

Establishment of national-level strategic investment funds

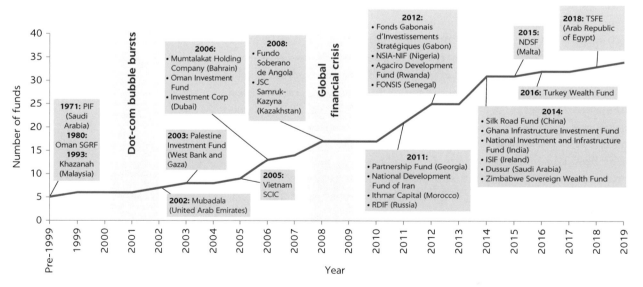

Source: World Bank.
Note: This figure is illustrative and is not a comprehensive list of national-level SIFs. Other strategic investment funds (SIFs) have emerged at the national level in countries like Indonesia and Morocco (in addition to Ithmar) since the pandemic. After the data collection period of this publication ended, the Oman SGRF merged with the Oman Investment Fund to establish the Oman Investment Authority in June 2020. Fundo Soberano de Angola has reduced its development-focused investment portfolio since 2017 to focus on savings and stabilization mandates. FONADIN = Fondo Nacional de Infraestructura (National Infrastructure Fund); FONSIS = Fonds Souverain d'Investissements Stratégiques (Sovereign Fund for Strategic Investments); ISIF = Ireland Strategic Investment Fund; NDSF = National Development and Social Fund; NSIA-NIF = Nigeria Sovereign Investment Authority – Nigeria Infrastructure Fund; PIF = Public Investment Fund; RDIF = Russian Direct Investment Fund; SCIC = State Capital Investment Corporation; SGRF = State General Reserve Fund (Local Initiatives Portfolio); TSFE = The Sovereign Fund of Egypt.

SIFs' establishment. According to original World Bank estimates, membership of the International Forum of Sovereign Wealth Funds—a forum started in 2009 for traditional SWFs—now consists of 40 percent SIFs. In addition, governments have also formed SIFs at the subnational level. In China, for instance, as of 2017 more than 1,000 SIF-like structures, called government guidance funds, had been formed, primarily at the provincial and municipal levels of government (McGinnis et al. 2017). Numerous multinational SIFs have also been set up, frequently with a regional rather than a national focus and often backed by multilateral finance institutions.[4]

In the current COVID-19 (coronavirus) environment, governments have frequently turned to sovereign investment vehicles to address the economic effects of the pandemic, echoing the emergence of new SIFs in the aftermath of the global financial crisis. Since March 2020, in an economically strained pandemic environment, governments globally have provided equity capital to companies of high economic relevance, often through sovereign investment vehicles, thus creating the potential for greater state ownership of companies after the crisis. The International Monetary Fund's chief economist, Gita Gopinath, underscored this trend in July 2020 when she recommended that governments shift focus from debt-oriented support to "equity-like" support to aid companies recovering from the crisis to avoid hyperindebtedness (Reuters 2020). In the months following the World Health Organization's declaration of a pandemic, sovereign investment agencies have been used in multiple instances to rescue distressed industries. For instance, the government of Turkey allowed its US$33 billion strategic investment fund, the Turkey Wealth Fund, to acquire controlling stakes of private companies in distress via a bill passed in parliament in April 2020 (Kozok, Karakaya, and Ant 2020; Turak 2020).

Governments have also used sovereign funds to proactively invest in COVID-19-resistant sectors. Mubadala's venture capital arm, Mubadala Ventures, declared plans to set up a health care fund in response to increased investment need in life sciences and digital health technology in the pandemic environment (Azhar 2020). Similarly, the Russian Federation's strategic investment fund, Russia Direct Investment Fund, has been involved in funding the development of Sputnik V, a COVID-19 vaccine developed by a Russian medical research institution.[5] Governments have also announced plans to establish new strategic investment funds in the COVID-19 environment. In the last quarter of 2020, the government of Indonesia announced a US$15 billion SIF dedicated to investing in domestic sectors such as power, roads, and health care (Allard, Suroyo, and Widianto 2020). Likewise, Morocco revealed plans in August 2020 to set up a US$4.8 billion SIF to address the economic effects of the pandemic (North Africa Post 2020). As a recent *Euromoney* article points out, "it could be argued COVID-19 is the moment sovereign wealth funds were made for: a shocking disruption to national economies that calls for a stable, patiently invested buffer" (Wright 2020).

In the aftermath of the pandemic, SIFs may possibly also be formed with a multicountry, regional approach to accelerate recovery in sectors hit hard by COVID-19. Because a single-country SIF approach may result in capacity overstretch and duplication, some countries may be inspired to call for a regional approach. The Marguerite Fund, one of the case studies in this book, is an example of such a regional SIF approach conceived by the European

Investment Bank and the national development banks of European Union member states France, Germany, and Italy in the aftermath of the global financial crisis to stimulate greenfield infrastructure investments in the European Union. Although regional vehicles may lead to cost- and capacity-related synergies, aligning various government objectives and national priorities may prove challenging. Therefore, existing SIFs may also simply collaborate on investment opportunities through joint ventures with other regional SIFs (see chapter 2 and table 2.7 for examples of such collaboration between sovereign funds).

Despite their increased prominence, SIFs are not always the best policy solution to fill investment gaps in policy-relevant sectors and are not devoid of challenges. This book does not advocate for SIFs as a catch-all cure for government ills. Despite their potential, as discussed later in this book, SIFs come with a number of significant challenges and are not always the best instrument to fill financing gaps and overcome barriers to private capital.

The setup and operations of such funds can be fraught with risks, particularly in country contexts with weaker governance, inadequate rule of law, and insufficient financial market regulation. The diversity of SIFs' objectives and operating contexts corresponds to significant diversity in the ways SIFs are funded, governed, and managed. SIFs face a set of unique governance and operational challenges arising from their dual role as commercial and policy-driven investors. Adhering to a double bottom line mandate is complex, and SIFs particularly struggle to measure nonfinancial impact that is not quantifiable. In addition, by injecting funds into the domestic economy, public capital SIFs can risk fragmenting government spending and budget procedure, making overall macroeconomic consistency between the SIF and the sovereign's budgetary process vital. Ideally, clear-cut and publicly disclosed fiscal rules must allow for contribution into the fund during times of surplus and withdrawal from the fund during times of deficit.

A government-sponsored SIF must thread the needle between the following intersecting considerations and audiences.

- *Legitimacy and longevity*. A government-sponsored SIF must consider the fund's longevity, legitimacy, and mandate through the lens of the country's electorate and political organizations. Given the risk of shifting political sands, the fund must be protected via structural safeguards and broad-based political commitment spanning electoral cycles. The public sponsor must employ a thorough and inclusive process to establish the SIF's legitimacy and make its mandate visible to the citizenry, political parties, and business communities. Safeguarding the SIF's long-term legitimacy also requires submitting the fund to high standards of transparency and disclosure that recognize the ultimate accountability to the political bodies representing the taxpaying electorate.
- *Expected shifts in national priorities*. National priorities can change during the SIF's life cycle, compounding the operational and governance complexity of such an institution. The COVID-19 pandemic is an excellent example of the unpredictability of future events on a scale that a policy maker setting up a SIF even in early 2019 could not have foreseen, yet multiple SIFs globally have had to reconfigure their existing strategies on account of the pandemic.

- *Attracting private capital.* Given that the SIF is set up to attract private capital, the public sponsor must consider the landscape of commercial investors it targets; the signals potential partners will receive through the SIF's structural, legal, and governance choices; and the likelihood of mobilizing capital from these partners. Here the public sponsor must also consider appropriate modes of risk-sharing with investors to catalyze private capital while avoiding vulnerability to moral hazards (see the discussion in chapter 2 on concessionality and risks).

- *Risk of distorting markets.* The public sponsor setting up a state-sponsored entity that operates in the commercial space must be continually vigilant to the risk of distorting markets. The double bottom line mandate of the SIF introduces a complexity to the operations of the fund that is foreign to most purely private capital funds. Overemphasizing the policy objective while sacrificing returns could alienate the private capital the SIF seeks to attract. Conversely, the SIF could crowd out private capital and achieve limited policy impact if it focuses overly on financial returns.

- *Efficacy of the SIF and adherence to its double bottom line mandate.* To secure the efficacy of the SIF and fidelity to its double bottom line mandate, the public sponsor must optimize the fund's internal governance environment, ensure the public sponsor has ultimate control over the strategic direction of the fund, and cede operational control to professionals that can best drive results.

The legitimacy of a SIF thus hinges on a slew of factors, chief among which are the governance, legal, and disclosure frameworks that discipline a SIF's investment activities. A successful SIF (1) has deployed substantial capital additional to the capital already available in the private markets, (2) realizes the stated financial returns, (3) fulfills the policy objective and crowds in commercial capital, (4) has effectively and transparently navigated the complex network of public and private relations inherent in the SIF model, and (5) has limited political interference.

OBJECTIVE AND METHODOLOGY

This book seeks to provide a compendium of references for policy makers who are establishing SIFs or strengthening the operations of existing ones, particularly as governments examine the value of such funds as a policy instrument in the immediate aftermath and years following the COVID-19 pandemic. It is targeted to policy makers and senior executives in ministries of finance and sector ministries relevant to SIF operations. SIF executives, staff, and private sector investment partners will also benefit from the volume.

Research for this book, which took place primarily from 2018 to 2019, was initiated in response to the growing role of SIFs in mobilizing private capital for infrastructure finance, climate finance, small and medium enterprises finance, and other policy-driven commercial investment. Whereas the literature on SWFs provides a wealth of information related to investing abroad in foreign currency–denominated financial assets, limited guidance is available on the type of commercial, policy-driven domestic investment undertaken by SIFs. This book seeks to remedy that lacuna. Several of the organizational forms that SIFs take are novel and are being tested for the first time. With scant historical evidence to draw on, the discussions and guidelines presented here are supported by the practical experience of the dozens of SIF and financial sector executives who generously lent their time to be interviewed for this volume, and documentation that they provided or that was otherwise available in the public domain.

This book considers SIFs' potential as well as their limitations and seeks to provide suggestions grounded in a balanced view of SIFs' role. Most of the discussion, analysis, and recommendations herein will be relevant for all SIFs, regardless of their investment focus. Because most SIFs focus primarily on infrastructure, however, the book reflects that orientation; it puts forth this analysis while recognizing the heterogeneity of SIFs and of their contexts.

The book also seeks to complement the literature on SWFs and the Santiago Principles that provide guidance for them (see IWG 2008). The Santiago Principles are 24 generally accepted principles endorsed by the members of the International Forum of Sovereign Wealth Funds. These principles are self-applied, not legally binding, and not part of the Financial Stability Board's Compendium of Standards. Nevertheless, these principles represent a form of soft law that, having undergone a process of formal acceptance by sovereign funds and their owners, is often employed by governments globally as a reference point in drafting SIF laws. This book therefore builds on the general guidelines manifest in the Santiago Principles to articulate lessons pertinent to commercial, policy-driven domestic and thematic investment. It also builds on two World Bank policy research working papers: "Strategic Investment Funds: Opportunities and Challenges" (Halland et al. 2016) and "Sovereign Wealth Funds and Long-Term Development Finance" (Gelb, Tordo, and Halland 2014). It complements other knowledge products funded by the Public-Private Infrastructure Advisory Facility, particularly the recently published *Global Review of Public Infrastructure Funds* (World Bank Group and IDB 2020).[6]

In transmitting a practical perspective on SIFs' establishment and operations, this book leverages the concrete experience of several SIFs and their executives. The analysis and recommendations reflect the information collected in a set of six case studies. The case study approach reflects the heterogeneous and qualitative nature of the information available on SIFs, and the variety of structural and functional forms that SIFs adopt. The case studies draw on more than 50 interviews, primarily with senior SIF executives in the six selected SIFs and with executives in public and private financial sector institutions that work closely with SIFs. The interviews took place between 2018 and 2019. In addition to the case studies, the book draws on relevant literature in several areas.

This book does not prescribe ideal SIF models to be applied under specific contexts; such an approach would be unrealistic given the wide range of contexts in which SIFs can operate and the evolving evidence on the effectiveness of SIFs. Rather, it accepts the existence of the SIF as an institutional innovation of the public sector and seeks to provide guidance for policy makers in this evolving area of government intervention in markets.[7] SIFs still have a limited track record and, as the report shows, operate in a variety of contexts, indicating that a heterogeneity of conditions can prove hospitable for a SIF. The book therefore refrains from prescribing contexts in which SIFs would be most appropriately formed, aggregating guidance on detailed preconditions that need to be met for a successful SIF, or suggesting what specific organizational choices a SIF should make within specific contexts. Instead, it uses a predominantly descriptive approach and seeks to highlight principles and provide operational templates to practitioners and policy makers where little widely available, practice-based experience has yet been documented and disseminated.

The creation of a SIF is an exercise in complex decision-making; therefore, this volume presents a range of options for policy makers to consider as they seek to make choices that best safeguard the SIF's legitimacy, efficacy, and mandate. The ultimate decision-making is left in the hands of policy makers. This nonprescriptive approach does not imply that SIFs can exist in, or are an appropriate solution to, all environments. Quite the opposite—as discussed in the book, SIFs have limitations and policy makers must not embark on setting one up unless they have considered and exhausted the possibilities of alternate instruments to solve such problems, clearly identified the additionality that the SIF can bring, and confirmed the fund's viability in the market.

The six case studies (see table 1.1) were selected using specific criteria, with a view to reflecting the heterogeneity of SIFs. The publication distinguishes SIFs primarily on the basis of funding sources within two categories:

1. *Public capital SIFs*: SIFs that are fully capitalized by a government or other public entity. Within this category, public capital SIFs that are wholly capitalized and managed by a single government are sometimes referred to as sovereign development funds.[8]

2. *Mixed capital SIFs*: SIFs initiated and funded by a public entity but also including investment by commercial entities.

Half of the case studies are public capital SIFs, and the other half are mixed capital SIFs. Case studies from three different continents reflect geographic diversity, and the selected SIFs are in different stages in their life cycle. The case studies are also, by design, descriptive and do not in general offer judgment on the choices made by specific SIFs. High- and upper-middle-income economy cases like the Ireland Strategic Investment Fund and the Marguerite Fund show the diversity of environments in which SIFs operate and help distill lessons from cases in which governance standards are perceived to be high and investment markets and competitive conditions advanced. The case studies reflect multiple ownership and management models, as discussed in this volume. Note that these studies were written before the COVID-19 pandemic and do not reflect structural changes that sovereign or quasi-sovereign entities undertook to reconfigure SIFs after it.[9]

Because SIFs are a relatively recent phenomenon, the literature available on this type of investment vehicle is limited. However, literature in adjacent fields offers valuable insights that are relevant for SIFs. This book therefore includes reference to literature on SWFs, private equity funds, state-owned enterprises,

TABLE 1.1 **Classification of case study SIFs**

PUBLIC CAPITAL SIFS	MIXED CAPITAL SIFS
FONSIS (Senegal)	Asia Climate Partners
Ireland Strategic Investment fund	Marguerite Fund (EU and preaccession states)
Nigeria Sovereign Investment Authority – Nigeria Infrastructure Fund	National Investment and Infrastructure Fund[a] (India)

Source: World Bank.
Note: EU = European Union; FONSIS = Fonds Souverain d'Investissements Stratégiques (Sovereign Fund for Strategic Investments); SIF = strategic investment fund.
a. Set up by the government of India, this is the only case study that is a government-sponsored, mixed capital SIF.

fiscal management and transparency, and other related topics. When relevant statistical evidence is available in the literature, such evidence is taken into account. For empirical information on the case study SIFs, the volume is grounded in publicly available documentation, as well as documentation provided by the individual SIFs.[10]

STRUCTURE

This book is divided into two parts comprising a total of 13 chapters. The first part describes the establishment and operations of SIFs; each chapter in this part concludes with a list of key takeaways. The second part consists of six case studies that detail the structural and organizational features of global SIFs operating in a variety of contexts. Finally, three appendixes include four thematic reviews, a list of global SIFs, and a list of people interviewed in the course of the research for this book. The thematic reviews provide additional reference material on topics relevant to SIFs: (1) the role SIFs can play in catalyzing domestic institutional capital to infrastructure, (2) SIF partnerships with private equity funds, (3) risk management, and (4) measuring the double bottom line.

Within the chapters, this volume explores how the SIF sponsor organizes a series of contracts between parties of the fund's multilayered principal-agent architecture to balance competing considerations.[11] To rectify potential pitfalls of the principal-agent relationship (such as information asymmetry or moral hazard) and realize multiple objectives, the public sponsor employs frameworks or contracts discussed in this publication's chapters.

Chapter 2: Overview of Strategic Investment Funds. This chapter introduces SIFs conceptually. It considers SIFs' effectiveness, as well as their limitations, and seeks to present a balanced view of their role. It provides the definition of SIFs, outlines the main features of such funds, and discusses the rationales behind the establishment of SIFs, SIF mandates, and the principles that underpin these mandates. The chapter then discusses the macrofiscal implications of SIFs and the limits to their potential as policy instruments. It concludes by underscoring the importance of preparatory studies that provide a rigorous analysis that can either validate or refute the hypothesis that the SIF is the instrument of choice among a menu of alternatives.

Chapter 3: Legal Framework. This chapter discusses a menu of options and good practices to consider when constructing the legal framework for a SIF, allowing for the heterogeneity of environments within which SIFs are formed. It examines the three overlapping foundational elements that construct the legal framework for a SIF: (1) the legislation under which a SIF is brought into existence, (2) the legal structure adopted by the SIF, and (3) the domicile of the SIF. It discusses the private agreements facilitated by general contract law via which a SIF relates to its stakeholders and outlines other public legislation—domestic or foreign—that affects the operations of a SIF.

Chapter 4: Governance. The quality of a SIF's governance is a core determinant of its success. This chapter discusses the importance of good governance for SIFs and how these entities and their public backers and capital providers can embed robust governance techniques within the organization to ensure that SIF activities correspond to their mandate. It explores why governance is important, what foundational elements constitute the governance of a SIF, and the principles of a well-governed SIF. The chapter serves as a precursor to the succeeding chapters that further spell out the governance processes embedded within the SIF's investment and risk management frameworks and processes, as well as its transparency and disclosure requirements. The chapter focuses on the governance arrangements of the SIF itself, rather than the governance model transmitted by the SIF to its portfolio companies.

Chapter 5: Investment and Risk Management. This chapter discusses the SIF's investment and risk management frameworks. It elaborates on governance arrangements within a SIF by focusing on the accountability framework embedded within a fund's investment management and risk management frameworks. The chapter also discusses the constituent components of the investment management and risk management frameworks, the bodies responsible for their definition and formalization, and the unique features of both in the context of a SIF.

Chapter 6: Investment Process. This chapter discusses the investment process of a SIF—that is, the practical implementation of the investment framework of a SIF. A SIF's investment process is a subset of its governance framework, establishing guidelines and procedures to effectively implement the investment strategy and to ensure that the double bottom line mandate is met. Because SIFs are primarily equity investors, the investment process discussed in this chapter relates to unlisted equity investments.

Chapter 7: Transparency and Disclosure. This chapter discusses the importance of transparency and disclosure for a SIF. Transparency and disclosure are twin guiding principles that allow the SIF and its governing bodies to be held to account while the fund invests public resources in pursuit of a stated mandate. The chapter highlights how the principles of transparency and disclosure are exhibited in the fund's accountability structure, governance arrangements, and reporting arrangements.

NOTES

1. See the International Forum of Sovereign Wealth Funds' web page "About the IFSWF Membership" (https://www.ifswf.org/about-ifswf-membership). The full definition of SWFs, according to the "Sovereign Wealth Funds Generally Accepted Principles and Practices: 'The Santiago Principles,'" is as follows: "Special-purpose investment funds or arrangements that are owned by the general government. Created by the general government for macroeconomic purposes, SWFs hold, manage, or administer assets to achieve financial objectives, and employ a set of investment strategies that include investing in foreign financial assets" (IWG 2008, 3). These traditional SWFs are set up typically for savings or stabilization purposes and invest primarily in publicly traded financial assets, such as stock and bonds.

2. For instance, foreign funds and investors may be unaware of, or unwilling to commit resources to generate, an investment pipeline in small economies.

3. A World Bank (2019) study estimates that new infrastructure could cost low- and middle-income countries 2 percent to 8 percent of gross domestic product per year to 2030.

4. For an overview of regional and multinational SIFs, see appendix C.

5. See the Sputnik V and Russian Direct Investment Fund websites (https://sputnikvaccine .com/about-us/the-russian-direct-investment-fund/ and https://www.rdif.ru /Eng_COVID-19/).

6. Funding for that publication was jointly provided by the World Bank, Inter-American Development Bank, and Public-Private Infrastructure Advisory Facility. Public infrastructure funds are here defined as nonbank financial institutions, under government ownership, that provide financing support to infrastructure projects in a country, sector, or region. These types of funds are pools of public capital destined for public investment in infrastructure. They are fiscal funds: quasi-fiscal tools for governments. Like SIFs, fiscal

funds provide increased functionality to public investment by centralizing relevant skills in a specialized body. In contrast to SIFs, however, they are not necessarily commercial investors and are not specifically designed to mobilize private capital (Halland et al. 2016).

7. Considerable academic and operational research has debated the wisdom of governments investing natural resource–related and other public revenue domestically through SIFs. Although that debate is not the focus of this book, the reader is encouraged to review that literature, some of which is highlighted in appendix E.

8. Santiso (2008) uses the term "sovereign development fund" and highlights that SWFs could "grow to become major actors of development finance: Sovereign Development Funds."

9. For instance, the case study on the Ireland Strategic Investment Fund does not reflect that the government of Ireland has recently tasked the fund to manage a €2 billion Pandemic Stabilisation and Recovery Fund to financially support Irish medium and large enterprises (with more than 250 employees or annual turnover of more than €50 million) that have been affected by COVID-19. See the Ireland Strategic Investment Fund web page "Life Sciences and Healthcare" (https://isif.ie/pandemic-stabilisation-and-recovery-fund), accessed December 12, 2020.

10. Information provided by individual SIFs is sometimes generalized and anonymized, to respond to confidentiality requirements.

11. The overarching framework presented in this chapter to frame the decision-making process of government sponsors of SIFs borrows from contract theory and the applications of contract theory put forth by economists such as Kenneth Arrow and 2016 Nobel Prize winners Oliver Hart and Bengt Holmström.

REFERENCES

Allard, Tom, Gayatri Suroyo, and Stanley Widianto. 2020. "Exclusive: Indonesia Sovereign Wealth Fund Aims to Raise $15 Billion by Offering Multiple Funds." *Reuters*, November 16, 2020. https://www.reuters.com/article/us-indonesia-swf-exclusive/exclusive-indonesia-sovereign-wealth-fund-aims-to-raise-15-billion-by-offering-multiple-funds-idUSKBN27X0E3.

Azhar, Saeed. 2020. "Abu Dhabi's Mubadala Ventures Plans Health Fund as Coronavirus Drives Demand." *Reuters*, April 2, 2020. https://www.reuters.com/article/mubadala-inv-healthcare-fund/abu-dhabis-mubadala-ventures-plans-health-fund-as-coronavirus-drives-demand-idUSL4N2BP364.

Environmental Audit Committee, House of Commons. 2011. *The Green Investment Bank: Second Report of Session 2010–11*. Volume 1. London: The Stationery Office Limited.

Gelb, Alan, Silvana Tordo, and Håvard Halland. 2014. "Sovereign Wealth Funds and Long-Term Development Finance." Policy Research Working Paper 6776, World Bank, Washington, DC.

Halland, Håvard, Michel Noël, Silvana Tordo, and Jacob J. Kloper-Owens. 2016. "Strategic Investment Funds: Opportunities and Challenges." Policy Research Working Paper 7851, World Bank, Washington, DC.

IWG (International Working Group of Sovereign Wealth Funds). 2008. "Sovereign Wealth Funds Generally Accepted Principles and Practices: 'Santiago Principles.'" International Forum of Sovereign Wealth Funds. https://www.ifswf.org/sites/default/files/santiagoprinciples_0_0.pdf.

Kozok, Firat, Kerim Karakaya, and Onur Ant. 2020. "Turkish Wealth Fund to Get Critical Role for Post-Pandemic World." *Bloomberg*, April 14, 2020. https://www.bloomberg.com/news/articles/2020-04-14/turkey-proposes-law-to-enable-sovereign-fund-s-aid-for-economy.

McGinnis, Patrick, Shanthi Divakaran, Jing Zhao, and Yi Yan. 2017. "Government and Venture Capital in China: The Role of Government Guidance Funds." Background paper for *Innovative China: New Drivers of Growth*. Washington, DC: World Bank.

North Africa Post. 2020. "Morocco to Create $4.8 Bln Strategic Investment Fund." *North Africa Post*, August 4, 2020. https://northafricapost.com/42859-morocco-to-create-4-8-bln-strategic-investment-fund.html.

Reuters. 2020. "IMF's Chief Economist Urges 'Equity-Like' Govt Support for Virus-Hit Firms." *Reuters*, July 9, 2020. https://www.reuters.com/article/imf-world-bank/imfs -chief-economist-urges-equity-like-govt-support-for-virus-hit-firms-idINT9N2DM008.

Santiso, Javier. 2008. "Sovereign Development Funds: Key Financial Actors of the Shifting Wealth of Nations." OECD Emerging Markets Network Working Paper, OECD Development Centre, Paris.

Turak, Natasha. 2020. "Sovereign Wealth Funds Will Play a Bigger Role in Markets Post-Coronavirus, Turkey Fund Chief Says." CNBC World Economy, May 22, 2020. https://www .cnbc.com/2020/05/22/sovereign-wealth-funds-have-a-bigger-role-post-covid-turkey -fund-chief.html.

World Bank. 2019. "Overview of Infrastructure Investment Needs in Low- and Middle-Income Countries by 2030." Beyond the Gap, Policy Note 1/6, World Bank, Washington, DC.

World Bank Group and DRC (Development Research Center of the State Council, People's Republic of China). 2019. *Innovative China: New Drivers of Growth*. Washington, DC: World Bank.

World Bank Group and IDB (Inter-American Development Bank). 2020. "Global Review of Public Infrastructure Funds. Volume 1: Identifying Key Design Features and Success Factors for Public Infrastructure Funds." World Bank Group and IDB, Washington, DC. https:// ppiaf.org/documents/5982/download.

Wright, Chris. 2020. "Older and Wiser: How Sovereign Wealth Has Responded to Covid-19." *Euromoney*, September 10, 2020. https://www.euromoney.com/article/27ft5h 678f5ma5k6xkxkw/capital-markets/older-and-wiser-how-sovereign-wealth-has -responded-to-covid-19.

Part 1 Design of Strategic Investment Funds

2 Overview of Strategic Investment Funds

INTRODUCTION

This chapter introduces strategic investment funds (SIFs) conceptually. The chapter considers SIFs' effectiveness, as well as their limitations, and seeks to present a balanced view of their role. Specifically, it examines the definition of SIFs and outlines their main features. It provides an understanding of the rationales behind the establishment of SIFs and a discussion on SIF mandates and the principles that underpin these mandates. It then discusses the macrofiscal aspects of SIFs and the limits to their potential as policy instruments. The chapter concludes by underscoring the importance of preparatory studies that provide a rigorous analysis to either validate or refute the hypothesis that the SIF is the instrument of choice among a menu of alternatives.

Given the increasing prevalence of this vehicle, this book explores factors critical to establishing and operating SIFs that lend them legitimacy and permit them to fulfill their mandate effectively. Legitimacy ensures that the general public and governing parties understand and support the SIF's purpose (Ang 2010). A SIF's legitimacy comes from acceptance by key stakeholders of its mandate and their recognition that the SIF implements its mandate efficiently and according to predefined criteria. If such legitimacy is absent, key stakeholders will lack confidence in the aims or management of the SIF. A lack of legitimacy also jeopardizes the SIF's financial sustainability, because it exposes the entity to political interference in its investment decisions.[1] Each of the following chapters in this book therefore discusses key aspects of setting up and operating a SIF with the view that legitimacy is essential.

WHAT IS A STRATEGIC INVESTMENT FUND?

SIFs exhibit all of the following six characteristics:[2]

1. They are initiated, and fully or partly capitalized, by one or more governments, or by quasi-sovereign entities (for example, government-owned global or regional development finance institutions).

2. They invest primarily in unlisted assets[3]—either domestically or thematically (for example, by making climate-friendly investments)—to achieve financial returns as well as to fulfill a policy objective[4] (double bottom line), with the latter sometimes referred to as the pursuit of economic returns.

3. They aim to mobilize commercial co-investment at the fund or project level.

4. They provide long-term, or patient, capital, primarily as equity, but also as quasi equity and debt.

5. They operate as professional fund managers on behalf of their investors, targeting commercial financial returns.

6. They are established as pools of assets (or funds) through various legal structures, such as investment company, trust, statutory corporation, or limited partnership.

At their best, SIFs are professional financial intermediaries, operating at arm's length from government. They straddle the public sector and private sector spheres and are well placed to take advantage of their strategic position between the state and the market. By capitalizing on their public and private sector links, SIFs act as specialized intermediaries for governments that seek to finance sectors that are underserved by private finance. SIFs seek to mobilize capital from private investors and other sources, such as development finance institutions (DFIs) or sovereign wealth funds (SWFs), which may invest public capital but on commercial terms. The combination of both types of capital sought by SIFs is referred to here as commercial capital.

SIFs may be set up to exclusively enact a SIF mandate or may be part of a larger SWF or public policy purpose. SIFs may operate as a vehicle wholly devoted to a policy-driven double bottom line mandate or be embedded within a larger SWF with traditional functions such as stabilization and savings. India's National Investment and Infrastructure Fund (NIIF) is an example of the former model; the Nigeria Infrastructure Fund (NIF), embedded within the Nigeria Sovereign Investment Authority (NSIA), is an example of the latter approach. SIFs may also be set up within an entity that performs other public policy functions: Malaysia's Khazanah Nasional Berhad (Khazanah), for example, invests its capital with a policy-driven mandate while also performing the role of a holding company for select state-owned assets.

SIF OWNERSHIP AND MANAGEMENT MODELS

Both the funding sources and management models of SIFs can be either solely public or public-private (see table 2.1). A crucial aspect of fund structure and governance is how to structure the ownership and management models to maximize the SIF's operational independence while fulfilling the double bottom line mandate. These factors are discussed in the following chapters on the legal and governance aspects of the SIF, as well as on investment management and process.

As discussed in chapter 1, the ownership of a SIF is a function of its source of capital, and this book focuses on two categories of SIFs based on ownership: public capital SIFs and mixed capital SIFs. SIFs are supported by multiple management models (see table 2.2), resulting in varying investor control over the mandate and varying levels of market perception of the sophistication of the fund.

TABLE 2.1 **Ownership and management models for select SIFs**

SIF	FUNDING SOURCE	MANAGEMENT
Ireland Strategic Investment Fund	100% funded by government of Ireland (proxy owner: Minister for Finance)	Internally managed by state agency, National Treasury Management Agency (public agency for asset-liability management)
Nigeria Infrastructure Fund (under Nigeria Sovereign Investment Authority)	Funded at all levels of government of Nigeria through revenue allocation mode): federal 46%, state 36%, local government 18%	Government controlled, independent investment authority: no separation between fund and manager
National Investment and Infrastructure Fund (NIIF), India	Central government stake: 49% Commercial capital stake (domestic and international): 51%	Dedicated fund management company with public-private ownership NIIF Limited: Company 49% owned by government, 51% by other investors
Marguerite Fund 2010 (Marguerite I)	European Investment Bank and European state financial institutions (from France, Germany, Italy, Malta, Poland, Portugal, and Spain); European Commission	Dedicated private manager: Marguerite Investment Management
Philippine Investment Alliance for Infrastructure	Government pension fund, Asian Development Bank, Dutch pension fund manager APG, MIRA	Private fund manager: MIRA (globally recognized fund manager)

Source: World Bank; see case studies in appendix A.
Note: MIRA = Macquarie Infrastructure and Real Assets; SIF = strategic investment fund.

TABLE 2.2 **Management model for SIFs**

PUBLIC CAPITAL SIFS	MIXED CAPITAL SIFS
Government agency: Managed by a government department or agency	*Dedicated manager (private or public-private):* Managed by a dedicated fund manager wholly owned by one or more investors
Independent public authority: Managed by a semi-independent government entity	*Contractual manager:* Managed on a contractual basis by an existing private manager
Publicly owned company: Managed by a publicly owned company	

Source: World Bank.
Note: SIF = strategic investment fund.

- Public capital SIFs tend to be managed by government entities—whether existing departments managing other assets or semi-independent authorities—or government-owned companies set up with the express purpose of managing the SIF. Typically, in such structures there is no legal separation between the fund and its manager (see chapter 3 for more detailed discussion on legal issues regarding the fund and manager).
- Mixed capital SIFs tend to be managed by either dedicated professional managers, which are formed specifically to manage the SIF and may be owned by one or more of the SIF's investors, or existing private managers that have been selected (usually through a bidding process) to manage the SIF.

SIF OPERATIONAL MODELS

Heterogeneity of mandates leads to a variety of operating models for SIFs. The operating model of the SIF reflects its investment horizon as well as its investment strategy. SIFs can be established either as permanent structures or as finite life funds. The types of objectives that SIFs seek to achieve frequently require long-term capital; for infrastructure, long-term capital is an essential ingredient. Public capital SIFs tend to be established as permanent structures, which allows them to take a very long-term approach to their investments and redeploy their capital after exiting an investment. By contrast, mixed capital SIFs that have mobilized commercial capital tend to be formed as finite life funds, because commercial investors look for a structure that allows them to exit their investments and realize their returns after a defined period. For instance, the Philippine Investment Alliance for Infrastructure and Marguerite II[5]—both of which have attracted private capital—have tenors of 10 years. SIFs may also choose to make their investments directly or to allocate capital through intermediaries that make investments on their behalf (though a fund of funds model). SIFs usually co-invest alongside other investors to fulfill their crowding-in objective. NIIF has also employed the platform investing model, through which the SIF makes an initial investment in a sector (together with co-investors), which can be followed by other acquisitions in the same industry, thus allowing for synergies to develop between the various investments. Often SIFs employ multiple investment approaches or operating models, as shown in table 2.3.

TABLE 2.3 **Operating models of SIFs**

INVESTMENT APPROACHES	PUBLIC CAPITAL SIFS	MIXED CAPITAL SIFS
Project development	FONSIS (Senegal)	Africa50 Fund
	Khazanah (Malaysia)[a]	
Direct investment	Bpifrance (France)	Africa50 Fund
	FONADIN (Mexico)	Asia Climate Partners
	FONSIS (Senegal)	Marguerite
	ISIF (Ireland)	NIIF (India)
	Khazanah (Malaysia)	
	Mubadala (United Arab Emirates)	
	NSIA-NIF (Nigeria)	
	Russian Direct Investment Fund	
Co-investment	FONSIS (Senegal)	Africa50 Fund
	ISIF (Ireland)	Asia Climate Partners
	Khazanah (Malaysia)	Marguerite
	Mubadala (United Arab Emirates)	NIIF (India)
	NSIA-NIF (Nigeria)	
	Russian Direct Investment Fund	
Fund of funds	Bpifrance (France)	GEEREF
	FONADIN (Mexico)	NIIF (India)
	FONSIS (Senegal)	
	ISIF (Ireland)	
	Khazanah (Malaysia)	
	NSIA-NIF (Nigeria)	
	Mubadala (United Arab Emirates)	
Platform		NIIF (India)

Source: World Bank; see case studies in appendix A.
Note: FONSIS = Fonds Souverain d'Investissements Stratégiques (Sovereign Fund for Strategic Investments); FONADIN = Fondo Nacional de Infraestructura (National Infrastructure Fund); GEEREF = Global Energy Efficiency and Renewable Energy Fund; ISIF = Ireland Strategic Investment Fund; Khazanah = Khazanah Nasional Berhad; NIIF = National Investment and Infrastructure Fund; NSIA-NIF = Nigeria Sovereign Investment Authority – Nigeria Infrastructure Fund; SIF = strategic investment fund.
a. Khazanah development for the Iskandar project falls under this category.

DOUBLE BOTTOM LINE MANDATE

The SIF's mandate establishes the policy-defined boundaries within which it has the liberty to operate as an independent commercial (or near-commercial) investor,[6] at arm's length from the government or other sponsor. What follows from articulating the rationale for a SIF is the expression of a double bottom line mandate that moors the SIF's raison d'être (see table 2.4 for illustrative examples of SIF mandates). The first bottom line is the financial return on the investment, and the second bottom line refers to the expected impact on economic productivity and growth or on environmental and social variables. This mandate should be clearly defined and publicly disclosed,[7] and it should be directly based on the findings from detailed preliminary studies for the SIF. As one of the intrinsic traits of the SIF, the double bottom line mandate is typically articulated in the constitutive documents of the SIF. For example, the Ireland Strategic Investment Fund (ISIF) has a statutory mandate to invest "on a commercial basis in a manner designed to support economic activity and employment in Ireland" as set out in the National Treasury Management Agency (Amendment) Act 2014 (NTMA Act 2014), Section 39.[8] Similarly, the investment policy statement of NSIA-NIF states that the fund "seeks to make a positive financial return on its investments in the infrastructure sector in Nigeria. It also aims to attract and support foreign investment and enable growth."[9] The mandate is likely to reflect the institutional history and political environment of the SIF's home country; therefore, some countries will prefer mandates that are as close as possible to market-based, whereas other countries may prefer more government participation.

The double bottom line mandate of the SIF seeks to match the government's policy objective with the need to attract private capital. The policy goal set by the public sponsor includes but is not limited to growing the economy, creating jobs, opening up economic opportunities for women and minorities, adapting to or mitigating climate change, boosting specific sectors or regions of the economy, and diversifying away from commodity reliance (in countries where that is the main industry). In this book, unless otherwise specified, "economic return" or "economic impact" refers generically to the fulfillment of the SIF's policy goal. SIFs set up by quasi-sovereign entities may also address thematic objectives across a range of geographies, such as the need for environmental finance. The policy objective is key because the sovereign (or quasi sovereign) as the principal has a much wider lens in assessing what constitutes profit than a typical fund manager does (van der Tak and Squire 1995). Sovereigns are focused on maximizing net benefits to society, whereas fund managers are focused primarily on financial returns. Therefore, the SIF must pursue active economic, environmental, and social impact in addition to financial return.

But this dual objective presents the SIF with a potential operational conflict that it must constantly seek to balance and mitigate. On the one hand, overemphasizing the policy objective while sacrificing returns could alienate the private capital the SIF seeks to attract and generate politically motivated investments through a vehicle that invests outside of the country's budget process. On the other hand, if the quest for financial returns is overly highlighted, the SIF could gravitate toward investments that are highly attractive to the private sector but have limited policy impact (Halland et al. 2016). Thus, the mandate is designed to provide equal emphasis on both aspects: the policy objective is tempered by a financial return objective and vice versa.

TABLE 2.4 **SIF mandates, examples from case studies**

SIF	DOUBLE BOTTOM LINE MANDATE	ALIGNMENT WITH SOVEREIGN / QUASI SOVEREIGN'S POLICY PURPOSE	SECTORS OF FOCUS
Asia Climate Partners	To offer the largest, fully fledged private equity investment platform for environmental finance in emerging Asia[a]	To demonstrate the possibility of investing in green finance in Asia on a commercial basis while adhering to rigorous ESG practices; focus is predominantly on investments in companies established in ADB developing member countries	Renewable energy, resource efficiency, environmental industries
FONSIS (Senegal)	To catalyze additional financial resources from local and international third parties to cofinance key local projects in strategic industries[b] Investment strategy dictates it must achieve a rate of return in excess of the average cost of state borrowings[c]	To support implementation of Plan Sénégal Emergent, which aims to make Senegal an emerging economy by 2035 (although fund has flexibility to invest outside of the plan)	Agriculture, infrastructure, industry, energy, mining, ICT, financial services, real estate and tourism, health care, and education
Ireland Strategic Investment Fund	To invest on a commercial basis in a manner designed to support economic activity and employment in Ireland	To attract capital and stimulate economy after the global financial crisis (reflected in initial strategy) To address five key economic priorities: indigenous industry, regional development, sectors adversely affected by Brexit, climate change, and housing supply (reflected mandate after 2018)	Housing, water, energy, airport, ports, food, agriculture, information technology, life sciences, and so on
Marguerite Funds	To invest, on a commercial basis, in policy-driven infrastructure projects in the European Union and preaccession states, based on a list of eligible sectors and with particular focus on greenfield infrastructure	To stimulate greenfield infrastructure investments in the European Union, catalyzing private investment, and to set an example of long-term investment	Infrastructure: transport, energy and renewables, telecommunications, and water
National Investment and Infrastructure Fund (India)	To invest in infrastructure assets and related businesses that are likely to benefit from the long-term growth trajectory of the Indian economy To generate attractive long-term risk-adjusted returns for investors on a sustainable basis[d]	To catalyze foreign institutional equity capital to the Indian infrastructure sector	Infrastructure and related sectors
Nigeria Infrastructure Fund	To make a positive financial return on its investments in the infrastructure sector in Nigeria To attract and support foreign investment and enable growth	To follow a rolling five-year plan, developed each year, that seeks to develop essential and efficient infrastructure in Nigeria while also ensuring financial returns	Primarily infrastructure, with emphasis on agriculture, health care, power, and motorways

Source: World Bank; see case studies in appendix A.

Note: ADB = Asian Development Bank; ESG = environmental, social, and governance; FONSIS = Fonds Souverain d'Investissements Stratégiques (Sovereign Fund for Strategic Investments); ICT = information and communication technology; SIF = strategic investment fund.

a. See the Asia Climate Partners website (http://www.asiaclimatepartners.com/about.php?id=18), accessed December 31, 2019.

b. Based on a presentation by FONSIS chief executive officer at the International Forum of Sovereign Wealth Funds Annual Meetings, Juneau, September 2019.

c. See FONSIS case study in appendix A.

d. See the National Investment and Infrastructure Fund website (https://niifindia.in/).

The mandates of both public and mixed capital SIFs frequently focus on infrastructure investment, but some employ a more diversified strategy focused on other sectors. Many SIFs established in emerging market and developing economies focus primarily on infrastructure; examples include the Ghana Infrastructure Investment Fund, NIIF, and NSIA-NIF. Other SIFs have pursued broader approaches focused on sectors like real estate, tourism, agribusiness, health care, and financial services. For instance, in its first incarnation as the Fonds Marocain de Développement Touristique, the Moroccan SIF Ithmar Capital was set up to help implement the Vision 2020 strategic plan to propel Morocco into a global top-20 tourism hot spot. In 2016, this mandate was broadened to encompass all domestic productive sectors.[10]

Adhering to a double bottom line mandate is more complex than having a singular target, and SIFs struggle with both measuring and managing these dual objectives. In addition, nonfinancial impact is typically harder to measure than more easily quantifiable financial returns. As table 2.5 shows, SIFs typically use either a transaction-by-transaction approach or a portfolio approach to embedding the double bottom line mandate (see also box 2.1). ISIF, for example, has striven to diligently address both financial and policy objectives through a rigorous transaction-by-transaction screening and monitoring process that seeks to ensure both targets are met for each potential investment. By contrast, NSIA-NIF takes a portfolio approach: although overall it seeks to meet a financial return target, 10 percent of available investment every year can be dedicated to social infrastructure projects that may have a lower internal rate of return (see the NSIA-NIF case study in appendix A). Similarly, the European Investment Bank (EIB) requires that all its investee funds, including Marguerite, measure the economic rates of return of their investments and comply with minimum return thresholds. Marguerite I guidelines were thus based on EIB guidelines

TABLE 2.5 **Managing the DBL**

MANAGING THE DBL	EXAMPLES
Transaction-by-transaction approach	
Require projects to present potential for both financial and economic/social returns during project identification.	ISIF looks to satisfy three metrics—additionality, displacement, and deadweight—in each project (see box 2.1 for explanation); and its financial target is to produce returns above the cost of Irish government debt.
	ISIF must comply with restrictions of EU state aid and EC Competition Authority so that it does not compete with private sector capital.
Portfolio approach	
Prioritize financial targets for the bulk of the portfolio, and allow lower targets for special carveouts of the portfolio.	Although NIF is required to pursue financial returns (US CPI + 3%), the establishment law allows for 10% of NIF's investment in any fiscal year on social infrastructure projects that enhance economic development in underserved regions that present less return potential.
	For Khazanah, the financial return is more important and is prioritized in investments outside Malaysia, while there is a lower IRR target for domestic investments.
Require a certain percentage of projects selected to present potential for economic return.	EIB requires that a certain percentage of projects invested in by EIB-supported SIFs must be EIB eligible (that is, economic return must be present).

Source: World Bank.
Note: CPI = Consumer Price Index; DBL = double bottom line; EC = European Commission; EIB = European Investment Bank; EU = European Union; IRR = internal rate of return; ISIF = Ireland Strategic Investment Fund; Khazanah = Khazanah Nasional Berhad (Malaysia); NIF = Nigeria Infrastructure Fund; SIF = strategic investment fund.

BOX 2.1

ISIF's approach to managing the double bottom line requirement

The Ireland Strategic Investment Fund (ISIF) uses a transaction-by-transaction assessment to ensure adherence to the double bottom line mandate. Specifically, it looks for projects that satisfy the following three metrics (meeting the three economic impact criteria is a precondition for any investment to be submitted to the investment committee).

1. *Additionality*. ISIF must pursue investments that produce additional economic benefits to gross value added or gross domestic product, which are likely to arise as a result of the investment under consideration, over and above what would have taken place anyway.
2. *Displacement*. As a corollary to the previous requirement, ISIF must avoid investments whereby the additionality created from an investment is reduced or made smaller at the

overall economy level because of a reduction in such benefits elsewhere in the economy. Compliance with displacement criteria (which can affect competitors in the domestic sector) skews investments toward export-oriented sectors and new technologies for which market opportunity is growing fast. ISIF targets 80 percent high impact (long-term, sustainable benefit) and 20 percent low impact (short-term benefits such as a temporary boost in employment).

3. *Deadweight*. ISIF must avoid investments whose economic benefits would have been achieved in any event in the absence of intervention. ISIF requires potential investees to do a thorough survey of commercial funding available to them before seeking ISIF capital.

Source: World Bank; see appendix A for the full case study.

and other requirements from the other sponsors (see the Marguerite case study in appendix A).[11] In some SIFs, the double bottom line mandate may be inherent in the choice of target sectors. For instance, NIIF's scope of investments is bounded within the Indian infrastructure sector, providing it a de facto economic objective tied to infrastructure development; the NIIF funds are expected to pursue commercial returns within these bounds. Thus, NIIF does not expressly manage the double bottom line and does not currently track or report on impact indicators (see the NIIF case study in appendix A).

RATIONALE FOR SIFS

Additionality

The primary argument for setting up a SIF is the extent to which a SIF's intervention can address market or government failures—that is, contribute *additionality* both to what exists in the market and to what is provided by the government. Although such debates are beyond the scope of this volume, the activities of SIFs touch upon wider debates on the role of the state in market economies.[12] In general, the desirability of public sector intervention with respect to addressing barriers to capital can be justified as those emanating from either a market failure or a government failure.[13] In turn, this justification for public sector intervention forms the basis for articulating the SIF's additionality.

Additionality as a prerequisite means that the basic structure of a SIF resembles that of DFIs: it must invest only when there is a confirmed financing gap and must seek to provide nonfinancial value that facilitates private investment.[14] The requirement for additionality positions SIFs adjacent to development banks and DFIs that pursue investment on a near-commercial basis, but with elevated requirements for economic and social benefits, and the precondition that private capital is not crowded out. Additionality can be categorized as[15]

- *Financial*: providing new sources of finance, using a diversity of instruments, or mobilizing additional financing; or
- *Nonfinancial*: mitigating risk; triggering regulatory change; setting higher environmental, social, and governance (ESG) standards; building capacity; building an investor base; or having a demonstration effect.

Additionality also requires that a SIF serves the sovereign's policy purpose better than through budget expenditure and that the SIF has no overlapping mandates with existing state agencies. This means that, for a SIF to be justified, it must, for instance, not only produce more and higher-quality infrastructure for each dollar spent but also crowd in private capital to confirmed financing gaps. It also means that investments justified primarily by economic, environmental, or social returns—that do not satisfy financial return benchmarks—should be funded through the traditional government budget process, not by a SIF (Gelb, Tordo, and Halland 2014). That is, the SIF must (1) produce economic, environmental, and social returns equivalent to what the government could otherwise execute through its budget or other agencies; and (2) unlike typical public sector expenditure, produce financial profits that can flow back as dividends to the government. This requirement implies, in turn, that the SIF bring capabilities to implement this mandate—such as professionalized investment management—that cannot be otherwise found within the government and that have the capacity to source, structure, and execute investments with economic, environmental, and social returns. The following discussion therefore examines the SIF's appeal as a policy instrument set up to provide additionality.

Affiliation to the sovereign(s) allows SIFs to bring implicit commercial advantages to the table, thus catalyzing other commercial capital. SIFs typically step in when there is a scarcity of long-term capital in the market, and they offer both longer tenor financing and financial instruments (for example, equity) and products that are not broadly accessible in commercial markets in the target sector or geography. ISIF's investment horizon, for instance, can extend to 25–30 years, and ISIF can invest across the capital structure, from senior debt to start-up equity. SIFs typically also have the knowledge and networks to manage local complexities, particularly for foreign investors hesitant to invest in emerging markets. They often reduce foreign investor risk perception by reducing information asymmetries and helping alleviate context-specific risks.[16] SIFs can also mitigate government failures by troubleshooting regulatory risk for the broader ecosystem of investors. They do so by observing investment impediments through their operations and providing a feedback mechanism to regulators, essentially serving as an "instrument of economic intelligence" for the government (see Fernándes-Arias, Hausmann, and Panizza 2019).[17] NIIF, for instance, deliberately plays the role of policy feedback provider to uncover investor pitfalls in the infrastructure financing landscape. Although partnering with SIFs is no substitute for contractual protection such as political risk insurance, long-term infrastructure fund investors have a relatively stable partner in a SIF, with an open line to the government, which can be helpful especially at times of political leadership change. Table 2.6 provides a breakdown of more specific additionality that each of the case study SIFs seeks to provide.

SIFs can play a role in countering government and market failures in the infrastructure sector. Many emerging market and developing economy governments lack the human capital to transform projects into bankable, fully documented projects that can be tendered to investors. With their in-house investment expertise, SIFs can complement the project preparation capacity of their host country. Senegal's FONSIS (Fonds Souverain d'Investissements Stratégiques, or Sovereign Fund for Strategic Investments), for instance, acts as project developer in the infrastructure sector, unlocking a pipeline of strategic assets for other investors to co-invest. Especially in countries where they have not invested before, infrastructure funds can benefit from pipeline sharing agreements with SIFs. For example, Meridiam, a global infrastructure fund manager with

TABLE 2.6 **The additional value of SIFs: Case study examples**

SIF	MODE OF ADDITIONALITY
Asia Climate Partners	• Targets high-risk/frontier markets in Southeast Asia with limited private investment in green sectors
	• Takes greenfield projects with construction risk
	• Embeds ADB ESG standards; enhances credibility of portfolio companies
FONSIS (Senegal)	• Acts as project developer or codeveloper for greenfield projects
	• Provides demonstration effect on commerciality of projects with development impact
	• Intermediates between government and private investors
Ireland Strategic Investment Fund	• Has investment horizon that can extend to 25–30 years
	• Invests across capital structure—senior debt to start-up equity
	• Brings local presence and credibility as a sovereign-backed strategic fund
Marguerite Funds	• Focuses on actively developing new greenfield infrastructure projects
	• Has investment horizons of 20 or more years, providing tenors not supplied by market
	• Has local presence
National Investment and Infrastructure Fund (India)	• Demonstrates the feasibility and attractiveness of investing in Indian infrastructure through direct and indirect investment
	• Helps international institutional investors identify credible, professional local counterparts (for example, local developers)
	• Facilitates access to and dialogue with ministries and other government stakeholders in the infrastructure sector
	• Professionalizes infrastructure sector through investing with high-quality developers and facilitating knowledge transfer from foreign partners
Nigeria Infrastructure Fund	• Focuses on greenfield projects, including earlier-stage projects that require substantial involvement in design and development
	• Invests generally when there is a funding gap unfulfilled by private investors[a]
	• Provides demonstration effect for innovative projects

Source: World Bank; see case studies in appendix A.
Note: ADB = Asian Development Bank; ESG = environmental, social, and governance; FONSIS = Fonds Souverain d'Investissements Stratégiques (Sovereign Fund for Strategic Investments of Senegal); SIF = strategic investment fund.
a. Marguerite also participates in competitive tenders.

€6.2 billion in assets under management, identified Senegal as a priority market for its Africa fund but had no prior experience investing there. Its partnership agreement with FONSIS calls for transparency from both parties in pipeline sharing, potentially opening new investment opportunities[18] (see thematic review 2 in appendix B). Unlike private investors, SIFs may also identify and address ecosystem constraints. For example, NSIA-NIF played a key role in unlocking domestic pension fund capital for infrastructure financing by partnering with GuarantCo[19] to launch InfraCredit, an agency that guarantees long-term local currency bonds issued to finance infrastructure projects in Nigeria (see thematic review 1 in appendix B).

Observing the additionality principle means that SIF investments are typically (but not always) steered toward greenfield investments and unlisted assets, for which the financing gap is clearer. As table 2.6 shows, several SIFs in the infrastructure space focus primarily on greenfield projects, for which there is scarcity of capital, to ensure they offer additionality. Many private investors prefer to invest in less risky operational infrastructure, when project development and construction have been completed and the project is generating a steady flow of revenues. This risk aversion leads to a dearth of commercial financing for greenfield infrastructure projects.[20] SIFs can help address this gap by taking on early-stage risk in infrastructure projects. For example, in the aftermath of the 2008 global financial crisis, when infrastructure investment in Europe had significantly decreased, the EIB and several national development banks of the European Union set up the Marguerite Fund. With this 20-year SIF, they aimed to stimulate greenfield infrastructure investments in the European Union and set an example of long-term investment. In contrast, the NIIF Master Fund, co-owned by the government of India and a number of mostly foreign commercial investors, currently focuses primarily on brownfield infrastructure assets (see the NIIF case study in appendix A). NIIF's rationale is that foreign capital that has so far been reluctant to invest in Indian infrastructure can be persuaded more easily to first invest in brownfield infrastructure, which can serve a demonstration effect before the capital pursues riskier investments. Notably, NIIF's Strategic Opportunities Fund, which includes a focus on greenfield investment, has not yet attracted commercial capital alongside that of the government of India. SIFs also do not typically invest in publicly listed stocks because trading on a stock exchange implies an existing market for such assets. Here again, however, there may be exceptions.[21] For financial management reasons SIFs may invest capital yet uncommitted to the double bottom line mandate in a portfolio of listed assets. For instance, ISIF's portfolio has been transitioning a global, predominantly listed securities portfolio to a domestic investment–focused portfolio that reflects the double bottom line mandate set out in the NTMA Act 2014 (see the ISIF case study in appendix A).

In regions with limited private sector activity, SIFs may even be employed to kick-start industries in the local economy. The Palestine Investment Fund is an example of such a fund. With the lack of a thriving local economy, the fund originates projects and incubates companies as well as industries, employing a buy-and-hold strategy given the lack of liquidity. It is a dominant investor in West Bank and Gaza in several sectors including renewable energy, agriculture and agribusiness, health care, and hospitality (see box 2.2 for more details).

In addition, both country-specific and thematic SIFs have been deployed to tackle the problem of climate change. India's NIIF set up the Green Growth

BOX 2.2

Palestine Investment Fund

The Palestine Investment Fund (PIF) was set up in 2003 to function as a sovereign wealth fund. It was recast in 2006 as a strategic investment fund pursuing a double bottom line mandate to invest in underserved sectors in West Bank and Gaza. PIF is a public shareholding company under the companies controller, adhering to the standard laws and regulations applied under the local Companies Law. It currently has US$1 billion in assets under management.[a]

Given the lack of a thriving local economy, PIF originates projects and incubates companies and industries. It is a dominant investor in West Bank and Gaza in several sectors including renewable energy, agriculture and agribusiness, health care, and

hospitality. PIF's strategy is to establish businesses, rather than purchase stakes in existing companies, and it is often the only shareholder in a business. PIF currently has 16 strategic investments in small and medium enterprises, real estate, natural resources, and construction. It employs a buy-and-hold strategy given the difficulty of exiting. Exits occur mainly on the Palestine Exchange because of the dearth of strategic buyers to invest in the economy.

PIF also leverages strategic partnerships to invest in West Bank and Gaza. For example, in March 2019, PIF partnered with the European Investment Bank to finance 35-megawatt rooftop solar projects for 500 public schools in the West Bank (Hill 2019).

Source: World Bank.
a. For more information, see the PIF website (www.pif.ps/home/).

Equity Fund with the United Kingdom's Department for International Development in 2018[22] to invest in sectors aligned with ambitious national targets that drive India's market for climate mitigation and adaptation infrastructure investments.[23] The fund—which is mandated to invest in clean energy, clean transport, and water and wastewater management—was launched at a time when global policy and technological trends suggested it was opportune to invest in advanced climate mitigation and adaptation solutions. Confronting climate-related challenges has also been the province of some SIFs initiated by quasi-sovereign entities. Asia Climate Partners (ACP), for instance, is a US$450 million private equity fund targeting the renewable energy, resource efficiency, and environmental sectors in emerging Asia, launched in November 2014 as a joint initiative of three founding partners: the Asian Development Bank, ORIX Corporation, and Robeco.[24]

With the potential to solve market failures and the appetite to pursue long-term strategic problems, SIFs can make attractive partners not just for private investors but also for other sovereigns, allowing governments to benefit from the heft of intergovernmental partnerships. The commercially attractive characteristics of SIFs, combined with the appeal of intergovernmental relationships and bilateral investment, have led to a plethora of strategic investment alliances between SIFs or between governments through their SIFs or SWFs. These alliances are typically formed by sovereigns to invite capital and technology transfer and know-how to their home countries, or to secure market expansion for their entrepreneurs and businesses (see table 2.7 for an illustrative list of such alliances). In December 2016, for instance, the governments of Morocco and Nigeria agreed to finance a gas pipeline project through their respective strategic investment funds: Morocco's Ithmar Capital and Nigeria's

TABLE 2.7 **Illustrative list of strategic alliances between global SIFs and SWFs**

DATE	PARTNERS	STRATEGIC ALLIANCE / VEHICLE	MANDATE
2017–18	ADIA, Temasek (Singapore), and NIIF (India)	NIIF Master Fund	To invest in infrastructure sectors in India
July 2018	Compañía Española de Financiación del Desarrollo[a] (Spain) and State General Reserve Fund (Oman)	€204.4 million Oman-Spain Investment Fund	To invest jointly in Spanish companies with an interest in expanding internationally to Gulf Cooperation Council countries, particularly Oman
March 2018	Ireland Strategic Investment Fund and China's CIC Capital Corporation	€150 million fund (Donnelly 2018)	To invest in (1) high-growth Irish technology firms aiming to access the Chinese market, and (2) Chinese firms using Ireland as a base for operations in Europe (target sectors include Internet of Things and mobile devices, big data, robotics, and artificial intelligence)
December 2016	Ithmar Capital (Morocco) and NSIA-NIF	Joint venture for Trans-African Gas Pipeline Project	To finance gas pipeline project

Source: World Bank.
Note: ADIA = Abu Dhabi Investment Authority; NIIF = National Investment and Infrastructure Fund; NSIA-NIF = Nigeria Sovereign Investment Authority – Nigeria Infrastructure Fund; SIF = strategic investment fund; SWF = sovereign wealth fund.
a. Compañía Española de Financiación del Desarrollo manages two SIFs: Fund for Foreign Investments and Fund for Foreign Investment Operations of Small and Medium Enterprises.

NSIA-NIF (Ithmar Capital 2016). India's NIIF is another good example of a strategic alliance between governments, with the NIIF Master Fund serving as a platform through which foreign SWFs have partaken in, or boosted their commitment to, infrastructure investment in India. In October 2017, NIIF signed an investment agreement worth US$1 billion with the Abu Dhabi Investment Authority, which became the first institutional investor in NIIF's Master Fund and an owner of NIIF's management company (PTI 2017). This agreement was followed in September 2018 by Singapore's Temasek agreeing to invest as much as US$400 million in NIIF to boost infrastructure financing in the country (Economic Times 2018).

Crowding in commercial capital

The secondary, and interrelated, argument for setting up a SIF is also the SIF's raison d'être: to crowd in commercial capital. In addition to the condition for additionality is the requirement that government capital be used to stimulate and mobilize additional capital, or crowd in commercial capital. As discussed, SIFs are set up precisely to stimulate commercial investment in underserved sectors. This function is again similar to the requirement that DFIs and MDBs must use their capital to mobilize private resources. The World Bank, for example, typically employs a systematic approach to assessing its mode of intervention, focusing first on upstream reforms to determine where market failures really lie and where public capital may best be put to use. The idea is to ensure that policy actions focus first on correcting market failures to unfetter private capital before deploying scarce public capital to fill a financing gap.

Several SIFs have been effective in mobilizing additional capital per their mandate, at either the fund level or the project level. As discussed in a prior World Bank policy research working paper on SIFs, the concept of a public capital multiplier is useful to understand the efficacy of the SIF's objective to crowd in capital (see Halland et al. 2016).[25] The public capital multiplier is the ratio of total investment to public funds invested and can be calculated at both the fund level and the project level.[26] Few SIFs disclose official numbers for their multiplier effects; however, NIIF is an excellent example of a SIF that is inherently structured for a multiplier effect at the fund level, with the Indian government restricting its ownership to 49 percent. Given that NIIF investments at the project level mobilize further private capital, NIIF estimates that their intervention in the market can lead to a multiplier effect of 15–20x. Table 2.8 shows a breakdown of actual and estimated multipliers for the case study SIFs.

The principle of additionality must be met, however, before celebrating the SIF's multiplier effect. A multiplier ratio is an imperfect method of assigning success to a SIF because the ratio does not consider whether the SIF intervention was indeed necessary to mobilize commercial capital. A higher multiplier—often found in SIFs undertaking fund of funds strategies—may also indicate that the sovereign sponsor has less control over the policy objectives because mobilization of additional capital is typically accompanied by dilution of ownership (Halland et al. 2016). Therefore, additionality remains the cornerstone to justifying a SIF's establishment. One way that SIFs enforce the discipline when seeking a multiplier effect is by systematically assuming only minority stakes (and on commercial terms) in their investments, thus reducing the risk of crowding out the private sector. Marguerite, for example, acts primarily as a minority investor, and seeks thereby to minimize crowding out other private investors (see the case study in appendix A). Similarly, ISIF generally takes minority equity stakes in Irish companies and invests on equal terms with private investors to generate the multiplier effect and ensure compliance with the Market Economy Investor Principle as part of European Union state aid rules.[27]

TABLE 2.8 **Estimated multiplier effect of SIFs**

SIF	MULTIPLIER	INVESTMENT STAKE ASSUMED IN PROJECTS
Asia Climate Partners	—	Minority/majority
FONSIS (Senegal)	32x[a] (actual)	Minority/majority
Ireland Strategic Investment Fund	2.8x[b] (actual)	Primarily minority
Marguerite Funds	17.5x[c] (estimated)	Primarily minority
National Investment and Infrastructure Fund (India)	15–20x[d] (estimated)	Minority/majority
Nigeria Infrastructure Fund	—	Minority/majority

Source: World Bank; see case studies in appendix A.
Note: FONSIS = Fonds Souverain d'Investissements Stratégiques (Sovereign Fund for Strategic Investments); SIF = strategic investment fund; — = not available.
a. See the FONSIS study in appendix A.
b. See the Ireland Strategic Investment Fund case study in appendix A. The current multiplier at portfolio level is 2.8x.
c. For Marguerite II (see case study in appendix A). The European Investment Bank's investment in Marguerite II was backed by the European Fund for Strategic Investment and is based on the assumption that the multiplier of the European Investment Bank's €200 million investment in Marguerite II would be at least 17.5x.
d. National Investment and Infrastructure Fund estimate (see the case study in appendix A).

CONCESSIONALITY FOR A SIF

Ideally all SIFs should set their financial return targets at commercial levels, that is, at the levels customarily expected by private investors in the same instruments and sectors. In principle, SIFs are not providers of concessional funding (see box 2.3 on the definition of concessional finance). The acceptance of concessional returns, other than in predefined, exceptional circumstances (discussed in the next paragraph), would risk crowding out existing commercial investors and would be contrary to the principle of additionality that is core to the SIF definition. Although the boundary between commercial and concessional returns is not always easy to define, a clear commitment to pursue commercial returns will force the SIF to be disciplined in valuing its investments both at entry and at exit and avoid diluting returns.

At a minimum, SIFs should clearly define the exceptional circumstances in which concessional investments are allowed. If a SIF opts to allow for concessional returns, it is advisable that it

- Segregate these investments into ad hoc concessional pockets of the portfolio;
- Restrict such pockets to a minority of the portfolio (for example, 10 percent);
- Set and disclose clear policy or economic criteria that justify breaching the commercial return commitment; and
- Set an ad hoc process for the evaluation and approval of concessional investments.

NSIA-NIF is a good example of a disciplined and transparent approach to concessionality. As discussed previously, up to 10 percent of the NIF capital

---

BOX 2.3

Concessional finance and strategic investment funds

Concessional funding is "financing at softer terms through price, tenor, rank, or security, or a combination to reduce project risk" (World Bank 2020). It is typically provided by governments or donors (such as development banks) to catalyze private sector investment. Examples of concessional finance include early-stage equity investments whose prospective returns are not commensurate with investment risk, first-loss tranches or guarantees, and senior or subordinated debt investments at subcommercial terms (World Bank 2020).

In practice, the boundary between commercial and concessional returns is not always easy to define. Several factors make it difficult to set a commercial return target.

- The returns targeted by commercial investors are not set in stone but vary over time, reflecting financial market and macroeconomic conditions.
- Target returns are always forward-looking and reflect arbitrary assumptions about the future performance of the investee company or project.
- In emerging market and developing economies, there might be few past investments for use as precedents to inform the setting of a return target for a new transaction.
- The strategic investment fund—as a provider of additionality—may be the sole bidder for an asset, making it impossible to determine the asset's valuation (and, hence, expected returns) through a competitive process among multiple bidders.

Source: World Bank.

available for investment in any fiscal year can be invested in social infrastructure projects that promote economic development in underserved sectors or regions of Nigeria and may present less favorable financial return potential. NIF seeks to recover at least the total cost of operations during the life of the project (net of any government subsidies the project may receive). All potential projects are submitted to an outside committee set up for this purpose by the National Economic Council that decides whether NSIA may invest in them. A comprehensive feasibility study is required to demonstrate how a prospective project serves the public interest and has clear potential to provide economic and employment stimulus (see the NSIA-NIF case study in appendix A).

In such exceptional cases, catalyzing private capital in contexts of market failures may require the sovereign or quasi sovereign of the SIF to consider offering sweeteners to the fund manager, commercial investors in a mixed capital SIF, and co-investors in the fund's projects. This mechanism could take various forms, as depicted in table 2.9. One such form of sweetener is to directly or indirectly reduce management fees for nongovernment investors by the sovereign or quasi-sovereign entity taking on a larger proportion of these fees (typically 2 percent is the industry standard). This mechanism is pertinent when the sovereign or quasi-sovereign entity has co-investors at the fund level. But incentives have to be carefully designed to reduce moral hazard, and to ensure that co-investors in the fund still have an incentive to monitor the fund. Another mechanism is to provide downside protection or promise asymmetric positive returns to the nongovernment investors in the SIF or co-investors at the portfolio company level. Senegal's FONSIS, for instance, caps its returns—that is, it limits the profits the SIF can accept—on most investments to 12 percent, which can benefit its co-investors (FONSIS does not have an external fund manager or co-investors at the fund level). Public sponsors also offer other perks. For instance, the Asian Development Bank, which is a founding partner in the ACP fund, supports ACP in deal sourcing, due diligence, and fundraising, and through technical assistance facilities.

TABLE 2.9 **Mechanisms for embedding financial incentives for SIF co-investors and managers**

BENEFICIARY	REDUCED HURDLE RATE OR MINIMUM RATE REQUIRED BY INVESTOR	REDUCED MANAGEMENT FEES	CAPPED RETURNS	DOWNSIDE RISK
Co-investor at fund level	n.a.	The public sponsor accepts a higher proportion of management fees vs. other investors.	Government investor accepts capped returns.	For example, first-loss tranche can limit downside for fund level co-investors.
Co-investor at project level	n.a.	n.a.	SIF accepts capped returns.	For example, first-loss tranche can limit downside for project level co-investors.
Fund manager	A reduced hurdle rate allows the fund manager to share in the profits of the fund earlier or at a lower threshold.	n.a.	Government anchor investor's commitment to cap returns helps the fund manager mobilize additional investors for a larger fund size.	n.a.

Source: World Bank.
Note: n.a. = not applicable; SIF = strategic investment fund.

MACROFISCAL IMPLICATIONS OF A SIF

This book does not delve deeply into the macroeconomic and fiscal implications of a SIF. Those issues are amply discussed in publicly available literature by both academic scholars and practitioners.[28]

Note, however, that consistency of the SIF's investment activities with the sovereign's macroeconomic policies is particularly relevant for public capital SIFs, or mixed capital SIFs anchored by one government. Links between SIFs and the macroeconomy are a two-way street; that is, causality can potentially run from the macroeconomy to the SIF and vice versa. On the one hand, the SIF's rate of return on investments is likely to be strongly procyclical, rising when the domestic economy's business cycle is in a boom phase and falling when there is a contraction. On the other hand, SIFs can also create macroeconomic balance issues, particularly if the fund is large compared to the size of the economy in which it operates.[29] Because SIF investment activities inject funds into the domestic economy and risk fragmenting government spending and budget procedures, the government must ensure overall macroeconomic consistency between the SIF and the sovereign's budgetary process. Such macroeconomic management seeks to mitigate the risk that the economy lacks absorptive capacity to accommodate SIF investments and seeks to counteract inflationary pressure caused by SIF investments (see box 2.4 on the Santiago Principles' guidance relating to the macroeconomic implications of SWFs). Coordination with macroeconomic policy is particularly relevant for SIFs capitalized with natural resource exports in hard currency (Halland 2019). Unlike public capital SIFs, mixed capital SIFs are typically insulated from macrofiscal interdependence, especially when their anchor is a quasi-sovereign entity, because they are not considered part of the sovereign balance sheet and are usually not directly responsible for economic policy.

Governments considering SIFs employ multiple mechanisms to maintain overall macroeconomic coherence. By crafting the SIF mandate to ensure that these funds undertake only commercial investments and that spending with only a policy purpose is kept on budget, governments can ensure from the outset that SIFs do not fragment the government's budgetary process or operate outside of budget scrutiny. From a macroeconomic perspective, governments considering setting up SIFs should base allocations to the SIF on a macroeconomic modeling exercise that helps determine the optimal size and relative allocations by sector (for example, Halland, Awiti, and Lim, forthcoming). Governments of resource-rich countries may also seek to insulate the domestic economy from commodity price fluctuations and ensuing fiscal volatility by setting up stabilization funds that complement SIF activities and moderate budget volatility. For instance, NSIA-NIF is a subfund under the larger umbrella Nigerian SWF, which also includes a stabilization subfund focused on macroeconomic stability during economic distress.[30] Coherence with macroeconomic policies can also be maintained through governance arrangements and representation on oversight bodies. For instance, Ireland's respective secretary generals for the Departments of Finance and Public Expenditure & Reform serve as ex officio members on the National Treasury Management Agency Board, which sets ISIF strategy.[31] Likewise, Khazanah's board of directors includes a representative from Malaysia's Ministry of Economic Affairs to ensure that the fund's investment activities are consistent with national economic policies.[32] Similarly, NSIA's governing council includes

Santiago Principles and macroeconomic implications of SWFs

The Santiago Principles include the following generally accepted principles and practices (GAPPs) related to sovereign wealth funds (SWFs):[a]

GAPP 3. Principle
Where the SWF's activities have significant direct domestic macroeconomic implications, those activities should be closely coordinated with the domestic fiscal and monetary authorities, so as to ensure consistency with the overall macroeconomic policies.

GAPP 4. Principle
There should be clear and publicly disclosed policies, rules, procedures, or arrangements in relation to the SWF's general approach to funding, withdrawal, and spending operations.

GAPP 4.1. Subprinciple. The source of SWF funding should be publicly disclosed.

GAPP 4.2. Subprinciple. The general approach to withdrawals from the SWF and spending on behalf of the government should be publicly disclosed.

Source: IWG 2008.
a. These principles apply also to public capital strategic investment funds.

representatives from domestic fiscal and monetary authorities, who can ensure alignment with Nigeria's macroeconomic policies. If the SIF is part of an economic union and the sovereign does not set monetary policy, the coherence of SIF activities focuses on the fiscal. For instance, Senegal's FONSIS is part of the West African Economic and Monetary Union and does not set monetary policies.[33]

Fiscal integration of the public capital SIF is important because of the link between contributions into and withdrawals from the SIF and the government's overall budget surplus and deficit. Public capital SIFs, like SWFs, are part of the overall balance sheet of the government, so their activities must maintain coherence with the overall fiscal policy of the government (Al-Hassan et al. 2018). The fiscal interdependence between a sovereign's balance sheet and a proposed SIF is the reason why sovereigns with high levels of debt and costly debt repayment must consider the opportunity cost of setting up a SIF versus paying down debt. For instance, under Article 40.2(b) of the NTMA Act 2014, ISIF must "ensure that investments do not have a negative impact on the net borrowing of the general government of the State for any year." The conditions under which funds can be transferred to the SIF must be made clear ex ante so that all potential co-investors have a clear picture of what funds will be used to capitalize the SIF and under what conditions they can be withdrawn. For instance, the government of Ireland cannot make withdrawals from ISIF until 2025.[34] Clear-cut and publicly disclosed fiscal rules must ideally allow for contribution into the fund during times of surplus and withdrawal from the fund during times of deficit. The Nigeria Sovereign Investment Authority (Establishment, etc.) Act, 2011, or NSIA Act 2011, for instance, clearly specifies that NSIA can be funded only with hydrocarbon revenues that are in excess of Nigeria's budgetary requirements, and that the only form of payout from NSIA is through dividends to stakeholders after five years of consistent profitability in all three NSIA funds (see the NSIA-NIF case study in appendix A). Sovereigns also sometimes provide tax exemption to SIFs established by ad hoc law and must carefully consider whether such tax exemption is justified.[35]

Precommitment to rules for early withdrawals, including any safety valve allowing crisis access to SIF funds, is equally essential. Safety valve provisions must spell out the precise conditions that can be considered an emergency or crisis and specify the mechanism for using funds from the SIF for purposes beyond those originally contemplated. For instance, under Section 42 of the NTMA Act 2014, the Minister for Finance may direct ISIF funds to finance credit institutions to remedy an economic or financial crisis in Ireland.

When considering the setup of a SIF, it is important to bear in mind the fiscal risks the government may undertake through the SIF and, conversely, the risks the SIF is exposed to through the sovereign.[36] For instance, SIFs set up under a state holding company model, and funded by retained earnings related to a portfolio of state-owned enterprises (SOEs), can be exposed to uncertain and potentially large liabilities of those state assets. In addition, deterioration of the sovereign's credit risk can in turn affect the SIF's credit rating and hinder its ability to issue debt. Symmetrically, the fund might create fiscal risks for the government by its own transactions. For example, if the SIF issues debt or makes investments in subsidiary companies, it may indirectly incur contingent liability for the sovereign because of a perception of implicit government guarantee through the participation of a SIF.[37] The sovereign must therefore provide limits on the purpose and extent to which a SIF may incur debt. Implicit state guarantees could generate perverse incentives for the fund's management, in particular encouraging excessive risk taking. Ideally, the sovereign must also make an unambiguous statement of fund independence in its establishment law, including a renunciation of any implicit guarantees, and the law should make provisions for the SIF's bankruptcy and resolution. A SIF backed 100 percent by a sovereign that does not have defined procedures for bankruptcy and resolution risks perpetuating the perception that its liabilities are implicitly backed by the government budget. In the absence of such an unambiguous statement, a second-best policy would be for the sovereign to make any guarantees explicit. If the state accepts liability for a portion of the SIF's debts through a guarantee, then such a guarantee should be explicitly recorded in the government's budget. The sovereign must carefully manage the potential risks that could arise from perverse incentives for SIF management to transfer value from the SIF to external entities.

LIMITATIONS OF A SIF

Although SIFs are designed to bring advantages to the table, they are not an overall fix for investor constraints or a substitute for good fiscal management. Even a well-functioning SIF does not substitute for the benefits of a strong regulatory framework, overall strong governance, and rule of law as relevant to investment and doing business. Enabling environment pitfalls for private investment—like insufficiencies in legislation for commercial contracts—require policy reforms that cannot be efficiently addressed by a SIF. Public capital SIFs are also not a substitute for a good fiscal management framework. As discussed earlier, without a clear purpose that adds value relative to other policy alternatives, a SIF will simply serve to fragment the government's investment program and complicate government oversight of public expenditure and fiscal risk. Particularly for public capital SIFs, the government must have capable fiscal management to efficiently oversee a SIF's activities and liabilities.

SIFs also cannot bind future administrations to honor the establishing government's commitment to the institution or its mandate, and they must strategically buffer against political headwinds to come (Environmental Audit Committee 2011).[38] This is a key risk that SIFs have to manage strategically, such as through long-term external partnerships and alliances that can buffer the attempt of future governments to prematurely dissolve a SIF. Governments would likely balk at severing alliances or co-investments from multilateral bodies or other SWFs, making such partnerships particularly valuable to the longevity of a SIF. It is therefore striking to observe SIFs such as the NIIF actively cultivating such relationships with both multilaterals and SWFs: to date, NIIF has received investments from SWFs like the Abu Dhabi Investment Authority and Temasek, as well as from multilaterals like the Asian Development Bank and Asia Infrastructure Investment Bank. Public capital SIFs set up by one government, by contrast, are more exposed to political risk.

CHALLENGES TO ESTABLISHING A SIF

SIFs are complex entities because they sit between providers of public and private capital, and because they can exhibit properties of SWFs, SOEs, and private capital funds. Their proximity to the sovereign or quasi-sovereign entity allows SIFs to operate in a commercial space while still having some of the privileges of this affiliation, such as being able to provide regulatory feedback to governments. Public capital SIFs exhibit properties of SWFs because they are investment agencies of the sovereign and their activities must be consistent with overall macroeconomic policies of the country, as discussed earlier. They also exhibit properties of SOEs because their mandate is shaped by a public policy purpose such as better infrastructure. All SIFs have properties of private equity funds because they typically take direct investment in unlisted assets and are usually active investors that require board seats and can mobilize or crowd in capital from other investors.

SIFs are subject to higher public standards because of their affiliation with the sovereign, and public capital SIFs are often part of complicated authorizing and regulatory environments. Being a state (or quasi-state) actor investing public funds changes requirements and expectations for transparency and disclosure as well as the perception of risk. Proximity to the sovereign elevates reputational risk of the SIF beyond the risk of poor financial returns because sovereign or quasi-sovereign entities are held to higher public standards of responsible investment. The operational independence of the public capital SIF may be subject not only to its constitutive documents but also to the existing authorizing environment for SOEs. SIF regulatory frameworks may derive from both the establishment documents and the rule books for both private investment agencies and SOEs (see box 2.5 for the example of China). In a country without centrally codified SOE rules, regulatory coherence for SIFs may also be cumbersome to manage.

One of the central features of the public capital SIF—its alignment with national priorities—may also lead to operational complexity for the fund manager as national priorities change during the SIF's life cycle. As discussed earlier, most public capital SIFs are set up to align with national priorities, a requirement typically reflected in their mandates. Given that the SIF has an institutional longevity that can go beyond election cycles or macroeconomic cycles, national

BOX 2.5

Complex authorizing environment for China government guidance funds

Despite substantial variation in the way China's national and subnational strategic investment funds (called government guidance funds, or GGFs) operate, a World Bank study found that they are often subject to a complex authorizing environment, resulting in conflicting messages that can blur the strategic objectives and undermine investment performance of these entities (McGinnis et al. 2017).

Apart from reporting to their respective government sponsors, GGFs can be subject to regulation and supervision from a variety of agencies such as China's National Development and Reform Commission, the Ministry of Finance, the State-Owned Assets Supervision and Administration Commission of the State Council, the Chinese Securities Regulatory Commission, and the Asset Management Association of China.

Understandably, each of these bodies regulates from a different perspective, creating overlapping regulatory frameworks. For example, the National Development and Reform Commission's goal is to ensure that GGFs target their capital to strategic industries in support of the government's industrial development policies, whereas the Chinese Securities Regulatory Commission and the Asset Management Association of China are focused on supervising funds that have raised capital from the private sector to ensure that investors in these funds receive adequate protection. In addition to central government policies and regulation, local GGFs are also subject to administrative measures devised by lower levels of government. Moreover, State-Owned Assets Supervision and Administration Commission of the State Council guidelines, which apply to state-owned enterprises, including GGFs, emphasize value capital preservation and appreciation.

As discussed in chapter 7, frequent reporting may thus skew the long-term investment nature of the strategic investment fund, forcing it to be driven—at least partially—by short-term returns in order to abide by supervisory guidelines. These principles can conflict with the fundamental nature of private equity–style investing, which is high risk and may require several years to produce profits.

Source: McGinnis et al. 2017.

priorities may well be subject to change. A good example of the latter change is ISIF. ISIF was established by NTMA Act 2014, after the global financial crisis, to invest in sectors of strategic significance to the Irish economy such as real estate, small and medium enterprises, venture capital, infrastructure, and so on. In 2015, ISIF's initial investment strategy was published; in 2017–18, the government initiated a review of the investment strategy given the rapidly improving economic situation in Ireland. As a result of this review, the Irish government revised ISIF's investment strategy in February 2019 to re-center on five new economic priorities: indigenous industry, regional development, sectors affected by Brexit, climate change, and housing. Such a fundamental shift in core mandate may result in changes to the operational structure of the SIF.

To develop its capacity and implement a long-term mandate, a SIF needs enduring and broad-based political commitment that spans electoral cycles: the absence of such support can jeopardize the longevity and effectiveness of the fund. For example, in 2004, through the Venture Capital Trust Fund Act, the government of Ghana created a SIF, the Venture Capital Trust Fund (VCTF), that was to be funded by a 25 percent levy from Ghana's National Reconstruction Levy[39] derived from banks and financial institutions. The VCTF was funded by the levy for only three years, however, because the National Reconstruction

Levy was repealed in 2007 as a result of its perceived negative impact on businesses. VCTF's budget became inconsistent thereafter because the fund was solely capitalized by the government. With the change in Ghana's government in 2008, the political will surrounding the establishment of VCTF also diminished (Divakaran, Schneider, and McGinnis 2018). This is a particular risk for public capital SIFs funded by one government. In principle, mixed capital SIFs are less vulnerable to political cycles because the presence of private co-investors can act as a counterweight to political considerations and strengthens the commercial focus of the fund.

ISSUES TO CONSIDER BEFORE ESTABLISHING A SIF

Before establishing a SIF, policy makers must consider whether prevailing political, economic, financial, and sector-specific conditions are enough for the fund to be successful. First, as with SWFs, when the government is the public sponsor, it must employ a thorough and inclusive process to establish the legitimacy of the SIF within the citizenry, political parties, and financial and business communities. Without legitimacy, SIFs may be vulnerable to shifting political sands. Second, because SIFs are employed to mobilize private capital, the enabling environment for private investors is a consideration for the success of the SIF. The enabling environment is a broad concept that ranges from the existence of specific laws and regulations, such as for establishing a private fund, to governance considerations, such as the level of corruption of a country and the ability to enforce contracts. A SIF may not require that all these elements be addressed as necessary conditions before establishment;[40] however, to attract private capital, the SIF must operate within a legal and regulatory environment sufficiently strong to provide co-investors with confidence that contracts can be structured and enforced. Particularly in the case of public capital SIFs, a key factor of success is the continuing commitment of the public sponsor anchoring the SIF, which may be secured through legal and institutional safeguards that ensure the longevity of the fund and prevent deviations from the mandate (see chapters 3 and 4 on legal and governance considerations).

The public sponsor also sends important signals to potential private partners through its overarching structural decisions that determine how the SIF operates. In-depth discussion on good practices around these structural decisions forms the crux of the following five chapters of this volume. Private investors look for signals of assurance that the SIF's investments will be undertaken on commercial terms, albeit within the fund's politically defined mandate. The public sponsor's choice to allow the SIF to be managed professionally is one such signal. Mixed capital SIFs can also enhance operational independence by restricting government ownership to a minority stake. For instance, the government of India signaled its desire to attract and accommodate private capital by choosing to restrict its stake in both the NIIF and its fund manager to 49 percent. Public capital and mixed capital SIFs alike strengthen operational independence by adhering to best practices for governance, such as involving independent directors on their boards and committees and inserting legislative checks and balances on government intervention (see chapters 3 and 4). Public sponsors and SIFs also send signals of commercial orientation through whom they recruit for SIF investment teams—typically recruiting both management and staff overwhelmingly from investment banking, fund management, or consulting firms—or whom they select for the board. The public sponsor's capacity for effective ownership is also important. For instance, if fund management is outsourced, then oversight bodies within the government will need the requisite economic, financial, and legal capacity to efficiently oversee the performance of the private fund manager and to manage the contractual relationship (see chapter 4 on governance). Transparency in operations is another confidence-boosting signal for private partners. Because SIFs are investors of public capital, transparency is central to all the frameworks that guide SIFs' activities, including their interaction with the government budget and the country's fiscal framework (see chapter 7 on transparency and disclosure).

PREPARATORY STUDIES TO ESTABLISH A SIF

To establish the legitimacy of the SIF as a tool of intervention, the public sponsor must start with a preliminary study—or feasibility study—that establishes the analytical foundation upon which a SIF is based. Particularly when a government is the public sponsor, the establishment of a sovereign investment fund is a one-time occurrence, or in any case not a frequent one. If a public capital SIF's establishment is driven purely by political considerations or electoral cycles, the public sponsor could rush the process to establish the fund in a way that severely hampers the functionality and sustainability of the fund. For both public capital and mixed capital SIFs, a thorough preliminary study permits the sponsor to articulate a precise definition of the fund's mandate and allows for the definition of legal and regulatory priorities in the setup of the fund. Specific decisions on legislation, governance structure, and investment policy follow from there. Such sequencing is important. Adequate legislation and regulatory measures for the SIF can be duly considered only if a proper analysis of the fund's role and mandate has first been undertaken. Previous feasibility studies for other public financial institutions can provide important lessons (see box 2.6 on the feasibility study for the Green Investment Bank).

A well-conducted feasibility study accomplishes multiple objectives through a sequenced analysis that, at each stage, either validates or refutes the value of a SIF intervention. The key objectives of the study are to develop a holistic understanding of the investment landscape in the target area—who the investors are, where capital gravitates, who manages the capital, and so on—and validate whether there are gaps in financing caused by either market or government failures. This analysis allows the public sponsor to conclude whether the SIF could indeed provide additionality in this space and whether the SIF is a more desirable instrument to serve the articulated policy purpose compared with other alternatives that might achieve the same goals. If the SIF is established as the instrument of choice, the feasibility study must provide a refined articulation of its mandate and outline the organizational and operational parameters within which it will function. The study must identify a pipeline of assets that would be investment worthy if investment could be catalyzed into this space. The feasibility analysis for a government-sponsored SIF should also ideally ensure consistency between the SIF's investment activities and sovereign macroeconomic policies, and identify the fiscal risks the government may undertake through the SIF as well as the fiscal risks the SIF would be exposed to through the sovereign.

BOX 2.6

Preliminary study for the Green Investment Bank, United Kingdom

The Green Investment Bank (GIB) provides an example of a public financial institution for which a detailed preliminary study was implemented (Vivid Economics 2011, Box 2). Entitled "The Economics of the Green Investment Bank: Costs and Benefits, Rationale and Value for Money," the study provides an in-depth examination of the case for establishing a green investment bank in the United Kingdom. Although the GIB is not a strategic investment fund, it has a similar mission to invest in infrastructure with a double bottom line.

The GIB was established in recognition of the market failures and barriers to investment in green assets in the United Kingdom.

The 2011 study was implemented in four phases. The first phase identifies market and institutional failures and barriers to investment in green infrastructure and large-scale, late-stage green technologies. The second phase analyzes what drives the identified investment gaps, how they may be closed, and whether the GIB may have a role. The third phase comprises a broad value-for-money assessment of the GIB as an institution, and of each of its interventions. The final phase considers the impact of the GIB on UK growth and how the GIB may be used to maximize growth.

The preliminary phase of the study identifies 15 sectors with financing gaps. It analyzes which of the 15 sectors have market failures, or areas of capital shortage, that the GIB could feasibly address. The study then considers the magnitude and degree of permanence of these market failure and capital shortages. Sector-specific market failures identified by the report include externalities, information asymmetries, market power, and complements. The main financial market failure identified by the report relates to investor

unfamiliarity with new types of technology and business models related to carbon technologies, as well as limitations on companies' ability to expand their balance sheets.

To determine whether the GIB constitutes value for money for taxpayers, the study assesses how GIB interventions compare with other possible policy vehicles. This value-for-money approach is applied to each sector in two steps. In the first step, each sector is screened for four attributes: complementarity with other government policies, market additionality, timing and investability, and green impact. It is illustrative to look at how these four criteria were applied to some of the 15 sectors. The criterion of complementarity excludes flood defenses, which already had alternative public funding in place. The criterion of additionality ruled out onshore wind and photovoltaic electricity generation, for which private capital seemed to be available. The criterion of timing ruled out carbon capture and storage, a technology considered too young to be ready for large-scale investment. On green impact, the areas with the highest expected effect were selected; they included offshore wind, for which the risks of pushing into deeper water were not yet well understood by private investors. Only a limited number of private investors were therefore active in deeper waters, and the GIB could make a difference.

The second step includes an assessment of investment returns, in terms of returns to society (net present value per unit of capital invested) and private returns to the GIB (return on capital employed). The study also includes a discussion of the type of financial instruments that the GIB may employ, and on what terms.

Source: Vivid Economics 2011.

The feasibility study therefore helps establish the bounds within which the SIF can credibly operate while imposing minimal risk to the sovereign's balance sheet. A well-conducted feasibility study therefore requires specialized knowledge and experience in areas ranging from market dynamics, fiscal policy, and investment fund legislation, to governance and management of a fund. Because of the complexity and diversity of topics to be covered, such studies are typically implemented by teams of experts—typically from global consulting firms, academic organizations, or MDBs—handpicked for their expertise and knowledge of SIFs. See box 2.7 for a detailed review of feasibility study features.

KEY TAKEAWAYS

- SIFs are special-purpose investment vehicles backed by governments or other public institutions that seek a double bottom line of financial and economic returns. They invest in, and mobilize commercial capital to, sectors and regions where private investors would otherwise not invest or would invest to a limited extent.

BOX 2.7

Key features of a feasibility study to establish a SIF

A preliminary study for a strategic investment fund (SIF) may include the following elements, depending on the fund's objectives.[a]

Phase 1: Fund's key policy features and mandate. A review of the fund's desired role, mandate, and objectives, as well as the market situation and financing gaps within which it will operate. Such review includes the following:

- Selection of sectors to be targeted by the SIF, review of investor landscape, and an assessment of financing gaps in these sectors
- For the selected sectors, assessment of market failures that the SIF is meant to address
- If such market failures exist, determination of how big they are and whether they will likely lead to permanent or transitory funding gaps
- Consideration of the likely policy impact on the sectors in which the SIF will operate
- Consideration of alternatives to understand if the objectives of the fund can be best met through a SIF structure as opposed to some other form (including public finance)
- Ensuring consistency of SIF operations with macroeconomic, fiscal, and financial sector policy[b]
- Cost-benefit analysis of SIF as compared with other policy options
- Assessment of the preconditions that a SIF would need to operate efficiently in its home market, country context, and relevant sectors

- Consideration of how the SIF would be complementary to the private sector, address market failures, and crowd in instead of crowding out private capital
- Consideration of the public sponsor (if sovereign) capacity constraints that the SIF will relieve
- Environmental, social, and governance conditions

Phase 2: Design of the SIF's operational features. The feasibility study addresses questions related to the viability and sustainability of the SIF as an investment organization, at the level of the fund itself. The feasibility study may include elements such as the following:

- An assessment of the risks that the fund will face, and how these can be mitigated
- A consideration of the pipeline of projects that the fund can feasibly target for investment: would the SIF leverage other stakeholders (for example, the government sponsor) to facilitate the sourcing of a pipeline?
- Options for fund structuring and governance
- Options for investment strategy (including investable asset classes) and process
- Human capacity requirements of the SIF, in order for it to effectively contribute to the overall quality of public investment
- Financial simulations for the fund
- Legal assessment of the fund's role, operations, and relationship to counterparties

a. This list of elements draws, in part, on Vivid Economics (2011).
b. This analysis is relevant for a SIF that has a government sponsor, and it could take place within the feasibility study or separately.

- Public capital SIFs are fully capitalized by a government or other public entity; mixed capital SIFs are initiated and funded by a public entity but also include investment by commercial entities.
- SIFs are heterogeneous in nature. They can take several different structural and legal forms, depending on the objectives they are set up to achieve and the context in which they operate.
- SIFs are not always a solution and are not devoid of challenges. They cannot fix investor constraints or substitute for good fiscal management. SIFs cannot bind future administrations to honor the establishing government's commitment to the institution or its mandate.
- The primary argument for setting up a SIF is the extent to which a SIF's intervention can address market or government failures—that is, contribute additionality to both what exists in the market and what is provided by the government. The secondary, and interrelated, argument for setting up a SIF is also its raison d'être: to crowd in commercial capital.
- Consistency of the SIF's investment activities with the sovereign's macroeconomic policies is particularly relevant for public capital SIFs, or mixed capital SIFs anchored by one government. Fiscal integration of the public capital SIF is also important, and the government must limit the fiscal risk it undertakes through the SIF.
- The public sponsor initiating a SIF must first establish the rationale and legitimacy of the SIF through undertaking a feasibility study that seeks to validate the presence of market or government failures and to confirm whether the SIF is the instrument of choice among examined alternatives.
- In principle, SIFs are not providers of concessional funding. If concessional financing is considered, the feasibility study must at a minimum clearly define the exceptional circumstances in which such an approach would be allowed.

NOTES

1. Ang (2010) refers to sovereign wealth funds rather than SIFs, but his argument on legitimacy is valid also for SIFs. For sovereign wealth funds, the threat to the sustainability of the fund is political interference resulting in immediate drawdown of capital for budgetary purposes, instead of spreading the drawdown across generations. For SIFs, the risk to sustainability extends to political influence on investment decisions, threatening the financial sustainability of the fund as well as its focus on its mandate.
2. This definition is based on a previous World Bank policy research paper by Halland et al. (2016) but has modified elements.
3. That is, their strategic mandate does not include investing in publicly traded assets.
4. Typically, the fulfillment of economic, social, or environmental returns.
5. For more on the Marguerite Funds, see the case study in appendix A.
6. See discussion on SIF pursuit of commercial returns versus elements of concessionality.
7. Refer to the Santiago Principles (the generally accepted principles and practices, or GAPPs), specifically GAPP 2: "The policy purpose of the SWF should be clearly defined and publicly disclosed" (IWG 2008, 7).
8. See the ISIF web page "About ISIF" (https://isif.ie/about-us), and see the ISIF case study in appendix A.
9. See the NSIA Infrastructure Fund Investment Policy Statement as Approved on April 6, 2019 (https://nsia.com.ng/sites/default/files/downloads/Nigeria%20Infrastructure%20Fund%20Investment%20Policy%20Statement%20-%20April%2016%202018_0.pdf).
10. See the International Forum of Sovereign Wealth Funds web page on Morocco (https://www.ifswf.org/member-profiles/moroccan-fund-tourism-development).
11. For reference, see "The Economic Appraisal of Investment Projects at the EIB" (EIB 2013), applied by the EIB to its entire investment portfolio. Marguerite II follows a more

traditional fund market approach in that guidelines or requirements from sponsors are documented via side letters.

12. Musacchio et al. (2017) provide an overview of the arguments for and against government intervention in financial markets through public financial institutions. Although their discussion centers on national development banks, the arguments apply similarly to SIFs.

13. Government failures resulting from factors such as bureaucracy, lack of predictability in policies, and so on.

14. The concept of additionality is prevalent in the development industry, where MDBs and DFIs are expected to make contributions that are beyond what the market can currently provide such that the private sector is not crowded out.

15. This modified definition is based on AfDB et al. (2018).

16. Local presence offers significant advantages to investors (Storper and Venables 2004), including higher returns to investment (Coval and Moskowitz 2001).

17. The arguments in that paper, which discusses the efficacy of development banks, have parallels to that for the role of SIFs. The paper argues that, because market failures are not readily observable and governments do not always have the necessary information before setting up the mandate of a development bank, the development bank itself must serve as "an instrument of economic intelligence" and transmit information back to the government. This argument applies to SIFs also, which are similar to development banks per the previous discussion.

18. The agreement does not include any obligation to co-invest, leaving flexibility to both parties.

19. GuarantCo is the credit enhancement unit of the Private Infrastructure Development Group, an infrastructure development and finance organization funded by several bilateral and multilateral institutions. GuarantCo provides local currency–contingent credit solutions, including guarantees to banks and bond investors.

20. Infrastructure projects have high preparation costs driven by the need for technical feasibility studies, due diligence, negotiating concession terms with the sector regulator, or structuring complex financing packages. Compared with operational infrastructure, new infrastructure projects have high risk at the project preparation and construction stages because cost overruns and delays can compound the drawback that the project is not yet generating revenue.

21. Investments in public companies should occur only in the exceptional circumstances that, despite the potential for positive financial returns, commercial investors are not providing capital, for instance, because of extreme financial market volatility. Even in these exceptional circumstances, a SIF investment in a listed company should be weighed against other fiscal and financial policy options that could help stabilize the economy, a specific economic sector, or financial markets. The rationale for such investment by a SIF should be clearly motivated, documented, and disclosed to the SIF's investors and the public.

22. NIIF and the Department for International Development committed £120 million each into the fund, and EverSource Capital was selected as fund manager.

23. The Paris climate agreement, negotiated between 196 countries, required countries to articulate their own contributions (Nationally Determined Contributions, or NDCs) to keep global temperature rise below 2 degrees Celsius and mitigate global warming. NDCs are country-articulated targets of the United Nations Framework Convention on Climate Change, and are part of Article 4 of the Paris Agreement. Activated through the Paris Agreement, India's NDCs include a commitment to derive 40 percent of the country's energy needs in 2030 from renewable energy sources. In addition, India has committed to a 35 percent reduction (from 2005 levels) in carbon intensity by 2030 as part of the global climate deal.

24. Robeco is an international asset manager with assets under management worth €165 billion (of which €102 billion are in ESG-integrated assets), headquartered in the Netherlands and fully owned by ORIX. ORIX is a diversified financial conglomerate listed on the Tokyo Stock Exchange, with activities in corporate finance, real estate, banking, and insurance, among others. Its Eco Services Division is involved in renewable power generation, energy conservation and storage solutions, and waste processing (see the ACP case study in appendix A).

25. As described in Halland et al. (2016), this concept was first used in the development of the Europe 2020 Project Bond Initiative, adopted in 2012.

26. Fund (or investment vehicle) multiplier = total size of fund or facility / public capital invested in fund. Investment multiplier = total capital invested in project / public capital invested in project.
27. As a government agency, ISIF must ensure that its investments do not breach European Union rules preventing unfair financial support for private sector enterprise. Every ISIF investment is subject to a strict vetting and cost-based analysis process in this respect.
28. For a specific discussion on SIFs, please see Halland (2019); discussion on SWFs in general can be found in various papers, including Al-Hassan et al. (2018).
29. See especially Gelb, Tordo, and Halland 2014 and the references therein.
30. See the NSIA Santiago Principles Self-Assessment 2019 (https://www.ifswf.org/assessment/nsia-self-assessment-2019).
31. See the ISIF Santiago Principles Self-Assessment 2019 (https://www.ifswf.org/assessment/ireland-strategic-investment-fund).
32. See the Khazanah Nasional Berhad Santiago Principles Self-Assessment 2019 (https://www.ifswf.org/assessment/khazanah-nasional-berhad-2019).
33. See the FONSIS Santiago Principles Self-Assessment (https://www.ifswf.org/assessment/fonsis-self-assessment).
34. See the ISIF Santiago Principles Self-Assessment 2019 (https://www.ifswf.org/assessment/ireland-strategic-investment-fund). Excerpt for proceeds from the divestment of directed investments as per section 47(4) of the NTMA Act 2014.
35. Tax exemption generally relates to the legal structure of the SIF (see chapter 3 for more detailed discussion).
36. This section derives from consolidated World Bank Group comments for draft laws for various SIFs.
37. It is precisely the implicit guarantee of government participation that is attractive to private investors and that can crowd in private capital.
38. Pages 48–55 of the report contain oral testimony from the Green Investment Bank related to the political and regulatory risk and the Green Investment Bank's role as an adviser on policy.
39. The National Reconstruction Levy Act 2001 (Act 597) had previously been introduced by the government to mobilize financing for national development through a 1.5 percent to 7.5 percent levy on companies' profits before tax.
40. For instance, a country may not have regulation on the establishment of private equity funds or may choose not to establish SIFs using other governance arrangements (for instance, FONSIS, ISIF, and NSIA were not established as limited partnership structures).

REFERENCES

AfDB (African Development Bank), AsDB (Asian Development Bank), AIIB (Asia Infrastructure Investment Bank), EBRD (European Bank for Reconstruction and Development), EIB (European Investment Bank), IDBG (Inter-American Development Bank Group), ISDBG (Islamic Development Bank Group), NDB (New Development Bank), and World Bank Group. 2018. "Multilateral Development Banks' Harmonized Framework for Additionality in Private Sector Operations." AfDB, AsDB, AIIB, EBRD, EIB, IDBG, ISDBG, NDB, and World Bank Group. https://www.ifc.org/wps/wcm/connect/7d286672-0c03-47f7-ad41-fce55d3ef359/201809_MDBs-Harmonized-Framework-for-Additionality-in-Private-Sector-Operations.pdf?MOD=AJPERES&CVID=mppa97S.

Al-Hassan, Abdullah, Sue Brake, Michael G. Papaioannou, and Martin Skancke. 2018. "Commodity-based Sovereign Wealth Funds: Managing Financial Flows in the Context of the Sovereign Balance Sheet." IMF Working Paper 18/26, International Monetary Fund, Washington, DC.

Ang, Andrew. 2010. "The Four Benchmarks of Sovereign Wealth Funds." Working paper. https://www0.gsb.columbia.edu/faculty/aang/papers/The%20Four%20Benchmarks%20of%20Sovereign%20Wealth%20Funds.pdf.

Coval, Joshua, and Tobias J. Moskowitz. 2001. "The Geography of Investment: Informed Trading and Asset Prices." *Journal of Political Economy* 109 (4): 811–41.

Divakaran, Shanthi, Sam Schneider, and Patrick J. McGinnis. 2018. "Ghana Private Equity and Venture Capital Ecosystem Study." Policy Research Working Paper 8617, World Bank, Washington, DC.

Donnelly, Ellie. 2018. "ISIF and China's CIC Capital Announce €150m Fund to Focus on High-Growth Companies." *Independent.ie*, March 16, 2018. https://www.independent.ie /business/irish/isif-and-chinas-cic-capital-announce-150m-fund-to-focus-on-high -growth-companies-36711260.html.

Economic Times. 2018. "NIIF Inks $400 Mn Agreement with Singapore's Temasek." *Economic Times*, September 6, 2018. https://economictimes.indiatimes.com/news/economy/finance /niif-inks-400-mn-agreement-with-singapores-temasek/articleshow/65710868 .cms?from=mdr.

EIB (European Investment Bank). 2013. "The Economic Appraisal of Investment Projects at the EIB." Projects Directorate, EIB, Luxembourg.

Environmental Audit Committee, House of Commons. 2011. *The Green Investment Bank: Second Report of Session 2010–11*. Volume 1. London: The Stationery Office Limited.

Fernándes-Arias, Eduardo, Ricardo Hausmann, and Ugo Panizza. 2019. "Smart Development Banks." IDB Working Paper 1047, Inter-American Development Bank, Washington, DC.

Gelb, Alan, Silvana Tordo, and Håvard Halland. 2014. "Sovereign Wealth Funds and Long-Term Development Finance." Policy Research Working Paper 6776, World Bank, Washington, DC.

Halland, Håvard. 2019. "Note on the Fiscal Implications of Strategic Investment Funds." Stanford Global Projects Center Working Paper Series July 2019. https://papers.ssrn.com /sol3/papers.cfm?abstract_id=3417086.

Halland, Håvard, Christine A. Awiti, and King Yoong Lim. Forthcoming. "The Allocation of Oil Revenues with Resource and Strategic Investment Funds." World Bank, Washington, DC.

Halland, Håvard, Michel Noël, Silvana Tordo, and Jacob J. Kloper-Owens. 2016. "Strategic Investment Funds: Opportunities and Challenges." Policy Research Working Paper 7851, World Bank, Washington, DC.

Hill, Joshua S. 2019. "EIB & PIF to Provide $18 Million for Palestinian School Rooftop Solar Projects." *CleanTechnica*, March 18, 2019. https://cleantechnica.com/2019/03/18/eib-pif -to-provide-18-million-for-palestinian-school-rooftop-solar-projects/.

Ithmar Capital. 2016. "Morocco and Nigeria Announce Trans-African Pipeline, New Regional Gas Pipeline to Develop West African Economy." *PR Newswire*, December 5, 2016. https://www.prnewswire.co.uk/news-releases/morocco-and-nigeria-announce -trans-african-pipeline-new-regional-gas-pipeline-to-develop-west-african-economy -604733586.html.

IWG (International Working Group of Sovereign Wealth Funds). 2008. "Sovereign Wealth Funds Generally Accepted Principles and Practices: 'Santiago Principles.'" IWG. https:// www.ifswf.org/sites/default/files/santiagoprinciples_0_0.pdf.

McGinnis, Patrick, Shanthi Divakaran, Jing Zhao, and Yi Yan. 2017. "Government and Venture Capital in China: The Role of Government Guidance Funds." Background paper for *Innovative China: New Drivers of Growth*. Washington, DC: World Bank.

Musacchio, Aldo, Sergio Lazzarini, Pedro Makhoul, and Emily Simmons. 2017. "The Role and Impact of Development Banks: A Review of Their Founding, Focus, and Influence." Working paper. http://people.brandeis.edu/~aldom/papers/The%20Role%20and%20Impact%20 of%20Development%20Banks%20-%203-9-2017.pdf.

NERA Economic Consulting. 2015. "UK Green Investment Bank—Examining the Case for Continued Intervention." Review prepared for the Department for Business, Innovation and Skills and the UK Green Investment Bank, NERA Economic Consulting, London.

PTI (Press Trust of India). 2017. "NIIF, ADIA Sign Investment Agreement Worth $1 Billion." *Economic Times*, October 16, 2017. https://economictimes.indiatimes.com/news /economy/foreign-trade/niif-adia-sign-investment-agreement-worth-1-billion /articleshow/61103444.cms.

Storper, Michael, and Anthony J. Venables. 2004. "Buzz: Face-to-Face Contact and the Urban Economy." *Journal of Economic Geography* 4 (4): 351–70.

van der Tak, Herman, and Lyn Squire. 1995. *Economic Analysis of Projects*. Washington, DC: World Bank.

Vivid Economics (in association with McKinsey & Co.). 2011. "The Economics of the Green Investment Bank: Costs and Benefits, Rationale and Value for Money." Report prepared for the UK Department for Business, Innovation & Skills. https://assets.publishing.service.gov .uk/government/uploads/system/uploads/attachment_data/file/31741/12-554-economics -of-the-green-investment-bank.pdf.

World Bank. 2020. "The International Finance Corporation's Blended Finance Operations: Findings from a Cluster of Project Performance Assessment Reports." Independent Evaluation Group, World Bank, Washington, DC.

World Bank Group and DRC (Development Research Center of the State Council, People's Republic of China). 2019. *Innovative China: New Drivers of Growth*. Washington, DC: World Bank.

3 Legal Framework

INTRODUCTION

The legal framework of a strategic investment fund (SIF) is the set of rules that govern the SIF's conduct of business and investment activities (OECD 2015, 28). The legal framework of the SIF consists primarily of the laws used to establish the SIF and its legal structure, as well as the fund's domicile. The SIF is also subject to a set of private agreements, formed under applicable contract law, that legally bind the fund and its counterparties during the operations of the SIF. In addition, the SIF may be disciplined by public laws in the domestic and foreign jurisdictions in which it operates.

A well-constructed legal framework can empower the SIF to successfully execute its mandate. In contrast, a poorly conceived legal framework can diminish the SIF's efficacy. At the level of the fund, such a framework will provide the contractual and governance mechanisms, including independent oversight, disclosure obligations, investment policies, conflict of interest policies, and standards of conduct, that promote discipline, transparency, and accountability (Awadzi 2015). Critically, the legal framework helps provide a robust governance system[1] that allows the SIF to formulate and implement its objectives and investment policies.[2] In doing so, the legal framework minimizes risks; maintains the confidence of domestic constituencies (such as the general public), host country regulators, and co-investors; and supplies efficient dispute resolution mechanisms in the event of conflict among SIF stakeholders.[3] Conversely, a poorly structured legal framework exposes SIFs to both domestic and international governance and political risks[4] that may jeopardize the effective execution of a fund's mandate (Rose 2019). In turn this can sap managerial time and attention, create significant liabilities, increase transactions costs, and reduce returns.

No single legal framework or legal structure is appropriate for all SIFs, which are formed in a heterogeneity of environments. Like sovereign wealth funds (SWFs), SIFs operate in a range of regulatory traditions and political environments, which cause variance in the availability and choice of legal frameworks and structures. In addition, legal frameworks and structures also differ because of dissimilarities in fund mandates, the need (or lack of need) to attract co-investors, and the availability of alternative regulatory regimes, which may be appealing in some cases (such as when the SIF seeks international co-investors at the fund level).

Because SIFs are a subset of the SWF universe and, depending on their setup and mandate, display the characteristics of state-owned enterprises (SOEs) and purely commercial private capital funds, elements of good legal frameworks and structures distilled from each of these areas can be appropriate to SIFs. In addition, legal principles applicable to SWFs are by and large applicable to SIFs (see box 3.1 on foundational legal principles articulated in the Santiago Principles). Like SOEs, public capital SIFs come in a variety of legal forms and "typically reside at the intersection of public and private law, with significant variation between and within countries" (World Bank 2014, 28). Public capital SIFs may also be set up to operate under laws applicable to SOEs in the jurisdiction and therefore can be subject to the best practices of these enterprises. Conversely, mixed capital SIFs may be identically modeled to private capital funds, set up through commercial law, observing industry norms and practices. Therefore, principles for sound legal frameworks and good governance applicable to private capital funds may also be applicable to such SIFs.

This chapter discusses a menu of options and good practices to consider when constructing the legal framework for a SIF, allowing for the heterogeneity of environments within which SIFs are formed. From the perspective of policy makers setting up either public capital SIFs or mixed capital SIFs, it examines

- The three foundational, and overlapping, elements derived from public law that construct the legal framework for a SIF: the legislation under which a SIF is brought into existence, the legal structure adopted by the SIF, and the domicile of the SIF;

BOX 3.1

Santiago Principles: Key legal principles for SWFs

The Santiago Principles include the following generally accepted principles and practices (GAPPs) related to sovereign wealth funds (SWFs):

GAPP 1. Principle
The legal framework for the SWF should be sound and support its effective operation and the achievement of its stated objective(s).

GAPP 1.1. Subprinciple. The legal framework for the SWF should ensure legal soundness of the SWF and its transactions.[a]

GAPP 1.2. Subprinciple. The key features of the SWF's legal basis and structure, as well as the legal relationship between the SWF and other state bodies, should be publicly disclosed.

GAPP 15. Principle
SWF operations and activities in host countries should be conducted in compliance with all applicable regulatory and disclosure requirements of the countries in which they operate.

Source: IWG 2008.
a. See also GAPP 1.1 Explanation and commentary (IWG 2008, 12): "First, the establishment of the SWF should be clearly authorized under domestic law. Second, the legal structure should include a clear mandate for the manager to invest the SWF's assets and conduct all related transactions. Third, irrespective of the particular legal structure of an SWF, the beneficial and legal owners of the SWF's assets should be legally clear. Such clarity contributes to accountability in the home country and is often required under the recipient countries' regulations."

- The private agreements facilitated by general contract law via which a SIF relates to its stakeholders; and
- Other public legislation, domestic or foreign, that affects the operations of a SIF.

LEGAL FRAMEWORK FOR SIFS

The law used to establish a SIF typically cumulates within it the choice of legal structure and domicile. The following discussion first focuses on the law to establish the SIF and then concentrates in more detail on the role played by legal structure and domicile in defining the SIF's legal framework.

Two main types of legal approaches are used to establish SIFs: (1) SIF-specific law or decree, with varying degrees of reliance on commercial or SOE law; or (2) purely commercial (domestic or foreign) law. In general, public capital SIFs tend to rely on SIF-specific legislation, whereas mixed capital SIFs tend to use commercial law (see table 3.1).

TABLE 3.1 **SIF-specific law and legal structure for a variety of public capital SIFs**

SIF	SOURCE LAW / DECREE	LEGAL STRUCTURE
Fundo Soberano de Angola	Presidential Decree 48/11 dated March 9, 2011	—[a]
Egypt Fund	Law No. 177/2018 on the Establishment of Egypt Fund	—[b]
Ghana Infrastructure Investment Fund	Act 877: Ghana Infrastructure Investment Fund Act, 2014 Act	Body corporate/SOE
National Development Fund of Iran	Article 84 of the Fifth Development Plan of the Islamic Republic of Iran	—[c]
Ireland Strategic Investment Fund	National Treasury Management Agency (Amendment) Act 2014	Not a legal entity
Samruk Kazyna (Kazakhstan)	Presidential decree dated October 13, 2008 No. 669[d] and Government Resolution No. 962 of October 17, 2008[e]	Joint stock company[f]
Nigeria Sovereign Investment Authority–Nigeria Infrastructure Fund	Nigeria Sovereign Investment Authority (Establishment, etc.) Act 2011	Body corporate/SOE
FONSIS (Senegal)	Law 2012-34: Authorizing the Creation of a Sovereign Fund of Strategic Investments (FONSIS)[g]	Limited liability company under private business laws of OHADA[h]
Turkey Wealth Fund	Law No. 6741 on Establishment of Turkish Wealth Fund Management Company	Private corporation
Palestine Investment Fund (West Bank and Gaza)	Presidential decree in 2000[i]	Public shareholding company

Source: World Bank.
Note: OHADA = Organisation pour l'harmonisation en Afrique du drout des affaires (Organization for the Harmonization of Corporate Law in Africa); SIF = strategic investment fund; SOE = state-owned enterprise; — = not available.
a. Independent legal entity but legal structure is unclear.
b. Law No. 177 of 2018 on the Establishment of Egypt Fund (translation) mentions only that the fund will have "an independent legal personality."
c. Independent legal entity but legal structure is unclear.
d. "On some measures on competitiveness and sustainability of national economy" (https://www.ifswf.org/assessment/samruk).
e. "On measures on realization of the Decree of President of the Republic of Kazakhstan No. 669" (https://www.ifswf.org/assessment/samruk and https://sk.kz/about-fund/history-of-the-fund/).
f. Created through the merger of two state conglomerates, Sustainable Development Fund Kazyna and Kazakhstan's Holding for Management of State Assets Samruk.
g. Subject to an explicit requirement (included in Article 2 of the FONSIS Law) to be 100 percent owned by the state; at least 70 percent of the state ownership must be direct state owned, and up to 30 percent can be owned by state dismemberments.
h. Legal framework for corporate law adopted by a group of West and Central African countries.
i. See the Palestine Investment Fund Santiago Principles Self-Assessment (https://www.ifswf.org/assessment/pif).

SIF-specific legislation

Establishing a SIF under SIF-specific legislation provides visibility and specificity on the legal framework of the SIF and can accommodate the SIF's mandate to balance both commercial and policy objectives. SIF-specific legislation can be of value to policy makers, managers, and co-investors of SIFs, who mutually benefit from a single law that lays out the rights and responsibilities of the various parties governing and managing the SIF, as well as investing alongside it. Commercial law, by contrast, cannot always be thus customized,[5] and may not accommodate the core feature of a SIF: its double bottom line objective. Commercial legal frameworks may also not have sufficient accountability mechanisms (such as fiduciary duties) to ensure compliance with the SIF's objectives and reassure taxpayers and stakeholders. For example, Section 41.4 of the Nigeria Sovereign Investment Authority (Establishment, etc.) Act, 2011 (NSIA Act 2011), as a customized law for Nigeria's SWF, can (and does) require that the NSIA's Nigeria Infrastructure Fund (NIF) must review all written proposals submitted by all levels of owners (federal, state, and local governments) related to infrastructure investment.[6] Such a provision could not be instated in law if the NSIA was set up under only commercial law.

Public capital SIFs are often established using special SIF-specific legislation or decrees. Specialized legislation creates the fund, establishes its institutional relationships within the government, sets out a mandate for the fund, and provides for its management and supervision. In some cases, this SIF-specific legislation makes no reference to commercial law or commercial structures in constituting the SIF. The Ireland Strategic Investment Fund (ISIF), for instance, was created by an act of parliament, specifically the National Treasury Management Agency (Amendment) Act, 2014 (NTMA Act 2014).[7] ISIF is not a separate legal entity but is instead a pool of assets under the NTMA, and does not rely on commercial legislation (see the ISIF case study in appendix A for more discussion). Similarly, under Section 4(b) of the NSIA Act 2011, NIF is a ring-fenced pool of capital managed by NSIA under its own distinct investment policy.

The permanence of the SIF is typically better secured by SIF-specific legislation approved by the legislature rather than by decree. In most jurisdictions, legislative acts have higher priority than executive decrees, although that may not be the case in countries where executive power is supreme. Several SIFs, such as in Angola, Azerbaijan, and Kazakhstan have been set up by presidential decree, which is a law issued by a head of state without the approval of parliament. For example, Angola's SIF, Fundo Soberano de Angola, was set up in 2011 by Presidential Decree 48/11 as an SWF wholly owned by the Republic of Angola.[8] Presidential decrees have the advantage of automatically becoming permanent law,[9] but they can more easily be overturned by subsequent decrees upon a change in executive power.

SIF-specific legislation still comes with some risk because special legislation cannot anticipate every contingency and may also create an uneven legal playing field between the SIF and purely private funds. SIF-specific law may leave significant legislative and governance gaps in the legal framework, unlike the typically more robust and tested commercial law. Special legislation may not inspire confidence for potential co-investors that the fund will be managed independently and predictably. For example, because the NSIA (and, it follows, NIF) was not established by Nigeria's general law regime, its independence depends in practice on the range and thoroughness of checks and balances within the NSIA Act 2011, especially considering that the Nigerian state is NSIA's sole shareholder.[10] (See the case study in appendix A on Nigeria's SIF for discussion on these checks and balances.) Strong checks would need to be included in SIF-specific legislation to ensure independent decision-making. In other cases, when SIFs invest across borders, the use of standard commercial laws may also provide foreign regulators with more comfort and certainty on the SIF's internal governance structure. In turn this may favorably affect the way national security–related investment laws are enforced with respect to the SIF.[11] Like SOEs operating in a commercial space, SIFs not subject to commercial law may also be more at risk of creating an uneven playing field between private players operating in the market and the SIF (World Bank 2014). When the government is the sole shareholder, through a SIF-specific law it can exercise full discretion over the SIF's organizational and governance setup.[12] SIFs that fully comply with corporate law are at least subject to the same legal framework as any other for-profit investor.

To counteract some of these risks, special legislation is often created with varying degrees of reliance on commercial law for the SIF's legal structure and governance standards.[13] Assuming that commercial law is robust, and rule of law is respected, using commercial structures alongside special legislation can provide predictable pathways of governance and management for the SIF's managers. Together they can provide a tailored legal framework suited to an entity operating at the intersection of public and private law. In many cases, therefore, SIF legislation expressly allows for the use of standard commercial forms for the legal structure of the SIF. That is, special legislation authorizes the creation of a fund's operating entities, and these in turn may be formed as trusts, limited partnerships, and corporations, relying on the legal and governance standards applicable to those forms to supplement the fund's legal framework (see more detailed discussion in the subsection on legal structure). Senegal's FONSIS (Fonds Souverain d'Investissements Stratégiques, or Sovereign Fund for Strategic Investments) is an example of such a SIF. It was established in December 2012 by the Senegal National Assembly Law 2012-34: Authorizing the Creation of a Sovereign Fund of Strategic Investments (FONSIS), subsequently ratified by the President of the Republic. However, FONSIS is also a limited liability company under OHADA law (incorporated in October 2013) and, as such, is subject to all applicable provisions of corporate law[14] (see box 3.2).

In some cases, governments forming public capital SIFs may reject commercial legal structures but depend on standard SOE structures or SOE-related laws and regulations to address legal or governance gaps. SOE legal frameworks vary significantly from country to country. SOEs can be established as statutory corporations with their own law or legal foundation; be corporatized under company law, SOE law, or both; or be noncorporatized entities under an SOE or public enterprise law (World Bank 2014). A SIF may likewise be formed as a bespoke governmental entity under SIF-specific legislation—typically as a statutory corporation[15]—and may not make use of general commercial forms. For instance, NSIA was established by ad hoc parliamentary law (the NSIA Act 2011) in May 2011, as a statutory corporation or a body corporate, the legal structure used by all parastatals in Nigeria. As a body corporate, NSIA is a public authority; it is not a fund governed by securities law, nor is it a company in a strict sense, governed by corporate law. Under its enabling legislation it may sue or be sued and may acquire, hold, and sell assets necessary for the performance of its

BOX 3.2

Establishment laws that rely on commercial legislation: The case of FONSIS

The legal frameworks of strategic investment funds often rely extensively on both special and general laws. The legal framework of Senegal's FONSIS (Fonds Souverain d'Investissements Stratégiques, or Sovereign Fund for Strategic Investments), for instance, highlights the potential benefits of supplementing special legislation with standard commercial legal frameworks. The establishment of FONSIS was authorized by the Senegal National Assembly under Law 2012-34,[a] which was subsequently ratified by the President of the Republic. Law 2012-34 prescribes that the rules of organization and functioning of FONSIS "shall be determined by this Act, by the Statutes and the Rules of Procedure in accordance with the standards, in particular those of the OHADA Uniform Act on companies."[b] General legislation therefore complements special legislation in areas where the former may be inadequate.

As a limited liability company under OHADA law,[c] FONSIS is subject to all applicable provisions, but these provisions can be modified when necessary by the FONSIS-specific Law 2012-34. FONSIS's status as a Senegalese Société Anonyme also means its board has full power over investment decisions, with no need for government approval, thus enhancing operational independence. At the same time, FONSIS-specific law includes special provisions not covered by commercial law. Article 24 of Law 2012-34 submits FONSIS to the audit of government administrative bodies such as the General State Inspectorate and the Court of Auditors.

Also per Law 2012-34, Senegal owns 100 percent of the company's capital. Ownership can be open to other state entities, but the state's direct ownership shall not be less than 70 percent.

Source: FONSIS case study; see appendix A.
a. Law 2012-34: Authorizing the creation of a Sovereign Fund of Strategic Investments (FONSIS), adopted on December 27, 2012.
b. Article 3, Law 2012-34. OHADA (Organisation pour l'harmonisation en Afrique du droit des affaires, or Organization for the Harmonization of Corporate Law in Africa) is a system of corporate law and implementing institutions adopted by 17 West and Central African nations in 1993.
c. The 2014 Acte Uniforme Révisé Relatif au Droit des Sociétés Commericales at du Groupement d'Intérét Économique.

functions. NSIA is also "independent in the discharge of its functions," under Section 1(4) of the NSIA Act 2011. Similarly, the Ghana Infrastructure Investment Fund was set up under the Ghana Infrastructure Investment Fund Act, 2014, as a "body corporate with perpetual succession," which "may sue and be sued and have in all respects the powers of a body corporate."[16]

In general, primary legislation should establish basic principles that cannot be easily changed, whereas specific fund details can be enshrined in secondary legislation that can evolve over time. As with SWFs, there is great variety in the level of detail in SIF establishment legislation, partly as a reflection of different traditions and constitutional requirements among countries (Al-Hassan et al. 2013). Some countries have extensive primary legislation, with only modest supplementary secondary regulation. Others will rely heavily on secondary regulation, such as rules and policies written by the ministry of finance. As noted by Al-Hassan et al. (2013), for instance, the law establishing Norway's Government Pension Fund Global has only nine short sections but is augmented by a series of secondary regulations and policies by the Norwegian Ministry of Finance. In general, it is preferable to establish basic principles in primary legislation, which cannot be easily changed, and to prescribe specific fund details in secondary legislation, which may be amended as the fund evolves (World Bank 2015). Details can also be left to other constitutive documents, such as articles of association, depending on the type of legal structure used.

Typically, the first part of the SIF-specific law will describe the SIF's foundational elements, such as its mandate, legal structure, and ownership; who manages it; and the rules by which funds can flow in and out of the SIF. Although the form and detail of establishment legislation will vary from jurisdiction to jurisdiction, several provisions are commonly found in comprehensive primary SIF legislation:

- *Preliminary details.* Legislation will typically start by describing basic details, such as the name of the fund, the location of its principal offices, and the fund's legal domicile.
- *Objectives and mandate.* The law must describe the objectives or the mandate of the fund. It is important that the law states clearly that the SIF will pursue both a financial and a policy objective, and clarifies any hierarchy between these two objectives. For example, although the NSIA-NIF must seek financial returns, the NSIA Act 2011 (Section 41.5) provides that 10 percent of NIF's available investment capital in any fiscal year can be invested in social infrastructure projects that enhance economic development in underserved regions, even if they provide less return potential.
- *Legal structure and life of the fund.* The law must highlight the legal structure of the SIF and whether it has a finite life. If provisions are envisioned for the dissolution of the fund, they must be clearly specified and not compromise the long-term horizon that SIFs typically take.
- *Capital provider(s) and fund management.* The law must describe who capitalizes the fund or—if the SIF is set up as a corporation—provides its equity. It must also designate a fund manager or, in the case of a corporation, establish procedures for the appointment of its board and top management. The statute may state that the government or a specific ministry is the investor or shareholder (as the case may be) in the SIF but that the SIF itself is the legal owner of the assets. Typically, global practice is that, on the government side, the ministry of finance is the proxy capital provider to the fund (or shareholder, as the case may be), because the ministry of finance is usually responsible for the financial and fiscal implications involved with the SIF. Ideally, the law will also clarify any restrictions on legal ownership of fund assets or the management company.
- *Operational independence of fund manager.* The legal provisions should also state to what extent the management company or, in the case of corporations, the board of directors is independent from government influence, and how such independence is protected with suitable governance arrangements.[17] Ideally, the fund manager or board has operational independence but also is assured of the government sponsor's support.
- *Source of funds and withdrawal of funds.* The law must define the initial assets of the SIF and outline the rules for fund inflow. This requirement includes defining the terms under which the SIF may borrow (if at all) and the purpose of such borrowing, and whether profits and gains would be reinvested into the fund. If a partial source of funds for the SIF comes from the contribution of state assets (such as equity stakes in SOEs), the transfer of these assets must be clearly written in law to ensure that the SIF is sufficiently funded for its mandate, and any conditions under which the transfer would occur must be clarified (see box 3.3 for more details). The law must also define the terms, conditions, and limits under which funds can be withdrawn from the SIF, including by defining the dividend policy.

BOX 3.3

Specifying the transfer of state assets into a SIF with the SIF law

When the initial funds for investment of a strategic investment fund (SIF) partially or fully originate from the contribution by the government of state-owned assets, the law must clarify how the ownership of such assets will be transferred to the SIF.

It would be important to define up front the dividend policy specifically for the portfolio of state assets, and whether they would be fully reinvested in the SIF or would be paid out by the SIF to the government.

The SIF could also absorb uncertain and potentially large liabilities when state assets are transferred to it. Symmetrically, the SIF might create fiscal risks for the government (through debt or contingent liabilities) through its own transactions, for example,

if the SIF can borrow or issue bonds. The law must clarify if such liabilities are guaranteed by the state.

If the fund's liabilities are fully accounted for on the SIF's own books, then the law must make provisions for SIF bankruptcy and resolution. A SIF that does not have defined procedures for bankruptcy and resolution may be assumed to have its liabilities implicitly backed by the government budget. Such an implicit state guarantee would likely generate perverse incentives with respect to risk management. In addition, if the state guarantees a share of the fund's contingent liabilities, then this guarantee should be accounted for in the government budget (even if implicit). See the more detailed discussion in chapter 2.

Source: World Bank.

- *Restrictions on use of SIF capital.* Ideally, the legislation must state whether the fund's assets may be loaned or used as collateral by the SIF or the government. If the fund can provide guarantees to subsidiary companies that have third-party investment, the pricing and terms of these should be defined with high specificity to avoid the transfer of contingent liabilities from these entities to the SIF (and implicitly, in turn, to the government).
- *Restrictions on liabilities assumed by the state.* Because a SIF may create financial risks (debt or contingent liabilities) by its own transactions, the law should clarify whether and how such liabilities will be assumed by the state, and make provisions for the fund's resolution (or bankruptcy, if the SIF is set up as a corporation). The NSIA Act 2011, for example, protects other government assets from being subject to NSIA's liabilities.[18]
- *Fund structure and operating model.* The law will typically provide details on the main fund's structure and its operational model, as well as details on other related structures, such as subfunds, and how they are funded relative to one another. This is the case with the NSIA Act 2011, which spells out the three fund compartments. In some cases, such detail may be delegated to regulation or other fund documents.
- *Relationship with other state bodies or domestic law.* The establishment law ideally clarifies whether the fund and its manager are required to coordinate with other state agencies or ministries. The law must also ensure that its provisions do not contradict the provisions of any other law it references and must clearly whether exemptions (for example, on tax) are to be provided to the SIF (see table 3.2).

The second section of the SIF-specific law usually describes its operational elements, such as the SIF's governance structure, its investment policy and strategy, and its reporting requirements (see table 3.3).

TABLE 3.2 **Common features of primary SIF legislation: Foundational elements**

KEY ELEMENTS IN SIF-SPECIFIC LEGISLATION		IRELAND STRATEGIC INVESTMENT FUND	NIGERIA SOVEREIGN INVESTMENT AUTHORITY	MUBADALA INVESTMENT COMPANY
Preliminary details	Establishment law	National Treasury Management Agency (Amendment) Act 2014 (NTMA Act 2014)	Nigeria Sovereign Investment Authority (Establishment, etc.) Act, 2011 (NSIA Act 2011)	Law No. (2) of 2017 Concerning the Establishment of Mubadala Investment Company
	Fund name	Ireland Strategic Investment Fund	Nigeria Sovereign Investment Authority–Nigeria Infrastructure Fund (NSIA-NIF)	Mubadala Investment Company (Mubadala)
	Manager	National Treasury Management Agency (NTMA)	Nigeria Sovereign Investment Authority (NSIA)	n.a. (not a separate entity)
	Fund domicile	Ireland	Nigeria	United Arab Emirates

GAPP 2: Clearly define and publicly disclose the SWF's policy purpose.

Mandate / Policy purpose	Objective of fund/ mandate	Hold/invest assets on a commercial basis in a manner designed to support economic activity and employment in Ireland.	Support the development in Nigeria of basic, essential and efficient infrastructure … to stimulate the growth and diversification of the Nigerian economy, attract foreign investment and create jobs for Nigerians.	Board of directors will set.[a]

GAPP 1.2: Publicly disclose key features of legal basis, structure, and legal relationship between SWF and other state bodies.

GAPP 3: Ensure SWF activities are consistent with overall macroeconomic policies and coordinate with domestic fiscal and monetary authorities.

Legal structure and ownership	Legal structure	n.a.	Body corporate	Public joint stock company
	Fund life	Per government of Ireland decision[b]	Perpetual succession	99 years
	Fund ownership	Minister for Finance	Federal, state, local government[c]	Government of Abu Dhabi
	Management company ownership	NTMA is a state agency.	NSIA	Mubadala Investment Company owns the fund.
	Operational independence of manager	Yes[d]	Yes	Yes[e]
	Restrictions on fund share transfers, sales, purchases, and other uses	n.a.	Owners "shall not transfer, redeem, assign, dispose of, sell, mortgage, pledge or otherwise encumber any interest of any kind in the Authority."	No shares may be transferred sold, mortgaged, or waived without consent of Executive Council.
	Restrictions on transfer of liabilities created by the SIF to the state	n.a.	n.a.	Yes[f]
Relationship with government / other laws	Relationship with state bodies / other domestic laws	Acquisitions or transfers of interests in credit institutions are exempt from Part 2 and Part 3 of the 2002 Competition Act.[g]	Exempt from Investments and Securities Act 2007 and Banks and Other Financial Institutions Act 2004.	n.a.
	Tax treatment	n.a. (Not taxed because not legal entity.)	Exempt from taxes at all levels of government.	n.a.

continued

TABLE 3.2 *continued*

KEY ELEMENTS IN SIF-SPECIFIC LEGISLATION		IRELAND STRATEGIC INVESTMENT FUND	NIGERIA SOVEREIGN INVESTMENT AUTHORITY	MUBADALA INVESTMENT COMPANY
Fund structure and model	Single/Multiple compartments	Single fund	NSIA Act 2011 established three funds, including NIF.	Two funds, Mubadala and International Petroleum Investment Company (IPIC)
	% allocation into subfunds		Initial capital allocated to all subfunds, with each receiving minimun of 20%.	
	Fund of funds / direct investment			

GAPP 4.1: *Publicly disclose source of SWF funding*

Funds inflow	Initial source of funds / initial capital	Assets and liabilities of National Pensions Reserve Fund[h]	US$1 billion	Assets and liabilities per merger of IPIC and Mubadala
	Inflows to the fund (from the government budget) / reinvestment	Minister may make cash or noncash transfers to the fund with the approval of both legislative houses. Income/gains reinvested into fund.	Residual funds from Federation Account in excess of Budgetary Smoothing Amount Reinvest proceeds into fund.	Board of directors may increase (or decrease) authorized and issued capital for the company per articles of association.
	Fund borrowing	Not specified	Permitted with prior written approval by the Minister of Finance.	Company and affiliates can borrow as deemed convenient by board.

GAPP 4.2: *Publicly disclose general approach to withdrawals from SWF and spending on behalf of the government*

Funds outflow	Rules on fund withdrawal	No withdrawal before 2025, except for disposal of directed investments (NTMA Act 2014, Section 42). After 2025, no outflow more than 4% of fund's assets in preceding year.	Board can unanimously declare dividends from NSIA's uninvested/uncommitted funds if each subfund has realized a net profit and anticipated operational expenses are covered. Dividends cannot exceed 60% of profits at time of payment.[i]	The board may decrease or restructure the capital of the company in a manner specified by the board members.[j]

Source: IWG 2008; World Bank.
Note: GAPP = generally accepted principle and practice; n.a. = not applicable; SIF = strategic investment fund; SWF = sovereign wealth fund.
a. Report states that Mubadala's "mandate is to create sustainable financial returns, furthering our shareholder's strategic objective of a globally integrated and diversified economy."
b. Because the fund has no distinct legal entity, it exists as long as the government wishes it to.
c. Based on percentage contribution to fund.
d. The committee is independent, but the agency, which is technically the manager, is a government body.
e. Although Mubadala's board of directors includes senior public officials of the United Arab Emirates, the board delegates aspects of its authority for executive management to the chief executive officer and managing director, as well as to the investment committee.
f. Under Law 1, Article 24: Government's Liability for the Debt: i) The Government shall be directly liable for the Public Debt; ii) The Government shall not be liable for the debt or obligations of Government Institutions, Companies and Subsidiary Companies or any other company or entity in which the Government holds an ownership stake or which is under its control or which has an interest therein (https://www.abudhabi.gov.ae/-/media/sites/adgov/gazettes/2017/en/2017-e1-en.ashx).
g. Actions by or on behalf of the fund and its management in relation to these transactions are not covered by the following: EC Regulations (S.I. No. 48 of 2011), (S.I. No. 168 of 2003), (S.I. No. 255 of 2006), and Irish Takeover Panel Act 1997.
h. Except for some foreign assets/liabilities. The National Pensions Reserve Fund was established by the National Pensions Reserve Fund Act 2000, Section 18.
i. Upon approval, dividends paid into Federation Account and distributed to federal government, state government, federal capital territory, local government, and area councils in proportion to their respective contributions.
j. Article 4: "The Board of Directors may decrease or restructure the capital of the Company in the manner specified by him." Relating to the board of directors, Article 8, paragraph 1, section (j) says that the board may "divide, transmit, transfer, merge, unify, sell and mortgage any of the Company's funds or assets or the funds or assets of any of its affiliated companies, waive the same with or without fee or dispose of any of the same in all forms of legal disposal" (https://www.ecouncil.ae/en/Official-Gazette/Documents/1st%20edition%202017%20english%20final%20file.pdf).

TABLE 3.3 **Common features of primary SIF legislation: Operational elements**

KEY ELEMENTS IN SIF-SPECIFIC LEGISLATION		IRELAND STRATEGIC INVESTMENT FUND	NIGERIA SOVEREIGN INVESTMENT AUTHORITY	MUBADALA INVESTMENT COMPANY
GAPP 10: Clearly define accountability framework for SWF's operations in relevant legislation, charter, other constitutive documents, or management agreement.				
GAPP 16: Publicly disclose governance framework and objectives, as well as how SWF's management is operationally independent from owner.				
GAPP 13: Clearly define professional and ethical standards and disclose it to members of SWF's governing body(ies), management, and staff.				
Governance	Governing bodies	Agency board, CEO	Governing council, board, CEO, and executive management	Executive council, board of directors for company, board of directors for fund, managing group with managing director
	Constitution, tenure of board members, and hiring of board (selection and criteria)[a]	9 members (3 government, 6 independent) appointed by Minister for Finance; 5-year terms and no more than 2 consecutive terms	9 members (3 executive, 6 independent) appointed by nomination committee; 4-year terms for nonexecutive directors and chairman, max. of 2 terms[b]	At least 5 members, including managing director and chairman; 4-year terms, renewed automatically unless Amiri Decree issued for reformation
	CEO selection	NTMA CEO appointed by minister	Appointed by president	Appointed by board
	Committees	Investment committee at minimum and other committees as considered appropriate by NTMA	At minimum, board must establish compensation committee, audit committee, and risk management committee.	Board may form committees composed of own members or third parties; Establishment Law does not mandate formation of any committees.[c]
GAPP 19: Investment decisions should maximize risk-adjusted financial returns consistent with investment policy and based on economic and financial grounds.				
GAPP 19.1: Clearly articulate in the investment policy, and publicly disclose, if investment decisions are subject to other than economic and financial considerations.				
Investment policy	Alignment with national priorities	Investment strategy in accordance with mandate "to support economic activity and employment" and other functions in NTMA Act 2014, Section 39	NIF investments must to extent possible be aligned/consistent with "infrastructure priorities and plans developed by the appropriate ministries and agencies with responsibilities over the particular infrastructure asset sector."	In alignment with Abu Dhabi's "Vision 2030, the long-term plan for the transformation of Abu Dhabi's economy, with a focus on knowledge-based industries and a reduced reliance on oil"
	Double bottom line mandate	Must invest assets on a commercial basis in a manner designed to support economic activity and employment in Ireland; financial return target: >cost of Irish government debt.	Invest in infrastructure sectors that contribute to growth and diversification of economy; long-term return benchmark: US CPI + 3%. Allow 10% of investment in any fiscal year for social infrastructure projects with possibly lower financial returns.	Economic diversification and sustainability are key principles.
	Provisions on co-investment/ co-investors	Co-investment, joint ventures, partnerships permitted[d]	Co-investment permitted	Permits "participation with others"
GAPP 19.2: Manage SWF assets in a manner consistent with sound asset management principles.				
Investment strategy	Eligible investments / targeted sectors	Except for specific circumstances, may not directly invest in fossil fuel undertakings; indirect investment cannot invest more than 15% in fossil fuel undertaking.	Primarily infrastructure assets	Broad range of activities permitted

continued

TABLE 3.3 *continued*

KEY ELEMENTS IN SIF-SPECIFIC LEGISLATION		IRELAND STRATEGIC INVESTMENT FUND	NIGERIA SOVEREIGN INVESTMENT AUTHORITY	MUBADALA INVESTMENT COMPANY
	Eligible instruments	As appropriate	As appropriate	As appropriate
	Geographic restrictions	No restriction, but foreign investments must have a positive impact on Ireland's economy.	NIF's primary focus is domestic infrastructure.[e]	No restriction
	Ability for government / public sponsor to direct fund investments	Minister for Finance can direct ISIF to certain investments in specified circumstances, according to the NTMA Act 2014, Sections 42 and 42A.[f]	Not specified	Not specified

GAPP 12: Annually audit SWF's operations and financial statements per recognized international or national auditing standards in a consistent manner.

GAPP 5: Report relevant statistical data pertaining to SWF in a timely basis to owner, or as otherwise required, to include where appropriate in macroeconomic data sets.

GAPP 11: Prepare annual report and accompanying financial statements on SWF's operations and performance in a timely fashion and per recognized international or national accounting standards in a consistent manner.

GAPP 22.2. Publicly disclose the general approach to the SWF's risk management framework.

GAPP 23: Measure and report to owner on the assets and investment performance (absolute and relative to benchmarks, if any) of the SWF per clearly defined principles or standards.

Disclosure/ reporting	Audit requirements	Comptroller and Auditor General of Ireland to review and audit accounts within 4 months of end of financial year	Annual internal audit by the Nigerian branch of an internationally recognized accounting firm	One or more independent auditors appointed by board of directors
	Use of IFRS	Not specified in law	IFRS, or other globally recognized standard	Not specified in law
	Reporting process	NTMA to provide report to minister within 6 months of end of financial year; minister must provide copies to both legislative houses.	NSIA to provide annual report to president, Minister of Finance, Central Bank, National Economic Council, National Assembly, and each State House of Assembly within 3 months of end of financial year; NSIA must provide report to Governing Council every 12 months; summary of annual report and relevant documents must be made available to the public.	The company shall have one or more accredited auditors verify its accounts and financial statements.

Source: World Bank.

Note: CPI = Consumer Price Index; IFRS = International Financial Reporting Standards; ISIF = Ireland Strategic Investment Fund; NIF = Nigeria Infrastructure Fund; NSIA = Nigeria Sovereign Investment Authority; NTMA = National Treasury Management Agency; SIF = strategic investment fund SWF = sovereign wealth fund.

a. For more on this, please see chapter 4 on governance.

b. Executive directors serve for as long as they occupy their position.

c. However, website indicates that Investment Committee and Audit, Risk, and Compliance Committee have been formed.

d. The fund is open to private co-investment (NTMA Act 2014, Section 41(4)(d)).

e. NIF's objective is to develop infrastructure in Nigeria, but NSIA may exercise its powers "within or anywhere outside Nigeria."

f. For instance, under Section 42, the Minister of Finance, after consultation with the Central Bank, may direct NTMA to invest ISIF assets in specified securities of a credit institution, or underwrite the issue of any securities of a credit institution, if the minister considers it necessary, in the public interest, in order to remedy a serious disturbance in the economy and/or prevent potential serious damage to Ireland's financial system.

- *Governance.* The legislative provisions outlining the governance of the SIF are among the most important (for SIF operations) and the most detailed. As chapter 4 discusses, the governance framework outlined in the law should aim to insulate the fund and its investment decisions from political interference while ensuring that short-term political interests do not jeopardize investments for the long-term benefits of the country. In addition, autonomy and independence of the fund must be balanced with proper oversight and accountability. The functions of the owner of the fund should be clarified in law; if these ownership functions are shared by different entities (such as a governing council and a ministry), the respective responsibilities must be clear and not overlap.
- *Investment policy and strategy.* The investment policies and principles will usually clarify the double bottom line nature of the SIF and align investments with the fund's mandate and the sponsor's priorities.[19] As chapter 5 discusses, there should be clear limits on the scope of investable assets. The ability to invest too broadly may blur the mandate of the fund, and staff may not have enough investment experience in certain assets and markets to invest prudentially. If the government has any ability to influence the direction of the investments, the conditions under which it can do so must be clearly spelled out in the law. For example, Ireland's Minister of Finance can direct ISIF to certain investments but only under specified circumstances (such as economic or financial system instability), according to Sections 42 and 42A of the NTMA Act 2014.[20]
- *Disclosure regime and risk management.* Last, the establishment legislation also includes provisions relating to reporting, transparency, and audit procedures. The law should prescribe the publication of key information, such as the fund's annual report and financial statements, accounting standards, and the general approach of the SIF's risk management framework.

Commercial legislation

Unlike public capital SIFs, mixed capital SIFs are generally established on a commercial law basis, most commonly under company law and the regulatory framework for investment funds. Mixed capital SIFs, in seeking to align themselves with market norms for private capital funds, often register under commercial law and are also disciplined by alternative investment fund regulation. For example, Marguerite II, as a mixed capital fund, is set up under Luxembourg company law and its fund manager is a recognized European Union (EU) Alternative Investment Fund Manager. Similarly, all three funds (Master Fund, Fund of Funds, and Strategic Fund) of the National Investment and Infrastructure Funds (NIIF) are Category II funds under India's Securities and Exchange Board of India Alternative Investment Funds Regulations, 2012, but are also governed by trust law because the legal structure of each fund draws from the Indian Trusts Act, 1882.

Although public capital SIFs may in some cases also be formed entirely under commercial law, they are more likely to register under company law than submit to private equity regulation. A government might wish to establish a government-owned investment vehicle under domestic company law to enhance the accountability and transparency of board members and management. An example of this is the Malaysian SWF, Khazanah Nasional Berhad (see table 3.4). Khazanah was incorporated as a public limited company under Malaysia's Companies Act 1965. It is therefore subject to all provisions of Malaysian corporate and tax law, with no exception granted to it because of its ownership by the government. Such provisions discipline Khazanah's governance and disclosure requirements, as well as its hiring policies related to specific ethnic groups. Khazanah is also not tax exempt: it pays the same corporate tax rate applied to all Malaysian companies.

India's NIIF represents an evolution in the legal model for a SIF sponsored by a government in that NIIF is subject to private equity regulation. Although mixed capital funds set up by development finance institutions are typically subject to private equity regulation, India's NIIF is unusual as a mixed capital SIF sponsored directly by the government of India and subject to private equity regulation because of the need to attract investors at the fund level. As mentioned previously, all three funds of NIIF are Category II funds under the Alternative Investment Funds Regulations 2012 and are subject to the supervision of India's capital markets authority. This makes NIIF unique compared with other government-sponsored SIFs, which, as mentioned previously, either are created by SIF-specific legislation or may be formed under company law.

Because SIFs are akin to private capital funds, mixed capital SIFs typically draw a clear distinction between the legal identity of the fund and its manager. The separate legal identity of the manager can also reinforce its operational independence from the public sponsor. Private capital funds, like other investment funds, are distinguished from other types of companies by their unique organizational structure that distinguishes between the entity holding the assets

TABLE 3.4 SIFs formed entirely under commercial law

SIF	OWNERSHIP	SOURCE LAW / REGULATIONS FOR FUND(S)	SOURCE LAW / REGULATIONS FOR MANAGER
Asia Climate Partners	Mixed capital	Exempted Limited Partnership Law (2018 Revision)	Hong Kong's Companies Ordinance (Cap. 622) (2014)
Marguerite II	Mixed capital	Luxembourg's Law of August 10, 1915, on commercial companies (Company Law)	European Union Alternative Investment Fund Management Directive, licensed under Luxembourg law (Marguerite Investment Management)
National Infrastructure Investment Funds (India)	Mixed capital	Securities and Exchange Board of India (Alternative Investment Funds) Regulations, 2012, and Indian Trusts Act, 1882	Company Law, 2013 (NIIF Ltd)
Khazanah Nasional Berhad (Malaysia)	Public capital	Malaysia's Companies Act 1965	n.a.[a]
Mubadala Investment Company (United Arab Emirates)	Public capital	United Arab Emirates Federal Law No. 2 of 2015 on Commercial Companies	n.a.[b]
Palestine Investment Fund (West Bank and Gaza)	Public capital	Companies Law No. 12 of 1964	n.a.[c]

Source: World Bank.
Note: n.a. = not applicable; SIF = strategic investment fund.
a. Because Khazanah is an investment company, the regulation for management entity is not relevant. Khazanah's activities in the financial markets (for example, the sale of listed shares in its portfolio companies and related disclosure requirements) must comply with applicable securities law, but the vehicle itself does not fall under fund regulation.
b. No separate management entity.
c. No separate management entity.

(the fund) and the entity managing these assets (the manager) (Morley 2014). Because mixed capital SIFs seek to pool domestic public sector capital with private sector and foreign capital, they tend to adopt both recognizable private sector management and capital pooling structures. The funds of NIIF, for instance, are managed by NIIF Ltd, a separate management company set up under the Companies Act 2013, to facilitate its independence from political influence (see table 3.4).

In many jurisdictions, funds and fund managers as distinct entities are regulated by complementary but separate regulations. Following the 2008 global financial crisis, regulators around the world began to impose new regulations on alternative investment funds—of which private capital funds are a subset—and their managers because of concern for how these funds might affect systemic risk.[21] The focus of this regulatory attention is particularly on the fund manager, rather than the fund, and chiefly on those fund managers managing large assets. For example, in 2011 the EU adopted Directive 2011/61/EU on Alternative Investment Fund Managers (AIFMs), which requires certain disclosures, risk management practices, and measures to prevent conflicts of interest.[22] The AIFM Directive focuses on regulating the AIFM managing more than €500 million (unleveraged) or €100 million (leveraged). In the United States, funds and fund managers are regulated by the Investment Company Act of 1940 and the Investment Advisers Act of 1940, respectively.[23] Consequently, SIFs seeking to closely align with private capital fund characteristics typically ensure compliance with both fund-level regulations and regulations governing the fund managers. For instance, Marguerite II is managed by Marguerite Investment Management S.A., an independent company licensed as an EU AIFM under Luxembourg law. Similarly, Asia Climate Partners' general partner, Asia Climate Partners General Partner Limited, is a Cayman limited company, but its management company is a Hong Kong limited company, regulated by the Securities and Futures Commission of Hong Kong SAR, China.

SIF legal structures and domicile

As discussed previously, the choices of legal structure and domicile are deeply interlinked, and typically embedded within the law that establishes the SIF. On the one hand, the fund's domicile, as the jurisdiction in which the fund is based for business and tax purposes, is a key decision for the SIF sponsor. Different jurisdictions offer a menu of various legal structures, levels of regulation, investor protections, dispute resolution mechanisms, and tax treatment. In turn, the choice of domicile may significantly affect a fund's contractual arrangements, performance, risk-taking behavior, reporting, and fund survival (Cumming, Dai, and Johan 2015). The legal structure, on the other hand, may signify a SIF's operational independence. For example, a fund set up as a separate entity with an independent board may more easily access financing independently through the capital markets. This is, for instance, the case with Khazanah, which has successfully conducted multiple bond issuances. The legal structure plays a crucial role in offering a (standard) governance and management system to support the operation of the SIF. The SIF's legal structure also determines its tax treatment, influences the level of control investors may exercise, and determines disclosure and transparency requirements. The choice of domicile influences the legal structure selected, and conversely the choice of legal structure may influence the chosen domicile.

Legal structure

A broad range of factors affects the choice of legal structures, which vary widely depending on the legal tradition of the jurisdiction concerned. Legal structures are typically chosen on the basis of the options they provide in terms of the rights, duties, and fiscal treatment of parties investing in, controlling, and managing the fund (see table 3.5). Investment funds tend to be formed as companies in countries operating under common law and civil code legal traditions, as trust forms in certain common law countries, or as contractual forms, typically in countries without trust laws (World Bank 2015). As discussed earlier in this chapter, SIFs may also be created as bespoke government entities (typically statutory corporations). Globally, however, private equity–type funds are usually created using the limited partnership structure, which allows a set of limited partners to provide capital passively and take on limited liability while the general partners actively invest the capital (see table 3.5 and box 3.4). Despite these differences in structure and associated legal provisions, there is considerable convergence in the form and function of investment funds around the world.

Whereas public capital SIFs that invest domestically, and do not seek outside investment at the level of the fund, typically adopt bespoke structures under special legislation or use local commercial structures, mixed capital SIFs tend to adopt globally recognizable private sector management and capital

TABLE 3.5 **Examples of legal structures used by global SIFs**

COMMONLY USED SIF LEGAL STRUCTURES	KEY FEATURES
No legal entity / contractual forms	• No separate legal existence. • Pass-through taxation. • Liability, control rights, supervision, management, and life of the fund may be set by agreement or secondary legislation and so on.
Statutory corporation / body corporate	• Statutory corporation created by the state through specific legislation. • Does not have constitutional documents typically required under Companies Act, such as articles of association / memorandum of agreement. • The Act defines the entity's mandate, powers, governance structure, and so on. • Statutory corporation allows for separation from government to ensure independence. • Not incorporated and not subject to the insolvency regime unlike companies incorporated under Companies Act.
Investment company	• Incorporated as a separate legal entity. • Perpetual life / permanent capital vehicle. • Can be recognized as tax transparent (for example, limited liability company in some jurisdictions) or provided tax exemption. • Governance structure usually includes board of directors.
Trust	• Rights and obligations are governed by trust deed. • Governance structure revolves around the trustee, which manages the fund or outsources responsibility to a fund manager. • Investors purchase units in a trust. • Can be recognized as tax transparent.
Limited partnership	• Two types of partners: limited partners that passively contribute capital and take on limited liability, and general partners that represent the sponsor of the fund, take on unlimited liability, and invest the fund's assets through a management company in return for a fee and share in profits. • Finite life fund, typically 10 years for private equity. • Typically recognized as tax flow-through entity: the fund does not pay taxes, and income is taxable at the investor level.

Source: World Bank.

Note: SIF = strategic investment fund.

Core features of the GP/LP structure

Private equity and venture capital funds usually employ a partnership model—typically through a limited partnership agreement—to structure their fund (see figure B3.4.1).

Investors are known as limited partners (LPs), and the fund management company is known as the general partner (GP). The GP raises capital from a limited number of qualified investors that become LPs in the fund. Typically, LPs consist of pension funds, insurance companies, foundations, endowments, high-net-worth individuals , sovereign wealth funds, or development finance institutions. The GP is responsible for all management decisions of the partnership, has a fiduciary obligation to act for the benefit of the LPs, and bears full liability for its actions (Preqin, n.d.).

The partnership is set up for a predefined period of time (usually 10 years, with possible extensions), during which investments must be made and exited. The capital is invested typically in the first three to five years. After that period, the GP is expected to exit investments and distribute returns to the LPs. The GP is remunerated with (1) annual management fees (typically 2 percent of committed capital) to cover operating expenses, and (2) a share of the investment gains from the fund (so-called carry or carried interest, typically set at 20 percent of profits). Carried interest seeks to align the incentives of the GP with those of the LP investors in the fund and usually applies only after the fund has achieved a minimum return hurdle rate (for example, 8 percent) and can be paid on a deal-by-deal basis or a whole fund basis (Preqin, n.d.).

FIGURE B3.4.1

Commonly used private equity fund organizational model: The GP/LP structure

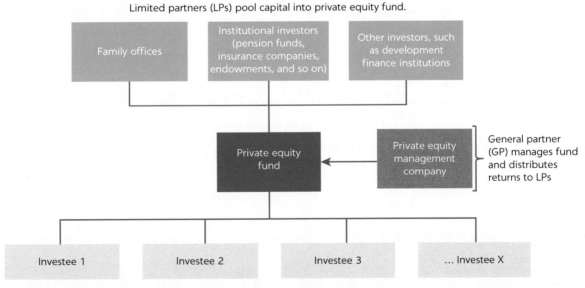

Figure Source: World Bank.

Box Sources: Divakaran et al. 2014; Preqin, n.d.

pooling structures. Because mixed capital SIFs seek to attract outside investors, globally recognized structures provide confidence to co-investors that the fund will operate predictably through mechanisms that have been tested through market discipline. Globally, investors are drawn to commonly used vehicles in well-known fund jurisdictions, such as the Delaware Limited Partnership (in the

US state of Delaware), which gives benefits like limited liability to investors. Established structures, such as trusts, limited partnerships, or corporations, also help provide some assurance that the SIF will be independent from political pressures (see table 3.6 for legal structures used by mixed capital SIFs).

Although the limited partnership structure is most commonly used among private equity funds globally, government sponsors of SIFs may resist the structural relegation to passive investors in such a model. Typically, the general partner (GP) / limited partner (LP) structure seeks to align the interests of the manager and the investors (see box 3.4). The fundamental characteristic of the GP/LP model is that the GP has more control, whereas the LP is a passive investor relying on the professional management expertise of the GP. In the case of SIFs, for which the public sector sponsor defines the strategic direction of the fund and provides the anchor capital to invest in a double bottom line strategy, giving up management control may be challenging (see chapter 4 for more detailed discussion on this topic).

Despite the risk that the public sector sponsor has less control in certain fund structures, it is important to bear in mind that there are greater hazards if the public sector sponsor adopts structures by which it can seize more control of the fund. Political interference, whether perceived or otherwise, from the public sector LP may sully the reputation of the fund, and both professional managers and potential co-investors may hesitate to participate. Other legal structures may not give the public sponsor limited liability as effectively as the limited partnership model does. A compromise is for the government sponsor to be represented in the advisory committee—built into the governance structure of the limited partnership model—to steer the strategic direction of the SIF (see chapter 4).

TABLE 3.6 **Legal structure and domicile for a variety of SIFs**

SIF	OWNERSHIP	LEGAL STRUCTURE	DOMICILE
Asia Climate Partners	Mixed	Exempted Limited Partnership Law (2018 Revision)	Offshore (Cayman Islands)
Marguerite II	Mixed	Luxembourg special partnership, or Societé en Commandite Spéciale (SCSp),[a] under Luxembourg Law of August 10, 1915, on commercial companies (Company Law)	Offshore (Luxembourg)
Ghana Infrastructure Investment Fund	Public	Statutory corporation (body corporate)	Domestic
National Infrastructure Investment Funds (India)	Mixed	Trust, under Indian Trusts Act, 1882	Domestic
Ireland Strategic Investment Fund	Public	No legal entity	Domestic
Khazanah Nasional Berhad (Malaysia)	Public	Public limited company, under Malaysian Companies Act, 1965	Domestic
Nigeria Sovereign Investment Authority	Public	Statutory corporation (body corporate)	Domestic
FONSIS (Senegal)	Public	Limited liability company, under OHADA framework[b]	Domestic
Palestine Investment Fund (West Bank and Gaza)	Public	Public shareholder company under Companies Law No. 12 of 1964	Domestic

Sources: World Bank (see case studies in appendix A); fund websites; available public documents.
Note: FONSIS = Fonds Souverain d'Investissements Stratégiques (Sovereign Fund for Strategic Investments); OHADA = Organisation pour l'harmonisation en Afrique du drout des affaires (Organization for the Harmonisation of Corporate Law in Africa); SIF = strategic investment fund.
a. The SCSp was introduced in Luxembourg in 2013. The SCSp is a variation of the long-established, standard Luxembourg partnership (Société en Commandite Simple, or SCS), the difference being that the SCSp does not have a legal personality separate from those of its partners and, as a result, can be structured more flexibly.
b. Acte Uniforme Révis Relatif au Droit des Socit Commerciales et du Groupement d'Intrêt Économique, 2014.

Domicile

The choice of domicile is relevant primarily for mixed capital SIFs anchored by nongovernment entities, whose choice may be influenced by a broad range of factors. Although a sponsor may have its primary operations in a home country, it may select another jurisdiction as the legal domicile for the fund. The choice of an offshore jurisdiction is driven by multiple considerations, such as the availability of a robust regulatory regime, the level of regulatory oversight desired by the fund and its investors, confidence in the rule of law, tax efficiency and neutrality, and the availability of appropriate investment instruments not existent in the host country. Reputable offshore domiciles typically also have a deep and experienced pool of service providers, including fund administrators, lawyers, accountants and auditors, and professional directors (RBC Investor & Treasury Services 2018) (see box 3.5). Despite those advantages, domiciling abroad requires acquiring familiarity with a new regime, hiring local expert advisers, and possibly incurring higher registration costs than in the SIF's home country. The choice of offshore domicile is most often exercised by mixed capital SIFs, which must consider the attractiveness of the domicile's legal framework for both the SIF sponsor and outside investors, and therefore often gravitate toward reputable fund jurisdictions.

For responsible investors, transparency is one of the key criteria of reputed jurisdictions. Transparency supports the fight against aggressive tax avoidance, tax evasion, corruption, money laundering, and other illicit financial flows.

BOX 3.5

Most popular domiciles

A number of well-established jurisdictions have been leading the race to attract funds. Historically, the most popular domiciles for alternative investment funds have generally been the Cayman Islands, the state of Delaware in the United States, Luxembourg, Malta, Ireland, Jersey, Guernsey, the Isle of Man, the British Virgin Islands, Bermuda, and Mauritius.

Fund sponsors often have regional preferences for domiciliation. European fund sponsors, for example, often domicile in Luxembourg. Sponsors from English-speaking countries are more likely to domicile in Ireland, in one of the Channel Islands jurisdictions, or in the United Kingdom. US fund sponsors are most likely to choose Delaware, the British Virgin Islands, or the Cayman Islands; and African and Asian sponsors more often domicile in Mauritius and the Cayman Islands.

Note that, from both an AML/CFT (Anti-Money Laundering/Combating the Financing of Terrorism)

and a tax angle, there are concerns that low tax jurisdictions or offshore centers are less transparent and, at times, less effective in providing relevant information—often specifically related to beneficial ownership information for legal entities incorporated under the laws of those jurisdictions. Some jurisdictions—such as Barbados, the Cayman Islands, Malta, and Panama—are currently on the Financial Action Task Force grey list, whereby the country has agreed to rectify certain AML/CFT deficiencies within a specific timeline.[a] These concerns may also be taken into account when deciding where to locate a strategic investment fund. As members of the Global Forum on Transparency and Exchange of Information for Tax Purposes, all these jurisdictions have committed to implement the international standards on tax transparency, including fighting the misuse of opaque structures that might conceal beneficial ownership.

Sources: Clarkson, Jaecklin, and Kaczmarski 2014; World Bank.
a. For more information, see the Financial Action Task Force list of jurisdictions under increased monitoring (https://www.fatf-gafi.org/publications/high-risk-and-other-monitored-jurisdictions/documents/increased-monitoring-march-2022.html).

In turn, this fight helps countries secure the stability and integrity of capital markets and mobilize resources to finance reliable public services highly sought by investors.[24] In addition, by revealing information on beneficial ownership, investors support tax transparency and financial integrity standards and the fight against illicit transactions.

Choosing a well-recognized fund jurisdiction allows SIFs to operate in a bigger arena than as a local actor. Commonly used fund jurisdictions offer predictability and are useful for dispute resolution through courts. They help investors manage legal risks and provide more credibility. SIFs trying to attract global investors also consider domiciles that provide tax treaty networks ensuring that cross-border investors are not double taxed.[25] Investors are also interested in whether taxes on income are treated as distribution to investors (which means investors bear the tax) or if they are treated as an expense (which means the GP bears the tax).

Mixed-capital SIFs, however, may still choose to set up their funds under applicable domestic laws, if these are deemed to be sufficiently tested and developed. NIIF, for instance, opted for onshore domicile, resulting in a trust structure commonly used by local private equity funds in India but not as familiar to foreign investors. NIIF's legal structure is subject to the Indian Trusts Act 1882, a law described as "archaic" by the government's own Minister of State for Finance (TNN 2015) before its first minor amendment in 2016, which relaxed the securities in which trustees can invest surplus trust money.[26] NIIF is therefore vulnerable both to inapplicable provisions in the Indian Trusts Act 1882 and to uncertain future amendments to the law. Despite this vulnerability, NIIF has attracted significant foreign capital, as discussed in this book. For mixed capital SIFs that invest only domestically or with co-investors that are primarily other domestic entities, the home jurisdiction may provide greater legal certainty and a favorable tax treatment, and thus may be an attractive venue even for the SIF's co-investors.

SIFs anchored by government sponsors are usually driven by political reasons to establish in their home country. As table 3.6 shows, public capital SIFs are typically domiciled in their home countries. For public capital SIFs, which do not need to consider whether the fund domicile is desirable to outside investors, the sponsor's home jurisdiction is typically found adequate as a domicile if the domestic legal framework provides a sufficiently robust structure. It is politically more difficult for a government sponsor to justify domiciling a SIF offshore. Retaining the SIF onshore also gives the government sponsor more control in managing potential regulatory hurdles. Table 3.7 shows the common factors affecting the sponsor's choice of legal structure and domicile.

PRIVATE AGREEMENTS IN SETTING UP A SIF

As discussed in the introduction to this chapter, SIFs set up under commercial law or partnering with co-investors must also construct part of their legal framework through private agreements or contractual provisions. The creation of these legal relationships mirrors the process for private investment funds. Much of the fund's internal governance mechanisms will be structured through key contractual arrangements articulated in key documents—the

TABLE 3.7 **Factors affecting the choice of legal structure and domicile**

FACTORS	RATIONALE	LEGAL STRUCTURE	DOMICILE
Suitability of legal and regulatory framework	A suitable legal environment provides flexibility and allows effective cooperation with international supervisory authorities, adheres to international standards, and offers strong investor protection rights. Responsive authorities offer a flexible, open, no-nonsense approach.		X
Availability of legal structures	Depending on legal tradition, some legal structures are unavailable in certain jurisdictions. Trusts, for example, are more typically available in common law countries.	X	X
Tax implications	Certain structures provide tax advantages relative to others; for instance, in partnerships and trusts typically no tax is paid at the entity level and investors are taxed on distributions. Investors also seek tax efficiency when choosing domicile, including tax treaty networks to avoid double taxation.	X	X
Life of the fund	Funds may adopt structures that provide for a limited or perpetual fund life; for example, limited partnerships may exist for a certain term, such as 10 years, whereas a corporation will typically have a perpetual existence.	X	
Control rights	Control rights vary according to the entity form, with some forms (such as corporations) providing more control to the investor than others (such as limited partnerships).	X	
Limitations on liability	Most funds adopting commercial forms will choose entity forms that limit liability for investors to the value of their investment.	X	
External financing / co-investors	SIFs seeking financing other than solely from the sponsor will tend to adopt standard commercial structures familiar to lenders, co-investors, and other market participants.	X	
Flexibility of legal structure	Certain legal structures may have more onerous, restrictive statutory provisions (such as companies and corporations), whereas others (such as trusts and partnerships) may enjoy relatively more flexibility in the structuring of the relationships among the parties.	X	
Administrative requirements	Certain legal structures may require detailed administrative and governance structures, and may impose ongoing disclosures, fees, and record-keeping requirements.[a] Administrative requirements may increase the complexity and costs of managing the fund.	X	
Service providers	Strong local service providers are present, with a skilled local workforce and a large number of local custodians.		X

Sources: Clarkson, Jaecklin, and Kaczmarski 2014; World Bank.
Note: SIF = strategic investment fund.
a. For example, structures set up in the European Union are subject to Directive 2011/61/EU on Alternative Investment Fund Managers. More generally, partnerships will typically be subject to less regulation than corporate entities.

most important of which include the private placement memorandum, the fund investors agreement, and the investment management agreement (see table 3.8). These documents will vary depending on the type of legal structure used by the fund (for example, a trust structure, a limited partnership structure, a contractual structure, or a company structure), and have different titles depending on the structure and the jurisdiction. Despite these differences, however, there is considerable convergence in the form and function of these documents across jurisdictions and legal traditions, because international investors tend to prefer common, predictable structures and frameworks for their investments. In addition, arbitration clauses are particularly important to SIFs formed under commercial legislation or investing with partner investors (see box 3.6).

TABLE 3.8 **Commonly used fund documents for SIFs set up under private equity norms**

DOCUMENT	PURPOSE	DRAFTER	SIGNATORIES
Private placement memorandum	Primary marketing or fundraising document	Sponsor counsel and managers	n.a.
Fund investors (shareholders) agreement[a]	Provides core legal terms for the fund and its investors, including fund objectives, contribution and distribution provisions, and fee arrangements	Sponsor counsel	Investors, sponsor, or managers
Investment management agreement	Authorizes and sets out terms under which manager will advise and manage the fund	Sponsor counsel and managers	Fund, fund managers

Source: World Bank.
Note: n.a. = not applicable; SIF = strategic investment fund.
a. Also known as the limited partnership agreement in a limited partner structure.

APPLICABILITY OF OTHER DOMESTIC, SUPRANATIONAL, AND INTERNATIONAL LAWS TO SIFS

The SIF may be disciplined by the public laws in various jurisdictions in which it operates: (1) the jurisdiction in which the SIF is established, which provides the foundation for the fund's institutional and governance structure and governs a range of operational issues of the SIF;[27] (2) the jurisdiction in which it is domiciled, which may be different from the jurisdiction of its home country; and (3) the jurisdiction(s) in which it invests, which applies when the SIF makes cross-border investments or engages foreign co-investors, and is subject to foreign laws, codes of conduct, best practices, and regulations.

Other domestic law

SIFs formed under SIF-specific law may also be subject to, or affected by, other domestic laws. As an entity operating in the financial sector, the SIF could potentially be subject to other domestic laws such as the broader financial sector regulatory framework. It may also be subject to the country's public-private partnership framework or sector investment restrictions that either drive or contract its pipelines. Despite efforts to construct a robust legal framework for a SIF, the fund's legal legitimacy could potentially be thwarted if the validity of its provisions is ambiguous or contradicts other applicable laws. For instance, in NSIA's case, the legal legitimacy of the fund was mired because state governments contested the legality of withdrawing hydrocarbon revenue from the Excess Crude Account to fund the NSIA (Amusan, Saka, and Omede 2017). SIF-specific law must therefore ensure that its provisions do not contradict the provisions of any other law it references, and that the hierarchy of laws observed by the SIF is clear.

Explicit or implicit reliance on SOE laws or structures, in particular, may subject the SIF to a variety of public sector laws and regulations that can conflict with the mandate of the SIF, hinder its ability to work with private players, and even fundamentally impede its operations. A SIF created as a statutory corporation, such as NSIA or the Ghana Infrastructure Investment Fund, may be subject to SOE laws or other public or private laws, including public sector employment rules, investment and budgeting regulations, procurement laws, public financial management laws, audit requirements, and sector-specific laws and regulations (World Bank 2014). When specific SOE laws are not in place, the regulatory requirements for the SIF as a public entity may be "scattered in various decrees

BOX 3.6

The significance of arbitration clauses for SIFs

A key decision in structuring the legal framework of a strategic investment fund (SIF) is whether to use an alternative dispute resolution process in the event of a dispute between the SIF and its partners or stakeholders.

In deciding on an appropriate dispute resolution mechanism, the SIF should also consider whether its domestic courts system has adequate expertise to adjudicate sophisticated financial matters. It may also consider domestic nonjudicial dispute resolution forums, and whether they are sufficiently developed. The SIF should also consider whether the home jurisdiction has ratified the New York Convention,[a] and any risk that the finality of arbitral awards would be called into question.

The most frequently used alternative dispute resolution mechanism is arbitration, a private process by which disputing parties agree that one or several individuals can make a decision about the dispute after receiving evidence and hearing arguments.[b] The choice of arbitral forum determines the laws and rules under which a dispute will be resolved and the location of the dispute resolution forum,[c] and it affects the cost and speed of resolution and the confidentiality of the dispute.

If a SIF or its sponsor chooses to include arbitration provisions in its legislation or fund documents, it will typically select both a choice of arbitral seat and a choice of an arbitration institution. The arbitral seat refers to the legal location of the arbitration, and typically determines the applicable substantive law, including local courts that may be used during the arbitration (K&L Gates 2012). The arbitral institution is the professional organization providing administrative support and procedural rules for the arbitration. Table B3.6.1 shows the most popular arbitral seats and arbitral institutions.

TABLE B3.6.1 **Popular arbitral seats and institutions**

ARBITRAL SEATS	ARBITRAL INSTITUTIONS
London, United Kingdom	The London Court of International Arbitration (LCIA)
Paris, France	International Chamber of Commerce (ICC)
Singapore	Singapore International Arbitration Centre (SIAC)
Hong Kong SAR, China	Hong Kong International Arbitration Centre (HKIAC)
Stockholm, Sweden	The Arbitration Institute of the Stockholm Chamber of Commerce (SCC)
Geneva, Switzerland	International Centre for Settlement of Investment Disputes (ICSID)
	International Centre for Dispute Resolution / American Arbitration Association (ICDR/AAA)

Source: SIA and White & Case 2018.
Note: Arbitral seats and institutions shown in order of popularity. The five most important factors for preferring certain seats were, in the following order (1) general reputation and recognition of the seat, (2) neutrality and impartiality of the local legal system, (3) national arbitration law, (4) track record in enforcing agreements to arbitrate and arbitral awards, and (5) availability of quality arbitrators who are familiar with the seat (SIA and White & Case 2018). The five most important factors for preferring certain arbitration institutions were, in the following order (1) general reputation and recognition of the institution, (2) high level of administration (including efficiency, pro-activeness, facilities, quality of staff), (3) previous experience of the institution, (4) neutrality and internationalism, and (5) access to wide pool of high-quality arbitrators (SIA and White & Case 2018).
Although arbitration has many benefits, drawbacks to arbitration include high costs, the lack of effective sanctions during the arbitral process, and the relatively limited power of arbitral forums compared to domestic courts (SIA and White & Case 2018).

a. Convention on the Recognition and Enforcement of Foreign Arbitral Awards adopted by the United Nations in 1958, which requires that the local courts in contracting states must recognize and enforce arbitral awards made in other contracting states.
b. See the American Bar Association's web page "Dispute Resolution Processes: Arbitration" (https://www.americanbar.org/groups/dispute_resolution/resources/disputeresolutionprocesses/arbitration/).
c. The location of the arbitral seat is "fundamental to defining the legal framework for international arbitral proceedings and can have profound legal and practical consequences in an international arbitration" (Born 2012, 105).

and regulations without any overarching law" (World Bank 2014, 28). In NSIA's case, the NSIA Act 2011 does not explicitly exempt the SIF/SWF from SOE laws, which can subject the fund to unpredictability regarding whether or not to apply SOE rules, such as being subject to audit by the Auditor General or having to follow public procurement rules. More significantly, NSIA's operations were affected in July 2015, when shortly after the Nigerian elections President Buhari dissolved the governing boards of all federal parastatals, agencies, and institutions—an unprecedented occurrence not anticipated by the NSIA Act 2011. NSIA therefore did not have a board from July 2015 to March 2017,[28] during which period it interacted with the Ministry of Finance directly and limited new investments. Ideally, governments must explicitly differentiate SIFs from SOEs (through special legislation or otherwise) to negate the risk of being subjected to laws and regulations that impede fulfilling their mandate (see box 2.5 in chapter 2 for a further example of the complexity of the authorizing environment of SIFs in China).

Under exceptional circumstances, SIF-specific laws or policies may exempt the fund from being subject to some domestic laws or regulations or may amend existing laws to suit the SIF's operations, but this approach risks creating an uneven playing field between the SIF and private funds. Equal application of commercial law is ideal because it helps create a level playing field with private players, providing no specific commercial or competitive advantage to the SIF (World Bank 2014). In some cases, however, SIF establishment laws clarify that certain state laws and regulations—such as on tax, investment funds, and SOEs, as well as securities laws and commercial laws—are not applicable to the fund. For example, according to Section 44 of the NTMA Act 2014, ISIF's investments in credit institutions are exempt from rules on competition and mergers and acquisitions (as applied in Part 2 and Part 3 of Ireland's 2002 Competition Act).[29] Exemptions should be limited to the strictly necessary—to mitigate the risk that a SIF is not able to implement its double bottom line mandate—and should be publicly disclosed, together with their rationale. In some cases, the government may be well justified in providing exemptions to the SIF because the objective is to allow the SIF to compete on a level playing field with private funds. For instance, compliance with public employment rules may prevent a SIF from hiring experienced investment professionals by offering competitive, market-level compensation. This limitation could affect the quality of the investment team and, ultimately, fund performance, which would justify an exemption from public employment rules. Regarding the example discussed previously, because NSIA's commercial viability and ability to interact on par with private entities could potentially be threatened by being subject to SOE rules, NSIA has used the board's ability to create policy to devise its own procurement rules.[30]

Supranational law

SIFs will also be subject to supranational regulatory frameworks in the jurisdictions in which they operate. Depending on the jurisdiction of the SIF and where it invests, SIFs may be subject to regional laws, such as EU directives. This is particularly the case for mixed capital SIFs, which may make cross-border investments that would implicate the legal systems of host countries; it also applies to public capital SIFs that may invest abroad and be subject to foreign legal systems or that are part of an economic bloc such as the EU. For instance, ISIF generally takes minority equity stakes in its domestic portfolio and invests on broadly equal terms with private investors to ensure compliance with the EU's Market Economy Investor Principle under EU state aid rules. As a government agency, ISIF must ensure that its investments do not breach EU rules preventing unfair financial support to the private sector. Every ISIF investment is therefore subject to a strict vetting and cost-based analysis process in this respect (see the ISIF case study in appendix A).

International law

Foreign laws, and the way they are applied, can have a critical impact on the origination and management of SIF transactions. The profitability of a mixed capital SIF's transactions, for instance, can be affected by income tax laws in the country where it invests. For example, the presence of a double tax treaty[31] will likely make investment in a fund much more appealing for foreign co-investors. The issue of sovereign immunity may also be critical for investors who may insist on a waiver of sovereign immunity for the SIF (if it would otherwise apply). However, co-investors may also seek to enjoy the benefits of dealing with a sovereign-affiliated entity by requiring a guarantee from the sovereign (for instance, a guarantee on an investee-company's debt, lowering the cost of such debt and enhancing the return on an equity investment).[32]

On the flip side, SIFs that invest abroad may also present special concerns to host countries because of their status as sovereign-sponsored entities, particularly because independence from the state sponsor varies greatly among SIFs. The Organisation for Economic Co-operation and Development identifies several concerns in this respect in connection with SOEs generally, which may also be applicable to SIFs (OECD 2009). Because SOEs are typically designed to fulfill a public interest purpose, like SIFs, an SOE is expected "to pursue objectives that differ from those of a privately-owned undertaking" (OECD 2009, 6). These objectives, for example, may include formal or practical obligations to subordinate profit maximization to the public interest purpose of the SOE, which may lead to actions that result in asymmetric preferential treatment in home markets versus foreign markets. SOEs may also serve the national interest through acquiring scarce resources or advanced technologies, or through subsidizing the foreign operation of public and private national business entities (OECD 2018b).[33] Perception of such practices among SIFs, which are designed to meet a double bottom line mandate, could result in concerns that the SIF is operating on an uneven playing field relative to host countries and to private players in the domestic market. Because SIFs may be perceived as being equivalent to SOEs, foreign governments may be concerned that distortions associated with foreign investments of SOEs may also apply to foreign investments of SIFs.

To alleviate these concerns, SIFs, like SWFs, must conduct their operations and activities "in compliance with all applicable regulatory and disclosure requirements of the countries in which they operate."[34] In return for their compliance with applicable laws and regulations, funds should expect that the host country will not subject the fund to restrictions or regulatory actions that other equivalent investors would not be subject to. Under the Santiago Principles, respect for applicable laws and regulations includes, among other things, disclosure "to the relevant regulators in such jurisdictions in compliance with applicable laws and regulations, including in connection with investigations or any other regulatory actions initiated by securities regulators or other relevant authorities."[35] Table 3.9 presents a broad (but not exhaustive) list of laws that may affect SIFs (see also box 3.7). Specifically, the Santiago Principles, as set out in IWG (2008), state that the fund should:

- Abide by any national securities laws, including disclosure requirements and market integrity rules addressing insider trading and market manipulation;

TABLE 3.9 **Other laws affecting SIF cross-border activities**

National security laws[a]	• Regulations will typically require advance notice provided to the regulators on transactions that may have a material impact on critical infrastructure and assets in the recipient country or may otherwise affect national security. Box 3.7 sets out an example of such regulation. • Proposed investments are screened by regulators. As part of this process, many regulations will require that the regulators look through special purpose vehicles engaged in the transaction to determine the ultimate investors in the vehicle. • Where necessary, potential negative impacts are mitigated through changes to the deal structure. In some cases, the transaction may be blocked by the regulator if mitigation is not possible.
Securities laws, investment funds laws, and fund adviser laws	• Recipient countries will typically impose regulations on how fund interests, debt instruments, equity investments, and other securities are sold to their citizens. • Countries often impose separate regulatory regimes for selling funds and the fund advisers (Morley 2014), and regulations often require significant disclosures by funds and advisers. Such disclosures are subject to antifraud rules enforceable by the regulators or, in some jurisdictions, the investors themselves. The regulations may also require the registration of the securities intended to be sold, which may involve significant review and comment on disclosures by recipient country regulators. • Securities regulators may also impose rules governing specific types of transactions, such as mergers or acquisitions.
Tax laws	• Tax considerations drive many structuring decisions for the fund and its investors, particularly for mixed capital SIFs. The importance of maintaining favorable tax treatment is critically important, and tax laws and regulations must be carefully navigated to ensure continued favorable treatment.[b] • Tax issues arise at four different levels: at the level of the investor, the fund, the portfolio investment, and the fund manager (Fenn and Goldstein 2002). The goal in each case is to eliminate or minimize tax obligations. In most cases, the fund is structured so that the fund does not pay tax, but so that the gains and losses pass through to the investors, who are then taxed individually. Investors will also tend to prefer that their investments remain anonymous, both in the recipient country and in their home jurisdictions. In other jurisdictions, however, transparency will be required. For example, investors from France and the Netherlands must invest in vehicles that provide transparency to their home-country regulators. • For SIFs operating outside of their home jurisdiction, the taxation of the fund sponsor itself varies depending on the jurisdiction. Some jurisdictions exempt fund income from taxation through specific legislation, administrative practice, or a double tax treaty (PwC 2012). Jurisdictions exempting SIFs and other state-affiliated entities from taxation may do so through the application of sovereign immunity doctrines,[c] which traditionally limit the application of a recipient country's laws to most areas of activity undertaken by sovereign entities within its borders. However, such grants of immunity are becoming increasingly narrow as cross-border investments by sovereigns increase. Some politicians, academics, and others have called for the elimination of sovereign immunity from taxation (Fleischer 2009).
Competition and antitrust laws	• Like private entities, SIFs will generally be subject to laws and regulations prohibiting anticompetitive behavior. • State-owned enterprises involved in anticompetitive conduct are regularly prosecuted in jurisdictions with established competition laws (OECD 2018a). In some jurisdictions, however, state-affiliated entities may be granted exemptions to these laws if they are engaged in activities in the general public interest. For example, Article 106(2) of the Treaty on the Functioning of the European Union provides a limited exclusion from competition laws for "services of general economic interest or having the character of a revenue-producing monopoly." Such exemptions will usually be read narrowly by recipient-country regulators.

continued

TABLE 3.9 *continued*

Public-private partnership laws	• Some jurisdictions will also impose specific regulations in connection with public-private partnerships (PPPs), which may apply to SIF activities depending on the structure of the SIF and its establishment legislation (if any). The European Bank for Reconstruction and Development and the Organisation for Economic Co-operation and Development have produced guidelines on the creation of PPP laws and regulations (EBRD 2006; OECD 2012). In particular, the guidelines encourage fairness, predictability, and enforceability of concession agreements used to structure the partnership. PPP legislation may also impose regulations relating to transparency, reporting obligations, guarantees, and security for lenders. • The contours of PPP laws and regulations will shape the ways in which projects are prepared and sourced. Depending on the regulation, this may expand or contract the pipeline of deals for the SIF.

Source: World Bank.

Note: SIF = strategic investment fund.

a. For SIFs operating in other countries, a major concern of any host country is that the SIF might invest in ways that jeopardize or affect the national security of the host country. A number of jurisdictions, including the European Union, Japan, the United Kingdom, and the United States, have recently revised investment regulations related to national security that may result in increased scrutiny for transactions involving state-owned enterprises.

b. Governments also recognize the need to provide taxation frameworks that encourage investments and development. In research on investment patterns in member states of the Association of Southeast Asian Nations, for example, Cevik and Miryugin (2018) conclude that "fair and efficient taxation is pivotal in funding public investment in infrastructure and human capital and thereby stimulating private investment."

c. See, for example, 26 U.S. Code § 892. Income of foreign governments and of international organizations (1990), which in most cases eliminates tax for investment activity by sovereigns, although the immunity does not apply to the investments characterized as commercial activity. Importantly for SIFs, the definition of commercial activity does not include governmental functions, which Internal Revenue Service regulations define as "activities performed for the general public with respect to the common welfare or which relate to the administration of some phase of government will be considered governmental functions." 26 CFR § 1.892-4T – Commercial activities (temporary regulations) (1988).

BOX 3.7

National security legislation: The US example

In response to increasing investments by state-controlled entities, many countries have recently introduced or strengthened their regulatory frameworks for reviewing the impact such investments may have on national security. Recent changes to the US regulatory framework, for example, expand the coverage of national security review beyond transactions that could result in a foreign entity's control of a US business.

Under the new legislation, the Foreign Investment Risk Review Modernization Act of 2018 (FIRRMA), transactions that merely include a noncontrolling investment may also be subject to review, if that investment gives the foreign entity access to

• Material nonpublic technical information in the possession of the US business;
• Membership, nomination, or observer rights on the board of directors; or
• Any involvement (except through the normal voting of shares) in substantive decision-making of the board regarding the use, development, acquisition, or safekeeping of personal data of US citizens; the use, development, acquisition, or release of critical technologies; or the management, operation, manufacture, or supply of critical infrastructure.

In contrast to the largely voluntary process prior to amendment, FIRRMA now requires a mandatory declaration for transactions involving critical technologies in which a foreign government has a substantial interest.

FIRRMA also subjects to review real estate transactions that may have national security implications, including transactions involving ports, real estate in close proximity to US government or military installations, or real estate that would otherwise provide foreign entities with the ability to conduct surveillance or other intelligence activities.

Source: World Bank.

Factors determining selection of legal counsel

Strategic investment funds engaged in cross-border investment will typically require the services of experienced global and local service providers to help manage legal and regulatory issues. Legal service providers will also be required for capital-raising transactions. Surveys of in-house counsel (Globality and The Lawyer Research Service 2018; Thompson Reuters and The Lawyer 2017) identify several key factors in the selection of appropriate outside counsel, including the following:

- Breadth of industry/sector expertise
- Responsiveness
- Experience of firm partners
- Existing relationships between the firm and the fund legal team and/or board
- Price and availability of alternative fee structures
- Innovative service delivery models (for example, use of technology, innovative staffing models)
- Size and reach of international network / relationships with host country law firms
- Capacity / number of lawyers at the firm
- Corporate social responsibility / responsible business practice initiatives

- Provide disclosure to local regulators, upon request and in confidence, of financial and nonfinancial information as required by applicable laws and regulation;
- Where required by applicable law or regulation, be subject to local regulators, and cooperate with investigations and comply with regulatory actions initiated by local regulators or other relevant authorities;
- Abide by any antimonopoly rules; and
- Comply with all applicable tax rules.

Obtaining the advice of experienced local counsel is key to navigating complicated legal and regulatory requirements. Relying on experienced counsel is particularly important for SIFs operating in foreign jurisdictions and for mixed capital SIFs that seek to attract and catalyze co-investment. Experienced local counsel can provide support in many areas, particularly (1) ensuring that projects meet the standards of the recipient countries and are not subject to lengthy and costly regulatory delays; (2) navigating the complex laws related to securities and investment funds, and fund adviser regulations; (3) facilitating access to and establishing relationships with regulators; (4) structuring transactions in compliance with regulatory requirements and minimizing regulatory costs; and (5) protecting the confidentiality of sensitive fund and project information. In some cases, a single, established firm may be able to provide all the different types of advice needed; however, SIFs may find it necessary to employ different firms for different areas of the law in order to secure the appropriate level of experience and capacity. Box 3.8 sets out some of the most important factors for funds in law firm selection.

KEY TAKEAWAYS

- A strong legal framework promotes discipline, transparency, and accountability in the SIF and can empower it to successfully execute its mandate. No single legal framework or legal structure is appropriate for all SIFs, which are formed in a variety of environments.

- Two main types of legal approaches are used to establish SIFs: (1) SIF-specific law or decree, with varying degrees of reliance on commercial or SOE law; or (2) purely commercial (domestic or foreign) law. In general, public capital SIFs tend to rely on SIF-specific legislation, whereas mixed capital SIFs tend to use commercial law. The choice of legal approach provides signaling effects to potential private co-investors on the operational independence and commercial orientation of the SIF.

- Public capital SIFs that invest domestically, and do not seek outside investment, typically adopt bespoke legal structures under special legislation or use local commercial structures. Mixed capital SIFs tend to adopt globally recognizable private sector management and capital pooling structures.

- Choosing a well-recognized fund jurisdiction as a domicile allows SIFs to operate in a bigger arena than as a local actor. Offshore domicile is primarily relevant for mixed capital SIFs anchored by nongovernment entities, for which a broad range of factors may influence the choice of domicile. SIFs anchored by government sponsors are usually driven by political reasons to establish in their home country.

- Explicit or implicit reliance on SOE laws or structures may subject a government-sponsored SIF to a variety of public sector laws and regulations that can conflict with the mandate of the SIF and hinder its competitiveness. Ideally, governments must explicitly differentiate SIFs from SOEs (through special legislation or otherwise) to negate the risk of subjecting SIFs to laws and regulations that impede fulfilling their mandate.

NOTES

1. In the Santiago Principles, the generally accepted principles and practices (GAPPs) for sovereign wealth funds (SWFs), GAPP 1.2 states, "The key features of the SWF's legal basis and structure, as well as the legal relationship between the SWF and other state bodies, should be publicly disclosed" (IWG 2008, 7). In addition, GAPP 6 states, "The governance framework for the SWF should be sound and establish a clear and effective division of roles and responsibilities in order to facilitate accountability and operational independence in the management of the SWF to pursue its objectives" (IWG 2008, 7).

2. See Santiago Principles GAPP 1, Explanation and Commentary (IWG 2008, 11).

3. With respect to the legal domicile of the SIF, a strong legal framework will also provide simple and manageable procedures for entering into investments and projects. The legal framework will provide for the protection of property rights and contractual rights, as well as effective enforcement of these rights. When establishing investment and enforcing investors' rights are "perceived as cumbersome and lack predictability" (OECD 2020, chapter 3), and if disputes "cannot be resolved in a timely and cost-effective manner" (OECD 2021, chapter 5), investors will be less willing to co-invest with the SIF.

4. Domestic political risks (for example, legitimacy), domestic governance risks (for example, corruption), international governance risks (for example, negative externalities created by SWF activity), and international political risks (for example, mercantilism, politicization).

5. Note that in some cases commercial laws are indeed customizable. Many commercial laws have default provisions from which to opt out, thus providing a highly customizable legal and governance framework for the entity. For example, some of Luxembourg's entity structures, like the SAS (société par actions simplifiées, or simplified shareholder company), are highly customizable.

6. For the full text of the NSIA Act 2011, see https://nsia.com.ng/~nsia/sites/default/files /downloads/NSIA%20Act.pdf.

7. For the full text of the NTMA Act 2014, see http://www.irishstatutebook.ie/eli/2014 /act/23/enacted/en/pdf.

8. See the fund's Santiago Principles Self-Assessment (https://www.ifswf.org/assessment /angola).

9. In some cases, they would need approval of the legislature.

10. State ownership is allocated between the Nigerian federal government, state governments, local governments, and the federal capital territory.

11. For example, a company established in accordance with standard company law provisions (setting out standards of independence for directors) may reduce regulator concerns over potential influence over the company by sponsor government officials, even when the government is a primary investor in the company.

12. Note that, as a sole shareholder, it would also have complete discretion in a commercial law framework although commercial law is often less customizable.

13. Per the Santiago Principles explanatory comments, SWFs are constituted in the same way: There are several ways in which the legal basis and structure of SWFs are disclosed. For SWFs that do not have a legal identity, their legal basis and structure is typically described in the provisions of publicly available legislation. The legal structure of SWFs that have a legal identity with capacity to act under public law is disclosed through the generally available constitutive laws of the SWF. Lastly, SWFs that are constituted as state-owned companies are normally governed by the country's company law (as well as other laws regulating private and public companies). In addition, some SWFs disclose key features of their corporate structure on their websites (for example, Australia, Canada (Alberta), the Republic of Korea, Kuwait, New Zealand, and Singapore) (IWG 2008, 12).

14. OHADA (Organisation pour l'harmonisation en Afrique du droit des affaires, or Organization for the Harmonization of Corporate Law in Africa) is a system of corporate law and implementing institutions adopted by 17 West and Central African nations in 1993.

15. This is typically the case for SOEs that have a specific policy goal in addition to profit maximization (see World Bank 2014).

16. For the full text of the Ghana Infrastructure Investment Fund Act, 2014, Act 877, see http:// www.odekro.org/Images/Uploads/Ghana%20Infrastructure%20Investment%20 Fund%20Act,%202014.pdf.

17. The NSIA Act 2011 provides a good example: in Article 25 the independence of the board is codified.

18. Section 4 of the NSIA Act 2011 describes that the funds are ring-fenced.

19. In some cases, the legislation itself may not describe the objectives but may make refer- ence to other legislation or policy documents, or delegate the development of a mandate to the fund's supervisory board. For example, the Turkey Wealth Fund legislation requires the board of directors to establish a "three years strategic investment plan com- prising the Company and its subsidiaries" (Article 3 of Law No. 6741 on Establishment of Turkish Wealth Fund Management Company [Türkiye Varlık Fonu Yönetimi Anonim Şirketi] and Amendments in Certain Laws published in the Official Gazette no. 29813, dated August 26, 2016).

20. For instance, under Section 42, the Minister for Finance, after consultation with the Central Bank, may direct NTMA to invest ISIF assets in specified securities of a credit institution, or underwrite the issue of any securities of a credit institution, if the minister considers it necessary, in the public interest, in order to remedy a serious disturbance in the economy or to prevent potential serious damage to Ireland's financial system.

21. The Group of 20's November 2008 summit was a defining point, leading to the decision that all significant financial market participants must be regulated to preserve financial stability and to protect investors.

22. Those managers are subject to the provisions of the AIFM Directive as transposed in their home member state. They are required to be approved by the regulatory authorities of their home member state but can also benefit from the management and marketing pass- porting regimes to provide these services in the territory of other European Economic Area member states.

23. As explained by Morley (2014, 1274–75), investment managers began separating the investment fund from the management companies that advise and oversee the fund nearly 100 years ago, and the separation of funds and managers is now ubiquitous in Europe and the United States. Many funds around the world also employ a similar separation between the fund and its managers, even if the labels of the entities used to create the fund and management vehicles differ from jurisdiction to jurisdiction.

24. Of the Global Forum on Transparency and Exchange of Information for Tax Purposes, 162 member jurisdictions have committed to implement the international standards to

fight against tax evasion and other illicit financial flows. Under the current World Bank Group Offshore Financial Centers Policy, intermediary jurisdictions with a controlling interest in an International Finance Corporation project must be domiciled in a jurisdiction that is "compliant" or "largely compliant" with the Global Forum's exchange of information on request standards to be eligible. This policy is currently being updated to reflect the evolution of the international standards on international tax and tax transparency.

25. Under the Organisation for Economic Co-operation and Development's Base Erosion and Profit Shifting project, countries are monitored to ensure their tax treaties are not misused for aggressive tax avoidance (treaty shopping).

26. Section 2, Indian Trusts (Amendment) Act 2016.

27. These issues include the fund's objectives and mandates, legal structure and ownership, relationship with the sponsor, funding, investment policies, and so on.

28. Despite the fact that NSIA is owned by all tiers of government (federal, state, and local), which complicates its identity as a federal parastatal.

29. This exemption is likely to allow the government to act in times of crisis, because ISIF funds can be directed to specific sectors during financial or economic crises.

30. Section 15 of the NSIA Act 2011 gives the board the ability to make policy within the confines of the act.

31. Bilateral agreements between two countries to ensure that taxes are divided equitably and that the cross-border investor is not paying taxes in both jurisdictions.

32. The NSIA Act 2011, Section 45, anticipated and prevented such a possibility by prohibiting the NSIA from providing "any guarantee or surety, whether for payment or performance, to or on behalf of the interest, rights or obligations of any person, company or entity involved or participating in or related to an infrastructure project, other than a wholly-owned subsidiary or affiliate of the Authority."

33. Certain kinds of infrastructure investments—such as network technology or critical infrastructure in utilities—in foreign jurisdictions may implicate national security concerns (see more on this in chapter 7 on transparency and disclosure).

34. See the Santiago Principles, GAPP 15 (IWG 2008, 8).

35. See the Santiago Principles, GAPP 15, Explanation and Commentary (IWG 2008, 19).

REFERENCES

Al-Hassan, Abdullah, Michael Papaioannou, Martin Skancke, and Cheng Chih Sung. 2013. "Sovereign Wealth Funds: Aspects of Governance Structures and Investment Management." IMF Working Paper 13/231, International Monetary Fund, Washington, DC. https://www.imf.org/en/Publications/WP/Issues/2016/12/31/Sovereign-Wealth-Funds-Aspects-of-Governance-Structures-and-Investment-Management-41046.

Amusan, Lere, Luqman Saka, and Adedoyin Jolade Omede. 2017. "Sovereign Wealth Fund and Fiscal Federalism in Nigeria (2011–14): An Assessment of Contending Issues." *Regional & Federal Studies* 27 (4): 441–63.

Awadzi, Elsie Addo. 2015. "Designing Legal Frameworks for Public Debt Management." IMF Working Paper 15/147, International Monetary Fund, Washington, DC. https://www.imf.org/external/pubs/ft/wp/2015/wp15147.pdf.

Born, Gary B. 2012. *International Arbitration: Law and Practice*. Kluwer Law International.

Cevik, Serhan, and Fedor Miryugin. 2018. "Does Taxation Stifle Corporate Investment? Firm-Level Evidence from ASEAN Countries." IMF Working Paper 18/34, International Monetary Fund, Washington, DC. https://www.imf.org/~/media/Files/Publications/WP/2018/wp1834.ashx.

Clarkson, David, Stefan Jaecklin, and Kamil Kaczmarski. 2014. "Domiciles of Alternative Investment Funds." Oliver Wyman. https://www.oliverwyman.com/content/dam/oliver-wyman/global/en/2014/dec/Oliver_Wyman_Domiciles_of_Alternative_Investment_Funds.pdf.

Cumming, Douglas, Na Dai, and Sofia A. Johan. 2015. "Are Hedge Funds Registered in Delaware Different?" *Journal of Corporate Finance* 35 (December): 232–46. https://www.sciencedirect.com/science/article/abs/pii/S0929119915001157.

Divakaran, Shanthi, Patrick J. McGinnis, and Masood Shariff. 2014. "Private Equity and Venture Capital in SMEs in Developing Countries: The Role for Technical Assistance." Policy Research Working Paper 6287, World Bank Group, Washington, DC.

EBRD (European Bank for Reconstruction and Development). 2006. "Core Principles for Modern Concessions Law." EBRD, London. https://ppp.worldbank.org/public-private -partnership/library/ebrd-core-principles-modern-concessions-law.

Fenn, Patrick, and David Goldstein. 2002. "Tax Considerations in Structuring US-Based Private Equity Funds." *International Financial Law Review*, January 24, 2002. https://www .iflr.com/Article/2027251/Tax-considerations-in-structuring-US-based-private-equity -funds.html.

Fleischer, Victor. 2009. "A Theory of Taxing Sovereign Wealth." *New York University Law Review* 84 (2). https://www.nyulawreview.org/issues/volume-84-number-2/a-theory -of-taxing-sovereign-wealth/.

Globality and The Lawyer Research Service. 2018. "Global Trends in Hiring Outside Counsel." The Lawyer. https://s3-eu-central-1.amazonaws.com/centaur-wp/thelawyer/prod /content/uploads/2018/01/17091634/Globality-Global-trends-in-hiring-outside -counsel.pdf.

IWG (International Working Group of Sovereign Wealth Funds). 2008. "Sovereign Wealth Funds Generally Accepted Principles and Practices: 'Santiago Principles.'" IWG. https:// www.ifswf.org/sites/default/files/santiagoprinciples_0_0.pdf.

K&L Gates. 2012. "Guide to Leading Arbitral Seats and Institutions." K&L Gates. http://www .klgates.com/files/upload/guidetoleadingarbitralseatsandinstitutions.pdf.

Morley, John. 2014. "The Separation of Funds and Managers: A Theory of Investment Fund Structure and Regulation." *Yale Law Journal* 123 (5): 1228–87.

OECD (Organisation for Economic Co-operation and Development). 2009. "SOEs Operating Abroad: An Application of the OECD Guidelines on Corporate Governance of State-Owned Enterprises to the Cross-Border Operations of SOEs." OECD, Paris. https://www.oecd.org /corporate/ca/corporategovernanceofstate-ownedenterprises/44215438.pdf.

OECD (Organisation for Economic Co-operation and Development). 2012. "Recommendation of the Council on Principles for Public Governance of Public-Private Partnerships." OECD, Paris. http://www.oecd.org/governance/budgeting/PPP-Recommendation.pdf.

OECD (Organisation for Economic Co-operation and Development). 2015. *Policy Framework for Investment*. Paris: OECD Publishing. https://www.oecd-ilibrary.org/finance-and -investment/policy-framework-for-investment-2015-edition_9789264208667 -en;jsessionid=H4pa1TMa3LxAwfRi4oTBBQiA.ip-10-240-5-135.

OECD (Organisation for Economic Co-operation and Development). 2018a. "Competition Law and State-Owned Enterprises." Background Note by the Secretariat, OECD, Paris. https:// one.oecd.org/document/DAF/COMP/GF(2018)10/en/pdf.

OECD (Organisation for Economic Co-operation and Development). 2018b. "Current Trends in Investment Policies Related to National Security and Public Order." OECD, Paris. http:// www.oecd.org/investment/Current-trends-in-OECD-NatSec-policies.pdf.

OECD (Organisation for Economic Co-operation and Development). 2020. *OECD Investment Policy Reviews: Egypt*. Paris: OECD Publishing.

OECD (Organisation for Economic Co-operation and Development). 2021. *OECD Investment Policy Reviews: Uruguay*. Paris: OECD Publishing.

Preqin. No date. "Preqin Pro: Glossary of Terms." Preqin Ltd. https://docs.preqin.com/pro /Preqin-Glossary.pdf.

PwC. 2012. "Sovereign Investment Funds: Tax Considerations for Global Investors." PwC. https://www.pwc.com/jp/en/tax-publications-financial-services/assets/sovereign -investment-funds-dec2012.pdf.

RBC Investor & Treasury Services. 2018. "Private Capital Fund Managers Consider Luxembourg and Ireland." *Nos Perspectives*, May 30, 2018. https://www.rbcits.com/fr /insights/2018/05/private_capital_fund_managers_consider_luxembourg_and_ireland.

Rose, Paul. 2019. "The Political and Governance Risks of Sovereign Wealth." *Annals of Corporate Governance* 4 (3): 147–271. http://dx.doi.org/10.1561/109.00000021.

SIA (School of International Arbitration, Queen Mary University of London) and White & Case. 2018. "International Arbitration Survey: The Evolution of International Arbitration." White & Case. https://www.whitecase.com/sites/whitecase/files/files/download/publications/qmul-international-arbitration-survey-2018-19.pdf.

Thomson Reuters and The Lawyer. 2017. "Standing Out from the Crowd: What Businesses Value from Their Law Firms." The Lawyer. https://www.thelawyer.com/knowledge-bank/white-paper/what-businesses-value-from-law-firms/.

TNN. 2015. "India Passes Bill to Amend Indian Trusts Act of 1882." *Times of India*, December 10, 2015. https://timesofindia.indiatimes.com/india/LS-passes-bill-to-amend-Indian-Trusts-Act-of-1882/articleshow/50114541.cms.

World Bank. 2014. *Corporate Governance of State-Owned Enterprises: A Toolkit*. Washington, DC: World Bank.

World Bank. 2015. "Mutual Funds in Developing Markets: Addressing Challenges to Growth." World Bank, Washington, DC.

4 Governance

INTRODUCTION

This chapter discusses the importance of good governance for strategic investment funds (SIFs) and how these entities and their public backers and capital providers can embed robust governance techniques within the organization. Chapter 3 sets out the key laws and regulations that underpin the governance of a SIF, and this chapter explores more closely why governance is important, what foundational elements constitute the governance of a SIF, and the principles of a well-governed SIF. The following chapters then spell out further the governance processes embedded within the SIF's investment policy, risk management, and transparency and disclosure requirements.

An entity's governance framework specifies the allocation of rights and responsibilities between its different stakeholders and articulates the rules and procedures for decision-making (World Bank 2014). Good governance contributes to the capacity of the entity to function consistently within its defined objectives and is an essential component to functional performance (North 1990; Williamson 1996). Research finds that good governance can affect investment returns by as much as 100 to 300 basis points per year (Ambachtsheer 2007; Ammann and Ehmann 2017). Even ideal institutions fail if poorly governed (Clark and Urwin 2008). The financial scandal involving the Malaysian SIF, 1Malaysia Development Berhad (1MDB), is a prime example of an institution that appeared to have good governance but for which in reality governance failures led to the theft of billions of dollars' worth of taxpayer money.[1]

A robust governance framework therefore bolsters a SIFs' legitimacy and is a prerequisite to effective long-term performance. Among the multiple factors involved in establishing a SIF, governance is core to establishing its legitimacy and implementing its mandate. A well-constructed governance framework aligns the SIF's governing bodies, providing incentives for proper oversight and management to ensure the objectives of the dual mandate are both met and monitored (see Gelb, Tordo, and Halland 2014).[2] Robust governance arrangements also insulate the SIF and its governing bodies from fluctuations in the political climate that can jeopardize the fund's long-term

BOX 4.1

Santiago Principles: Key governance principles for SWFs

The Santiago Principles include the following generally accepted principles and practices (GAPPs) related to sovereign wealth funds (SWFs):

GAPP 6. Principle
The governance framework for the SWF should be sound and establish a clear and effective division of roles and responsibilities in order to facilitate accountability and operational independence in the management of the SWF to pursue its objectives.

GAPP 7. Principle
The owner should set the objectives of the SWF, appoint the members of its governing body(ies) in accordance with clearly defined procedures, and exercise oversight over the SWF's operations.

GAPP 8. Principle
The governing body(ies) should act in the best interests of the SWF, and have a clear mandate and

adequate authority and competency to carry out its functions.

GAPP 9. Principle
The operational management of the SWF should implement the SWF's strategies in an independent manner and in accordance with clearly defined responsibilities.

GAPP 13. Principle
Professional and ethical standards should be clearly defined and made known to the members of the SWF's governing body(ies), management, and staff.

GAPP 16. Principle
The governance framework and objectives, as well as the manner in which the SWF's management is operationally independent from the owner, should be publicly disclosed.

Source: IWG 2008.

investment objectives or cause arbitrary changes in its mandate or strategy. Through ownership stakes or by assuming board seats on the companies they invest in, SIFs can also play a constructive part in the governance of their investee companies. With board seats, they can exert significant influence over the investee by instating directors with specific expertise. This chapter, however, focuses on the governance arrangements of the SIF itself, not the governance model transmitted by the SIF to its portfolio companies.

As with legal principles, governance principles applicable to sovereign wealth funds (SWFs), state-owned enterprises (SOEs), and private capital funds can also be applicable to SIFs. As a subset of the SWF universe, SIFs are by and large subject to the governance principles applicable to SWFs. See box 4.1 on foundational governance principles articulated in the Santiago Principles. Likewise, governance principles applicable to SOEs and to private capital funds have relevance for SIFs. This chapter therefore examines parallels in governance principles, as relevant, in SWFs, SOEs, and private capital funds, to inform the governance arrangements of a SIF.[3]

THE SIF'S GOVERNANCE CHALLENGES

The first governance challenge for SIFs arises from the principal-agent relationship: the SIF's public sponsor (or principal) must delegate decision-making to the fund manager (or agent). In actuality, the SIF, as with other SWFs and SOEs, is embedded in a multilayered principal-agent relationship.[4] The ultimate principal of a SIF is the taxpaying public that owns the wealth or public sector capital accumulated in, and allocated to, the fund. The taxpaying public is represented by a proxy owner, the public sponsor of a SIF, which is often the ministry of finance if the government is sole investor.[5] This proxy owner authorizes an agent (or manager) to make investment and divestment decisions on behalf of the principal such that the SIF yields net benefits to the primary principal.

The principal-agent challenge arises from the imperfect alignment of interests between the public sponsor that authors the mandate of the SIF and the manager that implements this mandate. By delegating decision-making to a manager, the public sponsor is susceptible to moral hazard risks caused by the information asymmetry between the two parties. This imperfect alignment of interests may manifest in different forms. For instance, in a SIF for which the governance framework is not well crafted, the SIF manager may focus disproportionately on the financial objective of the SIF, to the detriment of the economic objective, or the manager may take on excessive risk given that the cost of recklessness is disproportionately borne by the public sponsor and other investors. Actions of the agent to these effects would deviate from the best interests of the public sponsor, and the poorly designed governance framework—under which such actions occur—would result in costs borne ultimately by the taxpaying public. The principal-agent tension is thrown into sharper focus if the SIF is sponsored by multiple principals with differing ideologies, resulting sometimes in the absence of a singular objective. The SIF's governance structure therefore seeks to anticipate and correct for any deviation in rational economic decisions between the principal(s) and manager(s). The following sections discuss how SIF governance frameworks typically rectify principal-agent issues, usually by outlining acceptable risks within an investment policy (discussed further in chapter 5), incurring agency costs to closely monitor the manager, and presenting financial incentives to the manager in a manner that aligns with the public sponsor's interests.

The second governance challenge stems from the operational tension of simultaneously having to meet and balance the SIF's dual mandate objectives: financial and economic. As discussed in chapter 2, a SIF must seek to optimize the balance between meeting these objectives on the basis of its specific mandate. Conflict can arise from a lack of clarity on how to balance or prioritize the objectives, especially in cases when they may conflict. A lack of adequate monitoring of achievement in one or both objectives may result in the SIF's deviating from its mandate. The governance arrangements of the SIF, as discussed in the next section, therefore ideally outline the permissible methods for achieving and monitoring the dual objectives of the mandate.

As a (quasi) public sector entity, the SIF is also susceptible to a third governance challenge arising from the possibility of conflicts of interest that can jeopardize its mandate, distort private markets, or crowd out the private sector. Potential conflicts of interest and market distortions can arise from the public sector's dual role as both the SIF's provider of capital and the promoter of projects that the SIF may invest in, particularly when government is the sole provider of capital to the SIF. The conflicts of interest arise primarily because incentive structures for the government as a proxy owner, and the individual officials who represent this proxy ownership, are often not straightforward. In undesirable circumstances this complexity can lead to government officials using their public office for personal gain or advantage. Thus, the SIF needs to contend with the conflicts of interest and other risks that can arise through the representatives on SIF governing bodies or its relationship with government entities outside of the formal governing bodies. For example, the government, which often operates under competing priorities, could pressure a public capital SIF in certain circumstances to invest in politically motivated projects that may deviate from the long-term mandate of the SIF. On the flip side, the government could also give the SIF favored access to government public-private partnership project pipelines, favored pricing on government assets, and favored treatment by regulatory authorities—all of which could distort and crowd out private investors operating in the same sectors. The governance framework for the SIF ideally corrects for these issues through (1) an oversight structure that seeks to insulate SIF management from pressures to deviate from the mandate or distort the private market, and (2) the identification ex ante of the market gap the SIF must address without the risk of crowding out private capital.

KEY DECISION-MAKING BODIES AND THEIR FUNCTIONS

SIF governance structures typically consist of three levels of decision-making bodies that represent ownership, oversight, and management. The owner (or public sponsor), in addition to providing capital to the SIF, sets its driving objectives; the overseeing board sets the strategy to deliver on these objectives (with the input of the manager) and supervises the delivery; and the management carries out the objectives. The governance structure ideally works to (1) insulate the SIF and its investment decisions from political interference, (2) ensure that short-term political interests do not outweigh the long-term mandate, and (3) balance autonomy and independence of the fund with proper oversight and accountability.

The selection, composition, and characteristics of each governance body are important ingredients to the overall governance framework of a SIF. Each of these factors can either subtly, or more tangibly, undermine the integrity and efficacy of a SIF. Recruiting qualified and experienced decision-makers on governing bodies improves the likelihood that a fund's mandate and investment policy are aligned (Alsweilem et al. 2015). Nevertheless, institutions vary a great deal with regard to their capacity to select qualified board members, hire strong senior staff, and govern themselves as human capital–enhancing organizations (Ambachtsheer 2007; Clark and Urwin 2008). Ideally, no overlaps in membership should exist between the three governance bodies because such overlaps could create parallel chains of reporting. The principle of clarity should generally drive governance arrangements, and the respective roles and responsibilities of these three bodies should be transparently defined in the SIF's establishment law, bylaws, or governance codes or guidelines. Separation of responsibilities between the governance bodies is to some extent country-specific, reflecting legal and political circumstances. However, public sector participation ideally occurs in the higher-level governing bodies representing ownership, whereas private sector characteristics predominate at the oversight and management levels.

The specific characteristics of the governance arrangements derive primarily from the law establishing the SIF and from whether the fund and the fund manager are separate legal entities with different ownership compositions. As discussed in chapter 3, investor rights and governance arrangements are embedded within the law(s) that set up the SIF—such as trust law or company law—and the corresponding legal structure of the SIF. When the fund is not a legal entity, the SIF's governance arrangements stem entirely from the law that established it. In addition, the governance model can change if the public sponsor is financially invested in the management entity of the SIF. The differentiating organizational trait particularly of the limited partnership model, frequently used by mixed capital SIFs,[6] is a separation in legal identity between fund and fund manager: investment assets are housed in the fund, and management assets (or management responsibility) are located within management companies contracted to manage the fund.[7] SIF owners in limited partnership structures may exercise ownership rights over the fund but not the fund manager. This organizational distinction can in turn affect the governance arrangements of the SIF, as discussed in more detail in the following subsections.

Ownership structures

Ownership of the SIF by the public sponsor refers to the sponsor's role as provider of anchor capital. This may include (1) investor in a fund structure (for example, the Marguerite Funds), (2) shareholder in a holding company structure (for example, Khazanah Nasional Berhad), or (3) creation of a ring-fenced pool of assets within a ministry (for example, the Ireland Strategic Investment Fund [ISIF]). The ownership structure of a SIF is exercised through several options.

One common, simplified ownership model for public capital SIFs sponsored by a government has the ministry of finance (or its equivalent) as the proxy legal owner of the fund. Parliament (or the equivalent legislative body in a country), which represents the interests of the taxpaying electorate, is the body to which the SIF is ultimately accountable. However, the ownership function for a SIF is commonly exercised through the government's ministry of finance, which is typically also the legal owner of the SIF (see World Bank 2014).[8] For example, by law, Ireland's Minister for Finance is the owner of the Ireland Strategic Investment Fund (ISIF)[9] and is therefore also responsible for exercising the government's ownership functions (see table 4.1). The government may choose to set up a dedicated unit within the ministry of finance to concentrate the relevant capacity to perform this ownership function. In Norway, for example, the Government Pension Fund Global is managed by Norges Bank Asset Management, which is overseen by a dedicated Asset Management Department at the Ministry of Finance. In general, other ministries, such as those related to the sectors in which the SIF will operate, could also be candidates for proxying government ownership of the SIF (for instance, the Arab Republic of Egypt's Law No. 177/2018, which established the Egypt SWF, specified the competent minister as the Minister of Planning Affairs). However, the ministry of finance is generally considered to have the highest level of expertise in investment, finance, and economics to oversee a SIF's operations and its role in the overall economy and fiscal framework. Best practice on ownership models for SIFs generally avoids fragmented ownership between government entities because diffused ownership structures can complicate governance and diminish accountability and the ability to make decisions (World Bank 2014). Even if the ministry of finance assumes the ownership role, however, other ministries could provide an advisory role to the SIF. For instance, Section 40 of Ireland's National Treasury Management Agency (Amendment) Act 2014 (NTMA Act 2014) provides that the Irish Minister for Public Expenditure and Reform can advise on ISIF's investment strategy.

TABLE 4.1 **Ownership structures for public capital and mixed capital SIFs**

| | LEGAL OWNERSHIP OF THE SIF | | | | RIGHTS TO PARTICIPATE IN OWNERSHIP FUNCTIONS WITHOUT LEGAL OWNERSHIP | |
| | | SPECIALIZED OWNERSHIP OR POOLED FUNDS[a] WITHIN: | | | | |
	MINISTRY OF FINANCE	INDEPENDENT AUTHORITY	COMPANY STRUCTURE	FUND STRUCTURE	OTHER MINISTRIES	GOVERNING COUNCIL
Asia Climate Partners	n.a.	n.a.	n.a.	√	n.a.	n.a.
Marguerite II	n.a.	n.a.	n.a.	√	n.a.	n.a.
National Investment and Infrastructure Fund (India)	n.a.	n.a.	n.a.	√	n.a.	√
Ireland Strategic Investment Fund	√	n.a.	n.a.	n.a.	√[b]	n.a.
Khazanah Nasional Berhad (Malaysia)	n.a.	n.a.	√	n.a.	n.a.	n.a.
Nigeria Sovereign Investment Authority	n.a.	√	n.a.	n.a.		√
FONSIS (Senegal)	n.a.	n.a.	√	n.a.	n.a.	√[c]

Source: World Bank; see case studies in appendix A.
Note: FONSIS = Fonds Souverain d'Investissements Stratégiques (Sovereign Fund for Strategic Investments); n.a. = not applicable; SIF = strategic investment fund.
a. Pooled funds here refers to investment vehicles that collect investor capital and invest it in a manner that provides diversification for the investor and economies of scale for the manager.
b. Minister for Public Expenditure and Reform.
c. FONSIS's proxy ownership body (yet to be established) is a representative body called the Strategic Orientation Council, which is mandated to advise on investment strategy and strategic direction and is expected to meet annually under the chairmanship of Senegal's President or, if the President declines, the Prime Minister. The council will be composed of representatives of the local and international business, political, and academic communities and civil society.

A second structure common to public capital SIFs has the government delegate its ownership interests to an independent authority or state-owned corporatized entity that exercises the state's ownership interests in the fund at arm's length from the government bureaucracy. With this delegated ownership structure, the SIF is a separate legal entity owned entirely by the state but beholden to the SIF's own governance structure. The Nigeria Sovereign Investment Authority (NSIA), for instance, was created as an independent authority by the Nigeria Sovereign Investment Authority (Establishment, etc.) Act, 2011 (NSIA Act 2011) and is a federation agency owned by the federal, state, and local governments. Its governance structure, unlike that of ISIF, does not emanate from the existing bureaucracy[10] but is separately crafted for NSIA. Cumulating the state's ownership rights in an independent entity operating at arm's length from the state helps to reduce potential conflicts of interest that can arise if the government ownership interest is entirely exercised within a government department.[11] Several public capital SIFs therefore employ this ownership model. For example, Malaysia's Khazanah was incorporated in September 1993 under the Malaysian Companies Act 1965[12] as a public limited company to act as both a strategic investor and a holding company for Malaysian government assets.[13] Similarly, Senegal's FONSIS (Fonds Souverain d'Investissements Stratégiques, or Sovereign Fund for Strategic Investments), a separate legal entity incorporated under private OHADA business law,[14] is mandated to act as strategic investor and hold Senegal's state assets. The corporatization of such entities also allows them to be owned by multiple government agencies, including national development banks or development finance institutions. Khazanah is almost entirely owned by the Minister of Finance Incorporated,[15] but one share of the company is owned by the Federal Lands Commission (Incorporated). Although FONSIS is currently solely owned by the state, its establishment law allows ownership of FONSIS to be divided between other government agencies.[16]

An arrangement also common to public capital SIFs, usually driven by political economy considerations, is to incorporate a governing council[17] as a high-level governing mechanism within the ownership tier of the fund. This council represents broad government and societal ownership interests, plays an advisory role to the public capital SIF, and—depending on the jurisdiction—may or may not report directly to the parliament or other legislative body. Governing councils do not have legal ownership of the SIF but are often authorized by law to exercise specific ownership functions over the fund (see the discussion on ownership responsibilities in the next subsection). These councils are typically set up in public institutions and play a high-level advisory and supervisory role, such as providing input on the fund's strategy and policies, weighing in on any increases or decreases in capital, reviewing investment activities and performance, and assessing the hiring and firing of executives. For example, NSIA's current ownership structure, as mentioned earlier, is divided between the federal and subnational governments (see the case study in appendix A).[18] As a result, NSIA's governance structure includes a governing council representing these broad ownership interests (see box 4.2 for details).

Such councils can enhance the political legitimacy of the SIF and its operations by ensuring broad representation from the spheres of government, business, the financial sector, policy, academia, and civil society.[19] In the case of NSIA, for example, the federal government's use of a representative governing council helped ensure state-level support when the fund was established. However, the composition of the governing council must strike an optimal balance between representation and capacity. Governing council members with expertise in investment, corporate governance, and the sectors in which the SIF is active can enhance the ability of the council to provide useful oversight of the SIF.

BOX 4.2

Governing council: The example of the Nigeria Sovereign Investment Authority

According to the Nigeria Sovereign Investment Authority (Establishment, etc.) Act, 2011, the following government representatives, who are mostly proxy owners or have fiscal or monetary authority, have an automatic seat on the governing council: the President (who chairs the council), the 36 state governors, the Attorney General, the Minister of Finance, the minister in charge of the National Planning Commission, the governor of the central bank, and the chief economic adviser to the President, among others.

In addition, the President appoints to the council four reputable representatives of the private sector, two representatives of civil society (such as nongovernmental organizations or professional organizations focused on civil rights), two representatives of Nigerian youth, and four academics.

The governing council reviews the fund's strategies, policies, changes in capital, investment activities, and performance, as well as the hiring and firing of executives.

Source: World Bank; see case studies in appendix A.

Conversely, if council members do not have such capacity, their influence could be detrimental to the SIF. It is also important that the governing council's role be clearly specified by law or regulation and not overlap with or undermine other decision-making bodies, such as the board of directors. For instance, the NSIA Act 2011 states clearly that the governing council must observe the independence of the board and officers of NSIA.[20]

Whereas ownership structures for public capital SIFs focus on permanent capital vehicles, mixed capital SIFs pivot around pooled investment in a finite life legal entity, with investor rights dictated through contractual measures between the investor(s) and the fund manager. In the models described previously, pertinent to a public capital SIF, the SIF is usually formed as a permanent capital vehicle, thus assuming an enduring role within the government apparatus. Such permanent capital vehicles typify SIFs set up solely by one public sponsor (usually the government) with ultimate control over the SIF's longevity (see chapter 2). In contrast, as discussed in chapter 3, mixed capital SIFs often use finite life private equity–style legal structures (such as the limited partnership) and ensuing ownership and governance models. Finite life funds are convenient because they limit the tenure of the co-ownership relationship between the public sponsor and other investors, allowing a parting of ways once mutual objectives are met. For example, Asia Climate Partners (ACP) was formed by founding partners Asian Development Bank (ADB), ORIX Corporation, and Robeco pooling ownership interests in a 10-year limited partnership vehicle targeting the renewable energy, resource efficiency, and environmental sectors in emerging Asia. In this private equity–type ownership model of a SIF, investors exercise their ownership rights through contractual provisions described in chapter 3, which provide the contours of the fund's operation and its overall governance structure. The key governance document—usually the limited partnership agreement (described in greater detail later in this chapter)—lays out the rights and obligations of the investors and manager.

As a mixed capital fund sponsored by the government of India, the National Investment and Infrastructure Fund (NIIF) presents a hybrid ownership model, combining ownership features seen in both mixed capital and public capital SIFs. Specifically, the Ministry of Finance's ownership stake in NIIF is directly pooled with that of other investors as found in other mixed capital SIFs, and the ownership function is aided by a governing council representing government and business communities. The funds of NIIF are unit trusts that mimic the general partner (GP) / limited partner (LP) structure, pooling investments from the government of India (49 percent stake) and other domestic and international investors. The government's investments in the three funds of NIIF, as well as its stake in the manager of the fund (NIIF Limited), are made directly through the Ministry of Finance (that is, there is no separate ownership entity). The government's ownership interests are overseen by the Department of Economic Affairs of the Indian Ministry of Finance, which maintains an open communication channel with NIIF Limited. Therefore, the Ministry of Finance is the proxy legal owner of the stakes in the funds and manager, and is empowered to exercise the government's ownership rights. NIIF's Governing Council, chaired by the Minister of Finance and including members of India's business, investment, and policy communities, meets annually to provide general guidance on NIIF's strategy.[21] Both the Ministry of Finance and the Governing Council are headed by the Minister of Finance, thus ensuring consistency in strategic decisions.

Ownership responsibilities

Ownership responsibilities of the SIF public sponsor extend from analysis and planning before the SIF's establishment, through the SIF's operational phase, and to its closure. These responsibilities outlined in the constitutional documents of the SIF must focus on core rights, akin to those of shareholders of corporations, without infringing on day-to-day management of the SIF. Ownership functions should be limited to (1) defining the mandate and objectives of the fund; (2) capitalizing the fund and defining the withdrawal policy from the fund; (3) appointing a board of directors using a merit-based and transparent process; (4) overseeing the fund's operations and ensuring compliance with applicable laws, regulations, and corporate governance standards; and (5) monitoring and evaluating performance in line with the mandate of the fund and based on a defined framework (see table 4.2 for details). These responsibilities are essentially the same whether the public sponsor is the government or a development finance institution.

One of the key governance functions of the SIF public sponsor is to ensure that the SIF mandate is clearly crafted and factors in the requirement that the SIF not crowd out private capital. The public sponsor typically achieves this clarity of mandate by investing in feasibility studies (discussed in chapter 2), which

TABLE 4.2 **Public sponsor ownership functions in a SIF**

OWNERSHIP FUNCTION	ROLES AND RESPONSIBILITIES
Planning stage	• Commission preliminary studies and feasibility studies.
	• Determine the SIF's structure and governance arrangements.
Mandate	• Define the fund's mandate after consultation with stakeholders.
	• Establish broad outcomes that the fund is expected to achieve within this mandate, and agree to these outcomes with the SIF's board.
	• Monitor implementation of the mandate and objectives of the fund.
Macroeconomy	• Ensure consistency of SIF operations with macroeconomic, fiscal, and financial sector policy.[a]
Investment policy and strategy	• Approve the investment policy, with advice from the investment committee (or board).
	• Set the risk parameters of the SIF, in accordance with the risk tolerance of the political bodies that are the ultimate stewards of the SIF's assets (see Al-Hassan et al. 2013).
Board	• Ensure public sector representation on the SIF's board (if needed).
	• Appoint board of directors using a merit-based and transparent process (the board appoints the CEO and the investment committee).
	• Oversee the board's activities, and ensure the SIF's compliance with applicable laws, regulations, and standards.
Capital	• Allocate capital to the SIF from the government budget or other sources, subject to parliamentary approval.[a]
	• Set clear rules on dividend payments to the state and capital withdrawals, subject to parliamentary oversight.[a]
	• Approve SIF borrowing, if the SIF is permitted to borrow or otherwise assume liabilities on behalf of the state.
Management	• Establish the criteria and process for the selection and appointment of the CEO, who is then appointed by the board.
Documentation	• Determine the SIF's disclosure policy, in compliance with applicable laws.

Source: World Bank.
Note: CEO = chief executive officer; SIF = strategic investment fund.
a. Most relevant for public capital SIFs solely owned by the government.

are performed before the setup of the SIF and identify the market gap the SIF must address. These assessments, which serve as input into crafting the mandate of the SIF, are designed to address one of the key challenges faced when setting up a SIF, that is, ensuring that the SIF does not crowd out private capital by operating in markets in which no capital gap exists. For instance, Marguerite infrastructure funds were founded by the European Investment Bank and several European Union national development banks to commercially invest in policy-driven infrastructure projects in the European Union and preaccession states. These funds required considerable planning and analysis before establishment. The public sponsors therefore hired global consulting firm McKinsey & Company before setup to analyze the infrastructure funding gap and pipeline in the funds' target countries and used the analysis to strike a balance between investment objectives and policy-oriented objectives of the different sponsors.

Oversight

The public sponsor primarily remedies the principal-agent challenge discussed above through the SIF's oversight structure. The public sponsor constructs a robust oversight structure either through internalizing the management of the fund, taking an ownership interest in the fund manager (if a separate legal entity), or maintaining an advisory role over the implementation of the mandate by the fund manager. Commonly, the public sponsor internalizes the management of the fund within its bureaucracy or organizes the SIF as a corporate body—with investment assets and management assets housed in one entity (Morley 2014)—to increase alignment of interests between principal and agent. This is the case with SIFs formed as corporates (for example, FONSIS), formed as bespoke independent authorities (for example, NSIA), or housed within a government agency (for example, ISIF). If the fund and its manager are organized as separate legal entities, the public sponsor may also choose to take an ownership stake in the management entity to further align interests. For instance, the government of India (and key co-investors) has an ownership interest in both the NIIF subfunds and the manager, NIIF Ltd, which is a separate legal entity. Similarly, ACP's founding partners—ADB, ORIX, and Robeco—have ownership interests in both the limited partnership fund and its general partner. When the public sponsor is invested in the management of the SIF, oversight of the SIF is performed by a board of directors that actively monitors the SIF management on behalf of the owners, thus reducing the information asymmetry between principal and agent. Conversely, the public sponsor may choose to invest only in the investment assets of the fund and not in the fund management entity. This is the case with Marguerite II, which is organized as a Luxembourg special limited partnership (Societé en Commandite Spéciale, or SCSp) and is externally managed by Marguerite Investment Management, an independent external alternative investment fund manager not owned by the public sponsor or its co-investors. In this case, the oversight role of the European Investment Bank and other public sponsors is provided via investor supervision and approval rights in relation to strategy, waivers on investment restrictions, and other specific areas; it does not play the more active supervisory role of a board of directors.

Most SIFs are set up such that the public sponsor has ownership interests in both the SIF's investment assets and its management entity, thus ensuring greater control of how the SIF meets its mandate. The following subsections explore, first, how the oversight function plays out in such SIFs through a board of directors; how these boards are nominated, appointed, and configured; and how they actively monitor the mandate of the SIF and its management. They then explore the more hands-off oversight role played by public sponsors that own only the investment assets and have delegated management of the SIF to an external fund manager.

Oversight structure A: Board of directors

When the public sponsor is invested in the management of a SIF (through internalizing SIF management or taking an ownership stake in the management entity), oversight responsibilities rest with a governing body referred to in corporate governance parlance as the "board of directors."[22] The board sits at the nexus between the owner and manager governance tiers and plays an active role in guiding the SIF to meet its mandate and in monitoring the management of the SIF. Because most public sponsors choose to have control over how the SIF is managed, the board of directors is a common governing structure found in SIFs. The specific configuration of the board, its scope of responsibilities, its independence from the owner, and its resulting effectiveness vary greatly depending on country, context, and legal structure. This heterogeneity in approach is explored further in this subsection.

The key responsibilities for a SIF board are to ensure that the fund's double bottom line mandate is met, manage conflicts of interest, weigh in on strategy, hire the chief executive officer (CEO), and oversee management. The heft of such a portfolio of responsibilities makes the autonomy and empowerment of the board vital. A well-constructed board can be an important independent buffer between the owner and manager, allowing a separation between ownership and control.[23] It has a responsibility to act in the interest of the fund's mandate and its investors, and to do so with utmost care and diligence. The board must therefore have recognized authority over its portfolio, the ability to exercise its authority, and the independence to effectively intermediate between the owner and manager. This in turn makes it important that the board's role be spelled out clearly, depending on how the SIF is established, either under ad hoc legislation, general legislation, or the bylaws of the SIF and its board charter. Any actions by the public sponsor that short-circuit the board can undermine the board's efficacy and leave the SIF vulnerable to political interference.

Quality at entry therefore becomes critical to ensuring the board's authority, independence, and credibility. The public sponsor must bear in mind the importance not only of the board members' selection and composition but also of the manner in which they are nominated and appointed.

• Boards are composed of three types of directors: (1) executive directors from the management team; (2) nonexecutive directors who may be appointed from the public or private sectors, but who have ties to the owner or the SIF; and (3) independent directors, who have no ties to either the SIF or its owners (World Bank 2014). In mixed capital SIFs, if a board exists, its membership usually reflects the investors' respective capital allocation to the SIF. For example, ACP's board consists of one representative from each of the founding investors ADB, ORIX, and Robeco. Depending on country context, SIF board composition may also be guided by the country's SOE rules relating to boards. For example, Indian SOEs are allowed a maximum of two government board representatives (World Bank 2014). This rule seems to be reflected in the composition of the NIIF's six-person board, which has only two government representatives even though the government holds a 49 percent share of the SIF. Nonexecutive directors could be recruited from the public sector, private sector, or academia. For example, all six nonexecutive directors of NSIA are currently from the private sector. However, nonexecutive directors from the private sector or academia nominated and appointed by a public sponsor or government entity are to some extent still beholden to the appointing entity, which could affect their independence. For instance, the NTMA's nine-member board, which oversees ISIF, has six nonexecutive directors who are appointed by the Minister for Finance, giving them ties to the government.

• Ideally, most of the board should be composed of independent directors. The function of the board is not to be representative but to be independent in a manner that is in the interest of the owners (Block and Gerstner 2016). The makeup of the board should put a premium on independent directors, with no ties to the owner(s) or SIF (see box 4.3 for the definition of independent directors). Such directors can bring fresh thinking, specialized industry skills, and openness to debate, which can help guard against board capture by vested interests and can add value to the SIF's strategic direction (World Bank 2014).

BOX 4.3

Definition of an independent board member

An independent board member, or director, means a person who

- Has not been employed by the company or its related parties, including its major shareholder, in the past five years;
- Is not an adviser or consultant to the company or its related parties and is not affiliated with a company that is an adviser or consultant to the company or its related parties;
- Is not affiliated with a significant customer or supplier of the company or its related parties, including banks or other financial institutions owned by any of the major shareholders;
- Has no personal service contracts with the company, its related parties, or its senior management;
- Is not affiliated with a nonprofit organization that receives significant funding from the company or its related parties;

- Is not employed as an executive of another company where any of the company's executives serve on that company's board of directors;
- Is not a member of the immediate family of an individual who is, or has been during the past five years, employed by the company or its related parties as an executive officer;
- Is not, nor in the past five years has been, affiliated with or employed by a present or former auditor of the company or of a related party; and
- Is not a controlling person of the company (or member of a group of individuals or entities that collectively exercise effective control over the company) or such a person's close relative, widow, in-law, heir, legatee, and successor of any of the foregoing or the executor.

Related party means, with respect to the company and its major shareholders, any person or entity that controls, is controlled by, or is under common control of the company and its major shareholders.

Source: IFC 2012.

- To avoid the risk of politicization, public sponsors should ideally delegate the board nomination process to an independent nomination committee, or a recognized global recruitment firm, which identifies the pool of candidates. A SIF's board nomination process can itself become an avenue for considerable political influence and the formation of political alliances within the SIF. Lack of integrity in the process could result in a board member's being beholden to the public sponsor (or specific parties within the public sponsor), instead of acting with independence toward achieving the SIF mandate. The risk of political interference in the nomination process is likely to increase if a ministry or other high office of a public sponsor leads the process. To reduce political influence in the nomination process, the search for qualified individuals should be conducted within a structured and transparent nomination process led by an independent nomination committee, as a subset of the SIF board,[24] or by a reputed international recruitment firm (see box 4.4). For example, NSIA has a nomination committee to select board members, but this committee is led by the Minister of Finance (in consultation with the National Economic Council), which can reduce the potential for complete independence. The nomination process is strengthened if it is well-documented, with both the advertisement of board positions and the names of board nominees made available to the public (World Bank 2014). After selection, board appointments should be conducted in a timely manner and the public sponsor must disclose results to the public (World Bank 2014).
- Board members should be selected on the basis of clearly outlined criteria, with an emphasis on professional experience and fit and proper assessments.

BOX 4.4

Safeguards for government representatives on SIF boards

Safeguards for the appointment of government representatives to the board of a strategic investment fund (SIF) may be formalized in the SIF's founding law or in its articles of association, and may include the following:

- The appointment to a SIF board should be made only when no conflict of interest will arise.
- The appointment should be made on the basis of the relevant skills.
- The appointment should be made in the person's own right, and the delegation of the role to other officials should be prohibited.
- The appointee should be responsible for maintaining the same skills and governance competencies as other directors.

- The appointee should be subject to the same performance evaluation as other directors, including removal if deemed necessary.
- The appointee should share the same liabilities and reputational risks as other directors.
- The appointee should be subject to the same terms of appointment as other directors.
- The appointee should not be made chair or deputy chair.

Additionally, consistent with practice for state-owned enterprises in many members and nonmembers of the Organisation for Economic Co-operation and Development, SIFs could prohibit ministers and other political appointees from serving on the board.

Source: World Bank 2014.

Selection should be based on the identification of a range of skill sets and specialized knowledge that would be relevant to the competencies required for the board. Required board competencies may include financial and investment experience, as well as legal and corporate governance skills. For instance, NSIA's establishment law specifies that all board members must hold a university degree in economics, finance, or similar subject, and possess at least 10 years of finance or business experience at the senior management level.[25] The professional criteria for any public sponsor representatives on the board should be the same as for other board members. Prospective board members should have no conflicts of interest, and no tarnished reputations caused by embezzlement, fraud, or other such offenses. Their presence and participation on the board should instead infuse independence, autonomy, and professionalism to the governing body.

- Board size should be limited to a manageable size, usually fewer than 10 members.[26] The size of the board is important because it can affect the quality of debate, the cohesiveness of the board, and its ability to effectively oversee the SIF. Decision-making becomes a protracted process if the debating body is too large. At the same time, the board must also be large enough that it has the requisite specialized skills to add value to the SIF and is not overly cozy with management (World Bank 2014). Within the case studies, SIF board membership ranges from a low of three (ACP) to a high of nine (ISIF and NSIA) (see table 4.3).

TABLE 4.3 **Board composition of select case study SIFs**

SIF	BOARD SIZE	BOARD COMPOSITION (DIRECTORS)				BOARD CHAIR
		EXECUTIVE	PUBLIC SPONSOR/ GOVERNMENT	OTHER NONEXECUTIVE	INDEPENDENT	INDEPENDENT? (Y/N)
Asia Climate Partners (ACP)	3[a]	0	1 (33%)	2 (66%)	0	No chair
National Investment and Infrastructure Fund (NIIF), India[b]	8[c]	1[d] (13%)	2 (25%)	4[e] (50%)	1 (13%)	N[f]
Ireland Strategic Investment Fund (ISIF)[g]	9	1 (11%)	2 (22%)	6 (67%)[h]	0	N[i]
Nigeria Sovereign Investment Authority (NSIA)	9	3[j] (33%)	0	6[k] (67%)	0	N
FONSIS (Senegal)	5[l]	1 (20%)	4[m] (80%)	0	0	N[n]

Source: World Bank.
Note: FONSIS = Fonds Souverain d'Investissements Stratégiques (Sovereign Fund for Strategic Investments); SIF = strategic investment fund.
a. The current board members are the Deputy Director General, the Private Sector Operations Department of ADB, the Chief Operations Officer Asia Pacific at Robeco, and the Head of Energy and Eco Services Business at ORIX.
b. Board is at the level of NIIF Ltd., the manager of the fund.
c. Expected to be increased to 11, with government retaining 2 seats.
d. The only executive director is NIIF Ltd chief executive officer (CEO) / managing director (MD).
e. One director each from Abu Dhabi Investment Authority, Ontario Teachers, Australian Super, and one collectively from the domestic investors.
f. Chair is appointed at the start of every meeting.
g. ISIF board is the NTMA's board, which is in charge of all NTMA functions, including ISIF. One of its subcommittees includes the State Claims Agency Strategy, which is specific to the State Claims Agency, and not applicable to ISIF.
h. Six members, including the chair, are appointed by the Minister of Finance if, in the opinion of the minister, the person has expertise and experience at a senior level in one or more specialized areas such as finance, investment, or civil service of the state.
i. Chair is a nonexecutive member appointed by the Minister of Finance.
j. NSIA's Managing Director and two other NSIA executives, currently the chief operating officer and chief investment officer.
k. The distinction between nonexecutive and independent is unclear. In principle, they could be drawn from the public sector.
l. Currently 5 members, but FONSIS Law established that the board can have a maximum of 10 representatives.
m. Consists of the chair, a representative of the Presidency, and two representatives of the Ministry of Economy, Planning and Cooperation.
n. Chair is proposed by the President of Senegal, and the CEO may be considered for chair role.

- Although many SIFs have boards that include executive directors, it is common for the CEO to be the only executive on the board (Block and Gerstner 2016). This is the case with FONSIS, ISIF, and NIIF, as shown in table 4.3. To effectively divide roles and responsibilities between the board and management, management executives should ideally sit instead on advisory specialist committees providing input to the board.[27]

- The board should be chaired by an independent director. To ensure independence of debate, the chair of the board must ideally be an independent director who can facilitate the discussion and elicit a diversity of views. Highly qualified and respected board chairs must be charged with encouraging a culture of accountability and responsibility among board members (Clark and Urwin 2008). The chair of the board should not be occupied with day-to-day management, and having a CEO occupy the role of chair is generally frowned upon because the CEO could dominate board discussion and steer the course of debate. In general, a SIF's credibility as an independent and professionalized investment organization is enhanced by appointing as chair of the board an independent director with a private sector background and without direct links to the government. This preference may not be viable in some country contexts, where the practice may be for the boards of state-owned entities to be chaired by the government. For example, the chair of Khazanah's board is the Malaysian prime minister.

- Board members must be granted fixed terms of approximately three years, replacement of the board must be staggered, and board tenures should carry over across election cycles.[28] Board composition may need to be changed if, over the life of the fund, the SIF can benefit from a change in board skill sets, or to ensure that the board remains dynamic. In that case, however, there must be clear criteria for removing a director, so that SIF boards are not eliminated for arbitrary or political reasons. Finite board tenures are therefore recommended, with three-year board terms (combined with one to two renewals) being common. The NSIA Act 2011 (Article 20), for instance, allows nonexecutive board members to hold four-year terms, with one renewal. Similarly, ISIF's NTMA board members (except ex officio members) generally have five-year terms, renewable once.[29] Whereas unlimited tenures for board members can cause poor incentives, such as excessive risk-taking tendencies, limited tenures might encourage board members hoping for reappointment to focus on short-term investment horizons and be more risk averse. To minimize the influence of election cycles on the SIF's operations, board members' tenure periods should also carry over from one election cycle to the next (Al-Hassan et al. 2013). Furthermore, board members should be replaced in a staggered manner to avoid situations in which the entire board is replaced all at once, resulting in a lack of institutional memory. For instance, if governments follow the practice of dissolving parastatal boards after elections, public capital SIFs could potentially find themselves without a board following a change in government. As mentioned in chapter 3, this was the case for NSIA when newly elected President Buhari dissolved all boards of federal agencies and parastatals following Nigeria's 2015 elections, resulting in NSIA's operating without a board for two years.[30] For this reason, SIFs must ideally enshrine in law safeguards to ensure that their boards are protected from politically driven or election-driven dismissals.

- Board members should ideally be compensated on market terms (World Bank 2014). Because compensation is critical to the capacity to select competent board members, it should be competitively set to attract good talent. Restricting executive compensation to public sector pay can undermine the ability to competitively attract talent.

Once the board is constructed, the manner in which the board functions and conducts itself is critical to the success of the SIF.[31] As discussed earlier, the board must be empowered by the owner(s) to take on its portfolio of key duties (see table 4.4 for a list of key duties).

- The SIF board's primary task is to ensure that the double bottom line objectives are met, and to clarify how to prioritize these objectives especially when

TABLE 4.4 **SIF board functions**

OVERALL BOARD FUNCTION	KEY DUTIES
Supervise SIF mandate	• Establish and periodically review SIF strategy. • Approve any material amendments to SIF strategy. • Approve the fund's investment policy, submitted by SIF management / investment committee. • Develop selection policies and criteria for solicited and unsolicited proposals. • Approve the SIF investment strategy, and oversee its implementation. • Supervise the SIF trajectory toward the mandate established by the public sponsor. • Clarify the prioritization or approach with respect to meeting the dual objectives. • Provide approvals for investments, particularly those exceeding thresholds or risk limits if needed. • Oversee SIF representation in the boards of its portfolio companies. • Be vigilant in identifying and managing conflicts of interest that may lead the SIF to deviate from mandate. • Appoint subcommittees of the board. • Monitor portfolio performance and compliance with investment policies. • Approve annual budget and expenditure.
Appoint and supervise fund manager	• *Dedicated manager.* Appoint SIF CEO, and oversee appointment of senior executives. • *External manager.* If the SIF has a separate fund management company, conduct a competitive section process and appoint the fund manager. • Establish key performance indicators for the fund manager and oversee the performance of the manager.
Audit and risk management	*Audit* • Instate systems of internal and financial controls, and review and monitor the effectiveness of the systems. • Review and evaluate the internal audit process and outputs. • Select and appoint external auditors. • Review and evaluate outputs received from the external auditor through the audit committee. • Ensure the quality and integrity of the financial statements. • Ensure disclosure of related-party transactions and conflicts of interest. • Review compliance function. • Ensure compliance with accounting, legal, and regulatory requirements. *Risk management framework* • Articulate risk appetite, and prescribe the risk limits and thresholds for the SIF. • Ensure risks are identified, assessed, managed, and reported. • Ensure policies and procedures for risk management. • Monitor adherence to risk governance.
Compensation	• Devise, review, and approve compensation plans (including performance-related pay), policies, and succession plans for employees. • Ensure that compensation structure for employees is consistent with the SIF's long-term objectives.
Reporting	• Ensure that financial statements and other disclosures clearly present the SIF's performance. • Report to public sponsor and other SIF investors on the SIF's performance.[a]

Source: World Bank 2014 and original research for this publication.
Note: CEO = chief executive officer; SIF = strategic investment fund.
a. This follows from Principle 5 of the Santiago Principles: "The relevant statistical data pertaining to the SWF should be reported on a timely basis to the owner, or as otherwise required, for inclusion where appropriate in macroeconomic data sets" (IWG 2008, 7).

conflict may exist between them. Once a clear dual objective mandate has been drafted by the owner(s) and enshrined in law or bylaws, the board's responsibility is to ratify management's approach to balancing the two goals by endorsing an investment policy (discussed further in chapter 5). The board may instate processes and build capacity to meet and monitor both objectives. The board may also require the endorsement of subcommittees or sub management bodies to ensure that the dual objectives are met.

- Board members must be vigilant to identify and mitigate conflicts of interest that either jeopardize the SIF's interests or distort private markets to the detriment of the larger policy goal. As discussed earlier, SIF operations can be jeopardized by conflicts of interest that arise partly because the fund operates at the nexus of the public and private sector realms. Such conflicts of interest can be (1) commercial in origin, when the owner, board, or manager is engaged in related party transactions with a profit-related interest that conflicts with the SIF's mandate; or (2) political in origin, when public sponsor representatives at the owner or board level pursue, for political gain, competing interests contrary to the SIF mandate. Such pressures could translate to the SIF in various ways, including, but not limited to, pressure on SIF management to invest in projects for non-transparent and noncommercial reasons, or preferential treatment given to the SIF on pricing or pipeline that could harm private sector interests, leading to the crowding out (instead of crowding in) of private capital. Therefore, part of the board's responsibility is to be vigilant to the multitude of forms such pressure can assume. The board must ensure that SIF management is insulated from both clear and hidden coercions that nudge the SIF away from its long-term mandate. The structure and composition of the board can also play an important role here. For instance, by design, the government of India is a minority investor in NIIF with only two seats on a board otherwise filled with commercial investors. This arrangement tempers the ability of the government to use NIIF to further policy objectives that would be commercially unviable and deviate from NIIF's mandate. In general, the board must also instate safeguards to ensure that the SIF does not distort or crowd out private markets. As discussed in chapter 2, ISIF does this, for instance, through investment screening before an investment reaches the board for approval to ensure there is no deadweight—that is, the transaction is not displacing private capital. ISIF takes care not to compete with private capital by also requiring potential investees to do a thorough survey of commercial funding available to them before any ISIF investment (see ISIF case study in appendix A).
- Board members must also be alert to their own conflicts of interest and not vote or participate in discussions in which they have personal conflict. The board must ensure conflict of interest procedures are in place, so members have no vested interest in matters considered by the board. At NSIA, for example, board members must disclose the nature of their interest in advance of board consideration, cannot seek to influence a decision relating to that matter, and must leave the meeting during the discussion of that matter. In addition, no board member or other NSIA executive can be involved in a personal capacity, directly or indirectly, in the purchase of assets of or by NSIA (see the case study in appendix A).
- Board structure, processes, and procedures should be formalized in a manual (World Bank 2014). Policies that inform the way the board

functions and governs must be recorded in an operating manual or other documentation designed to reduce unpredictability in board behavior. Such policies include the code of conduct for the board and management. For instance, under Ireland's NTMA Code of Conduct for Members of the NTMA and its Committees, Investment Committee members are required to act objectively and independently (see ISIF case study in appendix A).

- The board ideally uses specialized committees to inform itself on key issues such as financial reporting or risk management, thus reducing the information asymmetry that underpins the SIF's principal-agent challenge. SIFs usually consist of the following specialized subcommittees: investment, audit, and risk management. They may also have committees focused on nominations and remuneration. Some development finance institutions, such as the United Kingdom's CDC Capital, have a separate board committee for development impact, which could be relevant to certain SIFs. Ideally, most members on these committees, including the chair, should be independent, and the committee reports directly to the board. An investment committee is unusual, however, in that the CEO and SIF management must ideally participate in investment and exit decisions, which are the most important executive actions taken by a SIF.

- The composition of the *investment committee* is important to the fund's ability to balance its policy and commercial objectives. Like the board, the investment committee's autonomy, independence, and ability to foster debate are of critical importance (Ohrenstein and White 2017). The investment committee of a public capital SIF should have no government representatives, given the risk of politicizing investment selection. Instead the committee should be powered by independent members and senior management operating at arm's length from the government. ISIF's investment committee has no government representatives and no ISIF executives, consisting instead of five independent members from the NTMA board and outside. By contrast, the majority government-represented board of FONSIS is responsible for approving all investments, and the investment committee (composed of four executive members and two board members) simply validates that disbursements are made per board decisions. In mixed capital SIFs structured as limited partnerships, the investment committee is usually fully empowered to make decisions on the acquisition and disposal of assets. For instance, Marguerite II's investment committee has sole responsibility for investment approval, subject to the investment's compliance with eligibility criteria set by the public sponsor and owners. In public capital SIFs, the board, rather than the investment committee, may be ultimately in charge of investment decisions. NSIA's board makes investment decisions on a majority basis, after screening and preparatory deal work has been overseen by the Executive Committee,[32] followed by screening by the Direct Investment Committee, which is populated by three nonexecutive board members.[33] The respective compositions of the Executive Committee and the Direct Investment Committee ensure that six of the nine board members are already comfortable with an investment by the time it reaches the full board for majority approval. NSIA's board currently has no government representation, but this is not enshrined in law.

- The *audit committee* is particularly important to the SIF as an investment agency with public assets and must be staffed by a majority of independent members. By selecting an external auditor and overseeing the internal and external audits as well as internal controls, this committee focuses on ensuring that financial reporting and compliance requirements are met. The committee also reviews financial statements and ensures disclosure of related-party transactions and conflicts of interest. Committee members have to be able to assess the accuracy and comprehensiveness of the information being transmitted to them. Therefore, ideally audit committees have at least two or three independent members who are in the majority, including the chair; and the committee has the requisite finance or accounting background.[34]

- A SIF's *risk committee* helps the board and senior management adhere to the risk policy prescribed by the board. It provides oversight of the SIF's risk management systems and procedures to identify, assess, manage, and report risks. The committee's responsibilities include ensuring that the SIF operates according to the risk parameters established by the government and the SIF's other investors. The risk committee provides advice to the chief risk officer and chief investment officer, as well as input to other board committees as relevant. The risk committee is itself supported by the chief financial officer and by the risk manager, and these executives are responsible to the committee for overseeing risk management across the SIF. In some cases, the risk committee may be combined with the audit committee to create a combined audit and risk committee (World Bank 2014). FONSIS, ISIF, and NIIF have adopted this model. Less often the risk committee is part of the investment committee, such as in the case of NSIA, whose Direct Investment Committee is also entrusted to play the role of the risk committee.

Oversight structure B: Financial incentives and limited partnership advisory committee or equivalent

When the public sponsor has no ownership interest in the management entity of the SIF, the principal-agent problem is addressed in large part by contractually aligning financial interests between investor and manager rather than by closely monitoring the manager via a board. As discussed in chapter 3, SIFs set up like private equity funds, which mobilize capital from third-party investors, typically employ or mimic the limited partnership structure (see box 3.4 in chapter 3). Governance is commonly effected through fiduciary obligations dictated by regulation (if the fund is set up under public law, such as investment fund legislation; see chapter 3), and contractual measures embedded in fund structure and financial incentives. Employing a finite life fund structure, for instance, provides the manager a clear timeline within which to show the investors results (Ribsteint 2009). The LP can curb the manager's risk-taking tendencies toward the end of the fund by limiting the investment horizon of the fund to within the first 3–5 years of a typically 10-year fund. Investors can also impose bespoke governance arrangements on the SIF through side letters requiring additional reporting or voting rights (Magnuson 2018). For example, in Marguerite II, side letters with some investors contain investment eligibility provisions—such as adherence to United Nations Principles for Responsible Investment—which apply to the fund as a whole. Financial levers are more easily deployed in mixed capital SIFs that may have more flexible compensation structures than public capital SIFs (see discussion later in this chapter).

Financial alignment of interest is commonly embedded in the structure of a limited partnership or equivalent structure through two levers:

1. *Profit sharing.* The manager is compensated by a management fee,[35] which is not tied to performance, and a share in the profits (or carried interest) of the fund beyond a hurdle rate.[36]

2. *Contribution of capital.* The manager is often required to contribute capital (usually about 1 percent) to the fund, thus establishing skin in the game for the manager.

There are limitations to such alignment of interests, however, as discussed in box 4.5.

When the public sponsor has no ownership interest in the management entity of a SIF, oversight responsibilities are also met via a limited partnership advisory committee or similar structure. This advisory committee represents the owners' interests in the SIF and is usually populated by the public sponsor and other key investors. The advisory committee has a more hands-off relationship to the management of the SIF than a board of directors does because the public sponsor and other investors have no ownership interest in the management entity.[37] The committee structure instead collapses the ownership interests in the SIF with the oversight responsibility of the board of directors. The SIF advisory committee provides oversight, serves as a sounding board on strategic matters, weighs in on conflicts, and provides waivers for investment or risk thresholds and other restrictions laid out in the limited partnership agreement, and other key matters.

Management

The third tier of a SIF's governance structure focuses on the management of the fund, driven primarily by whether the manager is in-house or dedicated

BOX 4.5

Limitations to aligning financial interests in a limited partnership model or equivalent structure

Despite using such financial levers to align interests, the public sponsor cannot fully eliminate the principal-agent problem. For instance, although carried interest helps to provide an incentive by allowing the fund manager to participate in profits, it does not eliminate the possibility that the manager may take excessive risk because, in the downside scenario, the manager may forgo a share in profits but does not give up management fees (Magnuson 2018).

The hurdle rate seeks to partially correct this misalignment at a portfolio level by not permitting the manager to participate in a share of profits until capital plus an agreed rate of return (usually 8 percent) has been remitted to the investors.

However, if the profit-sharing arrangement is not a sufficient motivator for the manager, the public sponsor and other investors may also bear the risk that capital is not fully deployed or is deployed in suboptimal investments. A key risk is that the fund manager may perceive the possibility of never seeing carried interest, so it is important to keep track of fund life and establish an attractive profit-sharing arrangement.

The public sponsor and other investors must therefore pay keen attention to the profile of the manager hired, to ensure that the manager is unlikely to be complacent about its own track record or to focus only on fixed management fees.

Source: World Bank, including interviews with International Finance Corporation (IFC) Private Equity Funds and IFC SME Ventures teams.

to the SIF (an internal manager) or is an external manager selected via a competitive process.[38] The selection of the SIF manager sends an important signal to the investment community in which the fund operates about the capacity of the SIF, its expected independence from the public sponsor, and its appeal as an investment partner to prospective co-investors. Whether private investors look to invest at the fund level in a mixed capital SIF, or as co-investors at the project level, the SIF's human resource capacity is crucial to its credibility as a partner. The options are the following:

- In the *internal manager scenario*, the public sponsor either assigns management responsibility of the SIF to an internal agency or recruits directly the individual investment professionals who will form the SIF's fund management team. The employment status of these professionals will vary with the legal setup of the SIF. For instance, they may be employed directly by the line ministry that supervises the SIF or by a new fund management firm set up to manage the SIF.

- In the *external manager scenario*, the public sponsor (1) appoints, through a competitive process, an external fund management firm with the qualifications to successfully implement the SIF's investment strategy; (2) negotiates a fund management agreement that disciplines the activities of the external manager; and (3) establishes processes to monitor the external manager's performance. Each of these three steps is discussed in detail later in this chapter.

Several factors affect the public sponsor's decision to appoint an internal or external fund manager, including the following:

- *The SIF's target investor mix.* Commercial investors place high importance on a fund management team's shared investment track record and proven working dynamics (for example, shared vision, complementarity of skill sets, and agreement among team members over roles, seniority, and remuneration). A public sponsor that aims to attract commercial investors to a SIF may therefore want to consider appointing an established external manager, rather than assembling the investment team from scratch. Marguerite, whose internal manager lacked a shared track record, highlighted this as one of the factors that hindered its ability to raise commercial capital for its first fund (see the case study in appendix A).

- *The availability of reputable investment talent in the target sector or geography.* A public capital SIF's sponsor that believes it has the talent in-house (or can organize such a team) within an internal agency may choose to do so, as the government of Ireland did by locating ISIF within the NTMA. If such talent is not easily accessible to the public sponsor, it may choose to seek an external manager. Because the private capital fund (PCF) industry is nascent or developing in many emerging market and developing economies, finding established and reputable external managers based in or interested in investing in these countries may prove difficult. If reputable external managers are already operating in the target sector or geography, they may be conflicted from managing a new fund. In these circumstances, a public sponsor may still prefer to appoint an internal manager, rather than settling for a second-tier external manager.

- *The extent to which the SIF's investment strategy diverges from the typical PCF investment strategy in the target sector or geography.* PCFs operate under precise assumptions in terms of investment time horizon, as discussed in chapter 5. A SIF that plans on longer-than-usual investment horizons may struggle to attract existing PCF managers. Similarly, an infrastructure SIF that targets early-stage greenfield projects may struggle to attract existing infrastructure fund managers, if the focus of the latter is on brownfield projects. Likewise, a SIF that pursues a very broad strategy—targeting, for instance, both direct and indirect investments, and investments in both equity and debt—may not appeal to PCF managers pursuing more specialized strategies. In all these cases, appointing an internal manager may be the best or perhaps the only option.

- *The procedures for appointing external versus internal managers.* It may be easier for a public sponsor to appoint individual investment professionals, under existing public hiring procedures, than an external fund management firm. As discussed later in more detail, the latter's selection process requires a sound understanding of the fund management industry and its legal and contractual frameworks, which the public sponsor may not have in-house. Conversely, an external manager, once hired, may facilitate the operations and reduce the running costs of a SIF through its established procedures and administrative infrastructure, as also noted in the generally accepted principles and practices (GAPPs), or Santiago Principles.[39]

SIFs sponsored by a national government generally opt for an internal manager (whether through an existing agency or by recruiting a new team), whereas SIFs sponsored by a development institution may often opt for an external manager. SIFs sponsored by development institutions often have the express mandate to attract commercial investors at the fund level, and have more targeted strategies in line with PCF standards; several development institutions also customarily invest in private equity (directly or indirectly) and therefore have the technical expertise required to appoint an external manager.

The SIF's principal-agent problem extends to remuneration for the fund manager, whether internal or external: incentives must drive both financial and economic returns. Performance-based pay for a SIF may need to be designed differently from the compensation structure generally used in the investment industry to reflect the SIF's dual objective mandate. Given the long-term investment horizon of SIF investing, for instance, the governance structure of the SIF must contemplate long-term incentives that drive individuals to perform in the interest of both the financial and the economic objectives of the fund. For an internal manager, public sector compensation schemes may impede the ability to flexibly remedy the principal-agent challenge through financial incentives (see discussion in the next subsection). For an external manager, long-term incentives could be achieved, for instance, by delaying the manager's right to carry (share in profits) until longer-term financial returns and economic returns are evident; by basing carry on the overall portfolio of the fund, rather than individual projects; or by allowing staff and managers to benefit from carry even after they leave the fund, which is likely when longer-term impact is discernible. At the same time, incentive structures should not deviate so radically from private sector fund management standards that they make it impossible to attract qualified fund managers to the SIF.

Internal fund manager selection

When the public sponsor has chosen for the SIF to have a dedicated or in-house management team, the CEO is ideally appointed by the SIF's board, not the public sponsor.[40] If the public sponsor retains the authority to hire and fire the CEO, it takes away one of the board's most important powers and dilutes its responsibilities. It also limits the accountability of the CEO to the board, and risks making the CEO beholden to the ownership entity or ministry (World Bank 2014). The public sponsor should instead establish the qualifications, criteria, and guidelines[41] for nominating, selecting, and appointing the CEO. It should also outline the criteria to remove the CEO from office.

Governments of developing countries and emerging markets often recruit SIF management (and staff) from their diaspora members working in international financial centers or reputed global organizations, and pair them with public sector technocrats who can manage the government apparatus. This is the case, for example, with the CEOs of FONSIS, NIIF, and NSIA, all of whom come from their respective country's diaspora. Diaspora members with global experience are thought to bring dynamic corporate backgrounds, create meritocratic cultures and opportunity for talented young professionals, and have low tolerance for politically motivated hiring. Having built their careers outside the country, however, diaspora members typically do not have a deep understanding of government networks and bureaucracy. Therefore, such recruits are frequently paired with senior public servants with extensive public sector experience and access to the ministries and government entities that are SIF partners. Such public sector recruits can bolster the SIF's value proposition of acting as a bridge for foreign investors to access local government networks. Even nongovernment public sponsors may value public policy experience in addition to investment experience.

The SIF CEO should be permitted to select his or her own senior executives and team. How senior executives and the SIF's team are selected and appointed has a strong bearing on the SIF's eventual efficacy. Given the importance of staffing, CEOs should ideally be allowed to select their own management team and staff, with the board reviewing the terms under which the CEO selects top management (World Bank 2014). NIIF's CEO, for example, was selected through a global search process, and among the core priorities he established to ensure manager independence was that NIIF Limited would be able to recruit its staff and executives without involvement from the government. Involving the public sponsor in the process would risk establishing a direct relationship between the public sponsor and SIF staff, thus allowing the CEO's authority to be undermined.

SIFs are highly skills-intensive organizations, requiring high-capacity management teams and staff with a range of experience, as demonstrated by the skill sets recruited by the various case study SIFs in this book. As investment organizations, SIFs must recruit on the basis of criteria that characterize staff of well-performing investment firms. Generally, these criteria encompass financial expertise, investment or operating expertise, and people skills, including access to broad networks.[42] Typical backgrounds include investment banking, fund management, consulting, infrastructure and project finance, multilateral development finance institutions, and sector-specific experience corresponding to the SIF's investment focus (see box 4.6 on staffing at NIIF). Although SIFs recruit heavily from the private sector, they also recruit talent from public sector backgrounds, for example, to staff economic impact teams. SIFs generally follow standard hiring processes of the investment industry, such as engaging well-reputed headhunters.

The compensation structures adopted by public capital SIFs—as quasi-public sector entities—are not always aligned with market terms, impeding their ability to compete aggressively for talent. Public capital SIFs are frequently subject to restrictions on compensation.[43] This inflexibility can lead to suboptimal performance, as indicated, for instance, by research showing that top-performing public pension funds base executive salary on market compensation rather than on government salaries (Bachher, Dixon, and Monk 2016). Whereas noncompetitive benefits will fail to attract qualified management and staff, generous benefits may be both politically and legally unviable and may skew public opinion against the SIF. As nongovernment entities, mixed capital SIFs with nongovernment sponsors tend to have more flexible compensation structures than public capital SIFs, so they can more easily attract qualified professionals. If a SIF uses industry compensation structures, its size affects its management fees (since compensation is a fixed percentage of total assets under management) and, in turn, its ability to attract top talent.

Public capital SIFs nevertheless do attract talent because of the perceived prestige and benefits of working with a sovereign fund. ISIF, for instance, has limited annual employee turnover, standing at 14 percent as of December 31, 2018. Many SIFs have attracted qualified management and staff despite offering below-market levels of compensation. Working with SIFs can offer perquisites: doing so provides professional visibility and access to both public and private sector networks and can be a valuable learning ground for young professionals seeking to gain investment and development experience. Meanwhile, more senior executives, and particularly diaspora members, may wish to leverage their skill sets and background to benefit their country's development or for broader economic impact.

Notwithstanding the limitations faced by public capital SIFs in offering compensation packages above public sector salary levels, such funds often have room for some performance incentives. SIFs commonly use performance-based pay, with bonuses linked to results, to enhance the commercial focus of managers and staff. For example, NSIA's compensation program is 10 percent performance based. Its overall remuneration structure is reviewed and approved annually by the board's Compensation Committee on the basis of market dynamics, with a view to be on par with the top quartile of the benchmark peer group (see NSIA

Staffing the NIIF

The National Investment and Infrastructure Fund's (NIIF's) staff includes 45 investment professionals with both international and local backgrounds in infrastructure investment and operations.

International experience for staff and managers of NIIF include the International Finance Corporation, the investment firm Actis, investment banks HSBC and Macquarie, professional services firms KPMG and Grant Thornton, and Khazanah Nasional Berhad. Domestic experience at NIIF includes the State Bank of India, investment firm HDFC Equity, the investment bank IDFC, and the industrial conglomerate Tata Group.

NIIF's chief executive officer and executive directors have more than 25 years each of experience. For staff, experience ranges from a minimum of typically 4 years for analysts, to over 18 years for senior principals.

Sources: NIIF management; World Bank case study (see appendix A).

case study in appendix A). Similarly, ISIF's typical remuneration package comprises a fixed base salary, discretionary performance-related pay where appropriate, and a career average defined benefit pension.

External fund manager selection

By choosing to recruit an external manager as the SIF's primary manager, the public sponsor largely circumvents the link to public sector pay scales. One of the advantages with SIFs run by external private management companies is that their compensation structure can deviate from public sector scales because they are completely outside the government apparatus. Fee levels for such managers therefore reflect the typical private equity combination of management fees and share of profits. The Philippine Investment Alliance for Infrastructure, a 10-year closed-end fund investing in Philippine infrastructure projects and businesses, is a good example of a SIF managed by an external, well-reputed manager (see box 4.7).

The public sponsor must ensure it undertakes a competitive recruiting process, and ideally involve the selected external manager in the design details of the fund to ensure ownership. The general sequence of events for PCFs involves the GP bringing an investment thesis it finds compelling to prospective investors to solicit capital. In the SIF case, this sequence is reversed: the public sponsor has a compelling economic mandate that it wants a professional manager to execute on commercial terms. The public sponsor therefore often uses a competitive request for proposal (RFP) process to identify a suitable primary manager for the SIF (see box 4.7 on the recruitment of the Philippine Investment Alliance for Infrastructure's manager). To secure the fund manager's ownership when the general sequence of events has been reversed, the public sponsor must ideally leave some details of the fund design open for the selected fund manager's input. In fact, the RFP process may offer

---

BOX 4.7

Recruiting an external manager for a SIF: PINAI

The Philippine Investment Alliance for Infrastructure (PINAI) is a 10-year closed-end fund, dedicated to equity and quasi-equity investments in Philippine infrastructure projects and businesses. PINAI was launched in July 2012 with 26 billion Philippine pesos (approximately US$625 million)[a] in committed capital and was fully invested by November 2015.

PINAI is an alliance of domestic and foreign investors, with a private fund manager. The domestic investor is the Government Service Insurance System (GSIS), a state-owned pension fund. The foreign investors are the Asian Development Bank (ADB); Macquarie Infrastructure and Real Assets (MIRA), an Australian asset manager with global expertise in infrastructure investing; and Dutch pension fund Algemene Pensioen Groep (ADB 2012). A subsidiary of MIRA was competitively selected to manage PINAI (ADB 2012).

Founding sponsors ADB and GSIS selected MIRA as the fund manager after a six-month competitive process during which the proposed investment mandate was presented by the sponsors to a group of 10 potential fund managers with established track records. Five of these managers expressed an interest in the mandate and made formal presentations to ADB and GSIS, after which three were shortlisted, and MIRA was eventually chosen (ADB 2012).

a. Based on the July exchange rate of US$1.00 = 41.60 Philippine pesos. The Philippine peso depreciated substantially over the following years. As of the end of October 2018, the exchange rate was US$1.00 = 53.40 Philippine pesos.

a platform for brainstorming on the design of the fund with prospective professional managers. Although Marguerite I was not technically managed by an external manager,[44] its hiring process offers some lessons for competitive recruitment and involving the manager in the design of the fund. In 2009, the European Investment Bank and cosponsors initiated the competitive selection of a CEO for Marguerite I. The CEO was also to be the first partner of the fund advisory company, was tasked with assembling the full investment team, and became proactively involved in defining an investment advisory agreement, fee structure, and long-term incentive plan aligned with the fund industry's best practices.

The external manager selection process can be organized in four phases: (1) identification of prospective managers, (2) screening and shortlisting of applicants, (3) detailed due diligence on shortlisted applicants, and (4) public sponsor's approval process for the selected manager.

In the first phase, the public sponsor identifies a long list of prospective managers potentially eligible to run the SIF. This phase usually involves an RFP and active search by the sponsor's representatives and advisers. An RFP may be required in accordance with public procurement rules applicable to the sponsor. Table 4.5 shows the indicative content of an RFP, to be tailored to the sponsor's specific requirements. The active search may involve browsing through PCF industry publications and databases, participation in PCF industry conferences, and networking by the sponsor's representatives and advisers.

Using an RFP process to identify a manager for the SIF has risks, but engaging in the process also has the advantage of signaling commitment to transparency by a public sponsor. The RFP process is limited to the players available in the market at that time. Perfectly qualified managers may not be ready because they are deploying another fund. The RFP process could also risk forcing teams to come together inorganically, resulting in suboptimal teams.[45] Nevertheless, a competitive RFP is still well suited to identifying an external fund manager, particularly for a proposed government-anchored SIF, because of the risks of actual and perceived political interference if using noncompetitive selection and the unpredictability of a timeline that comes with unsolicited proposals. Nontransparent recruitment of a fund manager is susceptible to corruption and can be costly for the public sponsor and SIF owners in the long term. The government of Angola, for instance, has been engaged in a protracted legal battle to sever the relationship between its SIF, Fundo Soberano de Angola, and the SIF's one-time primary asset manager, Quantum Global. The SIF claims that Quantum's engagement as manager was founded on improper arrangements between the former CEO and the head of Quantum (Milhench 2018).

In the second phase of the selection process, the public sponsor compiles a manageable short list of the most suitable applicants. Scorecards, on which applicants are evaluated and graded across a series of parameters, can be used to facilitate and document the shortlisting phase.

The third phase consists of an in-depth due diligence of the shortlisted applicants, based on interviews, visits to the managers' offices, and review of additional documentation. Some of the shortlisted candidates may be screened out in the early phases of due diligence, allowing the public sponsor to devote more time and effort to a smaller group of the best applicants. Due diligence topics will mirror the selection criteria used in the screening phase and summarized in table 4.5 (tailored to the SIF's specific features). The four core due

TABLE 4.5 **Indicative RFP content for external manager selection**

RFP SECTION	DESCRIPTION
Background	Background information on the rationale for the SIF's launch and the sponsor.
Purpose of the RFP	Brief description of the SIF the sponsor intends to launch, the sponsor's role, and its capital commitment.
Features of the proposed SIF	Summary description of the SIF's intended strategy, funding, governance, ESG requirements, and other elements deemed relevant. Subheadings could include the following: • Target sectors • Target geographies • Eligible investee companies and capital instruments • Target fund size • Capital commitments already secured from sponsor and other investors • Capital commitment sought from external manager • Commitment and drawdown periods • Indicative fee arrangement • Governance and, in particular, role of the investment committee and the advisory committee representing fund investors • Ability to meet the ESG criteria adopted by the SIF • Any undertakings and representations required from applicants (for example, compliance with anti-money laundering and other legislation)
Selection process	Description of selection process and timetable, including the following: • Submission of proposals • Proposal evaluation • Interviews with shortlisted candidates • Due diligence on shortlisted candidates • Final selection and sponsor's internal approval process
Selection criteria	The criteria deemed relevant for the selection of the manager, to be backed with written information by the applicants. Examples include the following: • Organizational structure of manager and suitability to proposed SIF • Description of the applicant's envisaged approach to fulfill the SIF's investment strategy, sourcing, and executing quality investments • Manager's track record in relevant sector • Manager's track record in relevant geography • Any competitive advantages of the manager (for example, deal sourcing capabilities, access to capital markets, and portfolio company support after the deal) • Description of the manager's team and its experience, credibility, and cohesiveness • Decision-making, risk management, and other processes suitable to ensure the SIF's achievement of its objectives • The manager's experience in fulfilling its fiduciary duties, including reporting and administration requirements • The experience of the fund manager in capital raising (if the proposed SIF seeks capital other than from the sponsor) • The proposed terms and conditions of the fund
Proposal submission	Procedures for submission and any representations by the sponsor (for example, the right to reject proposal or request additional documentation, nonliability for submission costs).

Source: World Bank.
Note: ESG = environmental, social, and governance; RFP = request for proposal; SIF = strategic investment fund.

diligence topics can be summarized as people, performance, pipeline, and process (the four Ps; see box 4.8).[46] The support of advisers in this phase can be beneficial, together with the use of industry tools and guidelines. The Institutional Limited Partners Association, for instance, has published a detailed fund due diligence questionnaire template (ILPA 2018). In addition to verifying that the external manager meets the expertise and reputability criteria required to run the SIF, due diligence also allows for a preliminary understanding of fund terms and economics between public sponsor and manager.

The fourth and final phase consists of the public sponsor's internal approval process for the selected fund manager. This process and its timing will vary

BOX 4.8

The four Ps of external manager due diligence

People. Fund management team composition, experience (individual and as a team), expertise in the strategic investment fund's target sector and geography, working dynamics, and incentive structure in previous funds managed (including distribution of incentives among various team members).

Performance. The team's verified investment track record from previously managed funds.

Pipeline. How the team intends to originate deals within the sectors and geographies targeted by the

strategic investment fund to comply with its double bottom line mandate, including any deals that the manager may have already identified.

Process. Based on its experience in previous funds, how the manager intends to run the strategic investment fund, including the investment process (from origination to exit); environmental, social, and governance compliance; investor communications and reporting; and desired legal terms.

Source: International Finance Corporation Fund of Funds team member interviews.

TABLE 4.6 **Indicative timeline for external manager selection**

RFP ISSUANCE	SUBMISSION OF PROPOSALS	PROPOSAL EVALUATION AND SHORTLISTING	INTERVIEWS AND DUE DILIGENCE OF SHORTLISTED MANAGERS	PUBLIC SPONSOR'S INTERNAL APPROVAL	TOTAL TIME
Day 1	+ 2 months	+ 1 month	+ 2 months	+ 2–3 months	7–8 months

Source: World Bank.
Note: RFP = request for proposal.

depending on the legal and governance requirements to which the public sponsor is subject.

In general, the overall external manager selection process can be time-consuming. Table 4.6 shows an indicative timeline. Experience of the International Finance Corporation and other development banks indicates that the whole process can take as long as eight months.

Hiring an external manager is a complex process: the public sponsor may want to hire advisers to support it through the process, and to ensure that the process is carefully documented. Consulting and research organizations specializing in the due diligence of private equity and other PCFs may serve as good partners for the public sponsor through the hiring process. Development institutions may also support public sponsors in the selection process, especially if they also plan to invest in the SIF. In compliance with the Santiago Principles and any applicable public procurement rules, it is advisable to document in writing every step of the process. GAPP 14 from the Santiago Principles calls for clear rules and procedures in dealing with third parties, including commercial fund managers and external service providers. Documentation may involve keeping written scorecards during the screening phase and full due diligence summaries for shortlisted managers. GAPP 15 calls for compliance with all applicable regulatory and disclosure requirements in the SIF's country.

Negotiating the investment management agreement
Once the selection is completed, the public sponsor and any other investors in the SIF will need to enter into a written investment management agreement disciplining all aspects of the relationship with the external manager. This is

standard practice in the PCF industry and is also recommended to SWFs by GAPP 18.2 of the Santiago Principles.[47] For PCFs set up as GP/LP structures, the agreement is commonly known as a limited partnership agreement (LPA). This section refers primarily to LPAs, because GP/LP structures are the most common among funds that invest in unlisted securities (see table 4.7).

LPAs must comply with the jurisdiction in which the partnership is formed and are often heavily negotiated. Table 4.7 lays out the typical terms of an LPA. An investor's negotiating power is influenced by the size of its capital commitment. Likewise, public sponsors that are large capital providers to a SIF may have greater leverage during negotiation. Some investors—institutional ones in particular—may have detailed requirements on certain LPA terms. Some LPA clauses may reflect generally accepted market standards, from which reputable managers may be disinclined to deviate. Commercial investors in a mixed capital SIF may also prefer to adhere to market standards.

TABLE 4.7 Typical terms of a limited partnership agreement

TERM	DESCRIPTION
Investment strategy	SIFs can opt to refer to the strategy detailed in the private placement memorandum, or also include detailed investment criteria in the LPA.
Investment restrictions	The LPA includes express limits to the investments the fund may make, mirroring or expanding on those contained in the private placement memorandum.
	In addition to the limits (discussed in chapter 5 in the sections on risk management), the LPA may expressly forbid, for example, hostile transactions, investments in other funds (unless the SIF operates as a fund of funds), borrowing above certain thresholds, foreign investments, investments in portfolio companies affiliated to fund executives, and investments in industries deemed unethical.
Closing dates	These are dates by which the fund may accept additional investors (usually limited to one to two years after the initial capital injection, to allow the manager to subsequently focus on investing rather than fundraising).
Term	The term is the life span of the fund and allowance for (typically limited) extensions.
Early termination	The LPA may include events that trigger the early termination of the fund (or the curtailment of new investment), by decision of investors that own a specified proportion of the fund commitments.
	These can include the failure of named key principals (key persons) to remain involved in the fund's management or the material breach of the LPA by the manager. Some funds also permit a no-fault divorce, subject to a prescribed financial settlement with the management team, if approved by a high proportion of the limited partners.
Noncompetition	The LPA may include a prohibition on the formation of similar competitor funds until the expiry of the investment period or investment of a high portion (for example, 75% of the capital commitments).
Indemnity	The LPA may indemnify or limit the liability of the general partner, the limited partners, the manager, the advisory committee, and each of their respective officers, employees, and agents. Exceptions are made in the case of a person who has acted in gross negligence or bad faith.
Transfers and withdrawals	The LPA may include restrictions to the transfer of limited partnership interests or withdrawals by limited partners.
Reporting	The LPA may include provisions on reporting of periodic financial, tax, and other information to investors.
Capital contributions	The LPA may specify size and timing of capital commitments to the fund, and provisions related to the drawdown of such commitments as the fund makes investments.
Distributions	The LPA may specify the timing and process through which a fund makes distributions to its investors and manager. So-called waterfall provisions discipline the sequencing of distributions to the limited partners and the fund management team, who are usually entitled to receive a share of the fund's profits (so-called carried interest) above a stipulated threshold.
Management fees	The fund manager will usually be paid a management fee periodically (for example, quarterly in arrears), in addition to the payment of carried interest. The LPA will set the management fee as a percentage of capital committed (in private equity funds, the typical range is 1.5%–2.5%). Other fees may be envisaged, for instance, for the reimbursement of deal-specific expenses incurred by the manager.

Source: Wylie and Marrs 2018.
Note: LPA = limited partnership agreement; SIF = strategic investment fund.

SIF public sponsors will want to ensure compliance with the SIF's policy mandate and may negotiate specific requirements through side letters. The SIF public sponsor must pay particular attention to the LPA provisions related to the fund's strategy, which must be consistent with the strategy laid out in the private placement memorandum and ensure compliance with the SIF's policy mandate, in addition to financial return requirements. The manager may also agree to side letters with some of the SIF's investors containing tailored arrangements not included in the LPA. Such side letters could reflect, for instance, specific environmental, social, and governance requirements or investment exclusion lists of certain public investors in the SIF. Marguerite's second fund (Marguerite II), for instance, complies with general investment eligibility criteria listed in the LPA to ensure adherence to the public sponsors' policy goals, and also signed side letters with some sponsors to ensure compliance with their specific environmental, social, and governance requirements. Side letters could also discipline, for instance, the ability of a public sponsor to publicly disclose information on the fund and its investments.

Monitoring the external fund manager

The primary means of monitoring the activity of the fund manager is the participation, by some of the SIF's investors, in an advisory committee or advisory board (as discussed earlier under the subsection on oversight). Such committees are common in most private equity funds. The committee discusses and provides advice to the manager on multiple issues, especially related to conflicts of interest or valuation, as set out in fund documentation (Wylie and Marrs 2018). The advisory committee, however, does not interfere with investment decisions, which are the sole responsibility of the manager's investment committee (Invest Europe 2018). The role and composition of the advisory committee should be articulated in fund documentation. Individual representatives on the committee should have enough fund investing experience to provide a meaningful contribution to discussions. Ideally, the advisory committee meets at least once a year (Invest Europe 2018).

In addition, the manager should keep investors duly informed through regular reporting of its investment activities. Specific regulatory requirements may apply in the SIF's jurisdiction (see discussion in chapter 7). PCF industry organizations have also published guidelines and reporting templates that a SIF could use. ILPA (2016), for instance, has published comprehensive quarterly reporting standards for private equity funds, (refer to chapter 7 for a detailed discussion on SIF disclosure).

Regular meetings between the sponsor (and other SIF investors) and the external manager are also advisable. By remaining in contact with the manager, investors can get a sense of how the pipeline is being executed, the performance of portfolio companies, the manager's success in adding value to portfolio companies, and other topics such as environmental, social, and governance compliance.

Finally, as described in table 4.7, the LPA will discipline the scenarios under which the fund can be terminated early. Early termination is determined, according to the LPA, by investors representing at least a specified portion of the fund's capital commitments. It usually applies if the manager triggers a material breach of the LPA or key executives fail to remain involved in the fund's management. Some funds also permit early termination outside of these circumstances (no-fault divorce), although in practice this faculty is rarely exercised and may require a financial settlement with the management team.

KEY TAKEAWAYS

- A robust SIF governance framework specifies the allocation of rights and responsibilities between the SIF's different stakeholders, and articulates the rules and procedures for decision-making in a way that bolsters the fund's legitimacy. SIF governance structures typically consist of three levels of decision-making bodies that represent ownership, oversight, and management.

- The SIF faces three key governance challenges: (1) the principal-agent challenge from an imperfect alignment of interests between the SIF's public sponsor (or principal) and its fund manager (or agent), (2) the operational tension of having to meet and balance the SIF's dual mandate objectives, and (3) possible conflicts of interest that can jeopardize the SIF's mandate, distort private markets, or crowd out the private sector.

- In most common ownership structures for government-sponsored public capital SIFs, either the ministry of finance acts as the proxy legal owner of the fund or the government delegates its ownership interests to an independent authority or state-owned corporatized entity. For mixed capital SIFs, ownership structures pivot around pooled investment in a finite life legal entity, with investor rights dictated through contractual measures between the investor(s) and the fund manager.

- Most SIFs are set up such that the public sponsor has ownership interests in both the SIF's investment assets and its management entity, thus ensuring greater control over how the SIF meets its mandate. The board of directors is a common governing structure found in such SIFs, and the autonomy and empowerment of the SIF board are vital to the efficacy of the fund. The selection and composition of board members are important, as are how they are nominated and appointed. Ideally, most of the board should be composed of independent directors, and the board should be chaired by an independent director. Such a composition, along with a professional SIF fund manager, helps insulate the fund from fluctuations in the political climate that can jeopardize the fund's long-term investment objectives or cause arbitrary changes in its mandate or strategy. The SIF investment committee should ideally have no government representation to ensure that no politicization of investments occurs.

- When the public sponsor has no ownership interest in the management entity of a SIF (external manager), the principal-agent problem is addressed in large part by contractually aligning financial interests between investor and manager rather than by closely monitoring the manager via a board.

- The SIF management is either (1) in-house or dedicated to the SIF (an internal manager) or (2) an external manager selected via a competitive process. If recruiting an external manager, the public sponsor must ensure it undertakes a competitive recruiting process, and it must ideally involve the selected external manager in the design details of the fund to ensure ownership.

NOTES

1. 1MDB was set up in 2009 under the Malaysian Ministry of Finance, with a board of advisers chaired by the Malaysian prime minister. The fund was allegedly used for political purposes to support the prime minister. The governance failures and scandal of the SIF, now declared insolvent, led to the ouster of former Malaysian Prime Minister Najib Razak.

2. World Bank (2014) provides an extensive discussion of the corporate governance of state-owned enterprises, including state-owned financial institutions.

3. The chapter relies on World Bank (2014), particularly in distilling parallels in governance principles for state-owned entities with SIFs.

4. See Rai (2012), which discusses multilayered principal-agent relationships with respect to national oil companies.

5. The principal, as discussed in chapter 2, may be another public entity such as one or more development banks. Private investors in the SIF are not considered here as the primary principal because they focus on only one of the SIF's objectives (financial returns) and not the others (policy returns and capital mobilization).

6. This organizational model is discussed in chapter 3 and is considered optimal for mixed capital SIFs in particular, which mobilize third-party capital, because investors pool their capital to diversify risk and each investor is liable to lose only up to the capital it has provided to the fund.

7. Morley (2014) argues that investment funds "are distinguished not by the assets they hold, but by their unique organizational structures, which separate investment assets and management assets into different entities with different owners." In this structure, the investments belong to funds, whereas the management assets belong to management companies.

8. Ownership is exercised not just by the legal owner but by the entities that have been delegated the responsibility to exercise the ownership rights.

9. Section 38(3) of Ireland's National Treasury Management Agency (Amendment) Act 2014.

10. ISIF's governance structure is in part embedded within the governance framework for its manager, NTMA.

11. Such conflicts of interest can emerge if the government department exercising ownership rights of a commercially oriented state actor also has influence over policy-making, regulatory, or supervisory functions of the state, which can potentially tilt the playing field to favor the government-owned entity.

12. Now the Companies Act 2016.

13. See the Khazanah Nasional Berhad Santiago Principles Self-Assessment 2019 (https://www.ifswf.org/assessment/khazanah-nasional-berhad-2019).

14. OHADA is the Organisation pour l'harmonisation en Afrique du droit des affaires (Organization for the Harmonization of Corporate Law in Africa). As referenced in chapter 3, FONSIS was created under the Founding Legislation n° 2012-34 approved by Parliament on December 27, 2012. This law in turn allowed FONSIS to be incorporated as a legal entity under private law.

15. Per the Ministry of Finance (Incorporation) Act 1957.

16. This is the current ownership structure, but the 2012-34 establishment law and the articles of association do permit other state-owned entities or governmental agencies to become shareholders as needed.

17. The terms advisory committee and governing council are sometimes used interchangeably, and other terms are also used to designate high-level SIF oversight bodies that are distinct from the board. For example, FONSIS's high-level oversight body is the Strategic Orientation Council. In this book, the term advisory committee refers to a body of investor representatives typically found in a limited partnership model, whereas the term governing council refers to an entity with broad government or societal representation.

18. Ownership is as follows: federal government 45.8 percent, state governments 36.2 percent, local governments 17.8 percent, and federal capital territory 0.2 percent.

19. The SIF often has a broad group of stakeholders, including political parties or nongovernmental organizations, that may lay claim to representing the interests of the taxpayers or citizenry, or parts of the citizenry.

20. Section 7(3) of NSIA Act 2011 states, "The Council shall, in the discharge of its duties, observe the independence of the Board and officers of the Authority."

21. At the time of writing, members include the Secretary of the Department of Economic Affairs, the Secretary of the Department of Financial Services, and representatives from the business and investment community.

22. This section draws its recommendations chiefly from chapter 6 of World Bank (2014). The term board of directors is most applicable to a corporatized entity or incorporated SOE;

however, it is used generally in this book to refer to the governing body that is in charge of supervising the fund on behalf of the owner.

23. See Block and Gerstner (2016), who refer to the discussion in Berle and Means (1932) of the concept of separating ownership and control.
24. The committee could be chaired by an independent director and consist mainly of independent directors.
25. An exception is made for one of the board members, which the Act specifies should be held by a legal practitioner.
26. World Bank (2014) suggests that 6–12 is the typical size.
27. Suggested by Alsweilem et al. (2015). Their recommendations are directed at SWFs, but these recommendations apply equally to SIFs.
28. According to World Bank (2014, 171), board members should be appointed for a fixed term, usually one to three years.
29. Schedule A, Section 3 A states, "Of the initial appointed members, the Minister shall appoint 2 members for a term of office of 3 years and 2 members for a term of office of 4 years."
30. President Buhari eventually appointed board members to NSIA in 2017, two years after the board was dissolved.
31. This section draws recommendations primarily from World Bank (2014).
32. Composed of NSIA's managing director, the chief operating officer, chief investment officer, as well as other senior management representatives.
33. A subcommittee of the board comprising three nonexecutive board members who decide on a majority basis—although in practice unanimity is sought in most investment decisions.
34. "Audit committees are usually required to have at least two or three independent members who make up a majority, including the chair. All members should be familiar with financial matters, and at least one should have a relevant financial or accounting background" (World Bank 2014, 193).
35. Usually 2 percent by industry standards. The management fee is usually charged on capital committed during the investment period of the fund and on capital invested after the investment period.
36. The hurdle rate is the minimum rate of return required by the investor before the investor permits the manager to share in profits. Industry standard is 20 percent for share in profits.
37. See discussion on the governance of private equity funds in Morley (2014).
38. The considerations in this section reflect input from a variety of expert sources, including interviews with fund manager selection experts at the International Finance Corporation (Maria Kozloski, former senior manager, IFC Fund of Funds, and Johanna Klein, IFC Asset Management Company), interviews with senior management of case study SIFs, evidence from the SIF universe, and guidelines published by recognized industry organizations. The latter include Invest Europe, the association representing Europe's private equity, venture capital, and infrastructure funds and their investors (600 members), and Institutional Limited Partners Association, a global organization representing more than 500 LPs with an aggregate investment in private equity funds of more than US$2 trillion.
39. See the Santiago Principles, GAPP 18.2, Explanation and commentary (IWG 2008, 21).
40. This discussion focuses on the creation of an in-house team from scratch, rather than the alternate scenario in which the public sponsor identifies an existing agency within its bureaucracy to manage the SIF.
41. Such as minimum qualifications, competitive contracting, and the development of a structured and transparent selection process (see World Bank 2014).
42. Warner (2006) suggests commercial experience, which we have translated into investment/operating experience in the context of the SIF.
43. These restrictions reflect common practice among public sector asset managers. According to Gratcheva and Anasashvili (2017), 60 percent of SWF investment managers and about 40 percent of public pension funds reported being subject to general public sector remuneration policies.
44. Marguerite I was managed by a dedicated fund manager that was not registered under the European Union's post–financial crisis Directive 2011/61/EU on Alternative Investment

Fund Managers (AIFMs). Marguerite Investment Management, an independent company owned by senior management, was appointed as the external alternative investment fund manager for Marguerite II. Still a dedicated manager, its legal status now allowed it to market to a broader group of investors across the European Union.

45. Interview with development finance institution professionals, including from the International Finance Corporation and Overseas Private Investment Corporation, that regularly recruit external fund managers.
46. From interviews with IFC Fund of Funds team members.
47. See the Santiago Principles, GAPP 18.2, explanation and commentary (IWG 2008, 21).

REFERENCES

ADB (Asian Development Bank). 2012. "Proposed Equity Investment: Philippine Investment Alliance for Infrastructure Fund (Philippines)." Report and Recommendation of the President to the Board of Directors, Project No. 45929, ADB, Manila. https://www.adb.org/sites/default/files/project-document/73632/45929-014-phi-rrp.pdf.

Al-Hassan, Abdullah, Michael Papaioannou, Martin Skancke, and Cheng Chih Sung. 2013. "Sovereign Wealth Funds: Aspects of Governance Structures and Investment Management." IMF Working Paper 13/231, International Monetary Fund, Washington, DC. https://www.imf.org/en/Publications/WP/Issues/2016/12/31/Sovereign-Wealth-Funds-Aspects-of-Governance-Structures-and-Investment-Management-41046.

Alsweilem, Khalid A., Angela Cummine, Malan Ritveld, and Katherine Tweedie. 2015. "Sovereign Investor Models: Institutions and Policies for Managing Sovereign Wealth." Discussion paper, Center for International Developent and Belfer Center for Science and International Affairs, Harvard Kennedy School, Cambridge, MA.

Ambachtsheer, Keith P. 2007. *Pension Revolution: A Solution to the Pensions Crisis.* New York: J. Wiley.

Ammann, Manuel, and Christian Ehmann. 2017. "Is Governance Related to Investment Performance and Asset Allocation? Empirical Evidence from Swiss Pension Funds." *Swiss Journal of Economics and Statistics* 153 (3): 293–339.

Bachher, Jagdeep Singh, Adam D. Dixon, and Ashby H. B. Monk. 2016. *The New Frontier Investors: How Pension Funds, Sovereign Funds, and Endowments Are Changing the Business of Investment Management and Long-Term Investing.* London: Palgrave Macmillan.

Berle, Adolph A., and Gardiner C. Means. 1932. *The Modern Corporation and Private Property.* San Diego, CA: Harcourt, Brace & World, Inc.

Block, David, and Anne-Marie Gerstner. 2016. "One-Tier vs. Two-Tier Board Structure: A Comparison between the United States and Germany." Comparative Corporate Governance and Financial Regulation Select Seminar Papers, Penn Law: Legal Scholarship Repository, University of Pennsylvania Carey School of Law, Philadelphia. https://scholarship.law.upenn.edu/fisch_2016/1.

Clark, Gordon L., and Roger Urwin. 2008. "Best-Practice Pension Fund Governance." *Journal of Asset Management* 9 (1): 2–21.

Gelb, Alan, Silvana Tordo, and Håvard Halland. 2014. "Sovereign Wealth Funds and Long-Term Development Finance." Policy Research Working Paper 6776, World Bank, Washington, DC.

Gratcheva, Ekaterina, and Nikoloz Anasashvili. 2017. "Domestic Investment Practices of Sovereign Wealth Funds: Empirical Evidence to Inform Policy Debates." In *The New Frontiers of Sovereign Investment*, edited by Malan Rietveld and Perrine Toledano. New York: Columbia University Press.

IFC (International Finance Corporation). 2012. "IFC Corporate Governance Methodology." IFC, Washington, DC.

ILPA (Institutional Limited Partners Association). 2016. "Quarterly Reporting Standards (Version 1.1)." ILPA, Washington, DC. https://ilpa.org/wp-content/uploads/2017/03/ILPA-Best-Practices-Quarterly-Reporting-Standards_Version-1.1_optimized.pdf.

ILPA (Institutional Limited Partners Association). 2018. "Due Diligence Questionnaire (Version 1.2)." ILPA, Washington, DC. https://ilpa.org/wp-content/uploads/2018/09/ILPA _Due_Diligence_Questionnaire_v1.2.pdf.

Invest Europe. 2018. "Invest Europe Handbook of Professional Standards." Invest Europe, Brussels. https://www.investeurope.eu/media/1022/ie_professional-standards -handbook-2018.pdf.

IWG (International Working Group of Sovereign Wealth Funds). 2008. "Sovereign Wealth Funds Generally Accepted Principles and Practices: 'Santiago Principles.'" IWG. https:// www.ifswf.org/sites/default/files/santiagoprinciples_0_0.pdf.

Magnuson, William J. 2018. "The Public Cost of Private Equity." *Minnesota Law Review* 102: 1847.

Milhench, Claire. 2018. "UK Judge Lifts Asset Freeze Order against Quantum Global in Angolan SWF Case." *Reuters*, July 31, 2018. https://www.reuters.com/article/angola-swf-litigation /uk-judge-lifts-asset-freeze-order-against-quantum-global-in-angolan-swf-case-idUSL5N 1UQ46M.

Morley, John. 2014. "The Separation of Funds and Managers: A Theory of Investment Fund Structure and Regulation." *Yale Law Journal* 123 (5): 1228–87.

North, Douglass C. 1990. *Institutions, Institutional Change and Economic Performance.* Cambridge, U.K.: Cambridge University Press.

Ohrenstein, Robert, and James White. 2017. "The Governance Implications of Increasing Levels of Direct Investment of Sovereign Wealth Funds." In *The New Frontiers of Sovereign Investment,* edited by Malan Rietveld and Perrine Toledano. New York: Columbia University Press.

Rai, Arun. 2012. "Fading Star: Explaining the Evolution of India's ONGC." In *Oil and Governance: State-Owned Enterprises and the World Energy Supply,* edited by David G. Victor, David R. Hults, and Mark C. Thurber. Cambridge, U.K.: Cambridge University Press.

Ribsteint, Larry E. 2009. "Partnership Governance of Large Firms." *University of Chicago Law Review* 76 (1): 289. https://chicagounbound.uchicago.edu/cgi/viewcontent.cgi? article=5460&context=uclrev.

Warner, Eric, ed. 2006. *Human Capital in Private Equity. Managing Your Most Important Asset.* London: Private Equity International. http://www.criticaleye.com/insights-servfile .cfm?id=692&view=1.

Williamson, Oliver E. 1996. *The Mechanisms of Governance.* Oxford: Oxford University Press.

World Bank. 2014. *Corporate Governance of State-Owned Enterprises: A Toolkit.* Washington, DC: World Bank.

Wylie, Andrew, and Nathaniel Marrs. 2018. "English and US Private Equity Funds: Key Features." Practice note, DLA Piper, September. https://www.dlapiper.com/en/us/insights /publications/2018/09/english-and-us-private-equity-funds-key-features/.

5 Investment and Risk Management

INTRODUCTION

This chapter discusses investment and risk management frameworks for the strategic investment fund (SIF). Building on earlier discussions of governance arrangements within a SIF, the chapter focuses on the accountability framework embedded within a fund's investment management and risk management frameworks. It discusses the constituent components of the investment management and risk management frameworks, the bodies responsible for their definition and formalization, and the unique features of both in the context of a SIF, as compared with private capital funds (PCFs) or sovereign wealth funds (SWFs).

INVESTMENT MANAGEMENT FRAMEWORK: KEY CONCEPTS

This section discusses the SIF's investment policy and strategy as core elements of the investment management framework. Chapter 6 follows up this discussion with a breakdown of the investment process in a SIF.

Investment policy

The investment policy is the chief contract between the SIF investors and the manager. It spells out the core parameters that the SIF needs to comply with in the implementation of its double bottom line mandate. Although some overlaps in content exist between the investment policy and strategy, the investment policy expresses the investor's vision for operationalizing the SIF's mandate by specifying the broad rules the manager of the SIF must observe. It breaks down core elements of these rules—discussed in detail later in the chapter—including the eligible investments that comply with the fund's policy purpose, the fund's investment horizon, return expectations, responsible investment policy, and the performance monitoring framework. The separation between investment policy and investment strategy is a feature of funds in which the anchor investor—such as a public pension fund or SIF—has delegated to an internal or external manager the responsibility for investing the assets of the fund (see table 5.1 on the broad distinction between investment policy and strategy for a SIF).

The investment policy serves multiple governance purposes. It commits and tethers the sponsor to a long-term vision for the fund, tempering the risk that subsequent and conflicting political priorities may undermine that vision.[1] The policy is an important aspect of concretizing the accountability framework of the SIF, requiring the fund to behave with predictability within stated boundaries (Alsweilem and Rietveld 2017) and providing a yardstick against which governing bodies can judge the intended activities of the manager.[2] It also provides the framework within which the financial performance and economic impact of the fund will be monitored and assessed.

The investment policy is usually outlined in the SIF's legislation, in ancillary regulation, or in policy documents of the sponsor, and is typically disclosed on the SIF's website. Because the investment policy is essential to the accountability framework of any public sponsor–anchored fund, including SIFs, best practice demands public disclosure of the policy[3] (see box 5.1 on the Santiago Principles, outlining the key guidance provided to SWFs on investment policy and strategy).

BOX 5.1

Investment policy–related guidance within the Santiago Principles

The Santiago Principles include the following generally accepted principles and practices (GAPPs) related to sovereign wealth funds (SWFs):

GAPP 18. Principle
The SWF's investment policy should be clear and consistent with its defined objectives, risk tolerance, and investment strategy, as set by the owner or the governing body(ies), and be based on sound portfolio management principles.

GAPP 18.1. Subprinciple. The investment policy should guide the SWF's financial risk exposures and the possible use of leverage.

GAPP 18.2. Subprinciple. The investment policy should address the extent to which internal and/or external investment managers are used, the range of their activities and authority, and the process by which they are selected and their performance monitored.

GAPP 18.3. Subprinciple. A description of the investment policy of the SWF should be publicly disclosed.

GAPP 19. Principle
The SWF's investment decisions should aim to maximize risk-adjusted financial returns in a manner consistent with its investment policy, and based on economic and financial grounds.

GAPP 19.1. Subprinciple. If investment decisions are subject to other than economic and financial considerations, these should be clearly set out in the investment policy and be publicly disclosed.

GAPP 19.2. Subprinciple. The management of an SWF's assets should be consistent with what is generally accepted as sound asset management principles.

GAPP 21. Principle
SWFs view shareholder ownership rights as a fundamental element of their equity investments' value. If an SWF chooses to exercise its ownership rights, it should do so in a manner that is consistent with its investment policy and protects the financial value of its investments. The SWF should publicly disclose its general approach to voting securities of listed entities, including the key factors guiding its exercise of ownership rights.

GAPP 23.0. Principle
The assets and investment performance (absolute and relative to benchmarks, if any) of the SWF should be measured and reported to the owner according to clearly defined principles or standards.

Source: IWG 2008.

Public capital SIFs usually formulate their investment policy (or clarify how the policy will be formulated) within the establishment law and ancillary regulation. The investment policy of the Ireland Strategic Investment Fund (ISIF), for example, is articulated in the National Treasury Management Agency (Amendment) Act 2014 (NTMA Act 2014). The Nigeria Sovereign Investment Authority (Establishment, etc.) Act, 2011 (NSIA Act 2011) provides broad investment guidelines, whereas investment policy for NSIA's Nigeria Infrastructure Fund (NIF) is published separately on the fund's website (NSIA 2019).[4] The establishment law for Senegal's FONSIS (Fonds Souverain d'Investissements Stratégiques, or Sovereign Fund for Strategic Investments) sets the fund's strategic orientation and delegates the definition of the investment policy to the fund's board.[5] Unlike public capital SIFs, mixed capital SIFs typically clarify the investment policy in the private placement memorandum, the main document used to market the fund to prospective investors, often commingling investment policy and strategy under a single umbrella. As anchor investor, the public sponsor plays a significant role—along with the internal or external fund manager—in defining the content of the memorandum. The policy or board documents of the public sponsor approving the latter's investment in the fund will also likely refer to the fund's investment policy or core elements of it. For instance, the proposal of the Asian Development Bank (ADB) to its board of directors to create Asia Climate Partners (ACP), together with asset managers ORIX and Robeco, contains the broad investment doctrine for the fund (ADB 2012).[6]

Investment strategy

The investment strategy translates the policy into detailed guidelines for the fund manager on permissible investments and transaction structures. Core elements of the investment strategy, discussed in detail later, include particulars on target sectors and geographies, admissible capital instruments, ability to take majority or minority stakes, size of individual investments, and co-investment strategy.

A rigorous definition of the investment strategy serves several purposes. The strategy is critical to guiding the investment activities of the external fund manager or internal investment team appointed to manage a SIF. It informs the structural elements of the SIF, such as its size, organization, and human resources needed for the implementation of the strategy.[7] For mixed capital SIFs that mobilize external capital at the fund level, the investment strategy is also a core component of the fund's marketing efforts and materials, helping fund managers target the most appropriate set of potential fund investors.[8]

The investment strategy is clarified within the investment policy statement of the SIF, in ancillary documents, or in the marketing material of the fund. In a typical PCF, whose fund manager has sole responsibility for developing the fund's thesis, the investment strategy is contained in the marketing materials the manager uses to mobilize capital from investors. By contrast, in the case of a SIF for which the public sponsor has conceived the fund's purpose, the investment strategy is crafted in response to the public sponsor's investment policy and may be articulated in different fund documents depending on whether the fund is solely capitalized by a government or is seeking co-investors alongside the public sponsor. For instance, the NSIA Act 2011 (Article 41.1) requires the manager to develop rolling five-year investment plans for NIF, and NSIA provides details on NIF's investment strategy within its annual reports. ISIF's establishment act, as mentioned previously, set the investment policy; however, it delegates the determination, monitoring, and review of the investment strategy to the fund's management body (NTMA), which does so by producing an ad hoc investment strategy document published on the website.[9] In conformity with the practices of PCFs, a mixed capital SIF such as ACP, Marguerite, and India's National Investment and Infrastructure Fund (NIIF) usually details its investment strategy within its private placement memorandum.

KEY ACTORS IN THE INVESTMENT MANAGEMENT FRAMEWORK

The formulation of the investment policy is a function of the delegated governance structure of a SIF; that is, the policy is constructed by the owner or (by delegation) the board. The SIF's investment policy is constructed like that of SWFs, for which a common governance arrangement is for the board to define the investment policy of the fund on behalf of the owner (Alsweilem and Rietveld 2017). Such an arrangement, for instance, is seen in NSIA's model, in which the board of directors issues the NIF's investment policy statement (NSIA 2019), or in FONSIS's case as referenced earlier. Frequently, the manager may also be involved in providing input into the investment policy, aided by its presence on the board or investment committee (Alsweilem and Rietveld 2017).

The SIF's investment strategy, by contrast, is usually established through an iterative process between the sponsor or board and the manager. A consultative process to develop the strategy may, in some instances, be explicitly required. For example, Articles 40.1, 40.3, and 41.5 of the NTMA Act 2014 require NTMA, as ISIF's manager, to formulate the investment strategy in consultation with the Minister for Finance and the Minister for Public Expenditure and Reform and with the advice of the NTMA investment committee. Such a process seeks to capitalize on the fund manager's expertise to design a commercially feasible investment strategy while also ensuring consistency with the policy objectives of the public sponsor. A poorly defined strategy may hinder a SIF's ability to hire qualified investment professionals, which, in turn, could affect a fund's performance and limit its ability to crowd in commercial co-investors at the deal level.[10]

Particularly in mixed capital SIFs that seek commercial co-investment at the fund level, with the fund manager playing a crucial role in the fundraising process, it is highly recommended that the public sponsor involve the fund manager in defining the strategy. For mixed capital SIFs, demonstrating deep expertise and providing concrete visibility on their target sectors and the investment opportunities represent important components of successful fundraising.[11] Commercial investors, for instance, may be deterred by a very narrow definition of the target sectors or permissible deal structures, which could restrict the fund's investment pipeline or undermine its ability to achieve the targeted returns. The prospect of poor fundraising or, if fundraising succeeds, poor returns will deter prospective fund managers, because fees paid to fund managers are customarily linked to both fund size and performance. The public sponsor of a mixed capital SIF must be willing to entertain an open dialogue with the prospective fund manager and embrace some of its investment strategy proposals. Marguerite is a good example in this respect. When the European Investment Bank and other public sponsors decided to launch the first Marguerite fund in 2009, they appointed a newly set up external fund manager, whose chief executive officer was extensively involved in defining for Marguerite an investment strategy as aligned as possible with fund industry best practices (see the case study in appendix A).

COMPONENTS OF THE INVESTMENT POLICY

Key elements of the investment policy include the following.

- *Policy purpose.* Investment policy statements generally start with an identification of the SIF's purpose and double bottom line mandate. This simple but vital statement sets the stage for the subsequent rules. It also adheres to two key generally accepted principles and practices (GAPP) set out in the Santiago Principles: (1) GAPP 18, which states that "the SWF's investment policy should be clear and consistent with its defined objectives, risk tolerance, and investment strategy, as set by the owner or the governing body(ies)"; and (2) GAPP 19.1, which states that, "if investment decisions are subject to other than economic and financial considerations, these should be clearly set out in the investment policy and be publicly disclosed" (IWG 2008, 8). NSIA-NIF's investment policy, for instance, complies with both by clarifying the objectives of the fund up front, stating its double bottom line objective, and indicating an overall elevated focus on financial returns: "The Fund seeks to make a positive financial return on its investments in the infrastructure sector in Nigeria. It also aims to attract and support foreign investment and enable growth" (NSIA 2019).[12] Similarly, Malaysia's Khazanah Nasional Berhad clarifies the bifurcation of financial and economic return objectives when it states that its "commercial fund aims to achieve optimal risk-adjusted returns, whilst its strategic fund undertakes strategic investments and holds strategic national assets with long-term economic benefits."[13]
- *Alignment with national priorities.* Public capital SIF investment policies are generally crafted to align with the sponsor's overall vision for socioeconomic development. For instance, Articles 42.1 and 42.2 of the NSIA Act 2011 require that NSIA-NIF investments align as far as possible with national infrastructure priorities, with a specific prioritization of federation-level economic benefits over local or regional ones. Similarly, ISIF's Investment Strategy 2.0 is informed by the objectives of Project Ireland 2040, which focuses on five priority themes (ISIF 2019). Public capital SIFs typically focus on national-level priorities, and mixed capital SIFs may reflect similar value systems. Marguerite I's management board had the ability to veto transactions if a proposed investment was potentially contrary to European Union (EU) policy objectives or publicly stated national policy in the country where the project was located.[14]
- *Eligible investments.* In line with the policy purpose discussed earlier, the public sponsor provides a broad definition of the eligible investments the fund can make, focusing on private markets. The priority placed on investing in unlisted assets is core to the definition of a SIF: it is hard to justify the additionality of investments in listed companies whose securities are routinely purchased and sold by other capital market investors. For example, Marguerite funds are required to invest, on a commercial basis, in policy-driven infrastructure projects in the EU and EU preaccession states, with particular focus on greenfield infrastructure, and based on a list of eligible sectors aligned with EU and national policies. These eligible sectors

include transport, energy and renewables, telecommunications, and water. This generic definition of eligible investments is usually broken down further in the investment strategy (as discussed in the next section).

- *Investment horizon.* The investment horizon indicates the tenure over which the fund is expected to be operationalized and returns are generated (Mulder et al. 2009). Notwithstanding the SIF's role as a provider of long-term patient capital (Halland et al. 2016), SIFs can have different time horizons dictated by their policy objective and the investor base they seek. As discussed in earlier chapters, public capital SIFs often tend to be structured as permanent capital vehicles with the flexibility for longer investment horizons because they are funded solely by the sovereign. For instance, NSIA-NIF's investment policy prescribes a 20-year investment horizon for NIF, in alignment with the long-term characteristics of infrastructure investment (NSIA 2019). Ireland's NTMA Act 2014 does not restrict ISIF's investment horizon, which ISIF clarifies can extend to over 30 years (see the case study in appendix A). A longer investment horizon enables public capital SIF involvement in, for instance, greenfield infrastructure deals (which have longer gestation periods) and corporate investments (or restructurings) that require a long time to bear fruit. Mixed capital SIFs, by contrast, frequently tend to be finite life funds, with a 10- to 15-year time span, because they seek investment from commercial investors that may be reluctant to commit capital for an indefinite period. The trajectory of the Marguerite funds provides a good illustrative example: Marguerite II's fund life was shortened from 20 years (life of the preceding fund, Marguerite I) to 10 years to enhance its attractiveness to private investors and in response to the preferences of most of its sponsors (see the case study in appendix A). Finite life SIFs must deploy their capital, exit the investments, and distribute the proceeds back to the fund investors within a contractually agreed term (usually 10–15 years). This requirement may prevent such funds from investing in greenfield projects at the early stages of development, such as the design phase.

- *Return expectations.* As discussed earlier, unlike traditional SWFs that invest primarily in publicly traded investments, SIFs focus on privately traded investments. A SIF's investment policy will set target returns to provide visibility, hold the SIF accountable to its investors, and discipline the manager's search for deal opportunities. Return targets for investment funds fall into two categories:

1. *Absolute returns.* Funds investing in unlisted securities and particularly private equity tend to set their returns on an absolute basis (for example, 20 percent gross internal rate of return).
2. *Relative returns.* Funds investing in publicly traded securities (stocks or bonds) set performance targets versus a benchmark index of publicly traded securities.

For SIFs that operate closely to the private equity model (limited fund life and focus on one specific layer of the capital structure, such as equity or mezzanine), the absolute returns target model is the most appropriate. For instance, Marguerite II targets a 10 percent net internal rate of return (see the case study in appendix A). However, this model is harder to apply to public capital SIFs that have the flexibility to invest across the capital structure (across different risk-return asset classes) and may not have the finite life of a private equity fund. In this case, it is advisable to

- Set a *minimum return threshold at the portfolio level*, possibly benchmarked to the SIF's cost of capital, such as the cost of sovereign debt if the sovereign is the primary contributor of capital to the SIF; and
- Define *specific return targets for the different asset classes* invested in, because the portfolio-level threshold may not accurately reflect the different risk or reward profiles of debt and equity.

Both thresholds are required because setting a minimum fund-level target linked only to the cost of sovereign debt, without a further specification of target returns for equity investments, would risk giving the SIF leeway to pursue equity deals at subcommercial equity returns. For instance, ISIF's investment policy, as articulated in the NTMA Act 2014, requires the fund as a whole to generate returns that are over the cost of long-term sovereign debt averaged over five years, although Article 39.4 of the act allows that the manager may aim for different returns for different types of investment in the portfolio.

- *Special carveout for investments with high economic returns.* SIFs vary in their approach to prioritizing the dual financial and economic return objectives. Some SIFs explicitly accommodate subcommercial returns in their investment policy, as long as doing so results in persuasive economic returns, and may anticipate changes in investment approach as a result of such strategy. Article 43 of Nigeria's NSIA Act 2011, for instance, allows NIF investments to have a lower target internal rate of return as long as they have compelling economic returns. Article 41.5 of the act allows 10 percent of NIF funds available for investment in any fiscal year to be invested in social infrastructure projects, even if they have less attractive commercial returns. In tandem, the NSIA-NIF investment policy provides for a long-term investment horizon to ensure that the fund can realize both a commercial objective and economic returns (NSIA 2019).[15] FONSIS's law gives much more clear-cut focus to the economic return objective by explicitly allowing FONSIS to make nonprofit investment decisions.[16] (See discussion in chapter 2 on exceptional circumstances that may justify concessionality in a SIF.)
- *Risk tolerance.* Risk management for any fund, including SIFs, is a complex, multifaceted exercise that could hardly be summarized in a high-level document such as the investment policy. (See the section in this chapter on risk management framework for a detailed discussion of all aspects of risk management.) Nevertheless, the investment policy ideally provides an indication of the SIF's overall risk tolerance, whether by direct reference to the topic or cautionary statements inserted throughout the document. NSIA-NIF's investment policy, for instance, opts for the latter approach. In a section called "Investment Principles," the policy (1) refers to portfolio diversification as an important tool of risk management and careful valuation analysis of each project as a way to reduce downside risk (as well as enhance returns); (2) solicits the design of measures to reduce liquidity risk;[17] (3) calls for portfolio diversification to take into account the fund's risk tolerance, and to avoid portfolio concentration risk; and (4) sets limits to the percentage of assets that could be dedicated to external funds or third-party fund managers, to avoid manager concentration risk (NSIA 2019).
- *Discretionary aspects of the investment policy and flexibility for modifications.* The public sponsor may choose to retain discretion over aspects of the investment policy for reasons such as national interest. For

instance, the NTMA Act 2014, Article 42, allows the Irish Minister for Finance, in consultation with the central bank, to channel ISIF funds to finance credit institutions during an economic crisis or in cases of insta-bility in the financial system.[18] In addition, the public sponsor may retain the flexibility to alter the investment policy in light of evolving economic conditions. For instance, ISIF's original investment strategy[19] was reviewed in 2017–18, in compliance with Section 40 of the NTMA Act 2014, which requires a periodic review of the strategy, and amended to reflect the rapidly improving economic situation of Ireland and changing opportunity set for ISIF (IFSWF 2019). The initial strategy reflected Ireland's need to attract capital and stimulate the economy in the after-math of the global financial crisis that severely affected the country. In July 2018, the Minister for Finance and for Public Expenditure and Reform announced a refocusing of ISIF within its overall policy mandate centered on five key economic priorities: indigenous industry, regional development, sectors adversely affected by Brexit, climate change, and housing supply (IFSWF 2019). A new ISIF strategy was therefore pub-lished in February 2019 (ISIF 2019). Similarly, NSIA's board decided in 2019 to increase the allocation to NIF from 40 percent to 50 percent of capital contributions to NSIA, reflecting the government's view of the importance of infrastructure to Nigeria's economic needs (NSIA 2018). Mixed capital SIFs may also modify their investment policy to reflect eco-nomic conditions. For instance, Marguerite I was launched right after the global financial crisis, when any investment in greenfield infrastructure in Europe was hard to fund. By the time of the launch of Marguerite II, abundant liquidity had returned to both the brownfield and shovel-ready greenfield segments (in certain EU member states and sectors perceived to be less risky), but a gap still persisted in development-stage projects and certain geographic regions and sectors. Therefore, unlike Marguerite I, which focused primarily on shovel-ready greenfield projects, Marguerite II can consider development-stage investments (see the case study in appendix A).

- *Responsible investment policy.* Given the policy-driven focus of SIFs, and the affiliation to the sovereign for a public capital SIF, a responsible investment approach is usually embedded within the investment policy of the SIF. For example, Marguerite's investment policy requires it to focus on environmen-tal, social, and governance (ESG) considerations, and the fund applies the European Investment Bank's ESG criteria within the investment process (see the case study in appendix A). Marguerite has also cosigned the United Nations Principles for Responsible Investment and aligns with the Equator III Principles and other ESG standards.[20] Similarly, India's NIIF and its underlying funds, investee funds, companies, and projects are required to align with ESG principles and assess ESG considerations during due dili-gence while monitoring and managing portfolio-level risk.[21] Likewise, adher-ing to rigorous ESG practices is part of ACP's core identity. The fund integrates ADB's ESG framework into all stages of its investment process (see the case study in appendix A).

- *Framework to review fund performance.* The investment policy also sets out the framework for monitoring the SIF's compliance with the terms set out in the policy. For example, NSIA-NIF's investment policy lays out the key per-formance indicators for the fund, clarifying the rationale for each, the governance body in charge of monitoring the indicators, and the time horizon over which the assessment will take place (NSIA 2019).

COMPONENTS OF THE INVESTMENT STRATEGY

The investment strategy gives particularity to the broad-brush strokes of the investment policy by detailing the approach(es) the fund manager will use to guide the fund's investment activities. The key elements of this breakdown (see table 5.1) are the following.

- *Fund structuring.* SIFs may choose to create distinct funds, deploying different investment policies and strategies but managed by the same fund manager. This approach is particularly useful when the remit contained in the public sponsor's investment policy for the fund is broad, and the manager seeks to distinguish between investment strategies within the wide mandate. The employment of the same fund manager to run separate funds may also be more cost-efficient, with savings in personnel, information technology, and administration costs. A good example is NIIF, which uses a multiple fund strategy to address the government of India's broad mandate to catalyze foreign capital for infrastructure and related sectors in India. The manager, NIIF Ltd., set up three distinct funds to serve this mandate. NIIF's Master Fund focuses on brownfield infrastructure projects in specific infrastructure sectors, establishing investment platforms that act as sector consolidators; the Fund of Funds provides anchor capital to infrastructure (and allied sectors) fund managers in India with strong track records; and the Strategic Opportunities Fund seeks to invest in assets and sectors that may require a longer investment horizon.
- *Target sectors.* Whereas SIF investment policies provide a broad description of eligible investments under generic definitions that usually overlook the diversity of industry subsectors and their business and financial drivers, the investment strategy gives clarity to this broad description using a breakdown of subsectors and geographies, which also helps clarify the required expertise of the investment team.[22] For instance, ISIF's mandate, described in the

TABLE 5.1 **Key elements of a SIF's investment policy and strategy**

INVESTMENT POLICY	INVESTMENT STRATEGY
Policy purpose of the fund (double bottom line mandate)	Fund structuring
Alignment with national priorities	Target sectors
Eligible investments	Target geographies
Investment horizon	Capital instruments
Return expectations	Minority/majority stakes
Special carveout for investments with high economic returns	Ticket size of investments
Risk tolerance	Co-investment/joint investment strategy
Discretionary aspects of investment policy and modifications	Strategic alliances between sovereigns
Responsible investment policy	Direct vs. indirect investment; internal vs. external management
Framework to review fund investment performance	

Source: World Bank.
Note: SIF = strategic investment fund.

NTMA Act 2014, simply states that the fund should invest "on a commercial basis in a manner designed to support economic activity and employment in the State."[23] ISIF's 2015 investment strategy elaborated by providing a list of 10 eligible investment sectors, an indicative portfolio allocation by sector based on estimated funding gaps (which helped determine ISIF's size), and commentary on the rationale for each sector's selection (ISIF 2015).

Box 5.2 provides a sense of the decision tree for SIFs focused on infrastructure as they identify the sectors of focus within the broad remit of the sponsor. Mixed capital SIFs whose investors include pension and other institutional funds may prioritize brownfield over greenfield investments. In general, pension funds opt to invest in large, mature operating assets that already yield cash flow.[24] As a condition to investing in a SIF, institutional investors may therefore require the SIF itself to prioritize less risky assets. Such risk aversion may be heightened when a SIF is managed by a newly assembled investment team, as opposed to an external fund manager with previous experience. Conversely, free of such constraints, public capital SIFs have greater flexibility to pursue riskier investments on the asset maturity and income generation spectrum.

BOX 5.2

Investment strategy: Snapshot on defining investment scope for infrastructure SIFs

For strategic investment funds (SIFs) focused on addressing infrastructure gaps, a rigorous definition of their infrastructure investment scope is an important component of the investment strategy. SIFs should consider the following parameters in defining the scope:

- Identifying a range of subsectors:
  - *Infrastructure sectors with monopolistic characteristics* (toll roads, ports, airports, utilities, water treatment facilities, power generation plants that sell power to utilities under offtake agreements). Projects in these sectors produce fairly predictable cash flows, driven by regulated tariffs paid by infrastructure users and long-term concession agreements (for example, the Marguerite funds and India's National Investment and Infrastructure Fund [NIIF]).
  - *Infrastructure sectors exposed to competitive forces* (telecom providers, merchant power plants, logistics and infrastructure services

companies). Competition exposes businesses in these sectors to a variety of risks, such as loss of market share or pricing power, which makes them riskier and more volatile investments (for example, Marguerite and NIIF).
  - *Enabling infrastructure*, or sectors at the crossroads of services and infrastructure, which can contribute meaningfully to the overall economic development of a country (health care, education, financial services companies specializing in infrastructure). The Nigeria Sovereign Investment Authority's Nigeria Infrastructure Fund has invested in private schools, cancer treatment and diagnostic centers (under public-private partnership models), an infrastructure debt fund, and an infrastructure bond guarantee company.[a]
- Identifying *stage of development*—the extent to which, at the time of investment, the infrastructure assets are already constructed—and

continued

Box 5.2 *continued*

income profile—whether the project already generates income and cash flows. Infrastructure investors commonly categorize projects as greenfield, brownfield, or secondary stage.[b]

- *Greenfield project* refers to an infrastructure asset that does not exist at the time of investment. The project may be in the planning, development, financing, or construction phase. Investors fund the building of the asset and its maintenance once it is operational. A greenfield project does not generate income—rather, it absorbs capital— during the development and construction phases. Income generation is delayed until the asset becomes operational. Investors therefore assume construction risk (such as unexpected delays or costs) and must have a sufficiently long investment horizon. The additionality of greenfield projects may be easier to justify for SIFs. Greenfield projects not only require new capital for development and construction but are also less palatable to existing institutional investors. Both funds managed by Marguerite, while retaining the flexibility to invest in brownfield projects, focus on greenfield investments.

- *Brownfield project* refers to an existing infrastructure asset that requires improvements, repair, or expansion; is usually partially operational; and may already generate income. Brownfield investments are usually less risky and require a shorter investment horizon. The additionality of brownfield investments can vary greatly, depending on the required infrastructure improvements, repairs, or extensions (and the related capital), which can be substantial (for example, in the case of restructuring of stranded assets, or greenfield additions). The additionality of a SIF's investment in brownfield projects

may also reflect a country's overall macroeconomic conditions. Marguerite invested in a shadow toll road in Spain after the global financial crisis, when high risk aversion toward the country limited capital inflows from private capital funds.

- *Secondary stage* refers to a fully operational asset that requires no investment for further development and already generates a steady income stream. These assets are sold in the secondary market by investors looking to exit their investments. The additionality of secondary stage projects may be less obvious but cannot be ruled out. For instance, a SIF may pursue a secondary transaction to demonstrate the feasibility of infrastructure investing in its country, or as the first step of a broader strategy to inject significant capital into the country's infrastructure sector. NIIF's Master Fund invested in Continental Warehousing, a terminal and logistics business previously controlled by three private equity funds, by using a special purpose vehicle ("platform," in NIIF's terminology) established to scale up investment in port infrastructure in India, crowding in capital at both platform and project levels. DP World, the Dubai-based port terminal owner and operator, injected capital in the platform company, of which it owns a 65 percent stake.

A SIF may later shift its positioning on project stage and income profile. For instance, NIIF first launched its Master Fund, which focuses on brownfield infrastructure projects. It subsequently concentrated on mobilizing commercial capital for a Fund of Funds, which focuses on indirect investments via existing or new infrastructure funds. Finally, it launched its Strategic Fund, targeting a broader range of investment strategies including greenfield investments with a long investment horizon of 20–25 years.

Source: Based on Della Croce 2011 and Preqin, n.d.; see also the case studies in appendix A.
a. The Nigeria Sovereign Investment Authority's Nigeria Infrastructure Fund portfolio companies are listed in the case study (see appendix A).
b. Definitions vary slightly across the literature; this study draws on those of Della Croce (2011) and Preqin (n.d.).

- *Target geography*. Because a SIF must comply with a policy mandate, its target geography is typically consistent with the domicile and policy objective of the public sponsor(s). SIFs with sovereign sponsors usually prioritize investments in the sponsor's domestic market. In contrast, the geographic scope of SIFs backed by a multilateral public sponsor or a group of bilateral sponsors from different countries can be broader—for instance, covering a continent, a political or economic union of countries, or a specific set of countries. In the case studies, all SIFs backed by a national sponsor invest exclusively or predominantly in their domestic markets: FONSIS invests in Senegal, ISIF in Ireland, NIIF in India, and NSIA-NIF in Nigeria. ACP (backed by the ADB) has a pan-Asian mandate. Nonsovereign sponsors may still impose geographic restrictions. For instance, Marguerite funds—backed by the European Investment Bank and the development banks of several EU member states—allow no more than 20 percent to be invested in a single EU member state and no more than 5 percent in preaccession member states.[25] Some SIFs backed by a national sponsor can also invest abroad. Their foreign investments, however, must be consistent with the domestic policy mandate, and will most likely represent a fraction of the portfolio. For instance, ISIF can make foreign investments if they are on a commercial basis and can have a tangible economic impact in Ireland; examples include investments in foreign venture capital funds that commit to back Irish companies. Note also that some SIFs are allowed to invest excess liquidity in the international capital markets. These investments are for capital preservation purposes and need not comply with the double bottom line mandate. FONSIS, for instance, is allowed to invest up to 25 percent of its assets (net of statutory reserves) in liquid, creditworthy foreign securities (see the case study in appendix A).
- *Capital instruments*. The investment strategy should clearly specify the instruments of focus. Different layers of the capital structure have different risk/return profiles and require different investment procedures and contractual documentation. The composition and skills of the investment team vary accordingly. SIFs in principle can invest in any capital instrument, if the investments offer the potential for commercial returns and, in compliance with the additionality principle, address a capital gap in the mandated sectors. Direct investments could include senior and subordinated debt, equity, and various forms of mezzanine capital (see box 5.3 for brief definitions of these instruments). Indirectly, SIFs can also invest in funds that focus on these instruments. Like PCFs, mixed-capital SIFs, whose investors include institutional ones, may have to select either equity or debt as their primary focus, in line with the emergence of private equity and private debt as distinct asset classes.
- *Majority versus minority equity investments*. For SIFs that focus on direct equity investments, a critical element of the investment strategy is determining whether the fund can take majority or minority interests in portfolio companies (or has the flexibility to do both). The size of the ownership stake in a portfolio company is a key determinant of the level of activism of a fund, in addition to the structure of the investment and the jurisdiction in which the portfolio company is located (Invest Europe 2018). Table 5.2 provides a breakdown of target stakes of case study SIFs, and box 5.4 provides a breakdown of generally used investor protection provisions in shareholder agreements.

BOX 5.3

Definitions of capital instruments investible by strategic investment funds

Senior debt refers to the first debt to be repaid if the borrowing company defaults. It is the highest-ranking debt in the capital structure and therefore the safest for a lender. It can be secured by assets of the borrowing company, such as real estate or equipment.

Subordinated debt has lower rights to receive principal and interest payments from the borrower compared with the rights of the holders of senior debt. Although subordinated debt can sometimes be secured, in general lenders rely on the borrowing company's cash flows for repayment.

Equity refers to an ownership stake in the company. Equity holders have rights over a share of the

company's profits and vote at shareholder meetings. They are also the last to receive remuneration in the event of default or liquidation of the company. Equity is therefore the riskiest layer of a company's capital structure.

Mezzanine capital is senior only to the company's common equity. It can be structured as debt (typically deeply subordinated and unsecured) or as preferred equity. Preferred equity usually has preference in dividend payments, meaning that, if a company pays dividends, it must pay dividends on preferred equity before it does on common equity.

Source: Based on Preqin, n.d.

TABLE 5.2 **Majority vs. minority stakes as targeted by case study SIFs**

SIF	INVESTMENT STRATEGY WITH REGARD TO TARGET STAKES
Asia Climate Partners	Can take majority or significant minority equity stakes. Board representation is required in all investments.
FONSIS (Senegal)	Takes minority equity stakes, with board representation as a necessary condition. Typical stake is up to 33% of the portfolio company's capital.
Ireland Strategic Investment Fund	Generally, takes minority equity stakes, on broadly equal terms with private investors.
Marguerite Fund	Invests primarily in minority stakes.[a]
National Investment and Infrastructure Fund (India)	Master Fund aims primarily for control positions in platform companies. If it takes a minority stake, it seeks protection through board representation or contractual rights (for example, veto) over key decisions such as investments, capex, leverage, related-party transactions, dividends, and exit options.
Nigeria Sovereign Investment Authority – Nigeria Infrastructure Fund	No specific guidance provided as to target stake size.

Source: World Bank; see case studies in appendix A.
Note: FONSIS = Fonds Souverain d'Investissements Stratégiques (Sovereign Fund for Strategic Investments); SIF = strategic investment fund.
a. Its first fund (Marguerite I) was subject to a formal requirement not to invest in more than 50 percent of each project's equity. The second fund (Marguerite II) is not subject to any formal limitations in terms of stakes acquired.

- *Majority investment.* A majority ownership stake, including by extension full ownership, grants a fund a majority of the votes at a shareholder meeting and, with it, control of the board and key corporate decisions, such as the appointment of management. Private equity funds that focus on buyouts seek majority or full control of their portfolio companies. By acquiring control, they are free to implement operational and financial improvements that, if the strategy plays out, will result in an increase in company valuation by the time of exit.
- *Minority investment.* A minority ownership stake does not grant control over the target company's management, strategy, and operations. It is commonly featured in growth equity deals,[26] in which the target company

Investor protection provisions in shareholder agreements

In minority transactions, strategic investment funds must protect themselves against downside risks arising from lack of control through proactive engagement with the majority owner and careful negotiation of the shareholders agreement. Minority private equity owners need to invest in building a relationship with the majority owner, understand its motivations, anticipate potential areas of misalignment, and plan for both the ownership and exit phases (Schneider and Henrik 2015). In addition, several provisions of the shareholders agreement—the main contractual document disciplining the relationship between shareholders of a company—can be negotiated to ensure alignment of interests between minority and majority owners.

General investor protection provisions in shareholders agreements include the following.

- Right to approve key actions:
  - Minority shareholder's right to approve board actions in critical areas, for instance, issuing stock, incurring debt, and acquiring or selling significant assets.[a] For practical purposes, this veto right should not extend to the day-to-day operation of the company.
  - Supermajority provisions requiring a portion of the minority shareholders to also approve corporate actions such as a merger or the sale of substantially all of the company's assets.

- Subjecting amendments of the shareholders agreement to the approval of some or all minority shareholders.
- Restrictions to the transfer of shares, including
  - *Right of first refusal*, allowing any nonselling shareholders to buy the stake of a selling shareholder on the same terms offered by a third party;
  - *Tag-along right*, allowing the nonselling shareholders to force the selling shareholder to include their equity in the sale to a third party, on the same terms;
  - *Drag-along right*, allowing the selling shareholder or the board to require the other shareholders to sell their stakes to a third party;[b] and
  - *Put and call provisions*, giving a shareholder the right to sell its stake to the company or other shareholders (put), or allowing the company or certain shareholders the right to buy another shareholder's stake (call).
- Preemptive rights in case of issuance of new equity, giving shareholders the ability to maintain their proportionate stakes by buying additional shares at the same price offered to other shareholders or third parties.

Sources: Greenberger 2001; Hewitt 2021.
a. The approval may be unanimous or include a percentage vote of the minority shareholders.
b. This provision is usually required by the controlling shareholder as a counterbalance to the tag-along right, as a way to prevent minority shareholders from jeopardizing the sale of the company by refusing to participate (see Greenberger 2001).

raises new capital through the primary issuance of shares. Minority deals are more common in emerging market and developing economies, an important consideration for SIFs that operate there.[27] Minority deals have several attractions for SIFs. First, when minority deals result from new equity issuance,[28] SIFs have the opportunity to support companies in their growth trajectory (Schneider and Henrik 2015). Second, minority deals allow SIFs to participate, together with other investors, in larger transactions that they would not be able to finance exclusively.[29] Third, they may facilitate co-investments in the target company, fulfilling the SIF's crowding-in objective[30] and mitigating the risk of crowding out private investors.[31] Fourth, if a SIF catalyzes the involvement of a majority co-investor with strong operating expertise and industry track record, it can improve the performance of the portfolio company, leading to higher financial and economic returns.[32] Fifth, minority deals are less likely to have hidden flaws given that other investors take or maintain an economic interest in the company (Schneider and Henrik 2015). Finally, even as minority investors, SIFs can act as troubleshooters in investments that require a heavy interaction with the local government, in particular in the infrastructure sector (for example, see the Meridiam thematic review in appendix B).[33]

For sellers of minority stakes, minority investors can be attractive for their specific expertise and credibility, beyond their infusion of capital.[34] A professional minority investor, for instance, can bring knowledge of adjacent industry sectors or new growth markets, and support the professionalization of portfolio companies' governance. In addition, SIFs—as well-recognized investors with high-level government affiliations—can credentialize their portfolio companies with commercial and financial counterparts, such as clients in new markets or future providers of capital. For instance, ACP considers its affiliation with the ADB, UK Department for International Development, and Japan International Cooperation Agency (its main public backers) a strong advantage for fast-growing portfolio companies that seek credentials to expand to new countries and that may consider, down the line, an initial public offering. The required compliance with the ADB's ESG standards also enhances the credibility of ACP's portfolio companies.

- *Individual investment size.* The SIF's investment strategy may also provide an indicative size for individual investments, sometimes referred to as "ticket size." Ticket size varies widely across funds, reflecting several factors, including (1) typical target company size in the sectors and geographies of focus or, for indirect investments, the typical size of an investee fund; (2) the SIF's size (total capital committed by its investors); (3) the SIF's focus on majority or minority deals; and, importantly, (4) the SIF's portfolio diversification strategy, which is a core component of risk management, as discussed in the next section. Marguerite II, for instance, targets €20 million to €100 million tickets, which—depending on sector, geography, and leverage—translate into project sizes of €50 million to €2 billion (see the case study in appendix A).

- *Co-investment/joint investment strategy.* Given that the raison d'être of a SIF typically hinges on attracting commercial capital, the investment policy or investment strategy highlights the importance of co-investments and joint investments with external investors. A key element of ISIF's investment strategy, for instance, is to attract co-investment from third-party investors, with the original target being 2.0x (ISIF 2019). The crowding-in of capital is viewed as particularly important because it leverages ISIF's finite resources to significantly increase the economic impact in Ireland. Article 41.4d of the NTMA Act 2014 permits NTMA wide flexibility in entering partnerships and joint ventures using ISIF funds. In tandem, ISIF's July 2015 investment strategy highlights its focus on attracting co-investment partners to multiply the impact of investments in Ireland's economy.[35] Likewise, the NSIA Act 2011 (Article 46.1) allows NIF funds to be used to develop infrastructure projects in Nigeria via co-investment strategies. NSIA's investment policy elaborates that NSIA will set up vehicles to attract international and domestic capital (NSIA 2019, Article 4.3) and gives wide flexibility to the manager to co-invest with infrastructure players or enter into joint ventures as it deems appropriate (NSIA 2019, Article 7.1).

- *Vehicles for strategic alliances between sovereigns.* Although not usually included in the investment strategy, as sovereign funds, public capital SIFs in particular operate within the realm of geopolitics and can serve as convenient vehicles for strategic and commercial alliances between sovereigns. In December 2016, for instance, the governments of Morocco and Nigeria agreed to finance a regional gas pipeline project through their respective SIFs, Ithmar Capital and NSIA-NIF (Ithmar Capital 2016). Between 2017 and 2018, the Abu Dhabi Investment Authority and Singapore's Temasek agreed to invest in NIIF's Master Fund to finance Indian infrastructure (see the case study in appendix A). Academic research has also shown that, when compared with global institutional investors in general, SWFs tend to invest noticeably more in countries with which they have a cultural affinity, perhaps because they find less information asymmetry when investing in what is familiar (Chhaochharia and Laeven 2008). Such alliances are, however, deal-specific and not usually part of the investment strategy.

- *Direct versus indirect investing and internal versus external management.* SIFs can choose to provide capital directly to companies (direct investing) or indirectly, by investing in third-party funds that provide capital to companies (indirect investing). A SIF's investment strategy should specify to what extent and according to which criteria the fund can engage in direct or indirect investing. In addition, the Santiago Principles recommend that SWFs disclose information on funds being managed either internally or externally, including the selection and monitoring process for managers.[36]

Direct investing gives funds greater control over investment decisions and management of portfolio companies, which is important for funds that focus on domestic economic development, and allows SIFs and SWFs alike to avoid the fees charged by third-party fund managers and the dilution they cause to ultimate investor returns (Wright and Amess 2017).

Indirect investing, by contrast, allows SIFs and SWFs alike to benefit from the skills and established systems of third-party managers in specialized instruments and markets, and to manage or reduce the costs of maintaining an asset management function in a particular market or instrument. To capture opportunities in specific markets and instruments, SIFs—like some private equity funds of funds—may act as cornerstone investors for new and emerging fund managers (Preqin 2017). In addition, the presence of other commercial investors in the SIF's portfolio funds can amplify the capital multiplier effect, as discussed in chapter 2. SIFs engaged in indirect investing should determine whether and under which conditions they are allowed to co-invest in portfolio companies alongside their investee funds.[37] A SIF that engages in indirect investing needs to ensure that its investee funds comply with its policy mandate and apply the same or equivalent ESG criteria. For instance, NSIA-NIF evaluates all direct and indirect investments against the same list of key performance indicators (financial and development impact related). Similarly, in order to qualify for an ISIF investment, third-party funds must comply with ISIF's statutory requirement of commercial return and economic impact.

Note that SIFs run by an external fund manager, already remunerated with fees levied on the SIF's returns, may be disinclined to pay further return-diluting fees to third-party managers. For example, the Philippine Investment Alliance for Infrastructure, externally managed by infrastructure fund manager Macquarie, engages only in direct investing. Conversely, SIFs managed by an internal team whose remuneration has a greater fixed component may be more open to indirect investing, to capture the benefits discussed earlier. SIFs that are internally managed or whose public sponsor is invested in the fund manager—for example, FONSIS, ISIF, NIIF, and NSIA–NIF—commonly pursue indirect and direct investing.[38] Typically a SIF limits the amount of assets that can be delegated to an external manager. For example, the NSIA-NIF Investment Policy Statement permits NIF to use external managers as long as they do not manage over 50 percent of NIF assets (NSIA 2019, Article 7.2).

Several aspects of a SIF's investment policy and strategy are unique and unlike those of PCFs or SWFs. Unlike traditional SWFs formed as stabilization or savings funds, SIFs invest in privately traded assets. The SIF's double bottom line objective results in an investment policy unlike that of both PCFs and SWFs in that it simultaneously seeks financial and economic returns. The choices of geography and sector in the investment policy of a SIF are often driven by economic or policy considerations; for PCFs, these choices are entirely driven by commercial investment pipeline and return factors, as identified by the fund manager. SIFs' often-explicit crowding-in objective also sets such funds apart, differentiating their investment approach from PCFs. For instance, SIFs often focus on co-investment and minority investment strategies to facilitate capital mobilization, and explicitly avoid crowding out private capital. Marguerite II's minority investment strategy, for example, seeks to minimize crowding out private capital, unlike standard infrastructure funds that prefer full control. Through their investment choices, SIFs seek also to differentiate themselves from PCFs and provide additionality to the investment landscape. For instance, ISIF's investment strategy is to capitalize on its "key differentiating features of flexibility, long-term timeframe and credibility as a sovereign investment partner to fill investment gaps and enable transactions which would not otherwise easily be completed."[39] Similarly, NSIA-NIF's investment policy allows it to add value to the infrastructure landscape by acting as project developer and sponsor, or by building capacity among local institutional investors.[40] SIFs may also provide capacity building to their public sponsor. India's NIIF engages in proactive discussions with central and local government authorities to steer new infrastructure development to commercial models.[41] Finally, SIF investment strategies may also reflect unique advantages not typically found in PCFs. For instance, IFC [International Finance Corporation] Asset Management Company's funds have relied on cost efficiencies achieved through investing alongside the IFC, thus capitalizing on access to the IFC's proprietary pipeline. Conversely, SIF investment approaches may also contain restrictions resulting from being subject to an authorizing environment that does not apply to PCFs. For instance, as a government agency, ISIF must ensure that its investments do not breach EU State Aid rules that prohibit unfair financial support for private sector enterprises.[42]

RISK MANAGEMENT FRAMEWORK: KEY CONCEPTS

The risk management framework for a SIF is a system that identifies, measures, manages, and regularly tracks all relevant risks that could potentially inhibit the fund's success (European Union 2011).[43] The risk management framework is therefore a critical component of the overall governance and accountability framework for a SIF. Because the mandates and investment policies of SIFs vary widely, risk management frameworks are bespoke systems that reflect the DNA of the specific fund and its particular risk appetite. The risk policies for a traditional SWF that invests primarily in publicly traded investments will be markedly different from the policies of funds investing primarily in private markets (like SIFs). Likewise, and at a more granular level, the risk policies for a SIF that invests directly in physical infrastructure will assume different characteristics from one that invests in infrastructure through a fund of funds model.

High risk management standards are important not only to meet a fund's investment objectives but also to preserve legitimacy and maintain a stable, transparent, and open investment environment.[44] The legitimacy argument is particularly cogent for SIFs because of their affiliation with a public sponsor. It is also important because SIFs' ability to attract investments at the fund level and co-investments at the project level rests, among other factors, on their perception as professional and trusted investors.

A robust risk management system is an expected feature for alternative investment funds in the private sector and for SWFs based on accepted governance standards. Global PCF industry best practices, such as the EU Directive 2011/61/EU on Alternative Investment Fund Managers (hereinafter, EU AIFMD), which was established after the global financial crisis, place a premium on strong risk management frameworks for alternative investment funds both to stem the systemic risk they can pose to the financial sector and to ensure investors are better protected. SIFs set up under the the EU AIFMD framework—like Marguerite II—must therefore comply with the stringent standards articulated in the directive (see box 5.5 on key aspects of the EU AIFMD). Key risk management requirements applicable to SWFs, and consequently to most SIFs, are also spelled out in GAPP 22 of the Santiago Principles (see box 5.6 on the Santiago Principles related to risk). The requirements of the EU AIFMD and the Santiago Principles broadly converge except that—as expected for sovereign investment agencies—the Santiago Principles recommend public disclosure of the risk management framework, which is not typically a requirement for regulated PCFs. In addition, the EU AIFMD provides more detailed guidelines on aspects such as safeguarding the risk management function through an independent reporting structure and ensuring that remuneration structures do not cause excessive risk-taking behavior.

Risk management requirements are usually embedded in the investment policy of the SIF, articulated in ancillary risk-specific policy documents of the SIF, or imposed by the investment fund regulatory framework in force in the SIF's jurisdiction. The risk management framework is usually formalized in one or a series of policies and procedures, depending on the variety of risks to which the SIF is exposed. Note that elements of a SIF's risk policy will be articulated within its investment policy and managed through the fund's investment strategy, so there will be some overlaps between the two frameworks. Provisions in the investment policy and strategy, including investment limits and restrictions, highlight the public sponsor's risk tolerance and have an implicit investment risk management purpose. For instance, ISIF has adopted a Portfolio Diversification Framework for the Irish Portfolio that sets investment limits based on maximum exposure by sector and by risk category (IFSWF 2019).[45] Noninvestment risks, by contrast, may be addressed by separate policies, such as employee codes of

EU AIFMD key requirements on risk management

The European Union's Directive 2011/61/EU on Alternative Investment Fund Managers, referred to here as EU AIFMD, establishes the following key requirements related to risk management.

Remuneration. Article 13 of the EU AIFMD requires that remuneration practices do not encourage excessive risk-taking, and instead provide incentives for managing risk in line with the risk profile of the fund.

Risk management. Article 15 requires that alternative investment fund managers

- Establish risk management as a functionally and hierarchically separate unit from investment management and other units to allow for independence and prevent conflict of interest.
- Ensure that the risk profile of the fund is aligned to its objectives, investment strategy, size, and portfolio structure.

- Establish a robust risk management system that identifies, measures, mitigates, and monitors all relevant risks for each investment strategy by
  - Conducting robust and well-documented due diligence procedures in line with the investment strategy and risk profile of the fund when considering an investment;
  - Identifying, measuring, managing, stress testing, and monitoring risks with each investment position and their effect on the overall portfolio; and
  - Identifying and maintaining maximum leverage limits for each fund.
- Review the risk management system at least once a year and adjust as necessary.

Liquidity management. Article 16 requires that alternative investment fund managers establish a liquidity management system that assesses and monitors liquidity risk in line with obligations of the fund.

Note: This summary is based on the provisions of the EU AIFMD (https://eur-lex.europa.eu/legal-content/EN/TXT/PDF/?uri=CELEX:32011L0061&from=EN). The EU AIFMD is transposed into national law in member states of the EU.

Santiago Principles: Key risk principles for SWFs

The Santiago Principles include the following generally accepted principles and practices (GAPPs) related to sovereign wealth funds (SWFs) and risk:

GAPP 22. Principle
The SWF should have a framework that identifies, assesses, and manages the risks of its operations.

GAPP 22.1. Subprinciple. The risk management framework should include reliable information and timely reporting systems, which should enable the adequate monitoring and management of relevant risks within acceptable parameters and levels, control and incentive mechanisms, codes of conduct, business continuity planning, and an independent audit function.

GAPP 22.2. Subprinciple. The general approach to the SWF's risk management framework should be publicly disclosed.

Source: IWG 2008.
Note: SWF = sovereign wealth fund.

conduct, business continuity manuals, and ESG policies, to name a few. Such policies are ideally disseminated within the organization to create a strong risk management culture at all levels of seniority (Al-Hassan et al. 2013). For instance, NSIA's investment policy discloses concentration limits with respect to investing in infrastructure subsectors or projects, or the use of external managers.

In addition, it lays out its risk framework in ancillary documents,[46] and outlines professional and ethical standards in documents such as the Compliance Policy and Conflict of Interest Policy.[47] All funds managed by NIIF, as alternative investment funds regulated by India's capital market authority, must comply with the risk management and disclosure requirements of India's AIF regulations (2012).[48]

COMPONENTS OF THE RISK MANAGEMENT FRAMEWORK AND KEY ACTORS

The SIF's risk management framework performs the following key functions:

- *Clarifies risk appetite.* It articulates the fund's qualitative and quantitative risk appetite in line with its mandate, size, investment policy, and structure.
- *Identifies and measures risks.* It identifies and assesses (quantifying where possible) potential risks that may impede the success of the SIF.
- *Establishes a governance structure* for risk management and a set of procedures that can mitigate and monitor risks (European Union 2011).

The public sponsor's risk appetite is commonly articulated in a risk policy document. The risk tolerance of a SIF cannot be distilled into one indicator but is usually a composite of several indicators that capture the adverse outcomes to which the SIF could be susceptible.[49] These indicators are used to assign an acceptable level of risk (for example, an acceptable probability of capital loss) based on the stated purpose of the SIF and the risk profile of its public sponsor.[50] For instance, NSIA-NIF's Investment Policy Statement requires the fund to seek a long-term return target of more than 5 percent of the US Consumer Price Index, but also clarifies that the fund's investments must be diversified within the infrastructure sector; that it cannot commit more than 25 percent of total assets to any one project or manager; and that no more than 35 percent of total assets can be committed to any specific infrastructure sector in Nigeria (NSIA 2019).

The clarification of risk appetite serves multiple purposes, chief of which is to sensitize stakeholders to how the fund's performance should be evaluated. The articulation of risk appetite is important because it prepares the public sponsor and co-investors for potentially unfavorable factors that could undermine the SIF's success and jeopardize reaching the fund's stated objectives (Al-Hassan et al. 2013). The articulation of risk tolerance is also important so that short-term fluctuations do not steer the public sponsor off course (Al-Hassan et al. 2013). In addition, explicit communication of risk tolerance helps ensure that other agents in the SIF's authorizing environment do not thwart the SIF's mandate by acting on contradictory views of risk tolerance. For instance, as discussed in chapter 2, a key agent influencing many of China's government guidance funds (SIFs set up at the national, provincial, and municipal levels) is the State-Owned Assets Supervision and Administration Commission of the State Council, which assesses the funds according to its principles—oriented toward state-owned enterprises—of capital preservation and appreciation (McGinnis et al. 2017). Such principles can conflict with higher-risk-oriented investment strategies that may take years to bear fruit.

Like PCFs and SWFs, SIFs are exposed to a wide range of risks, which can be identified in two categories:

1. *Investment risks.* These are risks affecting a SIF's individual investments and
    its portfolio, which should be rewarded by commensurate expected returns
    when an investment is approved (Al-Hassan et al. 2013). Such risks include
    the following:
    –   *Market risk* (for example, interest rate, foreign currency, equity, and com-
        modity price risks affecting a portfolio company's prospects). These risks
        could result in either unrealized or realized losses (capital loss) to the
        portfolio of the SIF.
    –   *Credit risk* (for example, a company's creditworthiness and indebtedness
        level, counterparty risks).
    –   *Liquidity risk* (for example, the inability to quickly sell an investment and
        convert it into cash).[51]
    –   *Portfolio company risk.* Risks specific to a portfolio company's business
        model, sector, organizational structure (for example, loss of core
        executives), and ESG compliance.
    –   *Third party risk.* Risks occurring as a result of co-investments or joint
        ventures with parties that have diverging financial and strategic interests.

2. *Noninvestment risks.* These are operational, regulatory, and reputational risks
    affecting the entire operation of a SIF. Unlike financial risks, risks affecting
    the entire operation of a SIF will not be rewarded by higher investment
    returns and can be addressed only through mitigating measures (Al-Hassan
    et al. 2013).
    –   *Operational risk* is the risk of loss from breakdowns in a SIF's systems
        and procedures or from factors outside the SIF's control. Examples
        include staff-related risk (incompetence and fraud), business continuity
        risk, process risk, and technology risk.
    –   *Regulatory risks* stem from changes in the laws and regulations
        governing the operation of SIFs, or changes in the application of such
        laws and regulations.
    –   *Reputational risk* is the possibility that negative publicity regarding
        a SIF's conduct, whether real or perceived, may negatively
        affect investment returns, result in expensive litigation or loss
        of counterparties, or damage the home country government's
        international standing.
    –   *Political risk* is the risk SIFs face from both global and domestic
        political events (see NSIA [2018], Risk Management, for examples
        related to NSIA in particular). It may result from shifts in geopolitical
        currents that affect a SIF's ability to attract and retain strategic or
        sovereign-affiliated co-investors or from transformative domestic
        politics that threaten to upend the SIF's legitimacy or alter its strategic
        focus.

The SIF typically captures the specific risks to which it is susceptible through
a customized methodology that can systematically monitor, mitigate, and report
on investment- and portfolio-level risk. Such a methodology identifies the top
risks and where they originate, creates a scoring system that integrates both
quantifiable and nonquantifiable risks,[52] and assigns acceptable levels of risk as
benchmarks. For instance, NSIA has developed a bespoke tool, employed by
NSIA-NIF's infrastructure team, to assess ex ante the risks for all infrastructure
projects. The tool considers several quantitative and qualitative factors including a project's fit with NIF's mandate, integrity checks of project counterparts,

and any technical, commercial, and financial risks. Factors deemed medium or high risk are included in the investment memo for approval along with proposed actionable mitigants. Such a system can then be used to monitor and judge the risk level of a transaction before investment and of a portfolio company after investment (see, for example, the thematic review of CDP Equity in appendix B).

The SIF's risk management framework is articulated based on the delegated governance structure of the SIF and seeks to mainstream risk-consciousness throughout the organization. The variety of risks affecting a SIF may require the involvement and cooperation of other bodies, in addition to the risk manager. This consideration applies particularly to noninvestment risks, whose nature is very diverse.

The SIF's top decision-making body—the public sponsor or its delegate, the board—usually has the responsibility for articulating the fund's risk appetite, approving its risk management framework, and overseeing the management and monitoring of risks. For instance, Khazanah's Framework of Integrity, Governance and Risk Management, adopted by its board in 2004 and updated in 2018, includes a risk management policy and guide to manage risks.[53] Less frequently, the public sponsor may delegate the authority to articulate the fund's risk appetite to the manager. ISIF's manager, NTMA, developed the risk management policy and framework and also the risk appetite framework for ISIF,[54] likely because NTMA is part of the Irish government apparatus and is therefore considered a suitable proxy to elaborate on the sponsor's risk tolerance. Once the risk policy is adopted, a SIF's board may delegate part of its risk oversight function to a subcommittee of the board or management that monitors whether the SIF is adhering to risk governance and risk appetite criteria. For instance, at NSIA, the Board Risk Committee supports the board in overseeing the identification, management, and monitoring of risks.[55] At ISIF, the Audit and Risk Committee and the Enterprise Risk Management Committee, composed of NTMA management, support the NTMA board in its function of overseeing risk management.

Risk mitigation is then mainstreamed within the SIF's management, often characterized through a "three lines of defense" approach whereby each tier has a responsibility to interrogate investment or operational decisions according to their risk impact on the SIF.

- *Investment team.* The first line of defense is primarily anchored by the investment team, which performs due diligence in line with the fund's risk profile. The SIF's investment committee then provides oversight, assessing investment risks based on the respective analyses of the investment and risk teams, and adjudicates final approval. NSIA's risk management framework, for example, relies on a first line of defense consisting of the investment team and support services like finance, legal, and information technology. Risk assessment for NSIA-NIF transactions is performed in the due diligence phase, and results are included in the investment memo provided to the Executive Committee, Direct Investment Committee, and board for decision-making (see the case study in appendix A). NSIA-NIF's Direct Investment Committee is accountable for assessing the risks of investment projects brought before it, undertaking a holistic risk-benefit analysis during its deliberations.
- *Risk management team.* The second line of defense usually focuses on the SIF's risk management team. The risk management function defines clear risk guidelines and reporting procedures based on the SIF's investment policy and strategy. The risk management team usually assesses risk at the

investment level by participating with the investment team in the due diligence process and providing feedback to the SIF's investment committee. The influence of the risk manager on the approval of an investment will vary by SIF. In many SIFs, risk managers do not have formal veto power over investment decisions but can challenge the investment thesis articulated by the investment team. SIFs share this feature with PCFs, for which the risk manager acts primarily as a second line of defense, making sure that all risks are assessed and measured to the highest standards (Invest Europe 2018). Some risk managers may also have the ability to escalate certain decisions to higher bodies (see the thematic review on CDP Equity in appendix B).

Once the investment has entered the SIF's portfolio, the risk team monitors and periodically reports on the risks posed by the portfolio, using benchmarks and mitigation criteria. A SIF's risk manager may need support from external specialists when dealing with risks in areas such as legal and regulatory compliance, marketing and public relations, treasury, tax, financial crime, labor relations, or information technology (Invest Europe 2018).

As discussed earlier, to eliminate conflicts of interest, best practice exemplified by the rules of the EU AIFMD calls for a functionally and hierarchically independent risk management role. For instance, in compliance with this directive, Marguerite Investment Management has a dedicated executive in charge of risk management, who is not a member of the investment committee, to ensure separation of functions.

- *Internal audit and compliance.* The third line of defense in a SIF consists of the internal audit and compliance groups, which ensure respect for laws, regulations, and policies under which the SIF is expected to operate, including those related to risk exposure. Such groups also provide independent assessments to the SIF's board and relevant subcommittees of the board overseeing audit and risk.[56] For instance, NSIA-NIF's compliance function regularly monitors the fund's portfolio concentration limits and other constraints.[57] Similarly, ISIF's internal audit team provides independent, reasonable, and risk-based assurance to key stakeholders on the robustness of the NTMA's governance, risk management, and the design and operating effectiveness of the internal control environment (NTMA 2020; see the case study in appendix A).

KEY TAKEAWAYS

- The investment policy is constructed by the SIF owner or (by delegation) the board. The policy spells out the core parameters that the SIF needs to comply with in implementing its double bottom line mandate, such as eligible investments, investment horizon, return expectations, responsible investment policy, and performance monitoring framework.
- Distinguishing features of the SIF investment policy include (1) a focus on both financial and economic returns; (2) alignment with the public sponsor's overall vision for socioeconomic development; (3) a focus on privately traded investments; (4) the public sponsor's ability to retain discretion over aspects of the investment policy, for national interest or to reflect changing economic conditions; and (5) a responsible investment approach.
- The investment strategy is usually established through an iterative process between the sponsor or board and the manager. It translates the policy into detailed guidelines for the fund manager on permissible investments and

transaction structures. Core elements of the investment strategy include target sectors and geographies, admissible capital instruments, ability to take majority or minority stakes, size of individual investments, and co-investment strategy.

- Distinguishing features of the SIF investment strategy include (1) the flexibility to invest through a range of capital instruments, subject to the investment's ability to attract commercial returns and exhibit additionality; and (2) a focus on co-investment and minority investment strategies to facilitate capital mobilization and avoid crowding out private capital.

- The risk management framework for a SIF identifies, measures, manages, and regularly tracks all relevant risks that could potentially inhibit the fund's success. A robust risk management system is an expected feature for alternative investment funds in the private sector and for SWFs based on accepted governance standards.

- The SIF's risk management framework clarifies risk appetite, identifies and measures risks, and establishes a governance structure for risk management. The SIF typically captures the specific risks to which it is susceptible through a customized methodology that can systematically monitor, mitigate, and report on investment- and portfolio-level risk. Risk mitigation is mainstreamed within the SIF's management, often characterized through a three lines of defense approach whereby each tier has the responsibility to interrogate investment or operational decisions according to their risk impact on the SIF.

NOTES

1. Alsweilem and Rietveldt (2017) compare this strategy to Ulysses contracts, named after the story in the *Odyssey* in which Ulysses has his hands tied to the mast of the ship so that he cannot be lured by the sirens.
2. As the NIF Investment Policy Statement of April 2019 well states, "It establishes a structure of guidelines and policies within which the executive management can exercise their delegated authority and against which recommendations to the Direct Investments Committee (DIC) and Board can be judged."
3. See the Santiago Principles generally accepted principles and practices (GAPP), GAPP 18.3: "A description of the investment policy of the SWF should be publicly disclosed" (IWG 2008).
4. The policy must be reconfirmed annually by the board.
5. See the FONSIS case study (appendix A) and Article 13 of Law 2012-34: Authorizing the Creation of a Sovereign Fund of Strategic Investments (FONSIS), passed by the Senegal National Assembly on December 31, 2012.
6. Commercially sensitive information has been redacted for the version published online.
7. See Invest Europe (2018), which discusses parallel insights with respect to PCFs.
8. See Invest Europe (2018), which discusses parallel insights with respect to PCFs.
9. ISIF has published two investment strategies since its establishment. Establishment acts and other documents mentioned in this paragraph can be found in the reference lists of the respective case studies.
10. As noted in the thematic review on Meridiam (see appendix B), the presence of highly qualified professionals (ideally with an international background) on a SIF's investment team facilitates co-investments with international PCFs.
11. In the private equity sector, there is increasing evidence that fund investors value a manager's ability to demonstrate deep expertise in a focused field, in the belief that sector-specific knowledge will lead to better-informed investment decisions (Preqin 2015).

12. Note that 10 percent of NIF funds available for investment in any fiscal year must be invested in social infrastructure projects, even if those projects have less than favorable commercial returns.

13. See the Khazanah Nasional Berhad Santiago Principles Self-Assessment 2019 (https://www.ifswf.org/assessment/khazanah-nasional-berhad-2019).

14. This option was never exercised, however; see the Marguerite Fund case study in appendix A.

15. Article 3.4.6 of the NSIA Act 2011 says, "Given its long-term investment horizon, the Fund can maintain the dual objective of realizing a commercial return and investing in infrastructure which might otherwise not be financed and developed."

16. Article 11 of Law 2012-34 says, "Le FONSIS joue aussi son rôle d'investisseur socialement responsable en faisant des investissements et actions à but non lucratif." (In English: "FONSIS also plays its role of socially responsible investor by making not-for-profit investments and actions.")

17. The risk that the fund may become a forced seller of assets to meet cash obligations.

18. Per Article 43 of the NTMA Act 2014, the minister has the authority to direct the investment, management, and divestment of such "directed investments."

19. ISIF's initial strategy from establishment in December 2014 to the end of 2018 focused on "developing a broad-based portfolio across industry sectors, regions and asset classes" (see the case study in appendix A).

20. See the Marguerite Fund case study in appendix A. For more information on the Principles for Responsible Investment, see the website (https://www.unpri.org); for more on Marguerite's ESG compliance, see https://www.marguerite.com/sustainability/.

21. See the NIIF case study in appendix A and the NIIF website)https://www.niifindia.in/investing).

22. Organization by industry can facilitate (1) deal origination in that industry, (2) evaluation of deal opportunities when they arise, and (3) understanding whether and how to add value to those opportunities (Gompers, Kaplan, and Mukharlyamov 2015).

23. See the full text of the act at http://www.irishstatutebook.ie/eli/2014/act/23/enacted/en/pdf.

24. If they participate in greenfield investments, it is usually on an opportunistic basis, or limiting such investments to a small portion of their portfolio (see Della Croce 2011).

25. The latter number may be increased to 10 percent with Advisory Committee approval (see the Marguerite Fund case study in appendix A).

26. However, growth equity deals can also involve the acquisition of majority stakes by the new investors.

27. For a number of reasons: (1) the share of businesses that are family owned or controlled is very high in many developing countries, and family owners in developing countries are often reluctant to cash out of their businesses, partly because of lack of sophisticated capital markets in which to invest and diversify their wealth; (2) for political reasons, emerging market governments often opt to sell only minority stakes in state-owned enterprises; and (3) in some countries, regulation prevents foreign investors (who may be co-invested in the SIF) from acquiring control of local companies (see Schneider and Henrik 2015).

28. As opposed to secondary sales of shares by existing shareholders.

29. Large transactions are frequent in the infrastructure sector or in privatization processes.

30. Co-investors could include existing company shareholders that agree also to purchase company shares in a capital increase.

31. ISIF, for instance, primarily takes minority stakes and invests on terms broadly equal to those granted to other investors, such that the fund generates a multiplier effect but also complies with EU rules preventing unfair financial support to the private sector.

32. For instance, one of NIIF's core goals when it gave a controlling position to DP World in a port platform established by NIIF was to allow investee companies to benefit from the experience of a well-established port terminal owner and operator. NIIF retained a 35 percent stake (see the NIIF case study in appendix A).

33. Meridiam—a global infrastructure fund manager that co-invested with FONSIS, with Gabon's SIF (Fonds Gabonais d'Investissements Strategiques), and with Ghana's SIF (Ghana Infrastructure Investment Fund)—noted that partnering with a SIF can highlight the long-term commitment to the country of a private fund and solidify the latter's standing as a serious counterpart (for instance, in the negotiation of regulatory agreements). The SIF can facilitate the dialogue with government decision-makers and help projects

navigate political change, an important factor affecting long-term infrastructure investments. Meridiam noted how such benefits of partnering with a SIF play out regardless of the size of a SIF's investment in an infrastructure project. See the Meridiam thematic review in appendix B for further considerations on the cooperation between SIFs and infrastructure funds.

34. This is also true for investments made by private equity funds (as noted by Schneider and Henrik 2015).

35. See the NTMA 2015 Annual Report (https://www.ntma.ie/annualreport2015/ireland _strategic_investment_fund.html).

36. GAPP 18.2 states, "The investment policy should address the extent to which internal and/or external investment managers are used, the range of their activities and authority, and the process by which they are selected and their performance monitored" (IWG 2008, 8).

37. Some SWFs co-invest with private equity funds in order to reduce fees and to gain experience in initiating deals, in addition to obtaining greater operational control over portfolio companies (see Wright and Amess 2017).

38. ISIF, for instance, pursues large-value, low-volume transactions through direct investments, and higher-volume, smaller-value transactions primarily through third-party funds; as of December 2018, indirect investments represented approximately 72 percent of the capital committed to ISIF's Irish portfolio. As discussed earlier, in order to expand its reach to a broader set of infrastructure sectors and opportunities in India, NIIF launched a Fund of Funds exclusively dedicated to indirect investing.

39. From the NTMA Annual Report (https://www.ntma.ie/annualreport2015/ireland _strategic_investment_fund.html).

40. Section 3.7 of NSIA (2019) says that NISA-NIF "may take on the role of project sponsor and developer as well as investor"; and Section 4.6.5 says that it may "improve capacity and project structuring skills and experience among local sponsors and other key participants."

41. A NIIF team, the Strategy and Policy Group, comprising public-private partnership and investment experts, works with these authorities when it sees the opportunity to set up a public-private partnership project instead of building infrastructure through public finance means (see the case study in appendix A).

42. See the ISIF Santiago Principles Self-Assessment 2019 (https://www.ifswf.org/assessment /ireland-strategic-investment-fund).

43. In describing the risk-related guidelines for alternative investment funds (AIFs), the EU's Directive 2011/61/EU on Alternative Investment Fund Managers (AIFMs) refers to the risk management framework as follows: "AIFMs shall implement adequate risk management systems in order to identify, measure, manage and monitor appropriately all risks relevant to each AIF investment strategy and to which each AIF is or may be exposed."

44. Al-Hassan et al. (2013) discuss this aspect of risk management for SWFs, but it is equally applicable to SIFs.

45. ISIF avoids the standard statistical approach to building portfolios, for example, calculating the correlation between categories or sectors, because it believes that lack of reliable Irish private markets data makes this approach unsound.

46. Such as a Market Risk Framework, Operational Risk Framework, Market Risk Management Policy, and Operational Risk Management Policy. See the NSIA Santiago Principles Self-Assessment 2019 (https://www.ifswf.org/assessment/nsia-self-assessment-2019).

47. See the NSIA Santiago Principles Self-Assessment 2019 (https://www.ifswf.org /assessment/nsia-self-assessment-2019).

48. See the Securities Exchange Board of India's page on AIF regulations (https://www.sebi .gov.in/legal/regulations/jun-2018/securities-and-exchange-board-of-india-alternative -investment-funds-regulations-2012-last-amended-on-april-17-2020-_34621.html).

49. See the discussion of SWFs in Al-Hassan et al. (2013), which also applies to SIFs.

50. See the discussion of SWFs in Al-Hassan et al. (2013), which also applies to SIFs.

51. NSIA (2019), for instance, notes that "the returns of a long-term portfolio can be undermined if the Fund becomes a forced seller of risk assets at an inopportune time in order to meet cash obligations, and policy will be designed to avoid this."

52. Qualitative risks may be measured using scales.

53. "The FIGR [Framework of Integrity, Governance and Risk Management] includes a Risk Management Policy, Schedule of Matters for the Board ("SMB"), Limits of Authority ("LOA") for the Management, a Code of Conduct and the appropriate policies and

procedures which guide our employees in their actions and behaviour." See the Khazanah Nasional Berhad Santiago Principles Self-Assessment 2019 (https://www.ifswf.org /assessment/khazanah-nasional-berhad-2019); see also the organization's "Who We Are" web page (https://www.khazanah.com.my/who-we-are/corporategovernance).

54. See the ISIF Santiago Principles Self-Assessment 2019 (https://www.ifswf.org/assessment /ireland-strategic-investment-fund).

55. See the NSIA Santiago Principles Self-Assessment 2019 (https://www.ifswf.org /assessment/nsia-self-assessment-2019).

56. See discussion on SWFs and internal audit and compliance in Hammer, Kunzel, and Petrova (2008).

57. Such as not providing guarantees to any infrastructure project, other than wholly owned subsidiaries or affiliates of NSIA (see the case study in appendix A).

REFERENCES

ADB (Asian Development Bank). 2012. "Proposed Equity Investment: Philippine Investment Climate Public-Private Partnership Fund." Report and Recommendation of the President to the Board of Directors, Project No. 45918, ADB, Manila. https://www.adb.org/sites/default /files/project-document/60119/45918-01-reg-rrp.pdf.

Al-Hassan, Abdullah, Michael Papaioannou, Martin Skancke, and Cheng Chih Sung. 2013. "Sovereign Wealth Funds: Aspects of Governance Structures and Investment Management." IMF Working Paper 13/231, International Monetary Fund, Washington, DC. https://www .imf.org/en/Publications/WP/Issues/2016/12/31/Sovereign-Wealth-Funds -Aspects-of-Governance-Structures-and-Investment-Management-41046.

Alsweilem, Khalid, and Malan Rietveld. 2017. *Sovereign Wealth Funds in Resource Economies: Institutional and Fiscal Foundations.* New York: Columbia University Press.

Chhaochharia, Vidhi, and Luc Laeven. 2008. "The Investment Allocation of Sovereign Wealth Funds." https://www.researchgate.net/publication/228206712_The_Investment _Allocation_of_Sovereign_Wealth_Funds.

Della Croce, Raffaele. 2011. "Pension Funds Investment in Infrastructure: Policy Actions." OECD Working Paper on Finance, Insurance and Private Pensions 13. Organisation for Economic Co-operation and Development, Paris.

European Union. 2011. "Directive 2011/61/EU of the European Parliament and of the Council of 8 June 2011 on Alternative Investment Fund Managers and amending Directives 2003/41 /EC and 2009/65/EC and Regulations (EC) No 1060/2009 and (EU) No 1095/2010." *Official Journal of the European Union* L 174, 1.7.2001. https://eur-lex.europa.eu/legal-content/EN /TXT/PDF/?uri=CELEX:32011L0061&from=EN.

Gompers, Paul, Steven N. Kaplan, and Vladimir Mukharlyamov. 2015. "What Do Private Equity Firms Say They Do?" Working Paper 15-081, Harvard Business School, Boston. https://www .hbs.edu/faculty/Publication%20Files/15-081_9baffe73-8ec2-404f-9d62-ee0d825ca5b5.pdf.

Greenberger, James J. 2001. "Minority Investor Rights in Private Equity Transactions." *Journal of Private Equity* 4 (2): 47–53.

Halland, Håvard, Michel Noël, Silvana Tordo, and Jacob J. Kloper-Owens. 2016. "Strategic Investment Funds: Opportunities and Challenges." Policy Research Working Paper 7851, World Bank, Washington, DC. https://openknowledge.worldbank.org/bitstream /handle/10986/25168/WPS7851.pdf?sequence=5&isAllowed=y.

Hammer, Cornelia, Peter Kunzel, and Iva Petrova. 2008. "Sovereign Wealth Funds: Current Institutional and Operational Practices." IMF Working Paper 08/254, International Monetary Fund, Washington, DC. https://www.imf.org/external/pubs/ft/wp/2008 /wp08254.pdf.

Hewitt, Christopher J. 2021. "A Shareholders Agreement Primer: The Corporate Pre-Nuptial Agreement." *VC-List*, June 13, 2021. http://vc-list.com/shareholders-agreement-primer/.

IFSWF (International Forum of Sovereign Wealth Funds). 2019. "Santiago Principles Self-Assessment: Ireland Strategic Investment Fund." IFSWF. https://www.ifswf.org/assessment /ireland-strategic-investment-fund.

Invest Europe. 2018. "Invest Europe Handbook of Professional Standards." Invest Europe, Brussels. https://www.investeurope.eu/media/1022/ie_professional-standards-handbook-2018.pdf.

ISIF (Ireland Strategic Investment Fund). 2015. "Investment Strategy: Executive Summary." National Treasury Management Agency. http://isif.ie/wp-content/uploads/2016/03/ISIFInvestmentStrategyExecutiveSummaryJuly2015.pdf.

ISIF (Ireland Strategic Investment Fund). 2019. "Investment Strategy 2.0: Towards 2040—Investing Commercially and with Substantial Impact." National Treasury Management Agency. https://isif.ie/uploads/publications/ISIF-Investment-Strategy.pdf.

Ithmar Capital. 2016. "Morocco and Nigeria Announce Trans-African Pipeline, New Regional Gas Pipeline to Develop West African Economy." *PR Newswire*, December 5, 2016. https://www.prnewswire.co.uk/news-releases/morocco-and-nigeria-announce-trans-african-pipeline-new-regional-gas-pipeline-to-develop-west-african-economy-604733586.html.

IWG (International Working Group of Sovereign Wealth Funds). 2008. "Sovereign Wealth Funds Generally Accepted Principles and Practices: 'Santiago Principles.'" IWG. https://www.ifswf.org/sites/default/files/santiagoprinciples_0_0.pdf.

McGinnis, Patrick, Shanthi Divakaran, Jing Zhao, and Yi Yan. 2017. "Government and Venture Capital in China: The Role of Government Guidance Funds." Background paper for *Innovative China: New Drivers of Growth*. Washington, DC: World Bank.

Mulder, Christian, Amadou Sy, Yinqiu Lu, and Udaibir Das. 2009. "Setting Up a Sovereign Wealth Fund: Some Policy and Operational Considerations." IMF Working Paper 2009/179, International Monetary Fund, Washington, DC.

NSIA (Nigeria Sovereign Investment Authority). 2018. "Enabling Sustainable Growth: Making an Impact on Nigeria's Future." Annual Report & Accounts 2018, NSIA, Abuja. https://nsia.com.ng/-nsia/sites/default/files/downloads/NSIA%20Annual%20Report%202018.pdf.

NSIA (Nigeria Sovereign Investment Authority). 2019. "Infrastructure Fund Investment Policy Statement As Approved on April 6, 2019." NSIA, Abuja. https://nsia.com.ng/-nsia/sites/default/files/downloads/Nigeria%20Infrastructure%20Fund%20Investment%20Policy%20Statement%20-%20April%2016%202018_0.pdf.

NTMA (National Treasury Management Agency). 2020. "NTMA Annual Report and Financial Statements 2019." NTMA, Dublin. https://www.ntma.ie/annualreport2019/downloads/8953-NTMA-Annual-Report-2019-Risk-Management.pdf.

Preqin. 2015. "Performance of Sector-Specific vs. Generalist Buyout Funds." *Private Equity Spotlight* 11 (5): 3. https://docs.preqin.com/newsletters/pe/Preqin-PESL-June-15-Performance-Comparison-of-Buyout-Funds.pdf.

Preqin. 2017. "Preqin Special Report: Private Equity Funds of Funds." Preqin. https://docs.preqin.com/reports/Preqin-Special-Report-Private-Equity-Funds-of-Funds-November-2017.pdf.

Preqin. No date. "Preqin Pro: Glossary of Terms." Preqin Ltd. https://docs.preqin.com/pro/Preqin-Glossary.pdf.

PwC. 2016. "Sovereign Investors 2020: A Growing Force." PwC. https://www.pwc.com/gx/en/sovereign-wealth-investment-funds/publications/assets/sovereign-investors-2020.pdf.

Schneider, Antoon, and Cristina Henrik. 2015. "Private-Equity Minority Investments, Can Less Be More?" The Boston Consulting Group, April 2, 2015. https://www.bcg.com/en-us/publications/2015/private-equity-minority-investments-can-less-be-more.

World Bank Group and DRC (Development Research Center of the State Council, People's Republic of China). 2019. *Innovative China: New Drivers of Growth*. Washington, DC: World Bank.

Wright, Mike, and Kevin Amess. 2017. "Sovereign Wealth Funds and Private Equity." In *The Oxford Handbook of Sovereign Wealth Funds*, edited by Douglas Cumming, Geoffrey Wood, Igor Flatotchev, and Juliane Reinecke. Oxford, U.K.: Oxford University Press.

6 Investment Process

INTRODUCTION

This chapter discusses the investment process of a strategic investment fund (SIF). Whereas chapter 5 details the process of establishing a SIF's investment policy and strategy, this chapter discusses the practical implementation of the investment framework of a SIF. Because SIFs are primarily equity investors, the investment process discussed in this chapter relates to unlisted equity investments.

A SIF's investment process is a subset of its governance framework, establishing guidelines and procedures to effectively implement the investment strategy and to ensure that the double bottom line mandate is met. The provisions of the investment process cover the whole life span of an investment in unlisted securities, which can be categorized in the following five phases: origination, evaluation, execution, ownership and supervision, and exit (see figure 6.1 for a schematic description). Each component of the investment process is discussed in a dedicated section below.

A diligent characterization of the SIF's investment process serves several purposes. The investment process guides the activities of the internal or external fund manager appointed to manage the SIF. A well-defined investment process allows the public sponsor to better supervise the SIF and improves public accountability. As stated in the generally accepted principles and practices (GAPP) set out in the Santiago Principles, "there should be clear and publicly disclosed policies, rules, procedures, or arrangements in relation to the SWF's general approach to funding, withdrawal, and *spending* operations" (IWG 2008, GAPP 4; emphasis added). A clear-cut investment process will ensure that the same analytical rigor is applied in evaluating and executing investments across a broad and evolving opportunity set as the SIF's policy mandates evolve. Outlining the investment process up front ensures that the investment team is required to apply rigor in evaluating, executing, and managing investments that may have lower financial returns but are justified by high economic returns. By establishing a clear investment process, a SIF reduces the risk that any misalignment of

FIGURE 6.1

Phases of the SIF's investment process

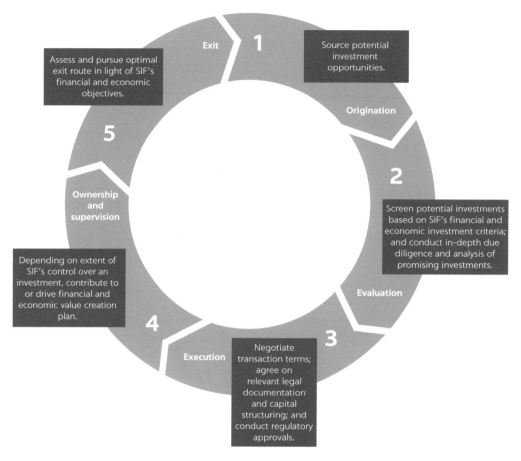

Source: World Bank; see case studies in appendix A.
Note: This figure depicts phases of the SIF's investment process related to unlisted equity investments. SIF = strategic investment fund.

incentives translates into suboptimal investment decisions.[1] The investment process also informs some of the structural elements of the fund, such as size, composition, and skill sets of teams (Invest Europe 2018). For mixed capital SIFs, a well-disciplined investment process is an important component of the fund's marketing efforts and materials (Invest Europe 2018). It provides transparency and confidence to investors that the fund manager will follow effective procedures to achieve the return objectives included in the investment strategy. In addition, a SIF with a well-disciplined investment process is likely to be perceived as a more efficient and reliable counterpart by private capital funds (PCFs) that may seek to co-invest with it.

The fund manager or senior members of the investment team typically drive the definition of the investment process, which is then formulated within the investment strategy or in ancillary documents. Defining the investment process requires a pragmatic understanding of, and expertise in, unlisted investments and related best practices. This requirement affects the choice of the body responsible for establishing the investment process. In mixed capital SIFs, the primary responsibility falls with the fund manager, in consultation with the public sponsor, as it does for the definition of the investment strategy.

In public capital SIFs, senior members of the investment team will most likely drive the definition of the investment process, subject to ultimate approval by the SIF's public sponsor. The investment process is usually formalized in the same document as the investment strategy. Mixed capital SIFs will formulate the investment process in a private placement memorandum; public-capital SIFs will lay out the investment process in ancillary documentation to the establishment act, as determined by a country's jurisdiction and the fund's legal framework.

INVESTMENT ORIGINATION

Investment origination, one of the core functions performed by the SIF's investment team, consists of sourcing potential investments that fit the fund's financial and economic return goals. A SIF's origination process, although sharing commonalities with that of PCFs, also presents distinctive features because of the SIF's affiliation with the public sponsor and potential to unlock opportunities through that affiliation. The following discussion first describes the origination routes common to SIFs and PCFs, and then focuses on those distinctive to SIFs.

SIFs rely on a variety of routes, also common to PCFs, to originate investments. These routes include the following.

- *Passive sourcing.* Potential investments are presented to the SIF by financial intermediaries, such as investment banks, which approach potential buyers on behalf of a company's shareholders (sometimes in the context of a formal auction) (Bain & Company 2017), or by other funds seeking co-investors in deals they have identified.[2] The SIF's credibility as a professional market operator and its track record of closing deals will increase its chances of being approached by such intermediaries.
- *Proactive sourcing.* The fund self-generates potential investment opportunities—often referred to as proprietary deals—leveraging the expertise and network of its investment team and formal and informal advisers, and its presence on the ground in the target market.[3] For example, in 2016, Singaporean SIF Temasek created formal advisory panels consisting of well-connected senior executives in Europe and the United States[4] to seek investment opportunities and advise on activities (Temasek 2016; Wells 2016). Proactive sourcing through tapping into institutional or temporary networks[5] may provide a fruitful origination route for newly launched SIFs focusing on investments overlooked by existing investors and intermediaries. Funds can also source additional investment opportunities by partnering with corporate acquirers that can share the benefits of their market position, infrastructure, potential synergies, and industry experience in return for a SIF's financial firepower and network.[6]
- *Cross-pollination,* a derivative of proactive sourcing whereby the investment team seeks to replicate successful investment theses and structures in new sectors or geographies (compatible with the fund's target universe). Collaboration and communication across the different sectoral and geographic teams of a fund will contribute to successful cross-pollination (Bain & Company 2017).

SIFs also access origination routes not commonly found in PCFs because of the public sponsor's access to target markets and the SIF's long investment horizon, which allows the fund to develop early-stage projects. These routes include the following.

- *The public sponsor proposes investment opportunities through formal or informal agreement.* Whether the SIF's sponsor proposes investments through a formal or informal agreement, it is crucial that the SIF retain full independence over investment decisions. Asia Climate Partners (ACP), for instance, occasionally receives investment proposals from its public sponsor, the Asian Development Bank, but maintains full discretion over investment decisions (see ACP case study in appendix A). A formal agreement to propose investment opportunities, if in place, should establish transparent procedures. The agreement may impose restrictions to ensure that the SIF is not administratively overburdened by less than robust proposals or steered toward unviable investments. For instance, in a public capital SIF, the agreement may (1) limit the number of government entities eligible to submit proposals, to avoid overloading the SIF with low-quality projects that lack support at the top echelons of relevant ministries; (2) specify a minimum level of documentation required for a proposal to be considered; and (3) include an obligation for the SIF to review all eligible proposals, avoiding favoritism toward certain government entities. Box 6.1 summarizes the provisions of such a formal agreement in place at the Nigeria Sovereign Investment Authority's Nigeria Infrastructure Fund (NSIA-NIF).
- *The SIF pitches to the public sponsor investment opportunities that require the sponsor's active cooperation.* For instance, India's National Investment and

---

BOX 6.1

Formalizing the process for investment proposals by the public sponsor: The NSIA-NIF example

The Nigeria Sovereign Investment Authority (Establishment, etc.) Act, 2011 (NSIA Act 2011) requires the Nigeria Infrastructure Fund (NIF) to review and analyze against the criteria of financial return all written proposals submitted to it by the Nigerian federal government and any state or local government.[a]

Investment proposals must be submitted in formal letters for consideration by NSIA-NIF. Before being sent to NSIA-NIF, such written proposals are usually approved at very senior levels in the presidential office, ministries, or other government bodies—ensuring that NSIA-NIF is not overloaded with requests that have little strategic priority for the government.

Upon receiving a written proposal, NSIA-NIF is required to review it, regardless of the government entity submitting it. The investment decision-making process is the same as for any other investment considered by NSIA-NIF, including three levels of due diligence and screening by the investment team, review and approval by the executive committee and direct investment committee, and—in the best scenario—final approval by the NSIA-NIF board.

NSIA-NIF independently analyzes investment proposals received from government entities and is free to reject transactions that do not meet its financial return requirements.

Source: World Bank; see NSIA-NIF case study in appendix A.
a. Article 41.4 of the NSIA Act 2011 says, "The Authority shall review and analyse against criteria of financial return all written proposals of the Federal Government, State Government, Federal Capital Territory, Local Government, and Area Councils submitted to the Authority and the Authority shall issue appropriately detailed parameters and procedures for the submission of such proposals."

Infrastructure Fund (NIIF) engages in proactive discussions with central and local government authorities to steer new infrastructure development to commercial business models, if they make sense. A team within NIIF, the Strategy and Policy Group, comprising public-private partnership and investment experts, works with these authorities when it sees the opportunity to set up a public-private partnership project instead of building infrastructure through public finance means. As an independent commercial entity, however, NIIF has no formal right to any infrastructure project that the government may consider developing, nor does it have the obligation to invest in policy-driven projects. The public sponsor may also use the government apparatus to facilitate the sourcing of certain deals. For example, Indian missions abroad are apprised of NIIF activities and can facilitate cross-border strategic alliances.

• *The SIF invests in developing early-stage investments that do not immediately generate a cash flow and may take longer to exit.* For instance, Senegal's FONSIS (Fonds Souverain d'Investissements Stratégiques, or Sovereign Fund for Strategic Investments) is explicitly mandated to act as project developer (see box 6.2). NSIA-NIF is also proactive in project development: of eight projects closed in the first half of 2018, half were sourced and developed by the NSIA-NIF investment team (the rest were brought to NSIA-NIF's attention by external sponsors). SIFs may also pursue multiple origination routes, as shown in box 6.3, which describes the multifaceted origination approach of Africa50, a SIF that develops and invests in infrastructure projects across Africa.

BOX 6.2

FONSIS: Originating investment opportunities as a project developer

The investment strategy of Senegal's FONSIS (Fonds Souverain d'Investissements Stratégiques, or Sovereign Fund for Strategic Investments) explicitly envisages that the fund develops strategic investment projects to attract investment partners. In such capacity, FONSIS prioritizes greenfield projects and is often the very first source of capital, well before any other commercial source.

For example, in its developer role, FONSIS, together with the International Finance Corporation (as part of the its Scaling Solar program), led the early-stage development of two solar power plants located in Kael (Diourbel) and Kahone (Kaolack). As part of its mandate to hold Senegalese interests in the project, FONSIS actively participated in the project's structuring, coordinated with relevant government stakeholders, and was involved, as an investor, in negotiating the financing package.

It was estimated that these solar projects would have a cumulative nominal capacity of 60 megawatts

and would represent 37 percent of the total installed solar capacity in Senegal when finalized. The cost for the two projects totaled €47.5 million. FONSIS contributed cash equity and some subordinated debt (in the form of quasi equity), and it holds a minority stake of 20 percent in both projects. A consortium composed of Meridiam, a global infrastructure fund based in Paris, and Engie Development, selected as the project's private developer after tender adjudication, contributed the rest of the equity. A pool of lenders comprising the European Investment Bank, the International Finance Corporation, and French development finance institution Proparco provided commercial loans. The projects will sell power to national utility company Senelec under a 25-year power purchase agreement. The projects also benefit from a government guarantee covering Senelec's obligations under the power purchase agreement.

Source: World Bank; see FONSIS case study in appendix A.

BOX 6.3

Africa50's multifaceted investment origination strategy

Africa50, a strategic investment fund launched in 2015 by the African Development Bank (AfDB), has the mandate to improve infrastructure in Africa by developing bankable projects and catalyzing investments, leverage public funds to raise private capital from long-term institutional investors, and operate commercially with an appropriate financial return while promoting economic development. Africa50 is a legally and financially independent entity owned by 28 African governments, two African central banks, and AfDB. At the time of writing, it had received over US$870 million in committed capital.

Africa50 pursues multiple routes to originate investments:

- *Thesis-driven screening.* Through a combination of data analysis, country studies and visits, and networking with governments and other funds, Africa50 is able to narrow the origination effort to specific sectors and regions.
- *Participation in the infrastructure investing ecosystem.* Africa50's investment team has a strong background in infrastructure investing in

Africa and an extensive network, which result in frequent investment solicitations from other market participants.
- *Connections to government and development institutions.* Africa50 receives investment proposals for consideration from the many African governments to which it is affiliated, as well as from AfDB. AfDB, in particular, proposes equity investments in projects to which it is a provider of senior debt. No formal agreement or obligation is in place for Africa50 to invest in deals presented by its sponsors, and the fund can also invest in African countries that are not among its shareholders.
- Africa50 has its own *project development operation*, under a stand-alone business line that absorbs approximately 10 percent of committed capital (the remaining 90 percent being dedicated to project finance). In this capacity, Africa50 typically commits low single-digit million dollar amounts for early-stage project development, in exchange for equity. It can also top up its equity investment through subsequent cash injections.

Sources: Africa50 website (https://www.africa50.com) and management interview.

INVESTMENT EVALUATION

A SIF's evaluation process siphons potential investments on the basis of their ability to deliver both financial and economic returns in compliance with the double bottom line mandate. The evaluation process progressively narrows the search from a large number of potential investment opportunities to a small number of particularly promising ones, which are subject to in-depth due diligence. If the opportunity passes the due diligence criteria, it is ultimately presented for approval to the SIF's decision-making body. This process is not unlike that of PCFs, which screen a vast number of investments before executing a handful each year. For every 100 opportunities considered, the average private equity investor deeply investigates fewer than 24, signs an agreement with fewer than 14, and closes only 6 deals (based on Gompers, Kaplan, and Mukharlyamov 2015). The fund devotes considerable effort and resources to evaluating transactions even if it will ultimately invest in only a very few.

The SIF's investment team screens investments and conducts due diligence, and the fund's investment committee or equivalent investment decision-making body provides advice and consent. The exact method varies between funds.

Some SIFs conduct screening and due diligence in different phases, with increasing staff commitment (in number or seniority) at each stage. In funds with a separate risk team, that team may be involved in the screening process from the early stages, as discussed in the previous chapter in the section on risk management. The SIF usually engages external advisers—such as legal, accounting, tax, and other consulting firms—to support specific aspects of due diligence. At the end of the evaluation process, the investment team summarizes its findings and recommendations in an investment memorandum, which is submitted to the SIF's decision-making body (for example, the investment committee or board) as the basis for investment approval or rejection. The investment memorandum not only provides a written record of the information considered in the evaluation process but also contains the core investment thesis against which the success of an investment will be measured during regular reviews (Invest Europe 2018). If the decision-making body requires further analysis and evaluation before a decision, revisions of the investment memorandum may be necessary (Invest Europe 2018). Figure 6.2 shows the example of NSIA-NIF, which conducts three levels of sequenced analysis before an investment is presented to the NSIA board for approval.

The purpose of in-depth investment due diligence—in PCFs and SIFs alike— is to obtain an in-depth understanding of the target company's prospects, the investment risks, the potential for financial returns, and ultimately the exit opportunities for the fund. Areas of investigation during the due diligence process include, subject to industry-specific adaptations (Invest Europe 2018), the following: the financial position of the target company; the quality of its management team; the sector(s) and geography(ies) of operation; technology and research and development efforts; protection of intellectual property rights; important regulations affecting the business; contractual arrangements with customers, suppliers, and other counterparts; pension liabilities; environmental, social, and governance (ESG) considerations; litigation risks; and insurance coverage. During due diligence the investment team also tests the company business plan's assumptions and evaluates investment risks and return prospects. The SIF's investors, regulators, and other stakeholders, as applicable, may require the team to carry out further checks, for instance, to ensure that the

FIGURE 6.2

NSIA-NIF investment evaluation process and responsibilities

Source: World Bank; see NSIA-NIF case study in appendix A.
Note: NSIA-NIF = Nigeria Sovereign Investment Authority – Nigeria Infrastructure Fund.

BOX 6.4

ISIF's adherence to double bottom line mandate through investment evaluation process

The Ireland Strategic Investment Fund (ISIF) evaluates all its investments according to three economic impact criteria, which are a precondition for any investment to be submitted to the investment committee for approval: (1) high additionality, (2) low displacement, and (3) low deadweight. See box 2.1 for a definition of these terms.

The process is as follows. First, the investment professionals in charge of studying a certain deal start an economic impact scorecard, filling in basic data such as revenue and employment potential. Next, ISIF's ad hoc economic impact team provides input into the scorecard. In parallel, the investment team produces a full investment proposal for the investment committee. The economic impact scorecard is sent for review

to an Economic Impact Implementation Group, which comprises ISIF's head of investment strategy, the chief economist of the National Treasury Management Agency (the public agency that controls and manages ISIF), and other members of the ISIF Investment Strategy Team and the National Treasury Management Agency Economics Unit. After review by the Economic Impact Implementation Group, the economic impact scorecard is submitted to the Portfolio Management Committee as part of the overall investment proposal. If approved by that committee, the proposal is submitted to the Investment Committee for consideration and, if thought fit, approval.

Source: World Bank; see ISIF case study in appendix A.

investment complies with relevant anti-money-laundering, anticorruption, or antibribery regulations (Invest Europe 2018).

SIFs are distinct from PCFs in their need to evaluate the prospective investment's compliance with the fund's economic impact criteria and objectives, in line with the double bottom line mandate. Compliance with the double bottom line is additional to ESG due diligence, which many PCFs also conduct in application of their own ESG policy or as required by their investors.[7] Some SIFs may employ feasibility studies to vet projects that meet the double bottom line requirement. For instance, as mentioned earlier in this publication, up to 10 percent of NIF capital available for investment in any fiscal year can be invested in social infrastructure projects[8] that may present less favorable financial return potential. As discussed in chapter 2, these potential Development Projects are submitted for approval to a committee set up by the National Economic Council,[9] and comprehensive feasibility studies must demonstrate the economic merit of the proposed project. Likewise, the Ireland Strategic Investment Fund (ISIF) follows a disciplined process to ensure that investments comply with the fund's economic impact criteria before they are submitted to the investment committee for the final investment decision (see box 6.4). Similarly, the board of FONSIS prescreens investment projects for their compliance with Plan Sénégal Emergent, a government plan for the structural transformation and growth of the Senegalese economy, which FONSIS is mandated to support. Once a project passes such screening and is ultimately approved by the board, FONSIS's investment committee implements the investment decision.

INVESTMENT EXECUTION

Once the SIF's decision-making body has approved a transaction, the investment team proceeds with negotiating and signing relevant transaction documents.

Commercial terms to be negotiated in transaction documents

Invest Europe (formerly the European Private Equity and Venture Capital Association) recommends that the documentation signed to acquire a portfolio company reflect the following commercial matters (terms will vary depending on whether a majority or minority interest is acquired):

- Ownership and control of the portfolio company after investment
- Share transfers (mandatory, permitted, and prohibited) and preemption rights
- Incentives for and obligation of the management team of the portfolio company
- Division of managerial responsibilities after investment

- Warranties, representations, and indemnities
- Investment performance milestones and any future obligations to provide further funding
- Board and shareholder consents required before the company takes specified actions
- Agreements with lenders to the portfolio company and intercreditor arrangements
- Quality, quantity, and frequency of information to be provided by the portfolio company
- Exit provisions such as tag-along and drag-along rights (see box 5.4 in chapter 5)
- Commitment by the portfolio company's management to comply with environmental, social, and governance practices

Source: Invest Europe 2018.

The transaction documents need to fully reflect the commercial terms agreed on between the SIF and its counterparts, in particular other shareholders (if any) and the management of the portfolio company. Box 6.5 summarizes the most important commercial terms. Transaction documents include

- A sale and purchase agreement between the fund and the seller(s) of the target company;
- A shareholder's agreement between the fund and its co-investors or remaining existing investors in the target company;
- Articles of association to discipline the governance of the target company; and
- Loan agreements with banks or other providers of acquisition debt.

The content of these documents varies depending on many factors, including local legal requirements and regulation, tax considerations, and deal-specific considerations such as whether the SIF purchased a minority or majority stake in the target company. Because of the complexity of transaction work, funds often engage specialized professional services firms to advise on legal, tax, and regulatory matters (Invest Europe 2018). Closing conditions before exchange of funds and actual change of ownership may involve regulatory approvals, consents by third parties, and the signing of employment agreements by key employees of the target company.[10]

INVESTMENT OWNERSHIP AND SUPERVISION

SIFs, like private equity funds, aim to increase the value of their portfolio companies through improving company strategy, operating performance, management, and governance (called *active ownership*; see box 6.6). The nature and structure of the investment, the size of the equity stake, and the jurisdiction in

Exercising active ownership

Funds exercise active ownership in several ways, including the following:

- Exercising their shareholder rights in order to affect key strategic decisions (as applicable).
- Appointing fund representatives to the company's board (the number of board appointees reflecting the size of the fund's equity stake) and therefore exerting influence on board decisions.
- Nominating board representatives to relevant board committees such as audit, nomination, and compensation.
- Designing (already in the deal evaluation phase) and working with the company's management to implement value creation plans encompassing operational, financial, and governance

improvements. A fund may appoint a portfolio management team specifically committed to this task.

- Engaging in regular discussions with the company's management.
- Conducting regular company visits.
- Enforcing and supporting the application of the fund's environmental, social, and governance standards.
- Establishing clear reporting guidelines, enabling the fund to conduct regular performance evaluations of portfolio companies. Reporting obligations will typically exceed those envisaged by applicable legislation and include, for instance, a series of key performance indicators specific to the company's business.

Sources: World Bank, based on Invest Europe (2018) and review of select SIF and private equity fund private placement memoranda.

which the portfolio company is incorporated all affect the fund's level of activism (Invest Europe 2018). Within this general context, SIFs approach active ownership in a distinct manner that reflects the double bottom line mandate and affiliation with public sponsors, specifically:

- SIFs can enhance the visibility and credibility of portfolio companies with prospective customers as well as future capital providers. For instance, ISIF's portfolio companies receive a credibility boost from their affiliation with a large government-backed fund.
- SIFs can attract co-investors with deep industry expertise that can support a portfolio company's implementation of financial and economic value creation plans. For instance, as discussed in chapter 5, NIIF was able to establish a platform with DP World, the Dubai-based port terminal owner and operator, to invest in ports, terminals, transportation, and logistics businesses in India. DP World controls the platform with a 65 percent stake, and the NIIF Master Fund is a significant minority investor with the remaining 35 percent of the equity. The platform will invest up to US$3 billion of equity to acquire assets and develop projects in the sector (see the NIIF case study in appendix A).

In addition to financial and operational metrics customarily tracked by PCFs, SIFs will want to track portfolio companies' compliance with the economic return mandate. ISIF, for instance, monitors compliance with its economic impact objectives semiannually at the portfolio company level and annually at the overall portfolio level. Every February and August, portfolio companies fill out an impact survey, with data such as revenues, employment, and exports. In addition, each year ISIF compiles an annual control report that measures the performance of all portfolio companies against financial and impact targets (see the case study in appendix A).

INVESTMENT EXIT

In principle, PCFs and SIFs have the same exit routes available to them, although constraints may exist depending on the financial markets within which the SIF operates. From a governance standpoint, the decision-making body in charge of the initial investment decision is usually tasked with approving the exit as well. The investment team is responsible for executing the exit transactions, for instance, by negotiating deal terms and related documentation. Exit decisions are usually a function of the portfolio company's having achieved the expected operational plan and exit market conditions.[11] PCFs and SIFs frequently base exit decisions on whether they have hit an internal rate of return or return on investment target, or if there is investor pressure to return capital.[12] Certain exit routes—particularly initial public offering (IPO) and sale to a financial buyer—may not be available in emerging market and developing economies that lack sufficiently developed financial markets. The following exit routes are available for private equity investments made by PCFs and SIFs alike:

- *Strategic buyer.* Sale of the portfolio company stake to a strategic buyer—that is, another company operating in the same or a related industry.
- *Financial buyer.* Sale of the portfolio company to a financial buyer, usually another private equity investor.
- *Co-investor.* Sale of an equity stake to a co-investor, usually according to provisions of the shareholders agreement (for example, exercise of put option).
- *IPO and follow-on offerings.* In this scenario, the portfolio company is listed on the stock exchange. The fund sells part of its stake at IPO, committing to retain the remainder for a lock-up period stipulated in the IPO documentation. Once the lock-up period has expired, and subject to market conditions, the fund is free to sell the remaining stake in one or more follow-on offerings. Public offerings are "slow-motion exits," often occurring over multiple years and leaving investors exposed to stock market fluctuations while they still hold an interest in the company (Bain & Company 2019).
- *Dividend recapitalization.* In this scenario, if credit market conditions are favorable, the portfolio company refinances its existing debt with a larger debt package and uses the proceeds to make large dividend payments to the fund or shareholder, allowing the fund to take money off the table (Bain & Company 2017). This strategy is particularly suited to businesses in sectors, such as infrastructure, that generate cash flow.

As pursuers of a double bottom line mandate and providers of patient capital, however, SIFs are driven by additional considerations when deciding on exit routes. These considerations include the following.

- *The ability to hold on to their investments longer.* As discussed in chapter 5, public capital SIFs in particular tend to have longer investment horizons than equivalent PCFs, in line with their mandate to be providers of patient capital. As a result, SIFs may invest in companies and projects that require a longer gestation period, as exemplified in particular by greenfield infrastructure investments. Unlike private equity funds that typically operate through a finite life fund, permanent capital structures often employed by public capital SIFs are not constrained by the need to exit by a fund life cycle deadline.
- *Demonstration effects and validation with private investors.* In pursuit of their double bottom line and as sources of additional capital, SIFs can invest in

companies or projects that are not conventionally targeted by PCFs or are deemed by PCFs to be too risky. Both ISIF and Marguerite, for instance, made investments in the respective target geographies during the global financial crisis and the ensuing European sovereign debt crisis when private investors suffered from heightened risk aversion. Both funds also target investments with high additionality that, by definition, struggle to attract PCF capital. By exiting investments made in such circumstances, SIFs demonstrate to PCFs the potential and viability of attractive financial returns in a certain sector, facilitating the future flow of private capital. In addition, SIFs looking to expand their investor base beyond existing sources of public capital may exit investments to show a proven track record of returns to prospective private investors in the fund. Marguerite, for instance, adopted this approach to enhance its credibility with private investors ahead of a new fund launch, as described in box 6.7.

- *Contribution to local capital market development.* A SIF, particularly one operating in emerging market and developing economies, may consider exiting a portfolio company through an IPO as a way to increase the size, visibility, and liquidity of the local equity market. For instance, InfraCredit, a provider of local currency guarantees to the Nigerian infrastructure sector and a portfolio company of NSIA-NIF, considers an IPO as an exit option in the long term partly to help develop local capital markets (see the InfraCredit thematic review in appendix B).
- *Reinvestment of capital.* As discussed in chapter 5, some SIFs have greater flexibility than closed-end PCFs to reinvest exit proceeds. These SIFs may want to exit portfolio companies in order to redeploy the capital and gains to new opportunities that fit their financial and economic return mandates.

BOX 6.7

Investment exit: The case of Marguerite

By the end of 2017, Marguerite's first fund (Marguerite I, launched in 2010) was fully invested. Marguerite I had received €710 million in capital commitments exclusively from public sources, including the European Investment Bank and several European state-controlled financial institutions.

To monetize part of the portfolio, return capital to investors, and enhance the credibility of the fund manager with private investors ahead of a new fund launch, Marguerite decided in 2017 to sell five renewable energy and concession-based assets to a new vehicle, still managed by the Marguerite investment team but fully backed by private capital. It ran a competitive sale process, with a financial adviser and vendor due diligence. Marguerite

Pantheon was set up as a Luxembourg special partnership (a société en commandite spéciale, or SCSp). Marguerite Pantheon is an investment vehicle wholly owned by a pool of funds and managed accounts run by Pantheon, a global private markets fund investor.

The Marguerite investment team is still in charge of managing Marguerite Pantheon. The fact that the five assets were deemed attractive by Pantheon and other bidders highlighted Marguerite's expertise and track record in selecting and executing financially attractive greenfield infrastructure investments. Marguerite's investors obtained an attractive price for the portfolio, within their expectations in terms of internal rate of return and cash multiple.

Source: World Bank; see Marguerite case study in appendix A.

- *Public perception with regard to ownership of portfolio companies.* Particularly in sectors that fulfill basic public needs, such as infrastructure, the ownership of an asset by a SIF can provide confidence that the asset will be run for public interest and not just to extract financial gains.[13] With this in mind, a SIF may carefully consider the timing of its exit as well as the reputation of prospective strategic or financial buyers. In the Indian infrastructure sector, for instance, aggressive underwriting of risks, excessive use of leverage by investors, and poor regulation led to many project failures in the 2007–12 period (Aiyar 2012). Mindful of these past developments, NIIF aims to be a credible and professional owner of infrastructure assets in the country.

KEY TAKEAWAYS

- A SIF's investment process is a subset of its governance framework, establishing guidelines and procedures to effectively implement the investment strategy and to ensure that the double bottom line mandate is met. The investment process guides the activities of the internal or external fund manager appointed to manage a SIF. A well-defined investment process allows the public sponsor to better supervise the SIF and improves public accountability.
- The investment process of a SIF focusing primarily on equity financing consists of the following five phases: origination, evaluation, execution, ownership and supervision, and exit.

    1. SIFs rely on a variety of investment origination routes also common to PCFs. But they also have access to origination routes not commonly found in PCFs because of the public sponsor's access to target markets and the SIF's long investment horizon, which allow the fund to develop early-stage projects.
    2. A SIF's evaluation process identifies and assesses potential investments on the basis of their ability to deliver both financial and economic returns in compliance with the double bottom line mandate, as well as investment risks and exit opportunities for the fund from the investment.
    3. Once the SIF's decision-making body has approved a transaction, the investment team negotiates and signs relevant transaction documents that vary depending on local legal requirements and regulation, tax considerations, and deal-specific factors.
    4. Although SIFs, like PCFs, aim to exercise influence over portfolio companies to optimize financial returns, their approach to active ownership has distinct features reflecting the double bottom line mandate and their affiliation with the public sponsor.
    5. As pursuers of a double bottom line mandate and providers of patient capital, SIFs are driven by additional considerations when deciding on exit routes, such as demonstration effects and capital market development.

NOTES

1. This is important because, as discussed in chapter 4 on governance, SIF investment professionals may not participate in the fund's returns the same way that PCF investment professionals do.

2. In a survey of 79 private equity funds with combined assets under management of more than US$750 billion, Gompers, Kaplan, and Mukharlyamov (2015) find that 46 percent of the closed deals were presented by investment banks, deal brokers, or other private equity funds. They note that large investments are more likely to go through an auction process.

3. Gompers, Kaplan, and Mukharlyamov (2015) find that 36 percent of deals closed by the private equity funds surveyed were "proactively self-generated." In their sample, smaller private equity firms were more likely to source proprietary deals, probably reflecting smaller deal sizes. In general, however, the generation of a proprietary deal flow remains a core priority for large and small private equity firms.

4. Including chief executive officers of major corporations such as Honeywell and PepsiCo.

5. See Bain & Company (2017) for an elaboration on useful networks for proactive investment origination.

6. See EY Global (2019) for discussion on partnerships between corporate acquirers and funds.

7. For instance, PCFs and SIFs that receive capital from development finance institutions are generally required to comply with those institutions' ESG criteria.

8. Projects that promote economic development in underserved sectors or regions of Nigeria.

9. All NIF's investments, including Development Projects, are ultimately evaluated by the same Direct Investment Committee and subject to final approval by the NSIA board.

10. See the DLA Piper web page "Mergers and Acquisitions: Overview of a Transaction" (https://www.dlapiperaccelerate.com/knowledge/2017/mergers-and-acquisitions -overview-of-a-transaction.html).

11. Of the private equity funds surveyed by Gompers, Kaplan, and Mukharlyamov (2015), 90 percent based their exit decisions on the portfolio company's achievement of the expected operational plan as well as on conditions in the exit markets (initial public offering and mergers and acquisitions).

12. More than 75 percent of the private equity funds surveyed by Gompers, Kaplan, and Mukharlyamov (2015) took into account hitting an internal rate of return or return on investment target, the opinion of the portfolio company's management, and competitive considerations. Over half of the funds surveyed considered in their exit decisions their investors' pressure to return capital. The pressure to exit investments is greater when the fundraising environment is robust and a proven return track record can facilitate raising a new and possibly bigger fund (Bain & Company 2019).

13. This consideration is in line with the government's primary objective in infrastructure projects to provide affordable and best value-for-money services to the end user (see PPIAF 2001).

REFERENCES

Aiyar, S. A. 2012. "Infrastructure Crisis Endangers Future Growth." *Times of India*, September 30, 2012. https://timesofindia.indiatimes.com/blogs/Swaminomics/infrastructure -crisis-endangers-future-growth/.

Bain & Company. 2017. "Global Private Equity Report 2017." Bain & Company, Inc., Boston. http://go.bain.com/rs/545-OFW-044/images/BAIN_REPORT_Global_Private_Equity _Report_2017.pdf.

Bain & Company. 2019. "Global Private Equity Report 2019." Bain & Company, Inc., Boston. https://www.bain.com/contentassets/875a49e26e9c4775942ec5b86084df0a/bain_report _private_equity_report_2019.pdf.

EY Global. 2019. "The New Imperatives for Deal Origination." Ernst & Young Global Ltd., April 10, 2019. https://www.ey.com/en_gl/private-equity/the-new-imperatives-for-deal -origination.

Gompers, Paul, Steven N. Kaplan, and Vladimir Mukharlyamov. 2015. "What Do Private Equity Firms Say They Do?" Working Paper 15-081, Harvard Business School, Boston. https:// www.hbs.edu/faculty/Publication%20Files/15-081_9baffe73-8ec2-404f-9d62-ee0d 825ca5b5.pdf.

Invest Europe. 2018. "Invest Europe Handbook of Professional Standards." Invest Europe, Brussels. https://www.investeurope.eu/media/1022/ie_professional-standards -handbook-2018.pdf.

IWG (International Working Group of Sovereign Wealth Funds). 2008. "Sovereign Wealth Funds Generally Accepted Principles and Practices: 'Santiago Principles.'" IWG. https:// www.ifswf.org/sites/default/files/santiagoprinciples_0_0.pdf.

PPIAF (Public-Private Infrastructure Advisory Facility). 2001. "Introductory Manual on Project Finance for Managers of PPP Projects." PPIAF. https://ppiaf.org/sites/ppiaf.org/files /documents/toolkits/Cross-Border-Infrastructure-Toolkit/Cross-Border%20 Compilation%20ver%2029%20Jan%2007/Resources/Treasury%20SAfrica%20-%20 Finance%20Introductory%20Manual.pdf.

Temasek. 2016. "Temasek Launches Americas Advisory Panel." News Release, June 16, 2016. https://www.temasek.com.sg/en/news-and-resources/news-room/news/2016/temasek -launches-americas-advisory-panel.

Wells, Peter. 2016. "Temasek Brings in Top European Advisers." *Financial Times*, January 20, 2016. https://www.ft.com/content/7addbded-0422-340f-9229-c3d7a9bc57a8.

7 Transparency and Disclosure

INTRODUCTION

This chapter discusses the importance of transparency and disclosure for a strategic investment fund (SIF). It follows the governance framework laid out in chapter 4 and highlights how the principles of transparency and disclosure are exhibited in the fund's accountability structure, governance arrangements, and reporting arrangements. This chapter also discusses the relatively recent global political and financial context within which transparency and disclosure of both sovereign-owned investment agencies and private capital funds have assumed heightened importance.

Transparency and disclosure are twin guiding principles that hold the SIF and its governing bodies accountable while the fund invests public wealth in pursuit of a stated mandate. *Transparency* is the principle that accepts and encourages scrutiny of, and within, the SIF such that it fortifies the fund's integrity as an institution. Transparency engenders trust (Rose 2015) and is a precondition to establishing a robust accountability structure (De Belis 2011) because it enables an environment within which the SIF and its governing bodies are answerable to both internal and external stakeholders. Transparency in a SIF strengthens its legitimacy and therefore its ability to endure as an institution regardless of changing political climates.[1] *Disclosure* is the complementary principle, making accessible the information that fosters transparency. Adhering to the principle of disclosure ensures that pertinent financial and nonfinancial information is conveyed accurately, comprehensively, and promptly to (1) governing bodies so they can assess the performance of the fund in compliance with the double bottom line mandate, inform their decision-making, and take corrective actions;[2] and (2) key stakeholders to encourage the scrutiny that safeguards the mandate of the SIF.[3] The transparency and disclosure framework is therefore embedded into the governance architecture of the SIF and enshrined in its establishment law, regulations, and policies. Together these two principles seek to mitigate and rectify the asymmetry of information inherent within the SIF's governance framework that arises between the public sponsor (principal) and the fund manager (agent),[4] and between the SIF and its external stakeholders.

GLOBAL TRANSPARENCY AND DISCLOSURE REQUIREMENTS

Transparency and disclosure requirements have increased globally over the past decade for all forms of investment funds and sovereign agencies. This trend has been driven by multiple factors, including higher standards of public accountability; increased investor expectations for responsible investment and environmental, social, and governance (ESG) disclosure; and changing global standards and regulatory norms.

Transparency requirements for sovereign-owned investment agencies in general came into sharp focus before the global financial crisis, when wariness of foreign state capitalism[5] amplified protectionist sentiments in developed countries like the United States. Protectionist sentiments were awakened in the United States when investments by sovereign-controlled foreign entities triggered worries about the risk of foreign access to industries, intellectual property, and technologies of national security importance (Jackson 2019). These concerns resulted in the enactment of a new law, the Foreign Investment and National Security Act of 2007, enlarging the scope of the interagency Committee on Foreign Investment in the United States to review investments by foreign entities in US assets. In addition, the 2008 global financial crisis highlighted the possibility of "a redistribution of financial *and* political capital" in the global landscape through the investment activity of Middle East and Asian sovereign wealth funds (SWFs) (Monk 2009, 1; emphasis in original). Several of these SWFs, for instance, rescued flailing US financial assets in a series of high-profile Wall Street investments in Morgan Stanley, Citigroup, and Merrill Lynch in the immediate aftermath of the crisis.[6] Although these investments delivered much-needed capital to the struggling banks, they also magnified protectionist concerns about the underlying motivations of foreign state-owned agencies taking stakes in US companies.[7] In 2018, continuing political concerns in the United States resulted in the enactment of the Foreign Investment Risk Review Modernization Act of 2018, which further broadened the purview of the Committee on Foreign Investment in the United States.[8] Note that such preemptive moves have not been restricted to the United States or developed countries. A more recent echo of a sovereign's protectionist move against incursions by foreign state-sponsored capitalists, for instance, was seen in the immediate aftermath of the COVID-19 (coronavirus) pandemic when the government of India effectively tightened investment from China in April 2020 by eliminating the automatic foreign direct investment route for countries with which it shared a land border.[9]

Partly to preempt a wave of protectionist moves targeting SWFs in the aftermath of the global financial crisis, the International Monetary Fund spearheaded the 2008 Santiago Principles through an International Working Group of SWFs focused on establishing a set of voluntary transparency-oriented provisions for these funds (see IWG 2008). The dominant thrust of the Santiago Principles was to provide greater transparency on the structure and operations of SWFs to allay protectionist worries in investment-receiving countries. These principles are also in line with an increasing dedication of global resources to establishing transparency standards—such as on fiscal transparency, monetary and financial policies, or corporate governance—within the international financial architecture.[10] Endorsed by over 20 countries at the time, the 24 principles aimed to agree on higher standards and methodologies for transparency, even if these standards were self-applied, not legally binding, and had to be customized to work in vastly different governance and economic contexts (De Belis 2011). Box 7.1 highlights the transparency-oriented provisions of the Santiago Principles.[11]

Likewise, transparency and disclosure in private capital funds—the private sector counterparts of SIFs—have assumed increased importance since the global financial crisis. One of the foremost global legislative reforms that increased transparency requirements in private equity funds was the European Union's Directive 2011/61/EU on Alternative Investment Fund Managers

BOX 7.1

Santiago Principles: Key transparency and accountability principles for SWFs

The Santiago Principles include the following generally accepted principles and practices (GAPPs) related to SWFs.

Governance

- *GAPP 1.2. Subprinciple.* The key features of the SWF's legal basis and structure, as well as the legal relationship between the SWF and other state bodies, should be publicly disclosed.
- **GAPP 6. Principle.** The governance framework for the SWF should be sound and establish a clear and effective division of roles and responsibilities in order to facilitate accountability and operational independence in the management of the SWF to pursue its objectives.
- **GAPP 10. Principle.** The accountability framework for the SWF's operations should be clearly defined in the relevant legislation, charter, other constitutive documents, or management agreement.
- **GAPP 13. Principle.** Professional and ethical standards should be clearly defined and made known to the members of the SWF's governing body(ies), management, and staff.
- **GAPP 16. Principle.** The governance framework and objectives, as well as the manner in which the SWF's management is operationally independent from the owner, should be publicly disclosed.

Policy

- **GAPP 2. Principle.** The policy purpose of the SWF should be clearly defined and publicly disclosed.
- **GAPP 4. Principle.** There should be clear and publicly disclosed policies, rules, procedures,

or arrangements in relation to the SWF's general approach to funding, withdrawal, and spending operations.
- *GAPP 4.1. Subprinciple.* The source of SWF funding should be publicly disclosed.
- *GAPP 4.2. Subprinciple.* The general approach to withdrawals from the SWF and spending on behalf of the government should be publicly disclosed.
- **GAPP 18. Principle.** The SWF's investment policy should be clear and consistent with its defined objectives, risk tolerance, and investment strategy, as set by the owner or the governing body(ies), and be based on sound portfolio management principles.
- *GAPP 18.3. Subprinciple.* A description of the investment policy of the SWF should be publicly disclosed.
- *GAPP 19.1. Subprinciple.* If investment decisions are subject to other than economic and financial considerations, these should be clearly set out in the investment policy and be publicly disclosed.

Procedures

- **GAPP 7. Principle.** The owner should set the objectives of the SWF, appoint the members of its governing body(ies) in accordance with clearly defined procedures, and exercise oversight over the SWF's operations.
- **GAPP 12. Principle.** The SWF's operations and financial statements should be audited annually in accordance with recognized international or national auditing standards in a consistent manner.

continued

Box 7.1 *continued*

Operational

- **GAPP 9. Principle.** The operational management of the SWF should implement the SWF's strategies in an independent manner and in accordance with clearly defined responsibilities.
- **GAPP 14. Principle.** Dealing with third parties for the purpose of the SWF's operational management should be based on economic and financial grounds, and follow clear rules and procedures.
- **GAPP 15. Principle.** SWF operations and activities in host countries should be conducted in compliance with all applicable regulatory and disclosure requirements of the countries in which they operate.
- **GAPP 21. Principle.** SWFs view shareholder ownership rights as a fundamental element of their equity investments' value. If an SWF chooses to exercise its ownership rights, it should do so in a manner that is consistent with its investment policy and protects the financial value of its investments. The SWF should publicly disclose its general approach to voting securities of listed entities, including the key factors guiding its exercise of ownership rights.
- *GAPP 22.2. Subprinciple.* The general approach to the SWF's risk management framework should be publicly disclosed.

Performance and reporting

- **GAPP 5. Principle.** The relevant statistical data pertaining to the SWF should be reported on a timely basis to the owner, or as otherwise required, for inclusion where appropriate in macroeconomic data sets.
- **GAPP 11. Principle.** An annual report and accompanying financial statements on the SWF's operations and performance should be prepared in a timely fashion and in accordance with recognized international or national accounting standards in a consistent manner.
- **GAPP 17. Principle.** Relevant financial information regarding the SWF should be publicly disclosed to demonstrate its economic and financial orientation, so as to contribute to stability in international financial markets and enhance trust in recipient countries.
- **GAPP 23. Principle.** The assets and investment performance (absolute and relative to benchmarks, if any) of the SWF should be measured and reported to the owner according to clearly defined principles or standards.

Source: IWG 2008.
Note: This box classifies the transparency and disclosure requirements based on the categories proposed in Dixon and Monk (2012). SWF = sovereign wealth fund.

(hereinafter, EU AIFMD) discussed in previous chapters. The EU AIFMD sought to mitigate the systemic risk posed by alternative investment funds to the financial system. It essentially set the global standard on the obligation for information flow from private equity fund managers to investors and regulators by putting in place minimum requirements for the form, content, and frequency of such information (see box 7.2 on the EU AIFMD's transparency requirements). The EU AIFMD was a watershed event for private equity and other alternative investment funds seeking to market in the EU, which were largely unregulated before the crisis. Similar regulatory attention to alternative investment funds in the United States was evidenced in the Dodd Frank Act in 2010, which changed the regulatory framework for private equity and venture capital funds so that any fund manager with over US$150 million in assets under management must register with the US Securities and Exchange Commission and be subject to its supervision and disclosure requirements.

In tandem, global investors increasingly require fund managers to be transparent with respect to pertinent information. Both institutional and retail

BOX 7.2

Transparency requirements of the European Union's Directive on Alternative Investment Fund Managers

The European Union's Directive 2011/61/EU on Alternative Investment Fund Managers (AIFMs) sets the standards for transparency and disclosure within three articles:

Article 22. Annual Report

- The AIFM must make available an annual report within six months of financial year end to investors and regulators.
- The annual report must contain the balance sheet, income statement, financial year activities report, material changes, carried interest, and remuneration for management and staff.
- Accounting standards must align with that of the EU member state / home state of the AIF. Accounting information must be audited and reproduced in the annual report, including any qualifications.

Article 23. Investor Reporting

The AIFM must provide relevant information for investors in each of the AIFs it manages, including the following:

- AIF investment strategy and objectives
- Domicile of AIF(s)
- Eligible assets of the AIF
- Associated risks and risk management systems
- Investment restrictions
- Conditions and/or restrictions on the use of leverage

- Procedures for changing investment policy and strategy
- Identity of AIFM, depositary, auditor, and other service providers, and their roles
- Description of any delegated management function
- Valuation procedures
- Liquidity risk management techniques
- Fees, charges, expenses borne by investor
- Manner of fair treatment of investors, and whether there is any preferential treatment offered to any investor
- Procedure and conditions for issue and sale of shares in AIF, and AIF net asset value
- Historical performance
- Management of conflicts of interest

Article 24. Reporting Obligations to Competent Authorities

AIFMs are required to provide detailed reporting to their regulatory authority, including information regarding the following:

- Instruments traded
- Exposures
- Categories of invested assets
- Illiquid assets and special arrangements
- Risk profiles and risk management systems
- Leverage employed
- A list of AIFs managed

Source: European Union Directive 2011/61/EU on Alternative Investment Fund Managers (AIFMs).

investors have increasing expectations regarding disclosure on sustainability and ESG topics. Concurrently, trade associations for private equity and venture capital general partners and limited partners have emphasized reporting requirements in their own recommendations for the industry. The Institutional Limited Partners Association recommends that investors have timely, clear, and comprehensive access to information such as on the management of investments, deviations from policy, the relationship between the manager and investees, or changes in the ownership of the general partner (ILPA 2019). In its handbook, Invest Europe, a trade association for European private equity and venture capital, provides recommendations aligned with those of the Institutional Limited Partners Association on reporting structure, content, and frequency (see box 7.3).

BOX 7.3

Invest Europe Handbook of Professional Standards 2018: Investor reporting guidelines

Invest Europe (2018) guidelines suggest the following reporting structure for private equity and venture capital funds, on a quarterly basis.

Fund information

- *Fund overview.* General information on the fund, investment focus, key economic terms for the general partner, fund operations, and governance
- *Executive summary.* Commentary on key developments, investment and activities, performance, and material changes
- *Fund performance status.* Information required to assess fund performance, including total commitments and paid-in capital, total investments, cumulative distributions to investors, cumulative management fees drawn, total net asset value, and gross and net internal rate of return
- *Fund financial statements.* Fund income statement, balance sheet, cash flow statement, summary of accounting, and valuation policy
- *General partner fees, carried interest, and fund operating expenses* (audit, tax, legal, and so on)
- *Fund bridge and leverage facilities.* Disclosure including identity of entities providing facilities, key terms, drawdowns, and interest incurred

- *Related party transactions and conflicts of interest.* Overview of such relationships and their resolution

Investment portfolio information

- *Portfolio summary.* Information on individual investments including holding period, geography and sector, and total returns
- *Portfolio asset detail* (semiannual, with quarterly updates). Detailed quantitative and qualitative information on each of the fund's current portfolio companies, assets, and funds, and valuation and methodology used

Investor information

- *Capital account.* Current and cumulative information on each limited partner's individual commitment in the fund, allowing for analysis of income and capital allocations
- *Drawdown notices* (per transaction). Accompanied by note on how funds will be used
- *Distribution notices* (per transaction). Accompanied by note with details on assets divested

Source: Invest Europe 2018, section 5.

In addition, SIFs as (partially) publicly owned entities are called to higher standards of disclosure based on changing reporting norms for state-owned enterprises (SOEs) worldwide. As a sovereign or quasi-sovereign entity, the SIF generally has higher public disclosure obligations. As the Organisation for Economic Co-operation and Development points out in the case of SOEs, for instance, government vehicles pursuing public policy objectives have a high level of disclosure obligation because these entities can have significant budget, fiscal, and social impacts (OECD 2016). The 2015 *OECD Guidelines on Corporate Governance of State-Owned Enterprises* is based on the underlying principle that SOEs are required to be transparent to the public (OECD 2015). The guidelines therefore call for reform efforts by governments to create robust transparency frameworks within the SOE sector and recommend high standards of disclosure, such as adhering to international accounting standards and conducting external audits of financial statements (OECD 2016).

Given this overall context, it is no surprise that transparency and disclosure of sovereign investment agencies is a richly discussed area of work, with multiple methodologies devoted to dissecting the elements of transparency, ranking

SWFs according to these methodologies, and propelling reform through healthy competition. Most transparency assessments and rankings have been developed for the wider universe of SWFs, but they have clear applicability to SIFs. Chief among these methodologies is the Truman SWF Scoreboard, first launched in 2008, with four successive iterations, the latest of which is the 2015 scoreboard examining 60 funds in 42 countries (Truman 2017).[12] The Truman scoreboard categorizes 33 elements of SWFs within four broad groups: structure, governance, transparency and accountability, and behavior (see box 7.4 on elements associated specifically with transparency and accountability).[13] Another SWF

BOX 7.4

Truman Scoreboard for SWFs (Transparency and Accountability) and Linaburg-Maduell Transparency Index for SWFs

Partial listing of Truman Scoreboard elements for transparency and accountability[a]

Investment strategy implementation

16. Are the categories of investments disclosed?
17. Does the strategy use benchmarks?
18. Does the strategy use credit ratings?
19. Are the holders of investment mandates identified?

Investment activities

20. Is the size of the fund disclosed?
21. Are the returns of the fund disclosed?
22. Is the geographic location of the investments disclosed?
23. Is information about the specific investments disclosed?
24. Is the currency composition of the investments disclosed?

Reports

25. Does the fund provide an annual report on its activities and results?
26. Does the fund provide quarterly reports?

Audits

27. Is the fund subject to a regular annual audit of its operations and accounts?
28. Is this annual audit promptly published?
29. Are the audits independent?

The Linaburg-Maduell Transparency Index[b]

Basic information

1. Manages its own website
2. Provides main office location address and contact information such as telephone and fax

Funding, structure, mandate

3. Provides history including reason for creation, origins of wealth, and government ownership structure
4. Provides clear strategies and objectives

Governance and conflicts of interest

5. Provides guidelines in reference to ethical standards, investment policies, and enforcement of guidelines
6. Clearly identifies subsidiaries and contact information
7. Identifies external managers

Financial information and performance

8. Provides up-to-date independently audited annual reports
9. Provides ownership percentage of company holdings and geographic locations of holdings
10. Provides total portfolio market value, returns, and management compensation

Sources: Truman Scoreboard developed in Truman (2008) and subsequently refined; SWF web page on the Linaburg-Maduell Transparency Index (https://www.swfinstitute.org/research/linaburg-maduell-transparency-index).
Note: SWF = sovereign wealth fund.
a. Only the grouping of questions under "Transparency & Accountability" have been provided here. Other questions in the 33-element scoreboard also have relevance to the structure, governance, and behavior of strategic investment funds.
b. This index provides one point for each of the items. The categorization shown here is based on the World Bank team's assessment, and is not expressly part of the methodology of the index.

index, developed by Carl Linaburg and Michael Maduell, is a 10-point scale called the Linaburg-Maduell Transparency Index, which focuses on elements such as clarity of strategy and objectives and independently audited annual reports (see box 7.4 on the full Linaburg-Maduell Transparency Index).[14] Despite disagreements between methodologies,[15] citing the rankings within such indexes is frequently used as shorthand to convey the high transparency standards maintained by individual SWFs. The governance structure of Norway's SWF, for instance, is considered exceptional partly because of a "profound commitment to transparency and public disclosure" (Alsweilem and Rietveld 2017). The fund receives a full 10/10 score in the Linaburg-Maduell Transparency Index and ranks highest on the Truman 2015 SWF Scoreboard with a total score of 98.

LEGAL AND REGULATORY CONTEXT

Although informed by global standards and norms, a SIF's transparency and disclosure framework emanates chiefly from the specific legal framework within which the fund is created and managed, leading to a variety of disclosure standards among global SIFs. As discussed earlier, the pressure for increased transparency for SIFs arises from international standards like the Santiago Principles, or standards in use in the global financial markets (Dixon and Monk 2012). These global standards are frequently translated into commercial laws pertaining to all investment funds, but not always into domestic ad hoc laws that set up the SIF. Therefore, an important question driving the transparency and disclosure framework of an individual SIF is whether the fund has a legal obligation to disclose specific information, and to whom. In less transparency-oriented political contexts, disclosure to the public may be viewed as less important than disclosure to the political elite (Alsweilem and Rietveld 2017; Hatton and Pistor 2012). The focus may be on transparency to the fund's own accountability structure, rather than to the public (Ang 2010). For example, the SWF of Qatar, the Qatar Investment Authority, has no legal or fiduciary requirement to disclose information to the public on the fund's operations. Instead, its board of directors has discretion over the frequency and extent of public disclosure.[16] The Kuwait Investment Authority is prevented by its establishment law from disclosing to the public particular information on the fund, such as its assets under management (Ang 2010). The Ireland Strategic Investment Fund (ISIF), by contrast, is required by law to provide specific information on the fund to the Minister for Finance, most of which is also disclosed in an annual report available to the public (see box 7.5).

The SIF's transparency and disclosure framework is also a function of the authorizing environment within which the SIF was founded. As discussed in previous chapters, the authorizing environment of public capital SIFs in particular can be complex because they are investment vehicles straddling public and private markets. In addition to being beholden to the public sponsor that created the fund, the SIF may be subject to the reporting requirements pertaining to SOEs as well as disclosure standards for investment funds perpetuated by the capital markets regulator in the fund's domicile. The SIF also may be guided by regulatory disclosure requirements of the sector in which it operates (OECD 2016). As discussed in box 2.5 and chapter 5 of this publication, for instance, in China many SIFs (known as government guidance funds) set up at the municipal, provincial, and national levels are expected to meet the annual reporting requirements of the State-Owned Assets Supervision and Administration

Legally required reporting obligations of the Ireland Strategic Investment Fund

Per Section 13 (1) of the National Treasury Management Act of 1990 (NTMA Act 1990), the National Treasury Management Agency (NTMA) is required to provide the Minister for Finance a report of the Ireland Strategic Investment Fund (ISIF) activities (consolidated with NTMA) within six months of the end of the year; the minister then reports to the Irish legislature, the Oireachtas.

In addition, per the NTMA (Amendment) Act 2014, NTMA must provide the following specific information on ISIF:

- The investment strategy pursued

- The investment return achieved by ISIF
- A valuation of ISIF's net assets
- A detailed list of ISIF's assets at the end of the year concerned
- The investment management and custodianship arrangements
- An assessment on a regional basis of the impact of ISIF's investments on economic activity and employment
- An assessment on a regional basis of the distribution of the investments made by ISIF

Sources: NTMA Act 1990 (https://www.irishstatutebook.ie/eli/1990/act/18/enacted/en/html); NTMA Act 2014 (https://www.irishstatutebook.ie/eli/2014/act/23/enacted/en/html).

Commission of the State Council and be guided by that commission's focus on asset growth and preservation. Such a focus on both short-term reporting and asset preservation, however, may produce a risk-aversion conflicting with the fundamental nature of government guidance funds investing in venture capital, which requires undertaking risk and may take several years to produce profits (McGinnis et al. 2017). Thus, the transparency and disclosure framework of a SIF has to be carefully constructed alongside unambiguous communication of the long-term-investor nature of the SIF; otherwise, the fund may sit at the intersection of several and sometimes conflicting messages from its authorizing environment.

The SIF typically translates its legal- or policy-driven transparency and disclosure obligations into practice by adopting well-accepted standards and corresponding benchmarks for financial institutions. It meets these standards and benchmarks through internal controls that are part of the SIF's governance framework (see World Bank 2014). Internal controls include the systems and procedures the SIF establishes to ensure the information reported to governing bodies and key stakeholders is comprehensive and accurate, that it is transmitted in a timely manner to inform key decisions, and that there are mechanisms through which information can be acted upon (World Bank 2014). Khazanah Nasional Berhad's transparency and disclosure standards, for instance, are underpinned by its in-house Framework of Integrity, Governance and Risk Management, adopted by the board in 2004 and updated in 2018. This framework creates the internal controls that guide Khazanah's overall operations and ensure decisions undertaken are based on comprehensive board information and oversight (Khazanah Nasional 2019).

TARGET AUDIENCE

Multiple external audiences, both foreign and domestic, are consumers of the SIF's transparency and disclosure obligations. They include the following.

- *General public and domestic institutional stakeholders.* In the multilayered principal-agent structure of the SIF, the taxpayer whose capital is used to fund the SIF is a key stakeholder, particularly for public capital SIFs. A public capital SIF's transparency in performance is observed with particular interest by a range of domestic political players that may scrutinize the alignment of the fund with its mandate (Foldal 2010; see also De Belis 2011). Government bodies that may have otherwise benefited from the public capital allocated to the SIF will be keen to receive accurate information on the fund's performance. If performance is in line with the stated policy and financial objectives, its disclosure will strengthen the SIF's institutional support. This examination of the SIF by political players can help instigate higher governance standards within the SIF. It may also add logistical obstacles that prevent the fund from being pillaged and its capital moved to other destinations (Alsweilem and Rietveld 2017). Public disclosure, in addition, forces the SIF to broadly engage with other government entities and civil society (Al-Hassan et al. 2013).
- *Investment partners.* The SIF's transparency is also of value to its potential investment partners, who seek, among other things, signals of the fund's operational independence, investment discipline, and commercial orientation through the information it discloses. In turn, the need to attract commercial partners can be a strong incentive to promote transparency within a SIF (De Belis 2011). For mixed capital SIFs, transparent disclosure can be especially important during the fundraising process, when the aim is to attract private capital.
- *Regulators.* As discussed earlier, the SIF may be subject to transparency and disclosure standards set up by ad hoc law, SOE requirements, or commercial law (see, for instance, box 7.2 on disclosure obligations set out by the EU AIFMD). Regulators of countries in which the SIF invests may also require disclosure,[17] which is particularly applicable to SIFs set up by multilateral development banks or development finance institutions that may invest in several countries.
- *Rating agencies and lenders to the SIF.* If the SIF issues debt, the lenders or bondholders, as well as credit rating agencies (if the SIF's debt is rated), will want to receive detailed, regular updates on the SIF's performance, with a focus on financial (rather than policy) aspects. These agencies will also observe the SIF's adherence to rigorous disclosure and accounting standards to assess risk (De Belis 2011).

Internal audiences for the SIF's transparency and disclosure obligations include the following.

- *Parliament or legislative body.* For public capital SIFs, parliament or the equivalent legislative apparatus is typically the ultimate stakeholder representing the taxpaying public within the accountability structure of the SIF. In some political systems, this ultimate authority may be the president (Alsweilem and Rietveld 2017, chapter 8). By assessing the financial accounts and performance of the SIF, parliament is in effect evaluating the performance of the government as an owner on behalf of the taxpayer (OECD 2016). ISIF's manager, the National Treasury Management Agency (NTMA), for instance, is accountable to the Public Accounts Committee and to Oireachtas Committees (Irish Parliament).[18] The NTMA's annual financial statements and annual report, which include details on ISIF's financial performance, are therefore presented to the Irish Parliament by the Minister for Finance.[19]

- *Public sponsor or investors.* The SIF public sponsor and board are both architects and consumers of the fund's transparency and disclosure framework. For mixed capital SIFs, the co-investors alongside the public sponsor are also key stakeholders for whom the transparency and disclosure framework of the fund is important. For both the investors and—through the delegated authority structure—the board, the framework provides the information for governance-related decisions on investment and risk management, and provides the intelligence necessary to assess and discipline the SIF's management and reduce the chances of misconduct (Al-Hassan et al. 2013). Note, however, that commercial investors in the SIF may be reluctant to disclose to the public performance and detailed portfolio information that is commercially sensitive and could affect their competitive positioning.

CORE COMPONENTS OF DISCLOSURE FRAMEWORK AND MECHANISMS OF DISCLOSURE

The key principles of high-quality financial and nonfinancial reporting are accuracy, comprehensiveness, comparability, relevance, and frequency (see World Bank 2014). Broadly, a SIF's transparency and disclosure framework provides (1) key features of the fund, including clarity on the mandate, ownership structure, legal basis, governance architecture, and policies adopted by the SIF, including the remuneration structure of its governing bodies; (2) a list of investments and fund performance with respect to both financial and economic returns; and (3) audited financial statements for the fund. Core elements of the SIF's disclosure framework are broken down in box 7.6.

The main mechanism for both financial and nonfinancial disclosure is a SIF's annual report, although a SIF usually provides salient information in ancillary documents published on its website (De Belis 2011). Disclosure is not expected to jeopardize the competitive positioning of the SIF, nor should it prove to be overly administratively costly (OECD 2015, 6).[20] SIFs commonly report on an annual basis but also may have semiannual or quarterly reporting. The annual report is embraced as a key instrument for public and investor disclosure by both the Santiago Principles and the EU AIFMD.[21] Particularly for public capital SIFs, annual reports are publicly accessible on the SIF website, which also typically contains key information on its governance structure, investment policy, responsible investment strategy, or ESG policies. As discussed earlier, ISIF publishes its economic impact report separate from the annual report, on a half yearly basis.[22] SIFs also disclose key financial and nonfinancial information through other mechanisms, and communication with the general public and domestic institutions—through seminars, media visibility, or up-to-date web presence—enhances the domestic legitimacy of the SIF.[23] Khazanah, for instance, organizes its stakeholder engagement via the media, fund managers, government agencies, civil society organizations, and members of parliament to increase understanding of the SIF (Khazanah Nasional 2019).

SIFs generally adopt either global International Financial Reporting Standards (IFRS) or local standards. The IFRS are accounting standards promoted by the International Accounting Standards Board; they provide a common accounting methodology that allows financial statements globally to be comparable.[24] Applying global or regional standards provides a point of comparison between the reporting of private and public sector entities and frees

BOX 7.6

Core components of disclosure for a strategic investment fund

Fund overview
- Ownership
  - Size of fund
  - Source of capital
  - Ownership structure

- Policy purpose and investment approach
  - Double bottom line mandate
  - Financial and economic targets
  - Funding, withdrawal, and spending rules
  - Investment policy, including eligible investments and restrictions
  - Investment strategy

- Legal framework
  - Legal basis and structure
  - Fund domicile
  - Legal relationship between the strategic investment fund and other sovereign bodies (if any)

- Governance framework
  - Division of roles and responsibilities between governing bodies, and selection procedures
  - Clarity on fund's operational independence
  - Internal vs. external managers
  - Preferential treatment offered to any investors
  - Professional and ethical standards
  - Related party transactions and management of conflicts of interest

- Risk management framework

Key developments
- Commentary on key developments, investment and activities, performance, and material changes

Detailed list of assets
- Information on individual investments including ownership stake, geographic location and sector, holding period, currency denomination, valuation methodology, and total returns

Fund performance
- Information required to assess fund performance, including total commitments and paid-in capital, total investments, cumulative distributions to investors, cumulative management fees drawn, total net asset value, gross and net internal rate of return, and economic impact assessment

Audited fund financial statements
- Fund income statement, balance sheet, cash flow statement, summary of accounting standards, and valuation policy

Compensation structure: Provides insight into the incentive structure for the fund's management

- General partner fees
- Carried interest
- Fund operating expenses borne by investor (audit, tax, legal, and so on)

Debt facilities
- Leverage policy
- Identity of entities providing facilities; key terms, drawdowns, and interest incurred

Sources: World Bank, based on European Union 2011; Invest Europe 2018; IWG 2008.

agencies from having to reinvent the wheel by developing their own standards (World Bank 2014). However, IFRS are not universally adopted. As shown in table 7.1, both Marguerite and the Nigeria Sovereign Investment Authority adhere to IFRS, whereas FONSIS,[25] ISIF, and India's National Investment and Infrastructure Fund (NIIF) follow local or regional standards.

Best practice dictates that the SIF be audited by an independent, well-reputed firm under the supervision of the board's audit committee (OECD 2016), although public capital SIFs are sometimes audited by the state comptroller and

TABLE 7.1 **Financial reporting standards of select SIFs**

SIF	FUND TYPE	FREQUENCY OF FINANCIAL REPORTING	ACCOUNTING STANDARDS USED	AUDITOR	PUBLIC ACCESSIBILITY
Asia Climate Partners	Mixed capital	Quarterly unaudited financial statements and audited annual reports of portfolio companies available to investors	—	—	Annual report not available online; website contains list and description of fund investments.
Marguerite	Mixed capital	Quarterly and annual portfolio performance reports available to investors	IFRS	Deloitte	Annual report not available online; website contains list and description of fund investments.
National Investment and Infrastructure Fund (India)	Mixed capital	Quarterly fund reports for investors and the board; semiannual portfolio valuations by independent evaluator	Indian Accounting Standard	Ernst & Young	Annual report not available online; website contains list and description of fund investments.
Ireland Strategic Investment Fund	Public capital	Annual, consolidated as part of NTMA annual report, with quarterly publication of a more limited set of information	Financial Reporting Standard 102[a]	Government of Ireland Comptroller and Auditor General	NTMA annual report, including financial statements, available on the website.
Nigeria Sovereign Investment Authority–Nigeria Infrastructure Fund	Public capital	Annual consolidated financial statements, with NSIA Monthly performance reports and quarterly portfolio reports for internal monitoring	IFRS	PricewaterhouseCoopers	NSIA annual report, including financial statements, available online.
FONSIS (Senegal)	Public capital	—	OHADA accounting system: Système Comptable OHADA	Ernst & Young and a local auditing firm State audit by General State Inspectorate and the Court of Auditors	Annual report available online, without financial statements.

Sources: World Bank (see case studies in appendix A); Santiago Principles self-assessments; SIF websites.
Note: FONSIS = Fonds Souverain d'Investissements Stratégiques (Sovereign Fund for Strategic Investments); IFRS = International Financial Reporting Standards; NIF = Nigeria Infrastructure Fund; NSIA = Nigeria Sovereign Investment Authority; NTMA = National Treasury Management Agency; OHADA = Organisation pour l'harmonisation en Afrique du droit des affaires (Organization for the Harmonization of Corporate Law in Africa); SIF = strategic investment fund; — = not available.
a. The financial reporting standard applicable in the United Kingdom and Republic of Ireland.

auditor general. Good practice also suggests publishing the independent audits of SIFs, but disclosure is purposeless if the party disclosing is not considered reliable (Wong 2009). External audits by a reputed firm are usually recommended because external auditors are independent and put their firm's credibility on the line to vouch for the financials of the fund. Article 38.2 of the Nigeria Sovereign Investment Authority (Establishment, etc.) Act, 2011 (NSIA Act 2011), for instance, requires that an external audit of the SWF's financial statements and operations must be conducted annually by an internationally recognized firm using IFRS as the accounting standard. Likewise, Khazanah's financial statements are audited by an independent external auditor and submitted to the Companies Commission of Malaysia (Khazanah Nasional 2019). For public capital SIFs, the public accountability element may dictate that the SIF be subject instead to public audits.[26] NTMA's financial statements, which include

ISIF, for instance, are audited by Ireland's Comptroller and Auditor General, a state body with the statutory remit to audit government bodies. In addition, ISIF's financial statements and operations are subject to NTMA's internal audit.[27] India's Comptroller and Auditor General typically serves as auditor for SOEs that are 51 percent or more owned by the government.[28] Because the government's share in NIIF is only 49 percent, NIIF is subject to external audit by Ernst & Young (see the NIIF case study in appendix A).

UNIQUE FEATURES OF THE TRANSPARENCY AND DISCLOSURE FRAMEWORK FOR SIFS

Public capital SIFs generally have higher public disclosure requirements than do mixed capital SIFs, which, like private equity funds, have an obligation to report primarily to their investors. Even though generally accepted guidance such as the Santiago Principles may require detailed disclosure on investments and performance only to the owner, it is advisable for public capital SIFs to disclose such information to the public.[29] ISIF offers a good example of this higher disclosure standard in practice: the NTMA annual report carries ISIF's balance sheet, financial statements, list of investments (including committed capital broken down by each investment), and investment return performance (see also box 7.7 on ISIF's approach to monitoring and reporting on economic impact).[30] Similarly, Article 37 of the NSIA Act 2011 requires the Nigerian SWF to make the fund's annual report, quarterly report, and key policy documents available to the public, and requires the annual report to be summarized and disseminated via widely circulated Nigerian newspapers. By contrast, as mixed capital SIFs, Asia Climate Partners, Marguerite, and NIIF have financial disclosure requirements typical of private equity funds and limited to the funds' investors, not the broader public. The public disclosure of all three SIFs is limited primarily to a list and description of fund investments on the website (see table 7.1 on financial reporting standards of SIFs). Because the public sponsor is the provider of anchor capital, ideally mixed capital SIFs must make best efforts toward disclosing nonfinancial information that may not be commercially sensitive but is critical to assessing whether the SIF is achieving its policy objectives.

For SIFs—and increasingly for private equity funds—the ESG policy is an important feature of nonfinancial disclosure. Global private equity funds in general are signaling increasing commitment to ESG principles in their investment approach, propelled by limited partner interest in sustainability and impact investing, and evidence that incorporating ESG measures limits exposure to risk and increases returns (Bain & Company 2020). For SIFs, ESG performance assumes even greater importance because of their status as sovereign or quasi-sovereign investment agencies: the standard of ethics SIFs promote with respect to the environment and social standards has reputational importance to their public sponsors. SIFs therefore are typically required to disclose ESG-related strategy, measures, and performance. Khazanah, for instance, states in its investment policy that, as a signatory to the United Nations Principles for Responsible Investment, it annually reports on the steps taken toward responsible investment.[31] Khazanah's Responsible Investment Policy outlines key investment principles, approach, and governance related to responsible investment.[32] Likewise, in the NTMA Annual Report 2019, ISIF discusses its Sustainability and Responsible Investment Strategy 2020, including key decisions such as

BOX 7.7

ISIF approach to monitoring and reporting on economic impact

The Ireland Strategic Investment Fund (ISIF) monitors compliance with its economic impact objectives annually at the Irish portfolio company level and the portfolio level. Every February and August, investee companies fill out an impact survey with data such as revenues, employment, and exports. In addition, each year, ISIF compiles an annual control report that measures the performance of all Irish portfolio companies against financial and impact targets. Once exiting investments, ISIF does not exercise any further active impact monitoring.

ISIF publishes an annual and a semiannual economic impact report with detailed metrics on ISIF's capital allocation and contribution to economic activity and employment. Table B7.7.1 provides a summary of these metrics. Initially, the focus was on fund-level portfolio metrics for publication; however, as the report has evolved, the reporting now takes account of sector-specific metrics that cannot be consolidated at the fund level (for example, megawatts of renewable energy, number of new housing units, and number of alternative small and medium enterprise financing platforms). The collection, verification, and reporting of economic impact data can be challenging given that they are relatively new concepts for investees to report on.

TABLE B7.7.1 **Comprehensive sample of metrics disclosed in ISIF's economic impact report**

AREA	METRICS
Capital	• Discretionary portfolio size • Capital committed • Capital committed by co-investors and multiplier • Market value of capital invested • Split of capital invested by region (Dublin and ex-Dublin) • Capital committed by strategy (Enabling Ireland, Growing Ireland, Leading Edge Ireland) and, for each, by subsector • List of new investments during period and ticket sizes • Fund returns • List of portfolio companies of investee funds

Economic activity	• GVA
	• Allocation of GVA by region
	• Exports generated by portfolio companies
	• Strategy-specific metric, for instance:
	  - Enabling Ireland: MW of renewable energy installed, tons of waste processed, housing units completed
	  - Growing Ireland: number of SMEs backed
	  - Leading Edge Ireland: list of VC funds invested and ticket sizes
	  - Case studies

Employment	• Total employment supported by Irish Portfolio companies and projects • Total wage bill • Split of employment by region (Dublin and ex-Dublin)

Source: World Bank; see ISIF case study in appendix A.
Note: GVA = gross value added; ISIF = Ireland Strategic Investment Fund; MW = megawatt; SMEs = small and medium enterprises; VC = venture capital.

developing a list of 211 fossil fuel companies in which it would not invest and having committed €349 million to renewable energy and forestry projects in Ireland as part of its climate-friendly investments (NTMA 2020). Mixed capital SIFs in particular are prompted or guided in their ESG policy and reporting by their development finance institution public sponsor. Asia Climate Partners, for instance, complies with the Asian Development Bank's general prohibited investment activities list and its ESG policies (see the case study in appendix A).

In addition, the SIF's double bottom line mandate requires that the fund disclose information on its economic performance. ISIF's economic impact is reported on a semiannual basis,[33] and includes items such as employment creation and contribution to economic growth nationally and by region, as well as sector-specific metrics, such as megawatts of energy installed by ISIF's renewable energy investee companies. The NTMA Annual Report 2019, for instance, reports that ISIF supported over 32,000 jobs up to the end of June 2019 (NTMA 2020).

SIF performance reporting should be accompanied by unequivocal communication emphasizing the long-term investment horizon of the fund so that attention does not focus on short-term performance (see Al-Hassan et al. 2013). Frequent reporting could undermine the long-term investment horizon of the SIF if such reporting is not accompanied by unambiguous messaging around the long-term investment nature of the fund, because short-term volatility in the SIF's performance may be misread by those who do not fully understand the long-term mandate of the fund, or by players seeking to undermine the fund for political reasons (Rose 2015). SIFs may be pushed into "a public demonstration of short-term performance," deviating from their long-term mandate (Dixon and Monk 2012). In such cases, transparency may undermine rather than aid the SIF, leading to transparency and disclosure standards that often focus more on annual, rather than quarterly, statements (De Belis 2011; Dixon and Monk 2012). As stewards of public capital, SIFs would generally do well to focus on higher public disclosure obligations and mitigate the risk of short-term orientation through the safeguards of explicit communication and emphasis on long-term returns.

KEY TAKEAWAYS

- Transparency and disclosure are twin guiding principles that allow the SIF and its governing bodies to be held to account as the fund invests public wealth in pursuit of a stated mandate. The transparency and disclosure framework is embedded in the governance architecture of the SIF and enshrined in its establishment law, regulations, and policies.
- Transparency and disclosure requirements have increased globally over the past decade for all forms of investment funds and sovereign agencies. SIFs, as holders of public capital, are expected to conform to high public disclosure standards.
- A SIF's transparency and disclosure framework emanates chiefly from the specific legal framework within which the fund is created and managed, leading to a variety of disclosure standards among global SIFs. The transparency and disclosure framework of a SIF must be carefully constructed because the fund may sit at the intersection of several, and sometimes conflicting, legal and regulatory requirements.
- Broadly, a SIF's reporting framework provides public disclosure of (1) key features of the fund, including clarity on the mandate, ownership structure, legal basis, governance architecture, and policies adopted by the SIF, including the remuneration structure of its governing bodies; (2) investments and fund performance with respect to both financial and economic returns; and (3) audited financial statements for the fund.

- The main mechanism for both financial and nonfinancial disclosure is the SIF's annual report, although the SIF also provides salient information in ancillary documents usually published on the website. SIFs generally adopt either the global IFRS or local standards. Best practice dictates that the SIF be audited by an independent, well-reputed firm under the supervision of the board's audit committee, although public capital SIFs are sometimes audited by the state comptroller and auditor general.

NOTES

1. Ang (2010, 6) discusses the issue of legitimacy with respect to sovereign wealth funds, but equally applicable to SIFs. He clarifies that, although transparency can enhance legitimacy, it is "neither a necessary nor sufficient condition to meet the legitimacy benchmark."
2. These consequences can vary depending on political and governance structure (De Belis 2011; see also Gelpern 2012). The conditions for accountability are discussed more in chapter 4.
3. According to TAI (2017), aspiring for transparency requires that information supplied be relevant, accessible, timely, and accurate.
4. See discussion in chapter 4; note that the transparency and disclosure framework also protects the fund manager from external or political pressures to deviate from the mandate by making visible the long-term mandate and investment policy of the SIF.
5. State capitalism is defined as "the use of government controlled funds to acquire strategic stakes around the world" (Lyons 2008).
6. The China Investment Corporation took a 10 percent stake in US investment bank Morgan Stanley; the Abu Dhabi Investment Authority injected US$7.5 billion into Citigroup during the early stages of the financial crisis, followed by a US$12.5 billion investment by Singapore's GIC Private Limited and the Kuwait Investment Authority acting as part of a consortium; and Temasek, also of Singapore, bought a US$5 billion stake in Merrill Lynch (Gopolan 2019).
7. For more discussion on the trend of sovereigns in investing across borders, see Rose (2008).
8. For a summary of the act, see https://home.treasury.gov/system/files/206/Summary-of -FIRRMA.pdf.
9. This move by the government was widely believed to be a response to fears that Chinese investors could be bargain hunting in India's corporate sector. India's Ministry of Commerce admitted in its press release of April 18, 2020, to a desire to quash attempts at opportunistic takeovers of Indian assets in the strained economic environment with the onset of the pandemic.
10. The Santiago Principles, however, are not part of the Financial Stability Board's Compendium of Standards (for a detailed discussion on the types of global standards and context for the Santiago Principles, see De Belis [2011]; see also Norton [2010]).
11. The successor to the International Working Group of SWFs, the International Forum of Sovereign Wealth Funds currently represents more than 30 sovereign wealth funds (https://www.ifswf.org/about-us).
12. The first scoreboard assessed 33 funds in 28 countries.
13. In 2015, the SWFs assessed scored best on elements of basic structure such as stating the objective of the fund and providing a legal framework, and scored least well on behavior elements such as policy on leverage or portfolio adjustment.
14. The index is a project of the Sovereign Wealth Fund Institute. Within this 10-point index, the Nigeria Sovereign Investment Authority has scored 9 points, and the Ireland Strategic Investment Fund and Khazanah Nasional have each scored 8 points. See the Linaburg-Maduell Transparency Index, Sovereign Wealth Fund Institute (accessed September 18, 2020), https://www.swfinstitute.org/research/linaburg -maduell-transparency-index.
15. For example, "Truman (2010, 94–96) is critical of the Linaburg-Maduell index for being superficial in some of its 10 elements (such as, Does the fund have a website?), not releasing the resulting scores for each element, and for combining many factors into some elements, such as portfolio value, returns, and management compensation, without providing any information about how the factors were weighted within each element" (Bagnall and Truman 2013, 14).

16. See the International Forum of Sovereign Wealth Funds web page, "Trends in Transparency: Santiago Principles Self-Assessments 2016" (https://www.ifswf.org/trends-transparency -santiago-principle-self-assessments-2016).
17. See discussion on accountability and SWFs in De Belis (2011).
18. See the ISIF Santiago Principles Self-Assessment 2019 (https://www.ifswf.org/assessment /ireland-strategic-investment-fund).
19. See the ISIF Santiago Principles Self-Assessment 2019 (https://www.ifswf.org/assessment /ireland-strategic-investment-fund) and NTMA Act 1990.
20. With respect to SOEs, OECD (2016) adds, "Disclosure requirements should not compromise essential corporate confidentiality and should not put SOEs at a disadvantage in relation to private competitors."
21. It should be noted that SIFs and SWFs may not always meet their own standards for publishing annual reports. Maire, Mazarei, and Truman (2021), for instance, find that 50 of the 64 SWFs covered by the fifth Truman SWF Scoreboard say they publish annual reports, but the authors could not find recent reports for 2 of them, and for 14 the most recent were from 2018. In addition, the authors found that 1 of the 19 SIFs/SWFs on the scoreboard does not say whether it issues a report and 4 issue only a summary report. Recent reports were available for 6 SIFs and only 2018 reports for 9 of them.
22. See the ISIF publications web page (https://isif.ie/news/publications).
23. See the discussion pertaining to SWFs in Al-Hassan et al. (2013); see also Rose (2017).
24. For more on the IFRS, see the IFRS Foundation website (https://www.ifrs.org).
25. Senegal's Fonds Souverain d'Investissements Stratégiques (Sovereign Fund for Strategic Investments).
26. As Alsweilem and Rietveld (2017) explain with respect to SWFs, "Expectations for public accountability add an often elaborate oversight infrastructure, involving a public auditor, a national regulator, external auditors, and sometimes a separate supervisory board (in addition to the board of directors)."
27. See the ISIF Santiago Principles Self-Assessment 2019 (https://www.ifswf.org/assessment /ireland-strategic-investment-fund).
28. According to India's Companies Act 2013, Article 2.45, a government company is "any company in which not less than fifty-one per cent of the paid-up share capital is held by the Central Government, or by any State Government or Governments, or partly by the Central Government and partly by one or more State Governments, and includes a company which is a subsidiary company of such a Government company." Per Article 143.5, the Comptroller and Auditor General appoints the auditor for government companies.
29. According to generally accepted principles and practices 23.0, the assets and investment performance (absolute and relative to benchmarks, if any) of the SWF should be measured and reported to the owner according to clearly defined principles or standards.
30. See the ISIF Santiago Principles Self-Assessment 2019 (https://www.ifswf.org/assessment /ireland-strategic-investment-fund). See, for example, NTMA (2020, 20–29).
31. See the Khazanah "Investment Approach" web page (https://www.khazanah.com.my /how-we-invest/investment-approach/).
32. Khazanah "Investment Approach" web page.
33. ISIF Santiago Principles Self-Assessment 2019 (https://www.ifswf.org/assessment/ireland -strategic-investment-fund).

REFERENCES

Al-Hassan, Abdullah, Michael Papaioannou, Martin Skancke, and Cheng Chih Sung. 2013. "Sovereign Wealth Funds: Aspects of Governance Structures and Investment Management." IMF Working Paper 13/231, International Monetary Fund, Washington, DC. https://www .imf.org/en/Publications/WP/Issues/2016/12/31/Sovereign-Wealth-Funds-Aspects-of -Governance-Structures-and-Investment-Management-41046.

Alsweilem, Khalid, and Malan Rietveld. 2017. *Sovereign Wealth Funds in Resource Economies: Institutional and Fiscal Foundations.* New York: Columbia University Press.

Ang, Andrew. 2010. "The Four Benchmarks of Sovereign Wealth Funds." Working paper. https://www0.gsb.columbia.edu/faculty/aang/papers/The%20Four%20Benchmarks%20 of%20Sovereign%20Wealth%20Funds.pdf.

Bagnall, Allie E., and Edwin M. Truman. 2013. "Progress on Sovereign Wealth Fund Transparency and Accountability: An Updated SWF Scoreboard." PIIE Policy Brief 13-19, Peterson Institute for International Economics, Washington, DC. https://www.piie.com/sites /default/files/publications/pb/pb13-19.pdf.

Bain & Company. 2020. "Global Private Equity Report 2020." Bain & Company, Inc., Boston. https://www.bain.com/globalassets/noindex/2020/bain_report_private_equity_report _2020.pdf.

De Belis, Maurizia. 2011. "Global Standards for Sovereign Wealth Funds: The Quest for Transparency." *Asian Journal of International Law* 1 (2): 349–82.

Dixon, Adam D., and Ashby H. B. Monk. 2012. "Reconciling Transparency and Long-Term Investing within Sovereign Funds." *Journal of Sustainable Finance & Investment* 2 (3–4): 275–86.

European Union. 2011. "Directive 2011/61/EU of the European Parliament and of the Council of 8 June 2011 on Alternative Investment Fund Managers and amending Directives 2003/41 /EC and 2009/65/EC and Regulations (EC) No 1060/2009 and (EU) No 1095/2010." *Official Journal of the European Union* L 174, 1.7.2001. https://eur-lex.europa.eu/legal-content/EN /TXT/PDF/?uri=CELEX:32011L0061&from=EN.

Foldal, Øyvind Ytrestøyl. 2010. "Mitigating Tensions between Domestic Politics and Global Finance–A Study of the Decision Making Process of Norway's Sovereign Wealth Fund." Masters' thesis, University of Oslo. http://dx.doi.org/10.2139/ssrn.1664344.

Gelpern, Anna. 2012. "Reconciling Sovereignty, Accountability, and Transparency in Sovereign Wealth Funds." In *Sovereign Wealth Funds and Long-Term Investing*, edited by Patrick Bolton, Frederic Samana, and Joseph E. Stiglitz, 205–8. New York: Columbia University Press.

Gopolan, Nisha. 2019. "China's $1 Trillion Sovereign Wealth Fund Has Gone Quiet." *Bloomberg*, April 7, 2019. https://www.bloomberg.com/opinion/articles/2019-04-07/cic-investments -have-gone-low-profile-a-new-chairman-won-t-help.

Hatton, Kyle J., and Katharina Pistor. 2012. "Maximizing Autonomy in the Shadow of Great Powers: The Political Economy of Sovereign Wealth Funds." *Columbia Journal of Transnational Law* 50: 1–81.

ILPA (Institutional Limited Partners Association). 2019. "ILPA Principles 3.0: Fostering Transparency, Governance and Alignment of Interests for General and Limited Partners." ILPA, Washington, DC. https://ilpa.org/wp-content/uploads/2019/06/ILPA-Principles -3.0_2019.pdf.

Invest Europe. 2018. "Invest Europe Handbook of Professional Standards." Invest Europe, Brussels. https://www.investeurope.eu/media/1022/ie_professional-standards -handbook-2018.pdf.

IWG (International Working Group of Sovereign Wealth Funds). 2008. "Sovereign Wealth Funds Generally Accepted Principles and Practices: 'Santiago Principles.'" IWG. https:// www.ifswf.org/sites/default/files/santiagoprinciples_0_0.pdf.

Jackson, James G. 2019. "The Committee on Foreign Investment in the United States (CFIUS)." CRS Report RL33388, Congressional Research Service, Washington, DC. https://crsreports .congress.gov/product/pdf/RL/RL33388/82.

Khazanah Nasional. 2019. "The Khazanah Report 2019." Khazanah Nasional, Kuala Lumpur. https://www.khazanah.com.my/our-performance/the-khazanah-report/.

Lyons, Gerard. 2008. "State Capitalism: The Rise of Sovereign Wealth Funds." *Law and Business Review of the Americas* 14 (1): 179.

Maire, Julien, Adnan Mazarei, and Edwin M. Truman. 2021. "Sovereign Wealth Funds Are Growing More Slowly, and Governance Issues Remain." PIIE Policy Brief 21-3, Peterson Institute for International Economics, Washington, DC. https://www.piie.com/sites /default/files/documents/pb21-3.pdf.

McGinnis, Patrick, Shanthi Divakaran, Jing Zhao, and Yi Yan. 2017. "Government and Venture Capital in China: The Role of Government Guidance Funds." Background paper for *Innovative China: New Drivers of Growth*. Washington, DC: World Bank.

Monk, Ashby. 2009. "Recasting the Sovereign Wealth Fund Debate: Trust, Legitimacy, and Governance." *New Political Economy* 14 (4): 451–68.

Norton, Joseph J. 2010. "The Santiago Principles for Sovereign Wealth Funds: A Case Study on International Financial Standard-Setting Processes." *Journal of International Economic Law* 13 (3): 645–62.

NTMA (National Treasury Management Agency). 2020. "NTMA Annual Report and Financial Statements 2019." NTMA, Dublin. https://www.ntma.ie/publications/ntma-annual-report-and-financial-statements-2019.

OECD (Organisation for Economic Co-operation and Development). 2015. *OECD Guidelines on Corporate Governance of State-Owned Enterprises*. Paris: OECD Publishing.

OECD (Organisation for Economic Co-operation and Development). 2016. "Transparency and Disclosure Measures for State-Owned Enterprises (SOEs): Stocktaking of National Practices." Discussion Paper for the Global Knowledge Sharing Network on Corporate Governance of State-owned Enterprises. https://www.oecd.org/daf/ca/2016-SOEs-issues%20paper-Transparency-and-disclosure-measures.pdf.

Rose, Paul. 2008. "Sovereigns as Shareholders." *North Carolina Law Review* 87 (1): 83. http://scholarship.law.unc.edu/nclr/vol87/iss1/3.

Rose, Paul. 2015. "A Disclosure Framework for Public Fund Investment Policies." *Procedia Economics and Finance* 29: 5–16.

Rose, Paul. 2017. "Sovereign Wealth Funds and Domestic Political Risk." In *The Oxford Handbook of Sovereign Wealth Funds*, edited by Douglas Cumming, Geoffrey Wood, Igor Filatotchev, and Juliane Reinecke. Oxford: Oxford University Press.

TAI (Transparency & Accountability Initiative). 2017. "How Do We Define Terms? Transparency and Accountability Glossary." *TAI Blogs*, April 12, 2017. https://www.transparency-initiative.org/blog/1179/tai-definitions/.

Truman, Edwin M. 2008. "A Blueprint for Sovereign Wealth Fund Best Practices." PIIE Policy Brief 08-3, Peterson Institute for International Economics, Washington, DC.

Truman, Edwin M. 2017. "Sovereign Wealth Fund Transparency and Accountability Explored." *Wake Forest Law Review* 52: 997.

Wong, Anthony. 2009. "Sovereign Wealth Funds and the Problem of Asymmetric Information: The Santiago Principles and International Regulations." *Brooklyn Journal of International Law* 34: 3. https://brooklynworks.brooklaw.edu/bjil/vol34/iss3/14.

World Bank. 2014. *Corporate Governance of State-Owned Enterprises: A Toolkit*. Washington, DC: World Bank.

World Bank Group and DRC (Development Research Center of the State Council, People's Republic of China). 2019. *Innovative China: New Drivers of Growth*. Washington, DC: World Bank.

Part 2 Case Studies

8 Case Study—Asia Climate Partners: Targeting Demonstration Effects for Foreign Investors*

The central value proposition of ACP is to offer the largest, fully fledged private equity investment platform for environmental finance in emerging Asia. ACP is looking to partner with established environmental businesses, with sound operating fundamentals and strong growth potential that benefit from the rapid macroeconomic and environmental dynamics in the target regions.

—*Asia Climate Partners website*

BACKGROUND AND MISSION

Asia Climate Partners (ACP) is a US$450 million private equity fund targeting the renewable energy, resource efficiency, and environmental sectors in emerging Asia. Launched in November 2014, it is a joint initiative of three founding partners: the Asian Development Bank (ADB), ORIX Corporation (ORIX), and Robeco. ORIX is a diversified financial conglomerate listed on the Tokyo Stock Exchange, with activities in corporate finance, real estate, banking, and insurance, among others. Its Eco Services Division is involved in renewable power generation, energy conservation and storage solutions, and waste processing. Robeco is an international asset manager with assets under management (AuM) worth €165 billion (of which €102 billion are in environmental, social, and governance [ESG]–integrated assets),[1] headquartered in the Netherlands and fully owned by ORIX.

ACP aims to demonstrate the viability of investing in green finance in Asia on a commercial basis, while adhering to rigorous ESG practices. It acts primarily as an equity investor in established, fast-growing businesses in large developing economies such as China and India as well as in frontier Asian markets. It leverages extensive support from its founding partners in deal sourcing, due diligence, and access to regional networks. By establishing a successful investment track record in green opportunities, it aims to attract more institutional

---

*Research for this case study was completed between 2018 and 2019. The text reflects the circumstances at that time.

investors, thereby unlocking significant financial resources for further invest-ments in the sector and region.

Of ACP's US$450 million AuM, US$200 million was provided by its founding partners, US$94 million by the UK government, and the remainder by a mix of public and private investors. The fund's management estimates that about 35 percent of the capital is private.[2] ADB alone contributed US$100 million (see figure 8.1). Other investors include the Japan International Cooperation Agency, the Japanese commercial bank Bank of Tokyo Mitsubishi-UFJ, the Japanese insurance company Sompo Japan, and the Japanese infrastructure developer Pacific Consultants Co.

The UK government invested through its Climate Public Private Partnership Program (CP3), which aims at demonstrating to private investors that investing in low-carbon and climate-resilient companies in developing countries is not only ethically right but also commercially viable. Through this demonstration CP3 aims to catalyze new sources of capital, such as pension and sovereign wealth funds, for climate adaptation and mitigation. CP3 targets the renewable energy, water, energy efficiency, waste management and recycling, sustainable agriculture, and forestry sectors in developing countries. ACP is one of two funds in which CP3 invested.[3] CP3 is a joint initiative of the UK Department for International Development and the Department for Business, Energy & Industrial Strategy, which contributed a joint investment of US$94 million to ACP. The two departments are not just investors; they also play an active role in the fund's limited partners advisory committee, and set out certain requirements in a side letter of the fund's limited partnership agreement (LPA) (see figure 8.2). They undertake quarterly and annual monitoring of ACP and have appointed a consultant to provide reports.

As a first-time fund with no previous track record, ACP struggled to raise capi-tal from international pension funds and institutional investors. It initially aimed for total AuM worth US$750 million. Even with backing from three

FIGURE 8.1

Breakdown of ACP's committed capital, by source

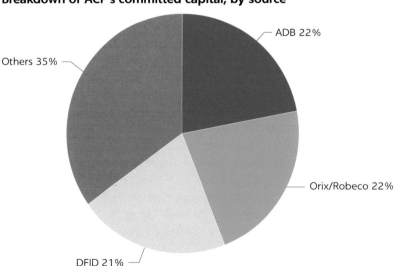

Source: ACP management.
Note: ACP = Asia Climate Partners; ADB = Asian Development Bank; DFID = UK Department for International Development.

FIGURE 8.2
ACP's structure

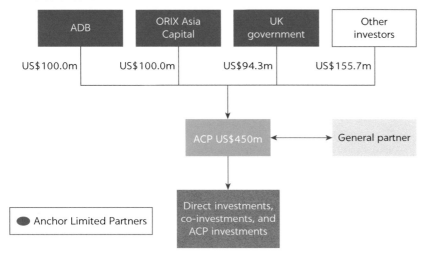

Source: ACP management.
Note: ACP = Asia Climate Partners; ADB = Asian Development Bank; m = millions.

well-recognized founding partners and lower fees than industry standards, achieving this goal was not possible. Nevertheless, at US$450 million, ACP is one of the largest private equity funds exclusively dedicated to climate-related sectors in Asia. The fundraising period ended in 2016, when ACP initiated its investment activities.

FUND STRUCTURE

ACP is set up with a traditional private equity general partner (GP)/limited partner (LP) structure, but the founding partners act as both GPs and LPs and play multiple roles, as outlined in the LPA. All legal arrangements pertaining to the fund and its LPs and GPs are under Cayman law. ACP charges lower management and performance fees than a typical private equity fund (1.5 percent management fee and 15.0 percent carried interest, compared with the 2.0 percent and 20.0 percent industry standards). Its investment team comprises 12 members with regional and sector experience, based in Hong Kong SAR, China.

The founding partners have a significant say over ACP's investment decisions, through their ownership of the general partnership and control of its board and investment committee. In addition to their investments in the fund, the founding partners have a stake in the general partnership, whose investment committee is composed of senior executives of each of the founding partners. To avoid conflicts of interest, investment decisions must be unanimous and are subject to certain voting excuse requirements. The limited partners advisory committee is also consulted in case of conflict situations.

Deal sourcing is done mainly by ACP's investment team, but from time to time the founding partners also source deals in which ACP can participate at its discretion. ADB, ORIX, and Robeco have an extensive presence, staff, and set of activities in Asia, with more than 30 offices and access to many transactions within the ACP mandate.

As an institutionally backed private equity fund, ACP is supported at several levels by the three partners:

1. ADB supports ACP in deal sourcing, due diligence, and fundraising, and through the provision of technical assistance facilities. ACP and ADB also have a formal staff secondment agreement.
2. ORIX, leveraging in particular its energy and eco services business headquarters and its East Asia business headquarters, supports ACP in deal sourcing and fundraising. ACP and ORIX also have a staff secondment agreement.
3. Robeco, in addition to initially providing staff seconded to ACP, also provided support services through general advice and access to Robeco's global network, sales, distribution, and investor relations (up to the fundraising's final closing date).

ADB may also provide debt, equity, or guarantees to companies or assets in which ACP makes an investment, with the terms and conditions of debt financing determined at arm's length. As discussed in more detail later in this case study, ACP takes significant minority or controlling equity stakes in investee companies, together with the project's promoter. ADB may typically provide a portion of the senior or subordinated debt and help attract other lenders. In one deal, ADB co-invested in the equity. In principle, ADB is free to deploy its full product suite, including guarantees, as it sees fit and to follow its own internal approval processes.

According to ACP management, the role of the founding partners, as described in the previous paragraphs, differentiates ACP from other Asian private equity funds focused on clean energy and energy efficiency. Those other funds are typically smaller (US$200 million AuM on average), target a limited number of sectors or countries, do not have access to ADB's services and network to mitigate sovereign and regulatory risks, do not have in-house capabilities to monitor ESG compliance, and charge higher fees.[4]

MANDATE FOR INVESTMENT

ACP can invest in renewable energy, resource efficiency, and environmental industries in China, India, and Southeast Asia, according to a list of eligible

TABLE 8.1 **ACP's target sectors and subsectors**

RENEWABLE ENERGY	RESOURCE EFFICIENCY	ENVIRONMENTAL INDUSTRIES
Solar	Energy service companies	Agribusiness, fisheries, and forestry
Wind	Energy efficiency	Environmental remediation
Biomass	Advanced materials	Process technologies
Sustainable biofuels	Smart grid	Water treatment
Hydro	Combined heat and power	Recycling and waste
Waste to energy	Storage	Sensors and instruments
Geothermal	Green buildings	Equipment manufacturing, assembly, and distribution for industries within target sectors
Hybrid power systems	Transportation improvements	
Energy storage		
Switching to renewable fuels		

Source: ACP management.
Note: ACP = Asia Climate Partners.

sectors detailed in the LPA. Table 8.1 shows the subsectors included by ACP in each category. Within this broad mandate, the LPA explicitly forbids investment in nonrenewable and nuclear power generation and hydrocarbon production.

ACP believes these sectors in Asia represent a large commercial investment opportunity, still not fully exploited. It notes that technology cost reductions have made clean energy production competitive in cost per kilowatt-hour in comparison with fossil-fuel power. Long-term macroeconomic trends (such as growth in population and gross domestic product per capita) and specific trends with large effects on the environment (such as growth in energy demand; carbon dioxide emissions; municipal solid waste; consumption of animal protein, paper, and wood; and decrease in water availability) call for more green investing and, ACP believes, offer greater opportunities in Asia than in Europe and North America.

Maximum portfolio exposure limits are defined by region, not by sector. ACP cannot invest more than 30 percent of its portfolio in China and in India, or more than 20 percent in any other individual Asian market.

The nature of the target sectors is such that, in ACP management's opinion, 60–70 percent of the portfolio will likely encompass investments in infrastructure. Examples include renewable power projects and water distribution and wastewater treatment. The current portfolio includes a solar power business in China, a wind farm in India, and an energy storage business in Indonesia.

ACP must comply with ADB's general prohibited investment activities list and ESG policies. ACP cannot invest in businesses that apply unfair labor practices, are involved in illegal activities under national or international laws, or operate in any of the following sectors: weapons, alcoholic beverages (excluding wine and beer), tobacco, gambling, radioactive materials, asbestos-related products, commercial logging, and environmentally damaging fishing practices.

INVESTMENT STRATEGY

ACP operates as a private equity fund, focusing on commercial investments in established midmarket businesses with proven technologies, good management, and strong growth potential. It targets 20 percent gross returns and invests in companies with enterprise value typically in excess of US$50 million and with positive earnings before interest, tax, depreciation, and amortization. It wins most of its investments in competitive auctions, where valuation is one key variable.

ACP may co-invest alongside other investors, taking significant minority or control equity positions and playing an active role in steering a company's strategy. It may also co-invest in investment funds or other entities sponsored by ADB, Robeco, and ORIX. In exchange for its stake in a company, ACP usually takes a seat on the company's board. Devoting an average ticket size of US$20 million to US$65 million, ACP plans to build a portfolio of 10–15 investments. Under a co-investment strategy ACP can target bigger deals, often in conjunction with its LPs or other investors.

PORTFOLIO AND TRACK RECORD

To date, ACP has closed four deals, summarized in table 8.2. At the time of writing, it was in the process of exiting one deal and was actively working on four to

TABLE 8.2 **ACP's portfolio companies as of November 2018**

TARGET COMPANY	COUNTRY	SECTOR	RATIONALE	CLOSING DATE
Panda Green Energy Group Limited	China (headquarters: Hong Kong SAR, China)	Renewable energy (solar)	Increase grid-connected solar projects; promote clean energy sources	2016
ColdEX	India	Cold chain logistics	Enable leading cold chain logistics group to build temperature-controlled warehouses, contributing to supply chain efficiencies and the reduction of food waste in India	2016
Skeiron Renewables	India	Renewable energy (wind)	Boost India's renewable energy mix	2016
NantEnergy (formerly Fluidic Energy)	Indonesia (headquarters: United States)	Energy storage	Promote rural electrification and clean energy use in Africa and Asia	2016

Source: ACP website; ACP management.
Note: ACP = Asia Climate Partners.

five deals to add to its portfolio in early 2019—in renewables, cold chain logistics, and sustainable agriculture.

ACP's proactive involvement at the portfolio company level takes place in five stages:

1. *Management.* ACP contributes to identifying key weaknesses (at the organization, strategy, or team level), developing a business plan, and hiring qualified professionals.
2. *Financing and operations.* ACP helps in attracting co-investors, budgeting, and providing access to the expertise and financial tools of its founding partners.
3. *Board participation.* ACP is a hands-on member, introduces best practices, and is represented in board subcommittees.
4. *Monitoring.* ACP sets internal key performance indicators, monitors market developments (technology, regulation), and conducts an annual ESG review.
5. *Exit preparation.* ACP aligns the expectations of management and co-investors regarding an exit strategy and timing, maintains financial-market-ready documentation, and promotes the visibility of the portfolio company.

ACP considers the full array of exit options typical of private equity deals, including a company's sale to a strategic or financial buyer, initial public offering, merger with another company (leading subsequently to a sale or initial public offering), sale of ACP's stake back to the company promoter, or recapitalization (if the company generates enough cash and has little debt). As a recent fund, ACP has so far not completed the exit of any deals, and information on actual returns in comparison with targets is also not yet available.

ADDITIONALITY AND MULTIPLIER CONSIDERATIONS

Notwithstanding its commercial focus, ACP aims for its investments to be additional, and to avoid crowding out other sources of private capital. ACP works toward these objectives by several means:

- In addition to relatively established and large markets such as China and India, ACP targets higher-risk, frontier markets, for instance, in Southeast Asia. It actively looks for transactions in locations where private investment in green sectors has not been forthcoming.
- Even in large Asian countries, local banks have limited expertise in renewables and other green sectors, and a fund such as ACP, together with ADB's loan products, could fill the gap.
- ACP is able to back project promoters with limited operational assets, and therefore also to take greenfield and construction risks.
- ACP offers more than capital; its affiliation with the ADB, Japan International Cooperation Agency, and UK Department for International Development is considered a strong advantage for fast-growing companies that seek contacts and credentials to expand to new countries and are considering an initial public offering down the line. The required compliance with ADB's ESG standards also enhances the credibility of ACP's portfolio companies. This perceived value added is illustrated by ColdEX, a portfolio company that values the credibility with new clients and in new markets that comes from an affiliation with ACP and its backers.

Because of its focus on commercial investments, so far ACP has made no direct use of concessionality at the deal level (for example, through grants, concessional loans, or guarantees). Any ADB loan or investment at the portfolio company level has been on commercial terms. Indirectly, however, ACP receives concessional help through the services provided, free of charge, by its founding partners. Furthermore, as the fund expands into frontier markets, it may consider applying for concessional loans or other tools if these tools positively affect the achievement of development impact in targeted investment.

ACP has indicated to investors that it could achieve a capital multiplier effect of over 100 times considering further equity and consequent debt leveraged. This is an informal commitment, not a hard target. This estimate is based on several undisclosed assumptions, including percentage equity stakes acquired and deal leverage.

GOVERNANCE

ACP's core decision-making and supervisory bodies are the GPs, its board of directors and investment committee, the investment adviser, and the limited partners advisory committee. See table 8.3 for a summary of the composition and functions of the various bodies.

In particular, the board of directors is composed of three senior executives, one from each of the founding partners, and is responsible for all major decisions outside the ordinary course of business, including budgeting, employment, and compensation. The current board members are the Deputy Director General, Private Sector Operations Department of ADB; the Chief Operations Officer Asia Pacific at Robeco; and the Head of Energy and Eco Services Business at ORIX. The board has no chairman, and all board members have equal rights and obligations. At the time of writing, ACP had no plan to add independent board members.

The investment committee includes representatives from ADB and ORIX. It recommends acquisitions and divestments to the GP and makes these decision on a unanimous basis.

TABLE 8.3 **Summary of ACP's governance bodies**

BODY	COMPOSITION	FUNCTIONS
General partner	• Legal entity registered in the Cayman Islands	• Primarily responsible for the management of the fund, including its portfolio management and risk management functions • Delegates certain investment management functions to the investment adviser
General partners' board of directors	• Has three voting members, one each from ADB, ORIX, and Robeco • Does not have a chairman (all three board members have equal rights and obligations)	• Is the main decision-making body of the general partner
Investment committee	• Comprises representatives from ADB and ORIX • Makes decisions on a unanimous basis	• Makes all investment decisions about a potential transaction
Investment adviser	• Legal entity under Hong Kong SAR, China, law • Most of ACP's investment team formally employed by the investment adviser, in addition to a secondee from ADB	• Responsible for the fund's management subject to the decision of the investment committee • Responsible for exercising the fund's rights in accordance with the instructions of the investment committee with respect to its interests in the fund's investments
Limited partners' advisory committee	• Comprises five representatives of limited partners, as appointed by the board of directors	• Advises the general partner and resolves issues involving potential conflicts of interest within the fund and such other items contemplated in ACP documents (for example, change in fund life and investment period) • Reviews such other matters as are customarily within the purview of an advisory committee

Source: ACP website, management interviews, and written feedback.
Note: ACP = Asia Climate Partners; ADB = Asian Development Bank.

The limited partners advisory committee has five members appointed by the LPs. It oversees the annual accounts, including portfolio valuation; is consulted on potential conflicts; and reviews fee generation at the portfolio company level.

STAFFING AND RECRUITMENT

ACP has a total staff (excluding board members) of 17, including 12 investment professionals with a background in investment banking, private equity, renewables investing, and asset management. The staff comprises one secondee each from ADB and ORIX. Investment professionals of the rank of director or managing director typically have 10–20 years or more of relevant experience. One staff member is dedicated to ESG compliance.

Staff recruitment follows the standard processes of the private equity industry. ACP engages an external headhunter to source suitable candidates when a new position opens. Resumes are received and interviews are conducted by all managing directors in the investment team. During ACP's setup phase, all three founding partners participated in and agreed to the recruitment of employees at the level of managing director; most staff had worked in similar funds operating in ACP's target sectors and were hired by the GPs through standard private equity industry processes that included external head-hunting firms.

Staff remuneration is market based with a fixed and variable component as in most funds.

ECONOMIC IMPACT AND ESG REPORTING

ACP applies ADB's ESG standards comprehensively throughout the investment process (see ADB 2001). ADB's ESG principles have detailed requirements in the areas of the environment, social equity, gender, labor, involuntary resettlement, and indigenous peoples, and a prohibited investment activities list (as mentioned earlier). These standards are adopted by ACP through its in-house Environmental and Social Management System. ACP also requires portfolio companies to use technologies to mitigate pollution, and practices consistent with internationally recognized standards such as the International Finance Corporation's environmental, health, and safety guidelines. ESG criteria are applied in the due diligence phase to identify material risks and then actively during company ownership. ACP's ESG system is largely in line with the requirements of the United Nations Principles for Responsible Investment (UNPRI), to which ACP intends to become a signatory.

ACP has an in-house, full-time ESG manager in charge of ensuring compliance with the Environmental and Social Management System and integrity procedures, analyzing data from portfolio companies, and monitoring and reporting on their compliance with ESG standards, including compiling an annual impact report. For larger portfolio companies, the work of the ESG manager is complemented by external consultants with specific country and sector knowledge.

ACP actively engages portfolio companies in focusing on ESG. The ESG manager coordinates with peers at the portfolio company as well as with its top management. ACP assists with review and implementation, sets out requirements in investment agreements, requires reporting annually or more frequently for investments with significant risks, and conducts annual visits and ESG audits.

ACP is in the process of expanding the metrics tracked by its annual impact report. Currently, ACP's impact report monitors the metrics summarized

TABLE 8.4 **Metrics contained in ACP's impact report**

METRIC	DETAILS
Total MW of clean energy installed	• By type (on grid, off grid) • By technology (wind, solar, hydropower, other)
MWh of clean energy generated	• By type (as above) • By technology (as above)
MWh of energy saved	• Specific to energy efficiency investments
Tons of CO_2e avoided	
Number of households with access to clean energy	• By type (household grid connection, dedicated energy access, district heating)
Jobs created	• In construction and operation phases • Males and females
Number of sustainable supply chain and clean technologies supported	• Total number of sectors represented in the investment portfolio
Private and public finance leveraged at fund level	• Essentially, fund AuM
Public and private finance leveraged (debt and equity) at co-investment level	• Total amount invested by third parties in ACP's portfolio companies
Public and private finance leveraged (debt and equity) at portfolio company or project level	• As above but includes debt raised by portfolio companies for specific projects

Source: ACP.

Note: ACP = Asia Climate Partners; AuM = assets under management; CO_2e = carbon dioxide equivalent; MW = megawatt; MWh = megawatt-hours.

in table 8.4. ACP plans to expand the list, seconding the growth of the investment portfolio and demand from LPs.

ACP had planned by 2019 to start publishing the annual impact report on its website and also on the websites of investee companies, to increase public awareness of its activities. At the time of writing, the impact report was delivered only to the LPs. ACP obtains data from portfolio companies biannually.

FINANCIAL DISCLOSURE

Portfolio reporting follows private equity best practices. It is handled by State Street Global Services, as the fund administrator, and is compliant with the standards of the European Venture Capital Association. Information provided includes

- Statements of committed and invested capital across investee companies and funds, regions, sectors, investment stages, currencies, and vintage years;
- Performance and valuation analysis of investee companies and funds;
- Description of material events at existing investee companies and funds as far as they can be made available to investors;
- Details of significant events, the team's views, and key market developments; and
- Quarterly unaudited financial statements and audited annual reports of portfolio companies.

Portfolio company valuation also follows the standard practices of the private equity industry. In order of priority, the methods used are the valuation used in the last financing round, comparable company valuation multiples, discounted cash flow, net asset valuation, and other industry benchmarks. Valuation is done by the fund manager, is updated whenever an event justifies a change in valuation, and is reported to the LPs quarterly.

NOTES

1. From the Robeco website (https://www.robeco.com/en/); figures as of March 2018.
2. Based on interview with management.
3. The other is the Catalyst Fund managed by the International Finance Corporation's Asset Management Company.
4. Interview with ACP management.

REFERENCE

ADB (Asian Development Bank). 2001. "Social Protection Strategy." Policy Paper, ADB, Manila.

9 Case Study—FONSIS: Pursuing a Triple Bottom Line of Economic Impact, Financial Returns, and Private Capital Mobilization*

BACKGROUND AND MISSION

FONSIS (Fonds Souverain d'Investissements Stratégiques, or Sovereign Fund for Strategic Investments) was established with Law 2012-34: Authorizing the Creation of a Sovereign Fund of Strategic Investments (hereinafter, FONSIS Law) passed by the Senegal National Assembly on December 31, 2012, and subsequently ratified by the President of the Republic. No further decrees were issued for the fund's establishment. In addition, Article 6 of the FONSIS Law envisages the launch of a future generations fund.

FONSIS is a limited liability company incorporated in October 2013 and fully compliant with the private business laws of OHADA, as is the case for all private companies in Senegal, which is a member state of OHADA.[1] Article 24 of the FONSIS Law also submits FONSIS to the audit of administrative bodies such as the General State Inspectorate and the Court of Auditors. Per the FONSIS Law, the government of Senegal owns 100 percent of the fund's capital but can open it to other state-owned entities. In any case, the state's direct ownership shall not be less than 70 percent.

FONSIS's broad mandate is to

- Invest or co-invest (with national and international partners) in strategic projects that generate a financial return and employment, predominantly via equity or quasi equity;
- Support Senegalese small and medium enterprises (SMEs) through different vehicles, including dedicated subfunds;
- Hold and manage equity stakes in state-owned enterprises and other assets on behalf of the state and create value for the state as a shareholder, supporting the ministry in charge of the state portfolio and, in the future, receiving remuneration for its services; and
- Maintain and invest some financial reserves for the benefit of future generations—in essence, acting as a traditional sovereign wealth fund.

---

*Research for this case study was completed between 2018 and 2019. The text reflects the circumstances at that time.

The government, via the Ministry of Finance, may also instruct the board of FONSIS to pursue other investment missions.

FONSIS's mandate is meant to support the implementation of Plan Sénégal Emergent (PSE), a development plan approved by the government in 2012 with the aim to make Senegal an emerging economy by 2035, although the fund has the flexibility to invest outside of the plan too. The plan includes an ambitious series of interventions and reforms in three core areas:

1. The structural transformation and growth of the economy, including development of the following sectors: agriculture, fisheries, agri-processing, social housing, mining, fertilizers, logistics, services, outsourcing, and tourism
2. Human capital, social security, and sustainable development, including focus on education, health, nutrition, water and sanitation, social security, emergency response, and the environment
3. Governance, institutions, peace, and security, including justice reform, promotion of human rights, local development, and decentralization

In compliance with the PSE, FONSIS has identified 10 target sectors, with infrastructure public-private partnerships (PPPs) featuring quite prominently among them. These sectors are agriculture, infrastructure, industry, energy, mining, information and communication technologies, financial services, real estate and tourism, health care, and education. As discussed in the subsection on portfolio and track record, infrastructure, mining, and energy (which includes solar power PPPs) account for 26 percent of total capital committed from 2014 to year-end 2018. Adding PPPs in the hospital sector, for which FONSIS undertook building construction and purchase of equipment, such percentage increases to 43 percent.

FONSIS was one of the sources identified to fund the vast investment required by the PSE. The plan identified a series of priority actions for the period 2014–18, requiring financing for a total of CFAF 10,288 billion (approximately US$17.9 billion).[2] The government planned to use budget sources in addition to other state-controlled financing vehicles including FONSIS; Fonds de Garantie des Investissements Prioritaires, a guarantee fund; Banque Nationale pour le Développement Economique, the national development bank; and Caisse des Dépôts et Consignations, a public investment institution. Even accounting for these additional sources, the government already in 2014 identified a shortfall of CFAF 2,964 billion (US$5.2 billion) to be covered primarily by the private sector through PPPs and by concessional loans, in order to preserve sovereign debt sustainability. After participating with all relevant stakeholders in the evaluation of the PSE's first priority action plan, ending in 2018, FONSIS was entrusted to lead the workshops on the funding model for the second priority action plan.

PSE has entered into its second priority action plan, which covers the period 2019–23. The budget for this plan is evaluated at CFAF 14,098 billion (approximately US$24.5 billion). The private sector is expected to cover CFAF 1,834 billion (US$3.2 billion); financial and technical partners, including development institutions with expertise in the relevant investment domains, are expected to cover CFAF 2,850 billion (US$5 billion).

FONSIS funding has fallen short of initial expectations. At inception in 2012, the government aimed to capitalize FONSIS with CFAF 500 billion (approximately US$870 million), predominantly by contributing stakes in state-owned enterprises and other assets. By the end of 2017, however, FONSIS had received only CFAF 10 billion (approximately US$17 million) in capital from the government, almost entirely in cash contributions from the state budget. See the subsection on fund structure for further details.

As a result of its limited capitalization, FONSIS had, at the time of writing, almost exclusively pursued the first two elements of its mandate (invest or co-invest in strategic projects with financial returns and employment potential, and support SMEs)—those most closely associated with the definition of a strategic investment fund as adopted in this book. At the time of writing, the launch of the future generations fund (or savings fund) was still in the planning phase. Senegal's demonstrated willingness to maintain a growth momentum through the 2019–23 Priority Action Plan triggered legal reforms that, at the time of writing, were being undertaken, notably a draft law addressing the allocation of oil and gas revenues expected to start flowing in 2022–23. Part of these revenues will be assigned to an intergenerational fund purposed with yielding steady returns for future generations, with FONSIS as sole fund manager. A law being drafted at the time of writing will reorganize FONSIS into two funds (a strategic fund and a generational fund), both managed by FONSIS S.A. Pending this reorganization, for simplicity in this case study, any reference to FONSIS will be to its capacity as a strategic investment fund, unless otherwise noted.

The yet to be launched generational fund would be capitalized with a portion of the revenues derived from recent oil and gas discoveries in Senegal and, according to the FONSIS Law, at least 15 percent of annual net income generated by FONSIS. Oil and gas companies Woodside and Exxon have received licenses from the government of Senegal to extract newly discovered, sizable reserves of oil and gas, respectively. Gas production is expected to start in 2021. The government will receive income in the form of revenue-sharing arrangements (nontax revenue) and corporate tax levied on the two companies. Thirty percent of the former will be used to capitalize the generational fund.

FUND STRUCTURE

Article 7 of the FONSIS Law establishes five potential sources of funding for FONSIS:

1. Equity capital provided by the state, mainly in the form of asset transfers, set initially at a minimum of CFAF 500 billion (approximately US$870 million). Any transfer of assets must be approved by presidential decree.
2. Borrowing, in consultation with the Ministry of Finance, from banks, other financial institutions, the capital markets, or other state entities. As in any other limited liability company, FONSIS's board of directors approves all borrowing. Borrowing is not guaranteed by the government of Senegal.
3. Remuneration of financial investments made by FONSIS and other remunerations received while carrying out its mission.
4. The allocation of part of the revenues of certain sectors such as mining, oil, and telecommunications. The amount of the allocation is determined annually in agreement with the Ministry of Finance, in accordance with applicable laws and regulations.
5. Donor funds that FONSIS may, in coordination with the Ministry of Finance, solicit from countries and institutions.

As of the time of writing, FONSIS had raised funds primarily through the first two means, and for amounts still below the target set in the FONSIS Law. Specifically,

- FONSIS received CFAF 10 billion (approximately US$17 million) in equity capital from the state, in the form of (1) cash allocations from the budget of CFAF 10 billion received in different tranches between 2013 and 2017, an amount sufficient to cover operating and personnel expenses and make small investments; and (2) asset contributions in the form of concessions to build and operate 250 kilometers of new toll roads, as well as a new railway line. Because these concessions do not yet generate revenue (120 kilometers of toll roads are under construction), their value is currently not recognized in FONSIS's balance sheet.
- In 2015 FONSIS obtained a CFAF 30 billion (US$52 million) credit line at commercial terms from Bank of Africa Senegal (BOA), with a first installment of CFAF 7 billion (US$12 million) drawn down at the time of writing. BOA, FONSIS, and the Senegalese government signed an agreement under which the state committed to deposit CFAF 3 billion (approximately US$5 million) each year into FONSIS's account at BOA. These state contributions are used to fulfill contractual repayments of the BOA line.
- In 2016, FONSIS received donor funding from the German development agency, Kreditanstalt für Wiederaufbau (KfW): CFAF 300 million (equivalent to US$500,000).

FONSIS is actively looking to expand its sources of funding:

- In 2017, FONSIS approached the Ministry of Economy, Cooperation and Planning with a proposal to relieve some budgetary pressures by entrusting FONSIS with the structuring of commercial projects, and dedicating budget resources only to noncommercial projects. As a result, some projects, originally meant to be funded by the government, were added to FONSIS's potential pipeline. FONSIS, following its normal investment process, will determine whether it can invest equity in these projects and raise additional debt. At the time of writing, this process was ongoing.
- Also in 2017, FONSIS applied for accreditation with the Green Climate Fund (GCF), a global fund created in 2010 by the United Nations Framework Convention on Climate Change to support climate mitigation and adaptation projects. Should FONSIS receive the accreditation, it would be able to access the GCF's suite of grant, concessional loan, and equity investment products for specific climate investments that meet GCF's investment criteria.

The government, via the Ministry of Finance, determines FONSIS's dividend payments to the state, which are capped at 60 percent of net income. For the first 10 years of FONSIS's existence, the state may not tap into FONSIS's financial reserves, for instance, for dividend payments. After that, according to Article 10 of the FONSIS Law, the state can use FONSIS's reserves to pay dividends only in case of force majeure, and in any event subject to a limit of 15 percent of total nonstatutory and nonlegal reserves.

Capital withdrawals from FONSIS are not allowed, unless approved by the President of the Republic, on advice from the Ministry of Finance, and ratified by an absolute majority of parliament.

FONSIS does not earn fees on its investment activities. As required by the FONSIS Law, internal rules establish a ratio of operating costs to size of FONSIS assets.

MANDATE FOR INVESTMENT

FONSIS's mission is to promote Senegal's role as an investor and partner of the private sector, with the aim to enhance direct investments in order to accelerate economic and social development through wealth and jobs creation for present and future generations.[3] It defines its mandate as triple bottom line: financial returns, economic impact, and maximizing private capital mobilization. Whereas private capital mobilization is an objective of all strategic investment funds, FONSIS emphasizes this objective by making external capital mobilization part of its triple bottom line because, for a developing country like Senegal with limited capital market access, it is essential to maximize the sources and amount of capital that can contribute to the country's economic development. FONSIS has not set a hard target for the multiplier effect but indicatively pursues a ratio of 10 dollars of external capital invested for each dollar that FONSIS itself deploys. To achieve its multiplier goal, FONSIS has prioritized the sourcing and development of a pipeline of investments to establish credibility with co-investors.

FONSIS contractually caps its returns in most investments in order to lower the funding costs for projects with positive economic impact, while ensuring that commercial investors are not crowded out. Although all FONSIS's investments are subject to a minimum internal rate of return (IRR) requirement of 12 percent, a return cap is meant to provide visibility to project promoters (with whom FONSIS co-invests) on FONSIS's exit terms and is negotiated on a deal-by-deal basis. When capping returns, FONSIS takes into account any existing potential commercial investors to ensure that FONSIS's terms are, at most, as favorable as, but never more favorable than, those offered by the other investors. This requirement ensures that commercial investors are not crowded out, for instance, by aligning FONSIS's capped returns with those of existing commercial investors in a project.

Project-specific capital mobilization has the advantage, in FONSIS's view, that projects can trigger new reforms or acceleration of pending reforms. In one example, a solar project promoted by FONSIS (Senergy) triggered a change in the terms of the power purchase agreement, which was based on previous fossil fuel–based power projects and inadequate for a solar PPP. The same revised power purchase agreement was subsequently used for another solar project. In another example, in order to invest in an imaging clinic, FONSIS pushed for health care reforms allowing for private management of hospital services.

INVESTMENT STRATEGY

FONSIS's investment strategy (including that of the generational fund) and risk policies are determined by the board, with the objective of achieving a rate of return in excess of the average cost of state borrowings (as determined in 2012).

FONSIS focuses on medium- and long-term investments with positive impacts on the economy and, with regard to the generational fund, on the creation of future financial reserves.

As a strategic investment fund, FONSIS plays three roles:

1. *Developer.* FONSIS develops strategic investment projects with the aim of attracting investment partners, soliciting expressions of interest; it prioritizes greenfield projects and is often the very first source of capital, well before any other commercial source.
2. *Restructurer.* FONSIS restructures and develops assets contributed to it by the state.
3. *Co-investor.* FONSIS co-invests in projects spontaneously presented by entrepreneurs, other investors, or the state.

As an example of its developer role, FONSIS, together with the International Finance Corporation (as part of the latter's Scaling Solar program), led the early-stage development of two solar power plants that subsequently attracted equity co-investments from infrastructure fund Meridiam and loans from development finance institutions. These two projects (the Kael and Kahone plants), together with two previous solar projects in which FONSIS invested in 2016 and 2017 (Senergy and Ten Merina, respectively), add about 120 megawatts of capacity to the Senegalese national electricity grid (see box 9.1 for details on all four investments).

FONSIS has not yet played the restructurer role with regard to specific assets contributed to it by the government. At the time of writing, its role was limited to advising the government on strategic development projects and supporting relevant negotiations.

As a co-investor, at the time of writing, FONSIS had taken passive stakes in projects or funds that are led and managed by external managers. For example, FONSIS took a 25 percent stake in Teranga Capital, a fund that is to provide equity and technical assistance to Senegalese SMEs, seeded by Investisseurs & Partenaires, a Paris-based investor in African SMEs and SME funds. Other passive investors in the fund include Senegal's main telecom operator Sonatel and insurance company Askia. In 2019, FONSIS started playing an active role in creating and co-managing funds, with the launch of the FONSIS/SAED[4] Agri SME Fund (a US$1.7 million fund to invest in agriculture projects in the north of Senegal); the We!Fund (a US$1.7 million economic empowerment fund to invest in projects that affect women); the pending launch of the SME Fund (a US$100 million fund to invest in all of Senegal in SMEs operating in water, sanitation, and hygiene; agribusinesses; health; education; and energy); and the pending launch (at the time of writing) of the REEF Fund (a US$50 million fund targeting the renewables and energy efficiency sectors) and the Blue Fund (a US$1.3 million fund dedicated to strategic water, sanitation, and hygiene projects).

Given its economic development mandate, FONSIS focuses predominantly on Senegal but can invest up to 25 percent of its assets (net of legal and statutory reserves) abroad, in compliance with exchange regulations in force. Shareholdings in foreign companies (mainly mining and oil companies) operating in Senegal are not affected by this threshold. FONSIS's financial investments abroad must be in liquid, creditworthy assets. At the time of writing, FONSIS had not made any such investment.

At the company level, FONSIS invests predominantly in equity or quasi-equity instruments, taking minority stakes and with board

BOX 9.1

FONSIS's solar investments

The Scaling Solar Senegal project derived from the ambition of the Senegalese government, through its Ministry of Petroleum and Energy, to develop a new energy mix integrating clean and affordable energy, through programs aimed at adding capacity to the national electricity grid via independent power producers. The Ministry of Petroleum and Energy, through the Regulatory Commission of the Electricity Sector, engaged with the International Finance Corporation (IFC) in 2016 to structure the program through an international call for tender. IFC recommended the participation of FONSIS (Fonds Souverain d'Investissements Stratégiques, Sovereign Fund for Strategic Investments) in the program, aiming to replicate the structure of the IFC's successful Scaling Solar program in Zambia, in which a national development fund played a key role as local institutional partner. As part of its mandate to hold the Senegalese state's interests in the project, FONSIS actively participated in the project's structuring, provided liaison with relevant government stakeholders, and was involved, as an investor, in negotiating the financing package.

The solar projects, located in Kael (Diourbel) and Kahone (Kaolack), were projected to have a cumulative nominal capacity of 60 megawatts and to represent 37 percent of the total installed solar capacity in Senegal when finalized in 2020. The cost for the two projects totaled €47.5 million. FONSIS contributed cash equity and some subordinated debt (in the form of quasi equity), and it holds a minority stake of 20 percent in both projects. A consortium composed of Meridiam, a global infrastructure fund based in Paris, and Engie Development, which was selected as the project's private developer after tender adjudication, contributed the rest of the equity. A pool of lenders comprising French development finance institution Proparco, the IFC, and the European Investment Bank provided commercial loans. The projects will sell power to national utility company Senelec under a 25-year power purchase agreement. The projects also benefit from a government guarantee covering Senelec's obligations under the power purchase agreement.

Previously, FONSIS invested in two solar projects, Senergy and Ten Merina, with a capacity of 30 megawatts each and operational at the time of this study. FONSIS holds a minority stake of 32 percent in Senergy and 10 percent in Ten Merina. Meridiam contributed the rest of the equity. The total cost for the two projects was €60 million. Of that total, €8 million was equity-funded, including about €1.5 million from FONSIS. The target equity internal rate of return is 12 percent. Proparco and the Belgian development finance institution BIO provided loans. These two projects also sell power to national utility Senelec under a power purchase agreement, with a government guarantee covering Senelec's obligations.

representation as a necessary condition. FONSIS can invest directly or through a subfund. The minimum ticket size is €450,000, leading to equity stakes generally below 33 percent. Exit options include put option to project promoter, sale to a private sector company (preferably domestic), sale to a financial investor, and initial public offering, among others. Exits may be dictated by the need to redeploy liquidity in other more profitable investments, achievement of IRR targets, or any contractual terms agreed to at the time of investment. FONSIS is also reviewing a potential debt investment, but it had not made a decision at the time of writing.

FONSIS seeks a target financial IRR in its equity investments that under no circumstances can be lower than 12 percent. Above that threshold, depending on economic and development impact considerations, the target IRR of an investment can vary and FONSIS can also opt to contractually cap its returns.

INVESTMENT PROCESS

FONSIS has several internal and external avenues to source projects. They include internal sourcing by FONSIS directly; request by the office of the President of the Republic, the Ministry of Finance, or other ministries; unsolicited proposals by project promoters; or presentation of projects by potential co-investors.

To be considered by FONSIS, a project must have a minimum set of prerequisite documents. For brownfield projects, these documents include the sponsor's proposal, a detailed data folder including the project's business plan and financial projections, a set of know-your-client documentation regarding the company and the sponsor, and historical audited financials. For greenfield projects, requirements are determined on a case-by-case basis. Typically, the promoter is requested to provide historical data from previous portfolio companies or relevant references in the sector. Other documents can be required by FONSIS to get the most accurate evaluation of the project.

For each of its functions—project developer, restructurer, and co-investor—as well as for debt investments, FONSIS has defined a precise sequence of activities, roles, and timetables that lead from investment sourcing to approval by the Investment Committee. The process varies for projects presented by a ministry or other public entity, and projects sourced otherwise. Figure 9.1 presents a graphic example. Steps include the receipt of a project idea, preliminary and detailed screening, establishment of a project committee for detailed

FIGURE 9.1

Investment decision process, FONSIS

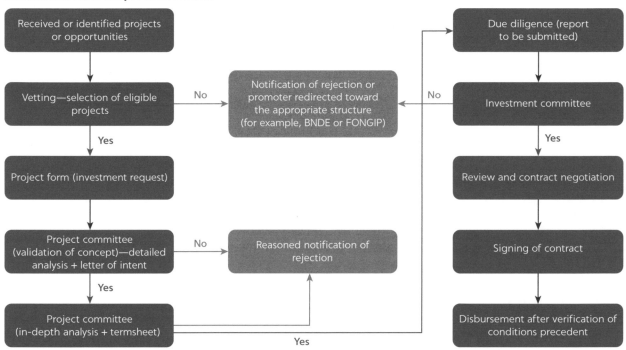

Source: FONSIS 2014.
Note: BNDE = Banque Nationale pour le Développement Economique; FONGIP = Fonds de Garantie des Investissements Prioritaires;
FONSIS = Fonds Souverain d'Investissements Stratégiques (Sovereign Fund for Strategic Investments).

transaction work, selection of co-investors (if any), presentation to the Investment Committee and approval, contract negotiations, financial closing, and ongoing monitoring and auditing of performance. As discussed in the subsection on governance, FONSIS's board prescreens projects for their compliance with the PSE and FONSIS's economic development mandate, but does so after the Investment Committee ascertains that the closing conditions are satisfied and that disbursements are made according to the board's resolution. The executive director in charge of the sector does the first vetting, with or without the help of the investment team depending on the project's complexity, and vetting is approved by the chief executive officer (CEO). When FONSIS rejects a project, it retains the ability to refer it to other state-owned finance entities such as the Banque Nationale pour le Développement Economique or Fonds de Garantie des Investissements Prioritaires, whose mandate may be more consistent with the features of the project in question.

PORTFOLIO AND TRACK RECORD

From inception to the end of 2018, FONSIS committed CFAF 30 billion (US$53 million) to 33 projects whose combined total cost is CFAF 957 billion (US$1.7 billion), generating a multiplier of 32x (see figure 9.2). The number of projects shows FONSIS's success in sourcing deals. At the time of writing, FONSIS had disbursed CFAF 5 billion (US$8.6 million) out of CFAF 30 billion committed, and deemed portfolio projects' performance in line with business plan and expectations.

Energy, agriculture, pharmaceuticals, and health care are, individually, the four largest sectors in terms of FONSIS's capital allocation (figure 9.3). Energy represented almost 24 percent of FONSIS's capital commitments from inception to the end of 2018. Health care PPPs and pharmaceutical ventures, together, broadly represented 42 percent of FONSIS's capital commitments over the

FIGURE 9.2

Investments approved by FONSIS since inception in 2013

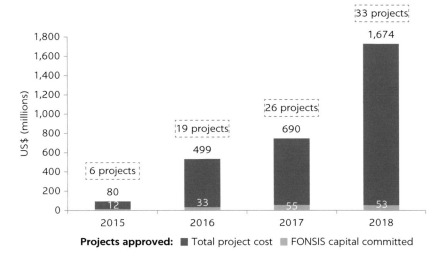

Projects approved: ■ Total project cost   ■ FONSIS capital committed

Source: FONSIS 2019.
Note: Multiplier calculated as ratio of total project costs to FONSIS capital committed. FONSIS = Fonds Souverain d'Investissements Stratégiques (Sovereign Fund for Strategic Investments).

FIGURE 9.3

Portfolio breakdown by sector, FONSIS

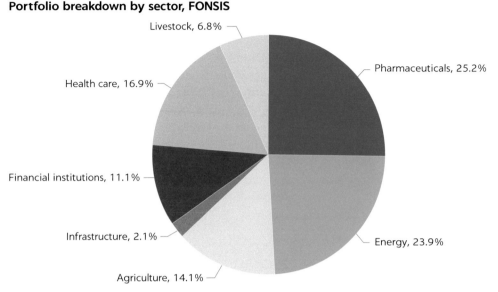

Source: FONSIS 2019.
Note: Figure shows sector shares of total disbursements as of December 2018, which were US$8.6 million.
FONSIS = Fonds Souverain d'Investissements Stratégiques (Sovereign Fund for Strategic Investments).

same period. FONSIS also has exposure, to a smaller extent, to financial institutions, real estate and infrastructure, and livestock breeding. Table 9.1 lists the projects approved to date. Other project approvals are ongoing.

In addition, FONSIS has launched the We!Fund, plans to launch the SME Fund, and is involved—as GP and LP—in the launch of other funds (Blue Fund, Project Development Fund, and REEF Fund), still pending at the time of writing. It plans to mobilize significant amounts of external capital for all these funds, in line with its triple bottom line mandate. Because FONSIS acts as promoter of these funds, this initiative falls under FONSIS's developer role—unlike the passive investment in Teranga. Given the risks, and novelty in Senegal, of SME investing and FONSIS's limited track record as a fund manager, to attract third-party investors FONSIS intends to partner with established fund managers and use its capital commitment as first-loss tranche (while retaining preferential participation in the upside). FONSIS would provide 5–10 percent of capital commitments, drawing from the BOA credit line.

Of the funds mentioned, REEF is a US$50 million renewable energy and energy efficiency fund focused on SMEs. The African Development Bank and the GCF would provide the majority of the capital. The fund would invest in SME equity and mezzanine debt. A funding proposal has been submitted by the African Development Bank to GCF for approval, and the search for a co-fund manager (in addition to FONSIS) is ongoing.

The SME Fund, being set up with KfW, is expected to be a US$100 million generalist SME fund that will invest in mezzanine debt only. FONSIS believes the investment opportunity is bigger in SME debt than equity, hence the larger size targeted for this fund compared with that for REEF. The fund is expected to benefit from a guarantee from the United States Agency for International Development's Development Credit Authority, covering any fund investment by commercial banks.

TABLE 9.1 **FONSIS projects approved from inception in 2013 to the time of writing**

PROJECT	SECTOR	FONSIS EQUITY STAKE (%)	DESCRIPTION
Biosoy	Agriculture	37	2,000-hectare farm
FONSIS SAED	Financial services	100	Fund launched by FONSIS in partnership with SAED (a local development agency), targeting agri-business SMEs in northern Senegal
Jambaar Immo	Infrastructure (real estate)	100	Newly established company in charge of redeveloping real estate assets (total project cost: US$64 million)
MF Touba	Health care	—	Construction and equipment of a five-floor building within Mathlaboul Fawzani National Hospital of Touba, in order to house its new medical platforms
Parenterus	Pharmaceuticals	23	Newly established, Senegal-based provider of intravenous solutions, with FONSIS contributing as a minority shareholder to the CFAF 9 billion (US$16 million) investment cost, together with the company's promoter and other local investors
Polimed	Health care	100	Medical imaging facility within the Mbour Public Health Center
Scaling Solar Senegal	Energy	20	Construction and operation of two solar plants with a cumulative nominal capacity of 60 MW in co-investment with Meridiam and ENGIE Development
Senergy	Energy	15	30 MW solar project; co-investment with Meridiam infrastructure fund
SIAA	Infrastructure	49	Development and management of special economic zones in Senegal
SOGENAS	Livestock	100	Newly established company launching high-productivity livestock in Senegal and developing dairy value chain; project solicited by the Ministry of Livestock and Animal Production in line with the sector priorities of the PSE
Solarys	Energy	100	Construction and operation of photovoltaic solar power plants for self-consumption (coupled with energy storage units) with a cumulative capacity of 17 MW (peak), on behalf of the National Water Company of Senegal
Ten Merina	Energy	10	30 MW solar project; co-investment with Meridiam
Teranga Capital	Financial services	22	SME-focused private equity fund, externally managed

Source: Information provided by FONSIS management.
Note: CFAF = West African CFA franc; FONSIS = Fonds Souverain d'Investissements Stratégiques (Sovereign Fund for Strategic Investments); MW = megawatt; PSE = Plan Sénégal Emergent; SAED = Société Nationale d'Aménagement et d'Exploitation des Terres du Delta du fleuve Sénégal et des vallées du fleuve Sénégal et de la Falémé (National Society for the Development and Exploitation of the land of the Senegal River Delta); SME = small and medium enterprise; — = not available.

ADDITIONALITY AND MULTIPLIER CONSIDERATIONS

FONSIS aims to deliver additionality and to avoid crowding out other sources of private capital in several ways.

- *As a project developer or codeveloper.* In this role FONSIS prioritizes greenfield projects and gets involved well before any other source of commercial capital. Through its preparation work, it opens the door for the subsequent entry of investors and lenders. For example, FONSIS mentioned its launch of a livestock company focused on introducing new breeds to Senegal; FONSIS at the time of writing was the only shareholder in this novel business and had budgeted five years of development work before the company is ready for external investments. FONSIS also invested in Parenterus, a newly established Senegal-based manufacturer of intravenous solutions, contributing as a minority shareholder to the CFAF 9 billion (US$16 million) investment cost, together with the promoter and other local investors; the project is seen as highly consistent with the PSE because of its potential to reduce imports of the products manufactured, create employment, and contribute to improvements in health care.

- *By generating demonstration effects.* Through its activities, FONSIS can demonstrate that certain projects with high development impact can be run as commercial enterprises, aiming to attract further commercial capital as a result. For example, FONSIS seeded Polimed, a diagnostics and laboratory business structured as a PPP and housed within an existing hospital. Polimed charges the same prices for its services as the Mbour public hospital, does not enjoy any subsidies, and employs doctors and nurses from the attached hospital (in addition to contractors hired ad hoc). FONSIS invested the equivalent of US$1.7 million to purchase equipment, build the facility, and hire contractors, and obtained a pilot concession from the hospital to run the facility starting in December 2015. The project is meeting FONSIS's IRR targets and could be used as a template for other similar projects in the health care sector.
- *As an intermediary between the government and private investors.* As a fully government-owned entity, FONSIS is well positioned to entertain new project ideas with ministries and other government bodies, even when projects challenge the institutional status quo. For instance, FONSIS was able to push the Polimed PPP idea despite initial resistance to a for-profit service provider expressed by the Ministry of Health. Meridiam, as a co-investor and codeveloper, also recognized the value added of FONSIS as an intermediary with government stakeholders.

As previously discussed, maximizing the capital multiplier is a core element of FONSIS's mandate, even if no hard targets are set. FONSIS justifies this approach with the large funding gaps necessary to support Senegal's economic development and the need to extend the search for capital beyond public and donor finance.

GOVERNANCE

FONSIS's main supervisory body is the Strategic Orientation Council, which has not yet been established. This council is mandated to advise on investment strategy and strategic direction and must meet annually under the chairmanship of Senegal's president or, if the president declines, the prime minister. Pending implementation of the council, the board performs these functions. The council will be composed of representatives of the local and international business, political, and academic communities, and civil society.

As a limited liability company and under private OHADA business law,[5] FONSIS's main supervisory body is the board of directors. The board is composed of FONSIS's CEO; chairman; two representatives of the Ministry of the Economy, Planning and Cooperation; and one representative of the presidency (see table 9.2). Its roles and responsibilities are described in Article 13 of the FONSIS Law as follows: "The Board deliberates on all measures concerning the

TABLE 9.2 **Summary of FONSIS governance bodies**

BODY	COMPOSITION	FUNCTIONS
Strategic Orientation Council	• Council yet to be implemented at the time of writing • Once appointed, will comprise representatives of the local private sector, the parliament, the academic system, or liberal professions	• Advises FONSIS on its investment philosophy and guides the fund toward its strategy • Powers, composition, and functioning determined by presidential decree
Board	• Up to 10 members, appointed by presidential decree for three-year terms (renewable one time) • Chairman proposed by the President of the Republic and elected by board • CEO a member while in office • Revocation of membership during term with approval of the President of the Republic • As of this report, five members including the CEO, the chairman, a representative of the presidency, and two representatives of the Ministry of Economy, Planning and Cooperation • No independent board member at the time of writing	• Deliberates on measures relating to the management of FONSIS and determines the investment and management policies of FONSIS • Outlines the fund's objectives and the orientation of its management • Exercises permanent control of the CEO's management • Appoints the CEO • Approves all investment projects, based on financial and economic considerations and the board members' expertise in various sectors (the Investment Committee ascertains that the closing conditions are satisfied and that disbursements are made according to the board's resolution) • Approves the annual accounts
Investment Committee	• Six members including the CEO, executive director in charge of business sectors, executive director in charge of finance and investor relations, chief legal officer, and independent members (2 board members) • One of the two independent board members chairs the Investment Committee	• Upon approval of investments by the board, validates each disbursement to make sure it is made according to the board's resolution • Evaluates investment-specific risks when validating each disbursement
Audit and Risk Committee	• Chaired by a board member and composed of the financial and administrative director and legal and regulatory affairs	• Evaluates internal risks and the respect of rules and procedures • Notifies the board of risks • Evaluates the risk management policy and the quality of internal controls
Recruitment and Remuneration Committee	• Chaired by the chairman of the board and includes a board member	• Approves the appointment of executive management and remuneration policies • Approves FONSIS's representation in the boards of its portfolio companies • Determines staff salaries and bonuses on recommendation by the CEO

Source: FONSIS 2017; Law 2012-34: Authorizing the Creation of a Sovereign Fund of Strategic Investments (FONSIS), passed by the Senegal National Assembly on December 31, 2012.
Note: CEO = chief executive officer; FONSIS = Fonds Souverain d'Investissements Stratégiques (Sovereign Fund for Strategic Investments).

management of FONSIS and defines the management and investment policy of the Fund. As such, it is responsible for the Fund's performance."

Board members are appointed by presidential decree. The FONSIS Law established that the board can have a maximum of 10 representatives, including up to 5 state representatives or civil servants, with 1 representative of the president, 1 representative of the prime minister, and 2 representatives of the Ministry of Finance. At the time of writing, the board is composed of the CEO (an ex officio member of the board with full voting rights); two representatives of the Ministry of Economy, Planning and Cooperation; and one representative of the presidency, and does not include any independent members. In 2019 a constitutional law[6] eliminated the position of prime minister, and a decree[7] split the Ministry of Economy, Finance and Planning into two separate ministries: the Ministry of Economy, Planning and Cooperation and the Ministry of Finance and Budget. The former Ministry of Economy, Finance and Planning's two board seats were transferred to the Ministry of Economy, Planning and Cooperation. The board elects a chairman proposed by the President of the Republic; the CEO may also be considered for the chairman role. Board members are appointed for three-year terms (renewable once), which can be revoked during their term with the approval of the President of the Republic.

FONSIS's CEO is appointed by the board on recommendation of the President of the Republic, for a five-year term (renewable once). With the approval of the President of the Republic, the CEO may be dismissed for gross misconduct, mismanagement, or unsatisfactory performance. The CEO must have at least 10 years of relevant experience in investment management, sovereign fund management, and banking (financing, mergers, acquisitions, capital markets, and so on), with at least 3 years as manager, general manager, associate or managing partner, or similar managerial position. The CEO must meet requisite standards of integrity. Figure 9.4 depicts FONSIS's organizational structure under the CEO.

Once investments are approved by the board, the Investment Committee validates each disbursement to make sure it is made according to the board's resolution. The Investment Committee comprises six members: the CEO, executive director in charge of business sectors, the executive director in charge of finance and investor relations, the chief legal officer, and two board members (one of whom chairs the Investment Committee).

FIGURE 9.4

FONSIS organizational structure

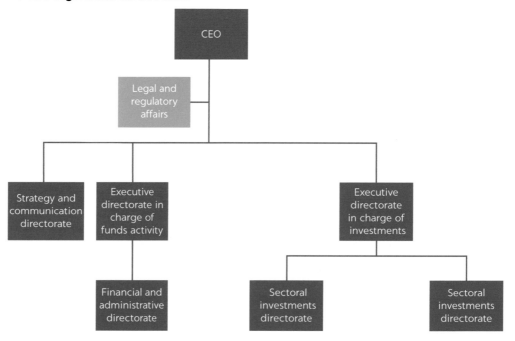

Source: FONSIS.
Note: CEO = chief executive officer; FONSIS = Fonds Souverain d'Investissements Stratégiques (Sovereign Fund for Strategic Investments).

STAFFING AND RECRUITMENT

FONSIS has a staff of 34, including 15 investment professionals with 10–20 years of relevant experience in Senegal and abroad. Professional backgrounds include investment banking, commercial banking, and investing. With the exception of board members who are government representatives, all FONSIS employees come from the private sector. FONSIS used an external Senegalese recruitment agency during the very early stages of recruiting. It subsequently put in place an internal process to hire staff, including public announcements of open positions, screening procedures, interviews with current staff, tests, and interviews with the executive directors.

The FONSIS Law establishes that management remuneration must be attractive and enable the hiring of qualified investment professionals. Personnel salaries and bonuses are set by the board on recommendation of the CEO. In practice, FONSIS cannot match the remuneration (salary plus bonus) of similar private sector funds, but the appeal of working for a high-profile institution in their native country has proven attractive for members of the Senegalese diaspora previously working in international financial centers.

ECONOMIC IMPACT AND ESG REPORTING

In its investment strategy FONSIS emphasizes the achievement of social and environmental impacts and the promotion of good governance practices. Specifically,

- FONSIS defines social and environmental impact as the creation of jobs with acceptable salary levels, local economic development, and the strengthening of value chains, coupled with minimal negative impact on the environment.
- From a governance perspective, FONSIS pushes portfolio companies to adopt transparent management and supervisory structures, performance and reporting systems, and accounting standards and procedures.

FONSIS implements its impact and ESG practices at all phases of the investment process, namely,

- In the *project selection phase*, FONSIS screens projects using predefined criteria including job creation, impact on local economy, coherence with the PSE, and minimal impact on the environment. In addition, projects must obtain clearance from the Ministry of Environment and Sustainable Development if required by it; such clearance is based on the completion of an environmental study.
- In the *project implementation phase*, once a project or company enters FONSIS's portfolio, FONSIS works proactively with it to implement the required ESG standards.
- In the *monitoring phase*, as a shareholder, FONSIS requires quarterly reporting of ESG compliance by its portfolio companies and participates in their governance bodies. The ESG standards follow international best practices, such as those promoted by the International Finance Corporation.

FONSIS has been a member of the International Forum of Sovereign Wealth Funds since 2019 (see IWG [2008] for the Santiago Principles).

FINANCIAL DISCLOSURE AND RISK POLICIES

FONSIS publicly discloses relevant financial information related to its operations in its annual reports. Reports are also published for the board of directors and the different committees.

As a limited liability company, FONSIS is subject to auditing requirements laid out by company law. International auditing firm Ernst & Young and a local firm have been appointed as auditors. In addition, according to Article 24 of the FONSIS Law, FONSIS is subject to control by the State General Inspection, the Court of Auditors, and the General Inspection of Finance.

At the time of writing, FONSIS had not yet formalized its risk policies.

NOTES

1. OHADA (Organisation pour l'harmonisation en Afrique du droit des affaires, or Organization for the Harmonization of Corporate Law in Africa) is a system of corporate law and implementing institutions adopted in 1993 by 17 West and Central African nations.
2. Senegal's currency is the West African CFA franc (CFAF) and is pegged to the euro. FONSIS is denominated in CFAF. Throughout this case study, any conversion to US dollars is based on an exchange rate of CFAF 575.00 to US$1.00, as of the beginning of October 2018.
3. See the "Who We Are" page on the FONSIS website (https://www.fonsis.org/en/who-we -are/our-mission).
4. SAED stands for Société Nationale d'Aménagement et d'Exploitation des Terres du Delta du fleuve Sénégal et des vallées du fleuve Sénégal et de la Falémé (National Society for the Development and Exploitation of the land of the Senegal River Delta).
5. More specifically, the Uniform Act on Commercial Companies and the Economic Interest Group (Uniform Act).
6. Constitutional law dated May 14, 2019.
7. Decree n° 2019-762 dated April 7, 2019.

REFERENCES

FONSIS (Fonds Souverain d'Investissements Stratégiques). 2014. "Schématisation des Procédures Internes d'Investissement et de Financement." FONSIS, Dakar.

FONSIS (Fonds Souverain d'Investissements Stratégiques). 2019. "Rapport Annuel 2018." FONSIS, Dakar. https://www.ifswf.org/sites/default/files/annual-reports/Fonsis -rapport-2019.pdf.

FONSIS (Fonds Souverain d'Investissements Stratégiques). 2017. "Rapport Annuel 2017." FONSIS, Dakar. https://www.fonsis.org/sites/default/files/rapport-annuel/Fonsis _Rapport_2017.pdf.

IWG (International Working Group of Sovereign Wealth Funds). 2008. "Sovereign Wealth Funds Generally Accepted Principles and Practices: 'Santiago Principles.'" IWG. https:// www.ifswf.org/sites/default/files/santiagoprinciples_0_0.pdf.

10 Case Study—The Ireland Strategic Investment Fund: A Strategic Investor in a High-Performance Economy*

A strategic investment fund must by nature be long term, but its mandate and strategy need to be flexible and adaptable, evolving to the needs of the economy.

—Eugene O'Callaghan, Director, Ireland Strategic Investment Fund

BACKGROUND AND MISSION

The Ireland Strategic Investment Fund (ISIF) is a fully state-owned €8.8 billion fund (as of December 31, 2018) with the double bottom line mandate to invest (1) on a commercial basis and (2) in a manner designed to support economic activity and employment in Ireland. It was established by act of parliament, specifically the National Treasury Management Agency (Amendment) Act, 2014 (hereinafter, the NTMA Act 2014).[1] ISIF invests both directly and indirectly through third-party managers, and has the flexibility to invest across the capital structure—from secured debt (rated or unrated) to venture equity.

ISIF is the successor of the National Pensions Reserve Fund (NPRF), established in 2001 to supplement the existing pay-as-you-go public pension system. NPRF was controlled by the NPRF Commission, acting through the National Treasury Management Agency (NTMA, or the Board) as fund manager. One of the statutory purposes of the NPRF was to meet as much as possible of the costs of social welfare and public service pensions from 2025 until 2055. Up to 2010, the Exchequer contributed an amount equal to 1 percent of gross national product annually into the NPRF. The NPRF Commission, through the NTMA, built a global, long-term portfolio of listed securities (stocks and bonds), real estate and private equity, commodities, and absolute return funds.

As a result of the global financial crisis, a significant portion of the assets of NPRF was used to recapitalize fragile Irish banks. In light of the particularly severe effects of the crisis in Ireland, at the direction of the Minister for Finance,

---

*This case study uses language directly from ISIF's Santiago Principles Self Assessment in some sections. The self assessment can be found at https://www.ifswf.org/assessment/ireland-strategic-investment-fund. Research for this case study was completed between 2018 and 2019. The text reflects the circumstances at that time.

in 2009 a total of €10.7 billion from the NPRF was invested in Allied Irish Banks plc and the Bank of Ireland, followed by a further €10 billion in 2011. Investments in the two banks were segregated into a Directed Portfolio subject to the direction of the Minister for Finance and oversight by the Department of Finance. The remaining pool of capital, termed the Discretionary Portfolio and worth approximately €4.5 billion in 2011, stayed under the control of the NPRF Commission. The annual contribution to the NPRF stopped in 2010 as a result of Ireland's worsened fiscal position.

In September 2011 the government announced its intention to establish a strategic investment fund to channel resources from the NPRF toward investment in sectors of strategic significance to the future of the Irish economy, which led to the announcement of ISIF and its mandate in mid-2013 and the formal establishment of ISIF in December 2014. This intention required legislative changes in the form of the NTMA Act 2014, providing, among other things, for the establishment of the ISIF and the transfer of all NPRF assets (both Directed and Discretionary Portfolios) to ISIF. Ownership of ISIF is vested in the Minister for Finance, with the NTMA responsible for control and management of the fund; consequently, NPRF's investment mandate ended. At the date of transfer from NPRF to ISIF, the total portfolio was valued at €22.1 billion, including €15 billion in the Directed Portfolio (subject to oversight and direction from the Minister for Finance) and €7.1 billion in the Discretionary Portfolio.

Following ISIF's establishment, its initial investment strategy was approved by the NTMA after consultation with the Minister for Finance and the Minister for Public Expenditure and Reform, and published in July 2015. The investment strategy was reviewed in 2017–18—in compliance with Section 40 the NTMA Act 2014, which requires a periodic review of the strategy—and amended to reflect Ireland's rapidly improving economic situation and changing investment opportunity for ISIF. The initial strategy reflected Ireland's need to attract capital and stimulate the economy in the aftermath of the global financial crisis that severely affected the country. By the time of the strategy review, Ireland's economy had improved well beyond expectations. ISIF submitted its own review material to the two government departments (Department of Finance and Department of Public Expenditure and Reform), and the Department of Finance published its review of ISIF in the fourth quarter of 2018 as part of the Budget 2019 materials (Ireland, Department of Finance 2019).

In July 2018, the Minister for Finance and Public Expenditure and Reform announced a refocusing of ISIF on five key economic priorities: (1) indigenous industry, (2) regional development, (3) sectors negatively affected by Brexit, (4) projects to address climate change, and (5) housing supply (Ireland, Department of Finance 2018). The latter priority is intended to address Ireland's housing shortage, one of the key issues that emerged with the economic recovery. The change in focus reflects the strong growth in the Irish economy and increase in capital inflows over the previous years, but also new challenges such as Brexit, the public debt level, the risk of economic overheating, national competitiveness, and global economic and geopolitical uncertainties.

To align with this new strategy and the ministerial review, a new ISIF business plan was developed (ISIF Investment Strategy 2.0), according to which a portion of ISIF funds would be reallocated through legislation to a new rainy day fund[2] and to two newly established agencies (ISIF 2019b). This reallocation is to occur over the medium term, with approximately 50 percent of it occurring in 2019. ISIF's Discretionary Portfolio was valued at €8.8 billion as of December 31, 2018 (ISIF 2018b). Of ISIF's capital, €3.5 billion will, subject to the requisite legislation, be reallocated as follows: €750 million has been committed to the newly established Home Building Finance Ireland (an agency dedicated to extending low-risk, working capital loans to small and medium housing developers); up to €1.25 billion to the Land Development Agency; and €1.5 billion to a rainy day fund, the primary purpose of which is to mitigate severe economic shocks beyond the normal fluctuations of the economic cycle. As a result, ISIF's size is reduced to €5.3 billion. ISIF's housing investments will seek to avoid overlap with Home Building Finance Ireland.

The following details of the case study reflect the position up to the end of 2018, before ISIF Investment Strategy 2.0.

FUND STRUCTURE

ISIF is not a separate legal entity; it is a fund[3] comprising a collection of assets, owned by the Minister for Finance and managed and controlled by the NTMA (subject to the direction of the Minister for Finance in respect of the Directed Portfolio element of the ISIF).

The NTMA Act 2014 established some general principles for the establishment and operations of ISIF. These principles include the following (see the subsection on governance for further detail):

- Adoption of a legal framework for ISIF including a specified policy mandate (investment objectives) and a framework for its management and control, which are publicly disclosed
- Minister for Finance ownership of ISIF[4]
- Status of the NTMA as controller and manager of ISIF, with responsibility for determining the investment strategy for ISIF
- Oversight provided by the Investment Committee of the NTMA on implementing the investment strategy

NTMA controls and manages ISIF, which does not include any third-party capital (figure 10.1). The NTMA is a public agency that provides asset and liability management services to the Irish government. In addition to managing ISIF, these services include borrowing on behalf of the government and managing the national debt, the State Claims Agency, the New Economy and Recovery Authority, and the National Development Finance Agency. NTMA has a staff of approximately 500, 45 of whom are allocated to the ISIF team. In addition, the ISIF team is supported by a number of NTMA corporate functions, including economics, finance, information technology, human resources, legal, communications, agency secretarial, risk, compliance, and internal audit.

MANDATE FOR INVESTMENT

The policy mandate for ISIF is that it be invested, on a commercial basis, in sectors and opportunities intended to generate positive economic impacts for Ireland. Specifically, according to the NTMA Act 2014, NTMA "shall hold or invest the assets of the Fund [ISIF] (other than directed investments) on a

FIGURE 10.1
Structure of NTMA and ISIF

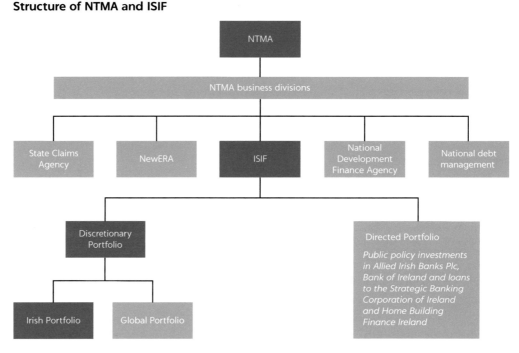

Source: World Bank.
Note: Dark blue boxes denote the units most relevant to ISIF's capacity as a strategic investment fund. ISIF = Ireland Strategic Investment Fund; NewERA = New Economy and Recovery Authority; NTMA = National Treasury Management Agency.

commercial basis in a manner designed to support economic activity and employment in the State."

The economic impact side of the mandate is based on three criteria against which ISIF evaluates all investment decisions:[5]

1. *Additionality* refers to the economic benefits to gross value added (GVA) and gross domestic product (GDP)[6] likely to arise from the investment under examination above what would have taken place in any case.[7] Elements of economic additionality at the investment level include GVA, employment creation, and qualitative features such as contribution to Ireland's enabling infrastructure, innovation capacity, and efficiency (for example, through sector consolidation).[8] ISIF investments may generate additionality in the medium to long term, through participation in existing or newly established businesses. Social and environmental considerations are specifically not embedded in the additionality test, which focuses on economic impact, but are covered by ISIF's Sustainability and Responsible Investment Strategy and adherence with the UNPRI and the Santiago Principles (as discussed in the subsection on economic impact and ESG reporting).

2. *Displacement* refers to instances when an investment's additionality is reduced at the overall economy level because of a reduction in economic benefits elsewhere in the economy. For example, an investee company that competes with other Irish companies would reduce the investment's overall impact on GVA of the whole economy. ISIF's investments seek to avoid displacement.

3. *Deadweight* refers to instances whereby the economic benefits of an investment would also have been achieved in the absence of such investment. ISIF focuses especially on avoiding financial deadweight—participating in investments that would have attracted private capital regardless of ISIF's participation.[9]

ISIF has a holistic approach to impact evaluation: investments must exhibit high additionality and low displacement and deadweight. Additionality is the necessary condition. ISIF has minimal tolerance for deadweight: it avoids competing with other sources of private capital and also requires potential investees to survey potential sources of commercial funding before an ISIF investment. Displacement can be harder to assess, especially in fragmented domestic sectors with many SMEs operating, some of which may suffer because of ISIF's investment in competing businesses. Compliance with the displacement criteria tends to skew investments toward export-oriented businesses and fast-growing sectors such as technology (information technology, pharmaceuticals, and biotech), and away from the domestic service and retail sectors.

ISIF sets no hard thresholds for any of the three criteria. Rather, ISIF applies a portfolio management approach to economic impact. Some investments are ruled out because of noncompliance with the criteria. Other investments may meet the criteria but have, for instance, relatively low economic additionality. In this scenario, ISIF may choose to invest only a small amount, keeping firepower for other investments with greater additionality. ISIF has targeted an 80 percent/20 percent split of its capital commitments between high-impact and low-impact investments; it defines high impact as producing sustainable, long-term benefits for the Irish economy and low impact as producing short-term benefits such as a temporary boost in employment or when additionality may be offset by displacement.

Meeting the three economic impact criteria is a precondition for any investment to be submitted to the Investment Committee for the final investment decision, under a precisely defined process. First, the investment professionals with the ISIF team who are focused on economic impact develop an economic impact scorecard, filling in basic data such as revenue and employment potential. In parallel, the investment team produces a full investment proposal for the Investment Committee. The economic impact scorecard is sent for review to the Economic Impact Implementation Group, which comprises ISIF's head of investment strategy, NTMA's chief economist, and other members of the ISIF Investment Strategy team and the NTMA Economics Unit. After the Economic Impact Implementation Group's review, the economic impact scorecard is submitted to the Portfolio Management Committee[10] as part of the overall investment proposal. If approved by that committee, the proposal is submitted to the Investment Committee for consideration and, if thought fit, approval.

ISIF collects and publishes economic impact data on a semiannual basis to measure the economic impact of investees and underlying investees (when ISIF invests in funds). The assembly and assessment of this data can be somewhat challenging given that economic impact is a relatively new concept (in the context of investing), but ISIF believes it has adopted a structured and consistent approach to the collection and analysis of such data.

A key element of ISIF's investment strategy is to attract co-investment from third-party investors. Co-investment is viewed as particularly important because it leverages ISIF's finite resources to significantly increase the quantum of economic impact in Ireland that can be achieved in the investment program.

ISIF targets investments that fall under three strategic drivers:

1. *Enabling Ireland.* Enabling sectors are those that create the foundations for sound economic growth and fix bottlenecks; examples include housing, of which Ireland has experienced a severe shortage; water; energy; and other infrastructure.
2. *Growing Ireland.* Growing sectors are those presenting significant expansion opportunities for the Irish economy, such as food, agriculture, and export.
3. *Leading Edge Ireland.* These drivers include new technologies and sectors, such as information technology and life sciences, in which Ireland has established a strong representation or reputation.

Infrastructure, under the broad definition adopted in this book, represents just over a quarter of ISIF's capital commitments. ISIF defines infrastructure as being its commitment to the airport and port sectors and infrastructure funds (representing about 10 percent of ISIF's capital commitments as of December 31, 2018). Adding commitments to the water (about 11 percent of ISIF's total capital commitments) and energy (about 6 percent of ISIF's total capital commitments) sectors, broad exposure to infrastructure stood at about 27 percent of ISIF's capital commitments as of December 31, 2018 (figure 10.2). Real estate, of which housing represents the largest portion, absorbs another 20 percent of committed capital. It includes the financing, development, and ownership of new residential housing stock.

FIGURE 10.2

ISIF's capital committed to Irish investments by sector, as of December 31, 2018

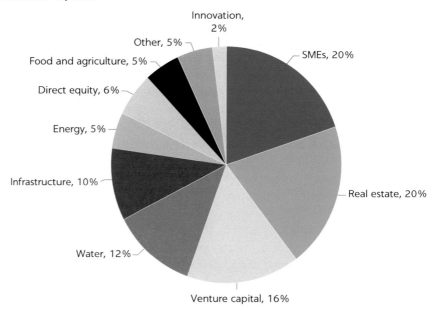

Source: ISIF 2018b.
Note: Figure shows sector shares of ISIF's committed capital in the Irish Portfolio as of December 31, 2018, which totaled €4.1 billion. ISIF = Ireland Strategic Investment Fund; SMEs = small and medium enterprises.

INVESTMENT STRATEGY

Consistent with its mandate, ISIF pursues commercial, risk-adjusted expected returns, varying according to the layer of the capital structure invested and the risk of the underlying investment.

At the Discretionary Portfolio level, ISIF aims for returns over the long term in excess of a rolling five-year average cost of Irish government debt.[11] When the investment strategy was defined in 2015, the Discretionary Portfolio return threshold was 4 percent. With the subsequent improvement in Ireland's economy, the rolling five-year average cost of Irish sovereign debt decreased to approximately 3.6 percent (December 2018). The required level of commercial return varies by transaction, sector, opportunity, and layer of the capital structure invested.

Within the Discretionary Portfolio, the Global Portfolio (as defined in the subsection on portfolio and track record) is designed, at the time of writing, to meet effectively its requirement to ensure that capital is available as investment opportunities in Ireland are executed and drawn down, while making a significant contribution toward ISIF's investment return objective. The legislative policy mandate for ISIF—to invest on a commercial basis in a manner designed to support economic activity and employment in Ireland—requires it to be transitioned, over a period of years, from a largely global portfolio into an Irish portfolio. Immediately converting the Global Portfolio into cash is not a preferred option, because the risk-free return on cash is negligible (at the time of writing). To achieve the capital preservation and return objectives for the Global Portfolio, ISIF—through third-party investment managers hired on a competitive basis—implements a dynamic, diversified, highly liquid, cautious investment strategy that includes a mix of asset classes including cash, debt instruments, equities, and alternative investments such as absolute return funds. The latter, by design, are expected to have low correlation to global markets, thereby delivering diversification benefits and lower volatility than equity markets.

ISIF is a long-term fund not subject to liquidity requirements, and it aims to be a permanent or patient capital source. The Minister for Finance may, after consultation with the NTMA, direct payments from ISIF to the Exchequer of up to 4 percent per annum of ISIF's value. No such payment can be made before 2025. In addition, the Minister for Finance has the right to direct that ISIF be invested in specified circumstances, according to Sections 42 and 42A of the NTMA Act 2014 (as amended). For instance, under Section 42, the Minister for Finance, after consultation with the Central Bank, may direct NTMA to invest ISIF assets in specified securities of a credit institution, or underwrite the issue of any securities of a credit institution, if the minister considers it necessary, in the public interest, in order to remedy a serious disturbance in the economy or prevent potential serious damage to Ireland's financial system.

In the Irish Portfolio, ISIF generally acts as a minority investor, on equal terms with other private investors, for the purpose of generating a multiplier effect and ensuring compliance with the Market Economy Investor Principle for the purposes of EU state aid rules. By acting as a minority investor, ISIF leverages sector expertise, co-investment, and scale. In 2018, 60 percent of the capital committed went to existing strategic partnerships and investments. If ISIF is a cornerstone investor, it may seek preferential terms compared with those offered to noncornerstone investors. When providing debt to a company, ISIF can be the sole or largest debt provider but seeks to represent less than

50 percent of the overall capital structure (debt plus equity). As a government agency, ISIF must not breach the above-mentioned EU rules preventing unfair financial support for private enterprises. Every ISIF investment is strictly vetted in this regard.

In the Irish Portfolio, ISIF invests both directly and through third-party managers, with a target size for direct investments of more than €10 million. In general, it pursues large-value, low-volume investments through direct investments, whereas it invests higher-volume, smaller-value investments through third-party platforms. As of December 2018 indirect investments represented approximately 72 percent of the capital committed to the Irish Portfolio, and direct investments represented the remaining 28 percent. Third-party funds must comply with ISIF's statutory requirement of commercial return and economic impact, in order to qualify for an investment. In its direct investments, ISIF can invest across the capital structure and over the long term—from secured debt (rated or unrated) to venture equity.

ISIF can make foreign investments both in its Irish and Global Portfolios. In the Irish Portfolio, to the extent that a foreign investment is made on a commercial basis and can have tangible economic impact in Ireland, such an investment would be regarded as consistent with ISIF's policy mandate. Furthermore, to the extent that it is not reasonably practicable for ISIF assets to be held or invested in accordance with the double bottom line mandate, such assets are to be held or invested on a commercial basis with a view to seeking a rate of return considered appropriate by the NTMA.

ISIF's investment strategy has regard to relevant policy objectives of the Irish government. The NTMA consults the Minister for Finance and the Minister for Public Expenditure and Reform when determining and reviewing ISIF's investment strategy and has regard to any views expressed by the ministers.

PORTFOLIO AND TRACK RECORD

ISIF's Discretionary Portfolio is making a transition from a global, predominantly listed securities portfolio (the Global Portfolio) to a portfolio that reflects the double bottom line mandate set out in the NTMA Act 2014. The transition will occur over a multiyear period as Irish investment opportunities, primarily in the areas of private equity and credit, are originated and executed. Cash to be redeployed in Irish Portfolio investments is freed through ongoing cash management of the Global Portfolio and liquidations of Global Portfolio investments as needed. As of December 31, 2018, capital committed to the Irish Portfolio was €4.1 billion, of which €2.8 billion had been drawn down. The remaining Global Portfolio was mostly composed of cash, debt instruments, equities, and alternative investments such as absolute return funds managed by global asset managers.[12] Table 10.1 provides a summary of ISIF's portfolio as of December 31, 2018.

As of that date, ISIF was slightly undershooting its return targets. From inception to the end of December 2018, ISIF generated an annualized return on the Discretionary Portfolio of +1.9 percent, as compared to its long-term target of greater than 3.0 percent. The 2017 return was +4.3 percent, made up of +4.5 percent on the Irish Portfolio and +4.1 percent on the Global Portfolio (NTMA 2018a, 19). Performance in 2018 was –1.0 percent, reflecting challenging market conditions in 2018 and the low interest rate environment (ISIF 2018b). The negative performance in 2018 was recovered in full as of June 30, 2019.

TABLE 10.1 **Summary of ISIF's portfolio as of December 31, 2018**

		INVESTED (EUROS, BILLIONS)	COMMITTED (EUROS, BILLIONS)
Discretionary Portfolio	Global Portfolio	6.2	n.a.
	Irish Portfolio	2.8	4.1
	Total	8.8	n.a.
Directed Portfolio	Bank stakes	7.8	n.a.
Directed Portfolio	Cash	0.2	n.a.
Total		16.8	n.a.

Source: ISIF 2019b.
Note: ISIF = Ireland Strategic Investment Fund; n.a. = not applicable.

TABLE 10.2 **Breakdown of capital committed to ISIF's Irish Portfolio as of December 31, 2018**

SECTOR OR ASSET CLASS	ISIF COMMITMENT (EUROS, MILLIONS)
Real estate	842
SMEs	789
Venture capital	622
Water	450
Infrastructure	396
Energy	240
Direct private equity	238
Food and agriculture	206
Other	192
Innovation	136
Total	4,111

Sources: ISIF 2019a, 2019b.
Note: ISIF = Ireland Strategic Investment Fund; SMEs = small and medium enterprises.

Commitments in the Irish Portfolio are diversified among sectors and asset classes consistent with the double bottom line mandate, as shown in table 10.2 and figure 10.3. (Table 10.3 also shows ISIF's infrastructure investment in the Irish Portfolio.) More than 70 percent of the commitments were indirect through external managers as of December 2018. ISIF uses third-party funds particularly when targeting SMEs, for which investment tickets are smaller. In terms of capital instrument, most commitments were to equity investments (58 percent) and the remainder to debt as of December 2018.

ADDITIONALITY AND MULTIPLIER CONSIDERATIONS

Although ISIF's additionality (under the definition described in chapter 2 and used throughout this book) was more straightforward during the Irish financial crisis and ensuing capital flight, ISIF still targets a distinct and complementary role versus private funds, in particular in the following respects:

- *Long-term investment focus.* ISIF's investment horizon can extend to over 30 years, whereas commercial banks do not typically lend for longer than

FIGURE 10.3

Breakdown of ISIF's Irish Portfolio commitments as of December 31, 2018

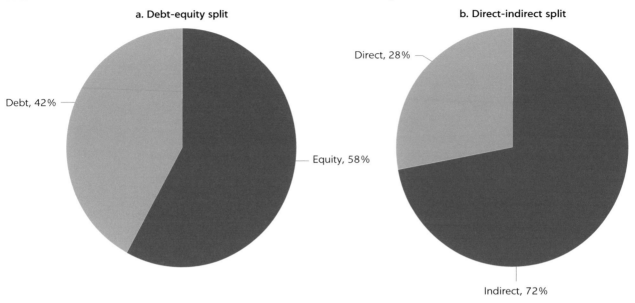

a. Debt-equity split

b. Direct-indirect split

Debt, 42%

Equity, 58%

Direct, 28%

Indirect, 72%

Source: ISIF 2018b.
Note: Figure shows sector shares of ISIF's committed capital in the Irish Portfolio as of December 31, 2018, which totaled €4.1 billion. ISIF = Ireland Strategic Investment Fund.

TABLE 10.3 **ISIF's infrastructure investment in the Irish Portfolio as of December 31, 2018**

COMPANY/FUND/PROJECT	SECTOR	CAPITAL COMMITMENT (EUROS, MILLIONS)	DESCRIPTION
Irish Water Refinancing Facility	Water	300	Refinancing for national water utility
Irish Infrastructure Fund	Infrastructure	250	Investing in Irish infrastructure assets: data towers, wind, primary care, national convention center
Irish Water	Water	150	National water utility
Greencoat Renewables	Energy	76	Renewable energy
Dublin City University	Infrastructure	55	Supporting the university's infrastructure development plan
Temporis	Energy	50	Renewable energy
Covanta Poolbeg Project	Energy	44	Waste-to-energy plant
Dublin Airport Authority	Infrastructure	35	Funding new runway
Encavis	Energy	35	Renewable energy
Aqua Comms	Infrastructure	25	Expanding subsea cable
Port of Cork	Infrastructure	18	Relocation of port
Shannon Airport	Infrastructure	14	Upgrading main runway
Total		1,087	

Sources: ISIF 2019a, 2019b; NTMA 2018a.
Note: ISIF = Ireland Strategic Investment Fund.

7 years and private equity funds look for exits typically within 5 years. For instance, ISIF has provided funding for infrastructure deals at 15-year or longer maturities. ISIF's approach to investing in private equity is based on the core principle of patient capital.

- *Flexibility of investment tools*. ISIF can invest across the capital structure, from senior debt, including variable maturities, to equity in start-ups. It can provide new funds or refinance existing capital structures.
- *Sovereign partner*. Businesses value the credibility and reputation associated with being investees of a sovereign-backed strategic fund. This feature can be valuable when approaching new clients or additional investors.
- *Presence on the ground and critical mass*. International funds often lack direct presence in Ireland. Local investors, by contrast, are often too small or do not have the resources to play a significant role in large projects. ISIF fills this gap and, as previously stated, can play a catalyst role for co-investors.

Although the achievement of a multiplier is implicit in its mandate, ISIF does not abide by formal targets. On an indicative basis, ISIF aims for a deal-level multiplier of two euros for every euro invested by ISIF. For example, if ISIF invested solely on its own, the deal-level multiplier would be 1.0x. The current multiplier at portfolio level is 2.8x. Note that ISIF counts both private and public sources as capital mobilized. Public sources of capital can include international development banks or the Irish government itself.

GOVERNANCE

A board, comprising a chairperson and eight other members, has overall responsibility for all of NTMA's functions, including managing ISIF. Six members, including the chairperson, are appointed by the Minister for Finance[13] if, in the opinion of the minister, the person has expertise and experience at a senior level in one or more of the following areas: investment, treasury management, business management, finance, economics or economic development, law, accounting and auditing, actuarial practice, risk management, insurance, project finance, corporate finance, the civil service of the government, or the civil service of the state. The other three members are the Chief Executive of the NTMA and the Secretaries General of the Departments of Finance and Public Expenditure and Reform, who are ex officio members of the board. Each member has a vote; however, in the case of an equal division of votes the chairperson has an additional casting vote. The term of office of an appointed member is five years, other than the initial appointed members of whom two members were appointed for three years and two members were appointed for four years.

The board has established four committees, each committee with its own terms of reference: Investment Committee, Audit and Risk Committee, Remuneration Committee, and State Claims Agency Strategy Committee. The Investment Committee is specifically dedicated to the management of ISIF. The State Claims Agency Strategy Committee is specific to the State Claims Agency. Remits of the Audit and Risk Committee and Remuneration Committee cover the NTMA as a whole (see table 10.4 for an overview of composition and functions of the NTMA committees).

TABLE 10.4 **Summary of ISIF's governance bodies**

BODY	COMPOSITION	FUNCTIONS
Board	Nine members including • Six nonexecutive members (including chairperson) with experience in finance, accounting, law, government civil service, and others—appointed by the Minister for Finance • Three ex officio members: the NTMA Chief Executive and the Secretaries General of the Departments of Finance and Public Expenditure and Reform (ex officio members) • Each member has a vote (chairperson has casting vote)	Overall responsibility for performance by the NTMA of its functions. The board has established four committees to assist in discharging its responsibilities: • Investment Committee • Audit and Risk Committee • Remuneration Committee • State Claims Agency Strategy Committee (specific to the State Claims Agency functions and therefore not relevant to ISIF)
Investment Committee	Five members appointed by NTMA: • Two non-ex officio board members • Three non-NTMA staff or board members appointed on the basis of their experience in business and finance • Chairperson appointed by NTMA and chosen from one of the two members who are also board members	The Investment Committee assists the board in the control and management of ISIF by making decisions about the acquisition and disposal of assets within such parameters as may be set by the board, advising the board on the investment strategy for ISIF, and overseeing the implementation of the investment strategy.
Audit and Risk Committee	Comprises four members appointed by the board from among its members	Assists the board in the oversight of • The quality and integrity of the financial statements, the review and monitoring of the effectiveness of the systems of internal control, the internal audit process, the compliance function, and the outputs received from the statutory auditor; and • The board's risk management framework including setting risk appetite, monitoring adherence to risk governance, and ensuring risks are properly identified, assessed, managed, and reported.
Remuneration Committee	Comprises four nonexecutive members appointed by the board	The Remuneration Committee assists the board through review and approval of the NTMA's overall remuneration policy, review and approval of any performance-related pay schemes operated by the NTMA, and approval of the total annual payments to be made under any such schemes.

Sources: ISIF website, management interviews, and written feedback.
Note: ISIF = Ireland Strategic Investment Fund; NTMA = National Treasury Management Agency.

The Investment Committee's composition and broad responsibilities are set out in legislation. It makes decisions about ISIF's acquisition and disposal of assets within the parameters set by the board, advises NTMA on the investment strategy for the fund, and oversees its implementation. The committee has five members, appointed by NTMA: two are selected from board members other than ex officio board members (the CEO and the Secretaries General of the Departments of Finance and Public Expenditure and Reform); the other three cannot be board members or NTMA staff and are appointed on the basis of their business and finance expertise. They are appointed by the board subject to the approval of the Minister for Finance. Investment Committee members are appointed for up to three years, extendable by two additional three-year periods. NTMA appoints the chairperson of the Investment Committee out of the two board members on the committee. The chairperson reports on the Investment Committee's activities to each meeting of the board.

FIGURE 10.4

ISIF investment decision process

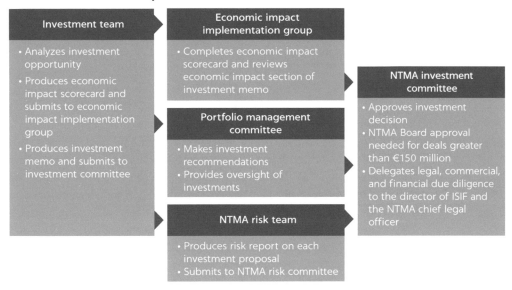

Source: Interviews with management.
Note: ISIF = Ireland Strategic Investment Fund; NTMA = National Treasury Management Agency.

NTMA's governance seeks to ensure that investment decisions are independent from political influence (figure 10.4). Under the NTMA Code of Conduct for Members of the NTMA and its Committees, Investment Committee members are required to act objectively and independently (NTMA 2018b). The quorum for a meeting is three, including one board representative. Decisions are made on a majority basis (one vote per member). The chairperson of the committee (appointed by NTMA) has the casting vote.

The board does not decide on individual investments, except for investments exceeding €150 million, which will be referred to the board for approval if they have first been approved by the Investment Committee.

The NTMA Code of Conduct also generally disciplines the conduct of NTMA and its board, committee members, and employees.

STAFFING AND RECRUITMENT

All ISIF staff are employed by the NTMA on individual contracts. The NTMA remuneration model is based on confidential, individually negotiated employment contracts, with competitive, market-aligned remuneration. The typical remuneration package comprises a fixed base salary, provision for discretionary performance-related pay when considered appropriate for the role or employee in question, and career average defined benefit pension.

Employee turnover at ISIF has been limited. The annual turnover as of December 31, 2018, for ISIF was 14 percent.

ISIF staff come from a diverse, generally private sector financial background, including private equity fund management, banking, energy, consulting, infrastructure, investment banking, corporate finance, and accountancy. ISIF encourages relevant team members to obtain the chartered financial analyst qualifications.

ECONOMIC IMPACT AND ESG REPORTING

ISIF monitors compliance with its economic impact objectives at the Irish Portfolio company level and the portfolio level. Every February and August, investee companies fill out an impact survey, with data such as revenues, employment, and exports. In addition, each year, ISIF compiles an annual control report that measures the performance of all Irish Portfolio companies against financial and impact targets. Once exiting investments, ISIF does not exercise any further active impact monitoring.

ISIF publishes an annual and semiannual economic impact report with detailed metrics on ISIF's capital allocation and contribution to economic activity and employment. Table 10.5 provides a summary of these metrics. Initially, the focus was on fund-level portfolio metrics for publication; however, as the report has evolved, the reporting now takes account of sector-specific metrics that cannot be consolidated at the fund level (for example, megawatts of renewable energy, number of new housing units, and number of alternative SME financing platforms). The collection, verification, and reporting of economic impact data can be challenging given that it is a relatively new concept for investees to report on.

ESG criteria are applied in ISIF investment activities, and measurement of some noneconomic impacts over the entire Discretionary Portfolio has commenced (although these are not yet published at the time of writing). ISIF has developed an ESG assessment framework focused on identifying material ESG risks, guiding due diligence, and monitoring key performance indicators through the investment life, in the Irish Portfolio. The framework is based on guidance from both the European Bank for Reconstruction and Development and the Sustainability Accounting Standards Board, combined with asset class–specific

TABLE 10.5 Comprehensive sample of metrics disclosed in ISIF's economic impact report

AREA	METRICS
Capital	• Discretionary Portfolio size • Capital committed • Capital committed by co-investors and multiplier • Market value of capital invested • Split of capital invested by region (Dublin and ex-Dublin) • Capital committed by strategy (Enabling Ireland, Growing Ireland, Leading Edge Ireland) and, for each, by subsector • List of new investments during period and ticket sizes • Fund returns • List of portfolio companies of investee funds
Employment	• Total employment supported by Irish Portfolio companies and projects • Total wage bill • Split of employment by region (Dublin and ex-Dublin)

Economic activity	• GVA
	• Allocation of GVA by region
	• Exports generated by portfolio companies
	• Strategy-specific metrics, for instance:
	  – Enabling Ireland: MW of renewable energy installed, tons of waste processed, housing units completed
	  – Growing Ireland: number of SMEs backed
	  – Leading Edge Ireland: VC funds invested in and ticket sizes
	  – Case studies

Sources: ISIF 2017, 2018a.
Note: GVA = gross value added; ISIF = Ireland Strategic Investment Fund; MW = megawatt; SMEs = small and medium enterprises; VC = venture capital.

tools based on the UNPRI. ISIF applies some exclusion criteria and has developed two carbon monitoring tools to estimate greenhouse gas emissions across the Irish Portfolio and to calculate carbon savings from its renewable and alternative energy investments.

ISIF aims to be a leading proponent of responsible investment in Ireland, by adhering to both the Santiago Principles and the UNPRI. As required by the UNPRI, ISIF reports annually on implementation of the principles; in July 2018 its UNPRI results were scored above median. ISIF is also a signatory of the Carbon Disclosure Project (CDP), a framework for investors to encourage companies to disclose their greenhouse gas emissions. ISIF promotes responsible investment in Ireland through forums such as CDP Ireland and the Sustainable Investment Forum Ireland. The NTMA has experience as a responsible investor in global markets (dating back to its time as manager of the NPRF) and translates that experience into the domestic investment landscape. This includes active ownership, wide-ranging portfolio ESG analysis to include carbon footprinting, and alignment with the Sustainable Development Goals.

ISIF has an investment exclusionary strategy with respect to cluster munitions and antipersonnel mines,[14] coal production and processing, and tobacco manufacturing. In addition to this strategy, the Fossil Fuel Divestment Act 2018 provides for the divestment by ISIF from fossil fuel undertakings (effectively, companies that derive more than 20 percent of their revenues from the exploration, extraction, or refinement of fossil fuels) within a practicable timeframe.

FINANCIAL DISCLOSURE AND RISK POLICIES

NTMA is required to prepare annual financial statements and an annual report, including with respect to ISIF's financial performance, which are laid before the Irish Parliament. NTMA is accountable to the Public Accounts Committee in accordance with the NTMA Act 1990. Section 49 of the act details that, for a given year, ISIF-related disclosures must include the following: the investment strategy pursued, the investment return achieved, a valuation of ISIF's net assets, a detailed list of the assets at the end of the year, the investment management and custodianship arrangements, an assessment on a regional basis of the impact of ISIF's investments on economic activity and employment, and an assessment on a regional basis of the distribution of the investments made by ISIF. ISIF's financial accounts are published annually in the NTMA annual report. The accounts show the breakdown of ISIF assets, at year-end market value, for the Directed, Discretionary, Irish, and Global Portfolios. The income statement shows capital gains (or losses), dividend and interest income, and ISIF's operating expenses. The accounts also list all securities held. ISIF publishes voting decisions with respect to equity investments across the Global Portfolio on its website.

As a state agency, NTMA's accounts are audited by the Comptroller and Auditor General. ISIF's activities are also audited by the NTMA Internal Audit function.

ISIF has adopted a Portfolio Diversification Framework for the Irish Portfolio, setting maximum exposure limits by sector and risk category.[15] Sectors include food and agriculture, energy, financial services, health care, infrastructure, information technology, and real estate. Risk is scored from 1 to 5 depending on the type of instrument and layer of the capital structure, as detailed in table 10.6. In addition, maturity, competitiveness, leverage, and downside protection

TABLE 10.6 **ISIF Irish Portfolio risk categories**

RISK CATEGORY	DESCRIPTION
1	Debt backed by strong cash flows and assets, strong covenants in place; debt with low probability of default and high recovery rate
2	Senior debt with standard covenants, backed by strong cash flows or assets
3	Subordinated debt, stretch senior debt, mezzanine debt, and so on; debt with higher likelihood of default or lower recovery rates; infrastructure equity or equity supported by well-established or regulated cash flows
4	Growth capital to companies with existing revenue; deeply subordinated debt
5	Equity in start-up or distressed companies

Source: ISIF management.
Note: ISIF = Ireland Strategic Investment Fund.

(for example, through contractual clauses or seniority in the capital structure) of each investment are considered. Investment limits are based on market value. ISIF's total exposure, including market value and undrawn commitments, is also monitored as an indicator of the portfolio's future evolution.

Limits are usually revised on an annual basis. The revised investment strategy published on February 1, 2019, is expected to skew the portfolio somewhat toward particular sectors (for example, real estate) and higher-risk-score investments—consistent with the refocus of ISIF's investment activities on regional development, housing, indigenous businesses, climate change, and sectors adversely affected by Brexit.

ISIF can diversify its portfolio abroad, for example, by investing in global funds that are expected to then invest in Ireland. These fund investments can enable ISIF to reduce its domestic exposure while still generating an economic impact in Ireland. For example, a €50 million investment in a €500 million global fund that invests €100 million in Ireland will provide capital to Irish businesses while ISIF is exposed to a pro rata share of the Global Portfolio's financial outcome.

ISIF also performs an all-weather analysis to test the Irish Portfolio's performance under different GDP growth and inflation scenarios, by examining the latter's impact on the discounted cash flows of individual investments and subsequently aggregating results at the portfolio level.

At the individual investment level, ISIF conducts a detailed analysis and adopts a disciplined approach to the design of capital structures. The risk team produces the risk categorization for each investment. The investment proposal is passed to the NTMA risk function, which analyzes the risks and passes its feedback to the Investment Committee (and, for deals exceeding €150 million, to the board) prior to investment approval.

NTMA's approach to risk management is based on the three lines of defense model and is designed to support the delivery of its mandates by proactively managing the risks that arise in the course of NTMA's pursuit of its strategic objectives. As the first line of defense, the ISIF unit is primarily responsible for managing risks on a day-to-day basis, taking into account NTMA's risk tolerance and appetite, and in line with its policies, procedures, controls, and limits. The second line of defense, which includes the NTMA risk, compliance, and other control functions, is independent of the ISIF unit's management and operations; its role is to challenge decisions that affect ISIF's exposure to risk and to provide comprehensive and understandable information on risks. The third line of defense, the internal audit function, provides independent, reasonable, and risk-based assurance to key stakeholders on the robustness of NTMA's governance and risk management, and the design and operating effectiveness of the internal control environment.

From a governance oversight standpoint, ISIF's risk management framework has three key elements:

1. The board sets the risk management policy and framework and the risk appetite framework. The former defines mandatory risk management standards and definitions that apply to all parts of NTMA and all risk categories. Detailed procedures discipline the application of these standards to the management of individual risk categories or processes. Board and management committees, including the Audit and Risk Committee and Risk Management subcommittees, support the board in performing the risk management function.
2. The Audit and Risk Committee assists the board in the oversight of the risk management framework to ensure risks are properly identified, assessed, managed, and reported.
3. An Enterprise Risk Management Committee oversees the establishment of appropriate systems to identify, measure, manage, and report enterprise risk. This committee comprises the most senior executive management team members (not the board). It performs a risk assessment twice annually for the purpose of identifying the main risks from an NTMA-wide perspective. These risks are then considered by the Audit and Risk Committee and the board.

ISIF has an increasing focus on monitoring investments in the Irish Portfolio as the fund moves into a more mature phase. Currently ISIF monitors investments on an ongoing basis (for instance, through quarterly calls and meetings), and this practice is formalized in quarterly reports to the Investment Committee and the annual control report that is presented to the Portfolio Management Committee. ISIF has recently appointed a Head of Monitoring with responsibility for monitoring all Irish investments.

NOTES

1. For the full text of the NTMA Act 2014, see https://www.irishstatutebook.ie/eli/2014/act/23/enacted/en/html.
2. The National Surplus (Exceptional Contingencies) Reserve Fund to be established pursuant to the National Surplus (Reserve Fund for Exceptional Contingencies) Act 2019 upon the commencement of this legislation.
3. "Fund" throughout the case study is used in a general sense, as distinct from any particular legal sense.
4. Ownership of ISIF vests with the Minister for Finance. In determining and reviewing the investment strategy of ISIF, the NTMA consults with the Minister for Finance and the Minister for Public Expenditure and Reform.
5. A description of the criteria can be found in ISIF (2015).
6. GDP is a measure of the market value of goods and services produced by organizations in an economy. GVA is the microenterprise-level measure of the value of goods or services produced, which—when aggregated across all enterprises and adjusted for taxes and subsidies—equals GDP.
7. Note that the term additionality as used by ISIF has a different meaning from the concept described in chapter 2 of this book and used throughout.
8. Although GVA is ISIF's preferred metric, the NTMA Act 2014 requires the annual report on ISIF to include an assessment on a regional basis of the impact of investments on economic activity and employment. Additionally, it is difficult to capture the GVA of enabling investments and therefore useful not to focus exclusively on this metric.

9. ISIF's definition of deadweight is, in essence, equivalent to the definition of additionality described in chapter 2 of this report and used throughout.
10. Senior ISIF team members responsible for making recommendations to the Investment Committee and Portfolio Management.
11. Using Eurostat's definition of cost of debt, which is based on the ratio of total annual interest cost to average sovereign debt outstanding.
12. Including Goldman Sachs Asset Management, JP Morgan Asset Management, Irish Life Investment Managers, Amundi Asset Management, and BlackRock Investment Management.
13. Appointments are subject to the Department of Public Expenditure and Reform Guidelines on Appointments to State Boards.
14. Prohibited investments under the Cluster Munitions And Anti-Personnel Mines Act 2008.
15. ISIF avoids the standard statistical approach to building portfolios, for example, calculating the correlation between categories or sectors. ISIF believes that lack of reliable Irish private markets data makes this approach unsound.

REFERENCES

Ireland, Department of Finance. 2018. "Minister Donohoe to Refocus the Ireland Strategic Investment Fund to Better Meet the Needs of a Strong & Growing Economy." Press release, July 5, 2018. https://www.gov.ie/en/press-release/a0cc86-minister-donohoe-to-refocus-the-ireland-strategic-investment-fund-to/.

Ireland, Department of Finance. 2019. "Budget 2019. Review by the Department of Finance of the Ireland Strategic Investment Fund." Department of Finance, Dublin. https://www.google.com/url?sa=t&rct=j&q=&esrc=s&source=web&cd=&ved=2ahUKEwim6vnU5tL3AhWBjYkEHZO6CtcQFnoECC0QAQ&url=https%3A%2F%2Fassets.gov.ie%2F180689%2Fee09022a-5b2f-45df-9e69-62e7ced3c553.pdf&usg=AOvVaw1fCDFADRk4K_dXSyaySBgA.

ISIF (Ireland Strategic Investment Fund). 2015. "Investment Strategy: Executive Summary." National Treasury Management Agency, Dublin. https://isif.ie/wp-content/uploads/2016/03/ISIFInvestmentStrategyExecutiveSummaryJuly2015.pdf.

ISIF (Ireland Strategic Investment Fund). 2017. "Economic Impact Report FY 2016." National Treasury Management Agency, Dublin. http://isif.ie/wp-content/uploads/2017/07/EconomicImpactReport31December2016.pdf.

ISIF (Ireland Strategic Investment Fund). 2018a. "Ireland Strategic Investment Fund H1 2017 Update: Including Economic Impact Report FY 2017." National Treasury Management Agency, Dublin. https://isif.ie/uploads/publications/ISIF-2017-Update-H1-2017-Economic-Impact-Report-22.01-Changes.pdf.

ISIF (Ireland Strategic Investment Fund). 2018b. "Ireland Strategic Investment Fund H1 2018 Update: Including Economic Impact Report FY 2017." National Treasury Management Agency, Dublin. https://isif.ie/wp-content/uploads/2018/07/ISIF-H1-2018-Update-published.pdf.

ISIF (Ireland Strategic Investment Fund). 2019a. "Investment Strategy 2.0: Towards 2040– Investing Commercially and with Substantial Impact." National Treasury Management Agency. https://isif.ie/uploads/publications/ISIF-Investment-Strategy.pdf.

ISIF (Ireland Strategic Investment Fund). 2019b. "Ireland Strategic Investment Fund H1 2019 Update: Including Economic Impact Report FY 2018." National Treasury Management Agency, Dublin. https://isif.ie/uploads/publications/ISIF-H1-2019FY-2018.pdf.

NTMA (National Treasury Management Agency). 2018a. "Annual Report & Accounts 2017." NTMA, Dublin.

NTMA (National Treasury Management Agency). 2018b. "Code of Conduct for Members of the National Treasury Management Agency and its Committees." NTMA, Dublin. https://www.ntma.ie/uploads/general/Code-of-Conduct-for-Members-of-the-National-Treasury-Management-Agency-and-its-Committees.pdf.

11 Case Study—The Marguerite Fund: An Infrastructure Fund Sponsored by Development Banks*

If you want to crowd in private investment with credibility, then you want to be as close to standard market practice as possible. Anything that deviates exposes you to being on unfair market terms: clauses that oblige you to go to board for exit, investors having a say on what the fund does, and so on.

– Barbara Boos, Head of Infrastructure Funds and Climate Action Division,
European Investment Bank

To get a project to the stage where it can be built, project development skills are sometimes more important than capital. Many investors are unfamiliar with project development, whereas Marguerite has this capacity. So, to get projects off the ground, we engage closely with sponsors over time.

– Nicolás Merigó, CEO, Marguerite Investment Management

BACKGROUND AND MISSION

The 2020 European Fund for Energy, Climate Change and Infrastructure (Marguerite I) and Marguerite II SCSp[1] (Marguerite II)—collectively called Marguerite for the purposes of this study—are infrastructure funds founded by the European Investment Bank (EIB) and several national development banks (NDBs) of the European Union. Their mandate is to invest, on a commercial basis, in policy-driven infrastructure projects in the European Union and pre-accession states, based on a list of eligible sectors and with particular focus on greenfield infrastructure. Although equity is the most commonly used tool, Marguerite can invest via equity, quasi equity, and mezzanine and subordinated debt. The funds are managed by an independent investment team. Marguerite I reached first close in December 2009, and Marguerite II did so in November 2017.

The idea to launch Marguerite I was conceived in 2008 by the EIB and the NDBs of three EU member states—France's Caisse des Dépôts et Consignations, Germany's Kreditanstalt für Wiederaufbau, and Italy's Cassa Depositi e Prestiti.

---

*Research for this case study was completed between 2018 and 2019. The text reflects the circumstances at that time.

In the aftermath of the 2008 global financial crisis, infrastructure investment in Europe had significantly decreased. In this context, the goals of Marguerite's founding sponsors were to stimulate greenfield infrastructure investments in the European Union, catalyzing private investment, and to set an example of long-term investment (by establishing a 20-year fund).

To ensure adherence with the policy mandate envisaged for Marguerite I, the sponsors decided to set up an independent investment advisory company rather than use an existing external fund manager. They hired McKinsey & Company to analyze the infrastructure funding gap and pipeline in the fund's target countries, negotiated a term sheet among themselves, and sought legal advice from Allen & Overy. The term sheet struck a compromise between the investment objectives of various sponsors—some more inclined to pursue market-oriented investments and others more policy-oriented. McKinsey & Company estimated the optimal fund size at €1.5 billion. Allen & Overy assisted in setting up a closed-end investment fund in Luxembourg, where the EIB is headquartered (adopting a SICAV/SIF structure,[2] supervised by Luxembourg financial regulator CSSF[3]).

In 2009 the sponsors initiated the competitive selection of a CEO, who was also to be the first partner of the fund advisory company and would be tasked with assembling the full investment team and delivering on the mandate. Nicolás Merigó, former head of Santander Infrastructure Capital, was selected and became proactively involved in defining an investment advisory agreement, fee structure, and long-term incentive plan aligned with the fund industry's best practices. He started in early 2010, and the bulk of the investment team was hired that same year. The role of Marguerite Adviser was similar to that of a traditional private equity fund manager (GP), although the fund was structured as a corporate entity.[4]

The first fund, Marguerite I, was launched in the first quarter of 2010 with €710 million of capital committed. The four original sponsors were joined by two more state-controlled financial institutions, Spain's Instituto de Crédito Oficial and Poland's PKO Bank Polski. The six institutions invested €100 million each in Marguerite I (figure 11.1). The European Commission provided €80 million, and two other state-controlled financial institutions from Malta and Portugal provided the remaining €30 million.

Despite its stated intentions and a significant fundraising effort, Marguerite I was not able to attract private investors at the fund level. Possible reasons include the newly composed investment team's slim track record, the perceived riskiness of the fund's greenfield strategy, concerns over public influence on investment decisions, and the timing of the fund's launch (right after the 2008 financial crisis). Although individual members of the investment team assembled by the CEO had proven expertise in infrastructure investing, the team lacked a shared track record. Governance rules were put in place to mitigate the sponsoring state banks' influence on investment decisions; however, these rules were not sufficient to alleviate private investors' concerns about investments being politically rather than commercially driven. In addition, risk aversion in the financial industry was still pronounced in the aftermath of the 2008 global financial crisis, and private investors were disinclined to invest in anything deviating from common practice, in terms of governance and investment strategy. Marguerite I was, however, successful in catalyzing private investment at the project level.

Simplified Marguerite I structure at closing

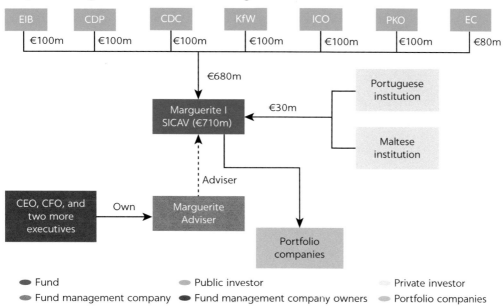

Fund
Fund management company
Public investor
Fund management company owners
Private investor
Portfolio companies

Source: Interviews with Marguerite management.
Note: The structure illustrated here was subsequently modified in December 2017 to comply with the Alternative Investment Fund Managers Directive. The new structure replicates that of Marguerite II, presented in figure 11.2. CDC = Caisse des Dépôts et Consignations; CDP = Cassa Depositi e Prestiti; CEO = chief executive officer; CFO = chief financial officer; EC = European Commission; EIB = European Investment Bank; ICO = Instituto de Crédito Oficial; KfW = Kreditanstalt für Wiederaufbau; m = million; PKO = PKO Bank Polski; SICAV = Société d'Investissement à Capital Variable.

Marguerite I was fully invested by the end of 2017, resulting in more than €10 billion overall project investment and posting financial returns in line with its target coupled with a high degree of diversification, transparency, and ESG compliance. The fund closed 20 investments in 13 EU countries. In interviews for this study, the Marguerite team expressed satisfaction with the quality of the portfolio, noting that all projects were implemented on time and on budget and that no project was subject to litigation or allegations of unfair business dealings.

To monetize part of its portfolio, return capital to its investors, and enhance its credibility with private investors ahead of a new fund launch, Marguerite decided in 2017 to sell five renewable and concession-based assets to a new vehicle, still managed by the Marguerite investment team but fully backed by private capital. A competitive sales process was run, overseen by a financial adviser and featuring vendor due diligence. Marguerite Pantheon was set up as a Luxembourg special partnership, or societé en commandite spéciale (SCSp). Marguerite Pantheon is an investment vehicle wholly owned by a pool of funds and managed accounts run by Pantheon, a global private markets fund investor. The Marguerite investment team is still in charge of managing Marguerite Pantheon. The fact that the five assets were deemed attractive by Pantheon and other bidders highlighted Marguerite's expertise and track record in selecting and executing financially attractive greenfield investments. Marguerite's investors obtained an attractive price for the portfolio, within expectations for the internal rate of return and cash multiplier.

Following, among others, implementation of the EU's Alternative Investment Fund Managers Directive (AIFMD), Marguerite I appointed Marguerite

Investment Management S.A., an independent company owned by senior management, as its external alternative investment fund manager in December 2017.

Marguerite also decided to adopt a more conventional structure for the second fund to invest in greenfield infrastructure. To enhance its attractiveness to private investors and reflect the preferences of most of its sponsors, Marguerite II was set up with a standard private equity general partner (GP)/limited partner (LP) structure (see figure 11.2). Like Marguerite Pantheon (see figure 11.3), it was established as a Luxembourg SCSp, with the management company having

FIGURE 11.2

Simplified Marguerite II structure

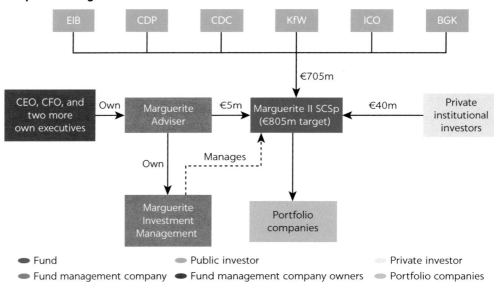

Source: Interviews with Marguerite management.
Note: BGK = Bank Gospodarstwa Krajowego; CDC = Caisse des Dépôts et Consignations; CDP = Cassa Depositi e Prestiti; CEO = chief executive officer; CFO = chief financial officer; EIB = European Investment Bank; ICO = Instituto de Crédito Oficial; KfW = Kreditanstalt für Wiederaufbau; m = million; SCSp = société en commandite spéciale.

FIGURE 11.3

Simplified Marguerite Pantheon structure

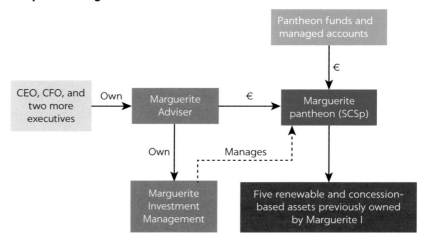

Source: Interviews with Marguerite management.
Note: CEO = chief executive officer; CFO = chief financial officer; SCSp = société en commandite spéciale.

a higher level of independence than was the case for Marguerite I, and notably with no sponsor representation at the executive management level (including investment decisions) (see the subsection on governance for a detailed discussion). The fund life was shortened from 20 years to 10 years (with two optional 1-year extensions), and the GP made a commitment of €5 million. Marguerite Investment Management was appointed as the external alternative investment fund manager.

Marguerite II was launched with strong backing from most of the original Marguerite I sponsors, resulting in a successful first close in November 2017, and additional interest from private capital. At the first close, Marguerite II received commitments for €705 million from the EIB, Cassa Depositi e Prestiti, Caisse des Dépôts et Consignations, Kreditanstalt für Wiederaufbau, Instituto de Crédito Oficial, and Bank Gospodarstwa Krajowego (the Polish development bank that replaced the original Polish sponsor). In June 2018, Marguerite II achieved a second close, raising an additional €40 million from a private institutional investor.

MANDATE FOR INVESTMENT

At the core of Marguerite's policy mandate is compliance with investment eligibility criteria established and monitored by the sponsors. The eligibility criteria envisage a focus on greenfield infrastructure, a choice of sectors that are consistent with EU and member states' policy objectives, and compliance with economic rate of return and ESG considerations. In Marguerite I, the private placement memorandum (the main document detailing the strategy and operations of a SICAV/SIF) listed the eligibility criteria. Compliance with the criteria was checked very early in the investment process, by submitting a short project idea document to the Management Board (which included representatives of the sponsors, independent members of the Investment Committee, and Marguerite Adviser management). The board had the ability to veto transactions if a proposed investment was potentially contrary to EU policy objectives or publicly announced national policy in the country where the project was located (this option was never exercised, however). In Marguerite II, this veto procedure does not exist and the eligibility criteria are addressed in the terms of the LPA and side letters signed with some investors. Eligibility provisions contained in side letters apply to the fund as a whole.

Unlike conventional private infrastructure funds, Marguerite's core mandate is to invest in greenfield infrastructure. Marguerite generally invests in shovel-ready projects for which most development work has been done (design, permits, and so on) and construction can start as soon as capital (equity and debt, usually in the form of project finance) is available. By focusing on greenfield investments, Marguerite differentiates itself from the typical private sector infrastructure fund, whose main focus is investing in brownfield, less risky, operational assets that already produce stable cash flows. Contrary to Marguerite I, Marguerite II has the ability to consider development-stage investments, for which some but not all the development work has been done. The broadening of the investment strategy reflects the change in investment environment between the launch of Marguerite I in

2008–09 and Marguerite II in 2017. Marguerite I was launched right after the global financial crisis, when any investment in greenfield infrastructure in Europe was hard to fund. By the time of the launch of Marguerite II, abundant liquidity had returned to both the brownfield and shovel-ready greenfield segments (in certain EU member states and sectors perceived to be less risky), but a gap still persisted in development-stage projects and certain geographic regions and sectors. Note that both Marguerite funds retain the flexibility to invest in brownfield projects, but only when the capital expenditures involved are very large (brownfield expansion). Some of these brownfield investments occurred in a period of high private capital risk aversion, therefore ensuring Marguerite's additionality; for instance, Marguerite I invested in toll highways in Ireland and Spain when those countries were in the midst of their sovereign debt crises.

The list of eligible sectors approved by the public sponsors and aligned with EU and national policies includes transport, energy and renewables, telecommunications, and water (table 11.1). In these four sectors, the sponsors have identified a combination of significant greenfield investment needs to meet EU and national policy objectives (especially for trans-European infrastructure), uneven infrastructure development across different EU countries and significant upgrade needs, potential for commercial financial returns (possibly in conjunction with local or EU subsidy schemes), and local technical and environmental assessment constraints.

In terms of geographic coverage, Marguerite's mandate included all EU Member States in the first fund and also preaccession countries in the second fund (the Balkans). Infrastructure projects connecting a Member State to a non–Member State are also allowed. As of December 2017 (end of the investment period of Marguerite I), the investment team reviewed more than 100 opportunities in 20 countries, closing 20 investments in 13 countries: Belgium, Croatia, France, Germany, Greece, Ireland, Italy, Latvia, Poland, Portugal, Romania, Spain, and Sweden. Marguerite has built a strong local presence across EU member states thanks to its institutional backing, investment track record, depth and range of nationalities in the investment team, and sourcing of EU-wide opportunities.

INVESTMENT STRATEGY

Marguerite operates as a traditional infrastructure private equity investor. Marguerite II has a 10-year term and a 5-year investment period, with potential to extend the fund life by two consecutive 1-year periods. It can invest in equity, quasi equity, mezzanine, and subordinated debt; equity is the most prevalent tool. The fund targets a 10 percent net internal rate of return, which is deemed commercial in light of the low interest rate environment (at the time of writing) and type of infrastructure investments pursued. It will consider all exit options opportunistically, including the sale of stakes to co-investors or industrial/financial buyers, and initial public offerings. The timing of the exit typically takes place once the project is fully operational and has proven its ability to produce stable cash yields, at which point valuation should peak.

Marguerite acts primarily as a minority investor, and seeks thereby to minimize the crowding out of other private investors. This approach differentiates it from standard infrastructure funds that prefer full control. Marguerite I was

TABLE 11.1 Marguerite II's eligible sectors

	TRANSPORT	ENERGY AND RENEWABLES	TELECOMMUNICATIONS	WATER
Policy drivers	• Quality of infrastructure varies enormously across the EU. • Significant greenfield CAPEX is required to meet EU's transport investment requirements (TEN-T). • Major expansion, upgrading, and maintenance requirements exist in all subsectors.	• Large greenfield CAPEX is required to meet EU objectives in renewables and energy efficiency. • Energy security concerns exist because of global volatility of energy supplies driving more investment. • New areas to be connected to existing European grids require significant upgrades.	• Demand for internet is high, and broadband usage is extensive. • Economic rate of return on broadband networks is high. • The European Commission announced targets for broadband and superfast broadband in Europe. • Local authorities are supporting broadband projects through subsidies.	• Sector has strong political dimension. • Mature market exists with wide range of delivery models/organizations across Europe. • Aging infrastructure needs upgrades (to mitigate leaks, and so on). • New markets include agriculture and industry.
Investment drivers	• Infrastructure PPP pipeline is fueled by persistent budget constraints in the EU. • Infrastructure investment is used as an economic stimulus tool. • Focus is on projects that are part of the TEN-T and that have a high deliverability ratio.	• Sectors supported by EU policies for climate change, energy security, and waste management. • Significant onshore and offshore transmission networks and upgrades for balancing (increased renewables capacity). • Focus is on higher priority projects supported by European Investment Bank funding (TEN-T or Projects of Common Interest).	• Financing is not sufficient for broadband networks in white/gray areas. • In many member states the ecosystem/framework to deploy broadband is not fully organized. • Need exists for a proactive equity approach from a fund like Marguerite II with a greenfield track record.	• Driven by implementation of EU directive on wastewater treatment, especially in Central and Eastern Europe, Italy, and Spain. • Sector is very suitable for PPP/concession.

Source: Marguerite management.
Note: CAPEX = capital expenditure; EU = European Union; PPP = public-private partnership; TEN-T = Trans-European Transport Network.

subject to a specific requirement not to invest in more than 50 percent of each project's equity. This requirement was relaxed for Marguerite II, which is not subject to any formal limitations in terms of stakes acquired. Partners can include construction companies, utilities, independent power producers, project developers, and operators.

In terms of position limits, Marguerite II is subject to various requirements, but they are not overly stringent. Its minimum ticket size is €10 million, and its maximum ticket size is 20 percent of total capital commitments—any investment exceeding 10 percent of commitments must be approved by the Advisory Committee. In practice, Marguerite II targets €20 million to €100 million tickets, which, depending on sector, geography, and leverage, translate into project sizes of €50 million to €2 billion. From a sector standpoint, Marguerite II is not subject to minimum or maximum allocation thresholds. From a geography standpoint, no more than 20 percent of Marguerite II can be invested in a single EU member state and no more than 5 percent in preaccession member states (but this may be increased to 10 percent with Advisory Committee approval). The Advisory Committee (see the governance subsection) can waive some investment mandate restrictions (for example, for investments exceeding certain thresholds).

The investment process follows the standard path typical of infrastructure fund managers, culminating in an investment decision taken independently by the Investment Committee. In the origination phase, Marguerite sources deals from direct market contacts, industrial and financial partners, banks, and advisers. A preliminary investment proposal is then submitted to the Investment Committee, which gives the go-ahead and approves a budget for transaction expenses. External advisers are hired to assist through due diligence and deal structuring. A full investment proposal is then submitted to the Investment Committee, including analysis of the deal structure, risks, valuation, financing, and other contractual arrangements. Given its focus on greenfield projects, Marguerite is hands on when it comes to negotiating investment and shareholder agreements, as well as project documentation (such as construction, operations and maintenance, and financing contracts). The Investment Committee has sole responsibility for investment approval (see more in the governance subsection). After closing, Marguerite generally takes one or more board seats to exercise oversight of company strategy, performance, and reporting.

In compliance with the AIFMD, Marguerite Investment Management has a dedicated executive in charge of risk management. This person is not a member of the Investment Committee, to ensure the separation of functions. Marguerite Investment Management has a full set of detailed risk management procedures for various types of risks applicable to Marguerite II's investments. Compliance with investment limits is verified by multiple levels of the management team during the due diligence and investment decision phases, and subsequently by both an asset management and risk management team.

PORTFOLIO AND TRACK RECORD

By September 2018, Marguerite I and II had closed 24 deals in 13 countries. The 20 deals closed by Marguerite I mostly followed the project finance model, with €9 billion of nonrecourse debt mobilized (roughly half from commercial banks and half from public sources), six investments refinanced, and five investments exited via sale to Marguerite Pantheon. Marguerite II had a successful start in 2018, with four new deals closed by September 2018. For confidentiality reasons, Marguerite does not publicly disclose realized project and portfolio returns. See table 11.2 for Marguerite portfolio companies.

ADDITIONALITY AND MULTIPLIER CONSIDERATIONS

Despite its focus on commercial investment opportunities, Marguerite aims to deliver additionality and minimize the risk of private investors being crowded out. Specifically,

- *Greenfield projects.* Marguerite focuses on greenfield projects, in contrast to private sector infrastructure funds that focus on brownfield, yield-producing assets. Marguerite II pushes further into earlier-stage greenfield projects that require substantial involvement in the design and development phases.
- *Investment only to fill funding gap.* Even when investing in brownfield assets, Marguerite seeks to fill a funding gap left by private sector funds. For instance, it invested in a shadow toll road in Spain at a time when risk aversion in that country was high after the country was severely affected by the 2008 global financial crisis (capital is flowing again to Spain, at the time of this writing).
- *Demonstration effect.* Sponsors are keen for Marguerite to be involved in innovative projects that can have a demonstration effect. Because of the risk associated with novel types of projects, private infrastructure investors tend to shy away from these deals in the first instance. For example, Marguerite was one of the first financial investors in greenfield offshore wind farms in Europe, demonstrating the commercial feasibility of these projects, which are now targeted by private investors.[5] Specifically, Marguerite invested in C-Power (Belgium) in 2011 and Butendiek (Germany) in 2013. At the time, infrastructure funds and institutional investors had not yet invested in green-field offshore wind farms. Two Danish pension funds coinvested in Butendiek primarily because of Marguerite's role as anchor investor.
- *Investment in riskier geographies.* Marguerite has also targeted Eastern European countries perceived by investors as higher risk. Marguerite will continue to do so in the future, with Marguerite II's scope expanded to preaccession countries. Marguerite I invested in Croatia, Latvia, Poland, and Romania—considered to be riskier investment environments than Western Europe.
- *Investment on a commercial basis.* Marguerite does not undercut competing funds on pricing. It generally targets double-digit returns, which was ambitious in 2010 when the fund was set up and, according to Marguerite management, still reflects commercial standards for greenfield investment.

According to Marguerite management, 90 percent of investments comply with these criteria, and the remaining 10 percent are more conventional infrastructure investments. The conventional investments include, for instance, a solar photovoltaic project in France. According to Marguerite and the EIB's assessment, the availability of private financing for greenfield, innovative projects remains limited in relatively riskier geographies and certain sectors. These geographic and sector limitations exist despite the current high availability of capital for brownfield infrastructure induced by the low interest rate environment.

TABLE 11.2 Marguerite portfolio companies

TARGET COMPANY	INVESTMENT DETAILS	COUNTRY	SECTOR	DESCRIPTION	TRANSACTION YEAR AND STATUS
City Green Light	39% equity stake	Italy	Energy efficiency	Support expansion of municipal lighting business	2018 In portfolio/operational and under construction
Haute Garonne	25% equity stake	France	Fiber broadband and telecoms	Support FTTH in rural regions	2018 In portfolio/under construction
Curtis	Mezzanine	Spain	Energy (biomass)	Support construction of biomass plant	2018 In portfolio/under construction
Heat	100% equity stake	Sweden	Renewable energy (wind)	Support construction of onshore wind farms	2018 In portfolio/under construction
Celsius	100% equity stake in SPV	Sweden	Renewable energy (wind)	Support construction of offshore wind farms with innovative offtake structure	2017 In portfolio/operational
Gestamp	90% shareholding	Portugal	Energy (biomass)	Support construction of two biomass plants with proven operating partners and an adjustment mechanism for downside protection	2017 In portfolio/under construction
Grand Est (Losange) FTTH	22% shareholding	France	Fiber broadband and telecoms	Support construction and operation of new high-speed FTTH network	2017 In portfolio/under construction
Pedemontana Veneta	Subordinated bonds	Italy	Transport (highways)	Support construction of highway that connects 34 municipalities, along with industrial areas	2017 In portfolio/under construction
Fraport Greece	10% equity stake	Greece	Transport (airport)	Invest in project company that operates 14 airports; stimulate tourism and commercial activities	2017 In portfolio/operational
2i Fiber	20% equity stake	Italy	Telecom infrastructure	Support platform for acquisition/consolidation of midsize Italian infra-based B2B telecom operators (Irideos plus three follow-on investments as of September 2018)	2017 In portfolio/operational

continued

TABLE 11.2 *continued*

TARGET COMPANY	INVESTMENT DETAILS	COUNTRY	SECTOR	DESCRIPTION	TRANSACTION YEAR AND STATUS
Rosace	37% equity stake	France	Fiber broadband	Promote FTTH concession projects in less densely populated areas	2016 In portfolio/under construction
AS Latvijas Gāze and AS Conexus Baltic Grid	29% equity stake in AS Conexus (from Latvijas Gāze spinoff)	Latvia	Natural gas pipeline and storage	Promote unbundling process and ownership of strategic storage infrastructure	2016 In portfolio/operational
N17/N18 Motorway	50% equity stake	Ireland	Transport (highways)	Support the construction and operation of highway (TEN-T project)	2014 In portfolio/operational
Zagreb Airport	21% equity stake	Croatia	Transport (airports)	Support project company's building of new passenger terminal	2014 In portfolio/operational
Poznań Energy-from-Waste	50% equity stake	Poland	Municipal waste plant	Support construction and operation of energy from waste plant	2013 In portfolio/operational
Aeolus	50% equity stake	Poland	Renewable energy (wind)	Support construction of onshore wind farm expansion (104 MW)	2013 In portfolio/operational
Chirnogeni Wind Farm	50% equity stake	Romania	Renewable energy (wind)	Support construction of onshore wind farm (80 MW)	2012 In portfolio/operational
Butendiek	22.5% equity stake	Germany	Renewable energy (wind)	Support construction of offshore wind farm (228 MW)	2013 Exited through sale in 2017
Autovía de Arlanzon (A-1) Motorway	45% equity stake	Spain	Transport (highways)	Support construction of motorway (TEN-T) in important corridor connecting cities and towns	2012 Exited through sale in 2017
Toul-Rosières 2	100% equity stake	France	Renewable energy (solar)	Support construction of 36 MW in 115 MW solar PV plant	2012 Exited through sale in 2017
C-Power	10% equity stake	Belgium	Renewable energy (wind)	Support construction of Thornton Bank offshore wind farm (326 MW)	2011 Exited through sale in 2017
Massangis 1	100% equity stake	France	Renewable energy (solar)	Support construction of 36 MW in 56 MW solar PV plant	2012 Exited through sale in 2017

Sources: Marguerite website and press releases; Marguerite 2018.
Note: The five assets exited were sold to Pantheon (Marguerite website). B2B = business-to-business; FTTH = fiber to the home; MW = megawatt; PV = photovoltaic; SPV = special-purpose vehicle; TEN-T = Trans-European Transport Network.

Marguerite monitors the multiplier effect of its capital investments, but it does not target specific multiplier levels. It sees the multiplier as the outcome rather than the driver of its investment decisions, which are strongly grounded in the portfolio eligibility criteria.

EIB's investment in Marguerite II was backed by the European Fund for Strategic Investment and is based on the assumption that the multiplier of EIB's €200 million investment in Marguerite II would be at least 17.5x (that is, facilitating about €3.5 billion of investment in new assets on the ground). As part of the European Fund for Strategic Investment process, EIB regularly tracks the multiplier of its investment.

GOVERNANCE

Marguerite's governance was designed as a compromise among the initial group of founding sponsors, with the specific intention of maximizing the fund's chances of success in inspiring the confidence of potential partners or investors. Thus, the fund's management was from the start separated from the direct influence of Marguerite's sponsors. As a result of the experience of Marguerite I and the introduction of the AIFMD, however, fund governance evolved between Marguerite I and II. Whereas Marguerite I retained its corporate structure as a SICAV/SIF, Marguerite II was incorporated as a Luxembourg SCSp. Both funds are now externally managed by Marguerite Investment Management (and advised by the four-person Marguerite Adviser) as their independent external alternative investment fund manager.

Marguerite II is based on a governance structure that differs from that of Marguerite I and is meant to prevent investor interference in the decisions of the fund management team (table 11.3). Marguerite I encompasses (1) a dual-layer supervisory board (nonexecutive board with general strategic policy and supervision powers) and management board (with executive powers) consisting of representatives of the investors, and (2) an investment/divestment process with some involvement of the investors. The governance model of Marguerite II does not entail any investors' involvement in executive decisions and prevents their interference in the investment decisions of the Marguerite team. As a result, the investors' role is restricted to participation in the fund's strategic and advisory committees.

Marguerite I was not set up with a conventional private equity GP/LP structure, one of the factors contributing to its failure to attract private investors at the fund level. As has been noted, Marguerite I was set up as a SICAV (société d'investissement à capital variable), a close-ended collective investment scheme under Luxembourg law. Marguerite Adviser, the Luxembourg-domiciled company owned by the senior management team, provided investment advisory services in compliance with an advisory agreement. Investment opportunities were subject to initial screenings conducted first by the management team and then by the management board, with the potential for deals to be rejected if they did not comply with the agreed-on policy objectives. In practice, some 100 ideas were presented (in a short memo format) for prescreening, and none got rejected. After this screening, investment decisions in Marguerite I were solely the responsibility of the Investment Committee, a subcommittee of the management board. The Investment Committee had five members—the CEO and chief financial officer of the advisory company and

TABLE 11.3 **Summary of Marguerite II's core bodies and functions**

GOVERNANCE BODIES	FUNCTIONS
Limited partners (LPs)	• Include the European Investment Bank (EIB) and other investors in Marguerite II • Make decisions via investor vote on fundamental matters such as the appointment or removal of the fund manager
Marguerite Adviser	• Controlled by four senior members of the investment team • Owns MIM and provides advisory services to Marguerite II and MIM
Marguerite Investment Management (MIM)	• Is an external alternative investment fund manager licensed under Luxembourg law, and fully controlled (via Marguerite Adviser) by the four senior members of the investment team (CEO, CFO, and two others) • Has overall responsibility for management, including investment decisions and administration of the fund, together with the Marguerite II general partner, and assisted by Marguerite Adviser • Has sole authority for portfolio management, investing, and risk management • Has ownership interest in Marguerite II through capital contributions by senior investment professionals
Investment Committee of MIM	• Includes the four partners of MIM and three independent members (all former CEOs from the power, utilities, and airport sectors) • Makes investment and divestment decisions by a majority, with MIM partners having, in effect, the ability to independently approve investments, subject to compliance with the eligibility criteria
Strategic Committee	• Includes senior representatives of the sponsors • Does not take part in any investment decision • Approves any material amendment to the strategic orientation of Marguerite II • Provides strategic consultation on the overall development of, and on key decisions relating to, the strategy of Marguerite II
Advisory Committee	• Includes representatives of the sponsors • Does not take part in any investment decision • Is responsible for granting approvals stipulated in the limited partnership agreement (for example, for investments exceeding certain thresholds or clearing conflicts)

Source: Marguerite management.
Note: CEO = chief executive officer; CFO = chief financial officer.

three independent members selected by the sponsors and coming from the private sector. Investment decisions were made by majority, although in practice unanimity was sought.

To reflect more standard fund industry practices in the European Union, and to facilitate fundraising from institutional investors, Marguerite II was set up as a Luxembourg special limited partnership (SCSp), a legal structure that has gained widespread acceptance for private equity and infrastructure funds (see box 11.1). The SCSp was introduced in Luxembourg in 2013, and more than 1,300 such partnerships were set up in the initial three years (PwC 2016). The SCSp is a variation of the long-established, standard Luxembourg partnership (société en commandite simple, or SCS), the difference being that the SCSp does not have a legal personality separate from those of its partners and, as a result, can be structured more flexibly.

The main advantages of the new structure used for Marguerite II are (1) the direct participation of the most senior investment professionals in fund results via their stakes in the GP, (2) the licensing of the fund management company as an external alternative investment fund manager under Luxembourg law, and (3) an expansion of the investment committee, resulting in the investment team having a clear majority in investment decisions. These changes ensure that the investment team has full independence in making investment decisions (within the eligibility criteria), skin in the game when it comes to fund performance, and a widely accepted legal accreditation.

BOX 11.1

Key features of the Luxembourg SCSp

- Despite not having its own legal personality, a société en commandite spéciale (SCSp) can own assets and has become a popular legal form for setting up carried interest structures such as private equity firms.
- An SCSp agreement, rather than general corporate law, details the decision-making and economic rights of the various partners.
- Limited partners are, in practice, passive investors whose liability is limited to the amount invested in the SCSp; they cannot be managers or part of the management board of the SCSp but may supervise the partnership through an advisory or supervisory board.
- General partners have unlimited liability, can (but do not have to) manage the partnership, and

- may have other rights such as the approval of accounts.
- The SCSp agreement details the economic rights of different partners, including payment of carried interest to general partners.
- An SCSp can have one or more managers, who may form a management board. Limited partners cannot be managers. General partners can be managers or appoint nonpartners to perform the role.
- Capital commitments by limited partners and commitment periods are contractually defined in the SCSp agreement.
- Accounting and disclosure obligations of the SCSp are less stringent than for similar corporate structures.
- Finally, an SCSp can borrow or issue debt securities.

Source: PwC 2016.

In Marguerite II, the mechanism to screen investments for their compliance with the sponsors' policy goals also differs from Marguerite I. Marguerite I addressed policy objectives via two separate instruments: (1) investment eligibility criteria in the private placement memorandum, and (2) a special eligibility verification procedure that the management board members could trigger with respect to investments that were potentially against EU objectives or public policy. The policy objectives of Marguerite II are addressed in the investment eligibility criteria stipulated in the LPA and certain side letters, and their compliance is monitored by the Advisory Committee. Side letters include the sponsors' various ESG requirements, such as adherence to the UNPRI.

STAFFING AND RECRUITMENT

Marguerite has a team of more than 20 investment professionals dedicated to business development, origination, transaction execution, and the asset management of portfolio companies. Reflecting the pan-EU mandate, the investment team represents 10 nationalities. The team has more than 250 years of cumulative experience in infrastructure financing, fund management, consulting, project finance, investment banking, and industrial companies.

The choice of a legal and incentive structure is aligned as much as possible with market standards, thereby facilitating the hiring of an experienced investment team. Marguerite's CEO negotiated a long-term incentive plan with the sponsors during the Marguerite launch phase in 2009–10, as an important precondition for attracting qualified professionals. Fee levels are confidential, but Marguerite's management confirmed that they reflect the typical private equity combination of management fees (at the lower end of the typical range for infrastructure funds) and share of carried interest.

ECONOMIC IMPACT AND ESG REPORTING

Marguerite applies the ESG criteria of the EIB and other public sponsors, and also endorses international ESG principles such as the UNPRI and the Equator Principles. ESG factors are fully integrated in every phase of investment analysis and decision-making, as detailed in table 11.4. Some sponsors require disclosure of ESG and impact metrics, such as renewable generation capacity installed and carbon dioxide savings.

EIB requires that all its investee funds measure the economic rates of return of their investments and comply with minimum return thresholds. Marguerite I guidelines therefore were based on EIB guidelines and requirements from the other sponsors.[6]

FINANCIAL DISCLOSURE

As is typical for private equity funds, Marguerite's financial disclosure is limited to the funds' investors, not the broader public. Such disclosure includes quarterly and annual portfolio performance reports, with portfolio valuation conducted internally. Marguerite funds are audited by Deloitte according to the International Financial Reporting Standards. Public disclosure is limited to a list and description of fund investments and press releases published on Marguerite's website and updated as new transactions are announced.

TABLE 11.4 **Marguerite's ESG assessment throughout the investment process**

DEAL PHASE	ESG IMPLEMENTATION
Project screening	• Potential investments are screened according to their social and environmental risks and have to meet minimum thresholds of economic return (in addition to financial returns).
Due diligence	• Marguerite estimates an economic rate of return and only proceeds with investments delivering a positive result in this respect. • Obligations to comply with environmental laws and regulations and to prohibit corruption are captured in project contracts (concession agreements, permits, construction contracts, operations contracts, and so on). • ESG considerations are included in the detailed investment proposal submitted to the Investment Committee.
Asset management	• An environmental and social officer was appointed to ensure ongoing compliance. • There is active ownership at the portfolio company level through board participation. • ESG risks identified during due diligence are carefully monitored throughout the holding period. • Environmental and social action plans reflecting the outcome of due diligence are implemented by the management teams of portfolio projects and companies.

Source: Marguerite 2018.
Note: ESG = environmental, social, and governance.

NOTES

1. For societé en commandite spéciale.
2. Société d'investissement à capital variable/specialized investment fund. A SICAV is a collective investment scheme common in several western European countries. Throughout this case study, the acronym SIF, when used in the expression SICAV/SIF, refers to specialized investment fund under Luxembourg legislation.
3. Commission de Surveillance du Secteur Financier.
4. The fund (Marguerite I) has a management board comprising representatives of the core sponsors (six), Marguerite Adviser (two), and three independent members. Investment decisions are made by a subcommittee of the management board comprising the independent members and the representatives of Marguerite Adviser. In addition, the management board has approval or veto rights over certain investment decisions (for example, those exceeding certain size thresholds). Marguerite Adviser plays a purely advisory role.
5. Although many offshore wind farms were built before the time of Marguerite's investments, they were funded by utilities or with bank debt, not by financial investors.
6. For reference, see EIB (2013), applied by the European Investment Bank to its entire investment portfolio. Note that Marguerite II follows a more traditional fund market approach in that guidelines or requirements from sponsors are documented via side letters.

REFERENCES

EIB (European Investment Bank). 2013. "The Economic Appraisal of Investment Projects at the EIB." Projects Directorate, EIB, Luxembourg.

PwC. 2016. "The Luxembourg Special Partnership: A Multi-Purpose Solution for the Real Estate Industry." PwC. https://www.pwc.lu/en/real-estate/docs/pwc-re-lux-special-partnership.pdf.

12 Case Study—National Investment and Infrastructure Fund: A Collaborative Model to Mobilize Foreign Investment*

When we look for international operating partners, we seek those who know the business, know India, are willing to commit to India for the long term and have a demonstrated track record of good governance.

—Sujoy Bose, CEO, National Investment and Infrastructure Fund

BACKGROUND AND MISSION

The key objective for setting up the National Investment and Infrastructure Fund (NIIF) was to catalyze foreign institutional equity capital for Indian infrastructure sector and related businesses. The launch of NIIF was announced in February 2015 by the government of India during the 2015–16 budget presentation. NIIF secured a capital commitment of about US$3 billion from the government.

Following the budgetary announcement of NIIF, the government held extensive consultations with relevant market participants in the funds industry (including sovereign and pension funds) to finalize the optimal structure for NIIF. Further, a global search process was carried out to shortlist and identify the CEO of NIIF, who came on board in October 2016.

Government capital in NIIF is allocated across three funds—the Master Fund, the Fund of Funds, and the Strategic Opportunities Fund (together referred to as NIIF)—all managed by the same investment manager (NIIF Limited) and governed by certain select core principles:

- The government would be a minority investor in each fund, with a stake of 49 percent, and the rest of the capital would be provided by commercial investors.
- Each fund invests on a fully commercial basis.
- The decision-making of each fund is carried out by its respective investment committee comprising NIIF management and in some cases independent professionals, with sole power over investment decisions. The investment committee(s) would not have government or investor representation, in line with global best practices in the fund management industry.

---

*Research for this case study was completed between 2018 and 2019. The text reflects the circumstances at that time.

- NIIF Limited would be majority owned by nongovernment, commercially focused investors, with a board constituted with majority representation by nongovernment investors and independent directors. NIIF Limited would be able to recruit its staff and executives without government involvement.

To fill a large equity financing gap for Indian infrastructure, NIIF aims to attract investors willing to consider large exposures and long tenors. By providing local access and expertise, NIIF aims to position itself as a beachhead for international capital looking to invest in Indian infrastructure through a collaborative investment approach.

According to the NIIF CEO, the NIIF structure is partly inspired by the collaborative investment model (Monk, Sharma, and Sinclair 2017), whereby institutional investors join forces to establish collaborative platforms for cost-sharing on deal sourcing, due diligence, and other stages of the investment process. NIIF Master Fund investors are also shareholders in the investment manager, thereby leading to an investor-owned fund management platform.

FUND STRUCTURE

NIIF Limited is the entity in charge of managing the three funds (figure 12.1). It was intentionally set up by the government as a company (not as a state-controlled development agency) to emphasize its role as a manager of commercial investments and the independence of investment decisions from policy objectives. Investors in the Master Fund receive an equity stake in NIIF Limited

FIGURE 12.1

NIIF structure

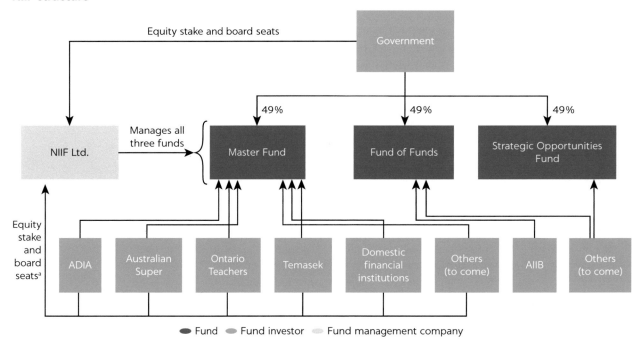

Source: World Bank elaboration.
Note: ADIA = Abu Dhabi Investment Authority; AIIB = Asian Infrastructure Investment Bank; NIIF = National Investment and Infrastructure Fund; Ontario Teachers = Ontario Teachers' Pension Plan.
a. Only for Master Fund investors. Allocation of board seat subject to contributing at least 10 percent of Master Fund capital.

and, above a certain investment size (see details in the governance subsection) also receive board seats. NIIF Limited earns fund management fees. Because the government's stake in the Master Fund and NIIF Limited is 49 percent, the government remains the largest investor and equity holder in NIIF with a substantial minority position (considering nongovernment investors as a single pool).

As an independent, commercial entity, NIIF has no formal right to any infrastructure project that the government may consider divesting, nor obligations to invest in policy-driven projects. NIIF does nevertheless engage in proactive discussions with central and local government authorities to steer new infrastructure development to commercial models, if it makes sense. A team within NIIF, the Strategy and Policy Group, comprising PPP and investment experts, works with these authorities when it sees the opportunity to set up a PPP project instead of building infrastructure through public finance means.

All three NIIF funds are AIF Category II funds under India's alternative investment funds (AIF) regulations and do not have any special dispensations under the law. NIIF funds are unit trusts under the common law model, which are set up to mimic the classic private equity GP/LP structure. Specifically, under Regulation 2(1) (b) of the Securities and Exchange Board of India (SEBI) (Alternative Investment Funds) Regulations, 2012, an AIF is any privately pooled investment fund, whether from Indian or foreign sources, in the form of a trust, company, body corporate, or limited liability partnership. Private equity funds are generally classified as Category II AIFs, which are closed-end funds, with long tenures determined at the time of setup.[1]

NIIF funds are designed with the explicit purpose of mobilizing commercial capital in a fund format. With the government's commitment of US$3 billion and its 49 percent stake, the NIIF funds are anticipated to have total commitments of just over US$6 billion. Note that fund economics are denominated in Indian rupees (US dollar amounts in this case study are based on an exchange rate of US$1.00 = Rs 70.00).

The three NIIF funds are at different stages of development, in line with the envisaged evolution of commercial infrastructure investing in India. NIIF deems direct investments in brownfield, operating infrastructure to be the likely entry point for commercial investors over the short to medium term, especially international ones that may not be very familiar with the Indian investment environment. As a result, NIIF prioritized the launch of the Master Fund, which focuses on brownfield infrastructure projects (see the investment strategy subsection). The Master Fund's fundraising is well advanced at the time of writing, with total capital commitments (including the government portion) of US$1.8 billion out of a target of just over US$2 billion.[2] NIIF subsequently focused on mobilizing commercial capital for the Funds of Funds, which focuses on indirect investments via existing or new infrastructure funds; the Fund of Funds received the first capital commitment in March 2019 and made its first investments in the green infrastructure and affordable and mid-income housing sectors. The Strategic Opportunities Fund began investing in the fourth quarter of 2018, using only capital committed by the government; at the time of writing, it has not yet mobilized commercial capital. The Strategic Opportunities Fund targets a broader range of investment strategies, including greenfield investments with a long investment horizon of 20–25 years, and investments in noncore infrastructure sectors. It made its first investment in October 2018, when it acquired IDFC Infrastructure Finance Limited, a nonbanking finance company that lends to operating infrastructure projects, with a loan book of US$643 million equivalent (NIIF 2018b).

The Master Fund is anticipated to have total commitments of just over US$2.1 billion, of which US$1 billion (or 49 percent) would come from the government (table 12.1). At the time of this report, the Master Fund had received commitments of approximately US$900 million from commercial investors, resulting in a total of approximately US$1.8 billion including the government's contribution. The largest investors, providing a commitment of US$250 million each, are the Abu Dhabi Investment Authority (ADIA), one of the largest sovereign wealth funds globally; AustralianSuper, Australia's largest superannuation fund; and the Ontario Teachers' Pension Plan (Ontario Teachers), Canada's largest single-profession pension plan (PTI 2019). Temasek, Singapore's sovereign wealth fund, committed US$100 million. Four prominent domestic financial institutions— Axis Bank, HDFC Group, ICICI Bank, and Kotak Mahindra Life Insurance— have also invested in the Master Fund (NIIF 2018a).

Investors committing to the Master Fund receive proportional ownership rights in NIIF Limited, the manager, and 3:1 co-investment rights with the Master Fund. For instance, ADIA, AustralianSuper, and Ontario Teachers secured co-investment rights of US$750 million each, and Temasek secured rights of US$300 million. Such rights provide ADIA, AustralianSuper, Ontario Teachers, and Temasek the ability to co-invest with the Master Fund in individual deals if they wish to do so. See further details on the co-investment strategy in the subsection on the Master Fund strategy.

The Fund of Funds is anticipated to have total commitments of US$1 billion, including the government's stake. In June 2018, the board of the Asian Infrastructure Investment Bank (AIIB) approved a US$100 million investment in the NIIF Fund of Funds (AIIB 2018).[3] As part of AIIB's proposed investment, NIIF has implemented ESG standards throughout its operations and, in all three funds, has recruited an ESG officer to ensure implementation.[4]

The government's role as anchor investor of the NIIF funds was a key determinant of the decisions by ADIA, AIIB, AustralianSuper, Ontario Teachers, and Temasek to consider investing in NIIF funds. The presence of prominent private Indian financial institutions as investors was regarded as an additional strength. Discussions with ADIA started in the context of a broad memorandum of understanding between the Indian and Emirati governments. AIIB, as a multilateral

TABLE 12.1 NIIF's anticipated fund size and investors at time of writing

	FUND OF FUNDS	MASTER FUND	STRATEGIC OPPORTUNITIES FUND
Government maximum commitment (US$, billions)	0.5	1.0	1.5
Total anticipated fund size (US$, billions)[a]	Just over 1.0	Just over 2.0	Just over 3.0
Investors at the time of writing (excluding government)	AIIB (US$100 million, potentially increasing to US$200 million)	ADIA (US$250 million); AustralianSuper (US$250 million); Ontario Teachers (US$250 million); Temasek (US$100 million); four domestic financial institutions[b]	None

Source: World Bank elaboration.
Note: ADIA = Abu Dhabi Investment Authority; AIIB = Asian Infrastructure Investment Bank; NIIF = National Investment and Infrastructure Fund; Ontario Teachers = Ontario Teachers' Pension Plan.
a. If NIIF succeeds in attracting commercial investors matching (with a 51 percent stake) the government's maximum capital commitment.
b. Canada Pension Plan Investment Board, Canada's Public Sector Pension Investment Board, and the US International Development Finance Corporation have also invested since the case study was written.

development bank, was also naturally predisposed to partnering in a vehicle backed by the government.

NIIF has established a strong relationship with India's Ministry of External Affairs and is leveraging India's foreign offices to obtain introductions to foreign sovereign wealth funds (SWFs) and pension funds (both public and private). The CEO of NIIF is provided the opportunity, through various forums, to brief Indian ambassadors and high commissioners on the strategy and activities of NIIF. Several ambassadors and high commissioners are well versed about NIIF and highlight the NIIF investment opportunity to authorities in the countries where they are posted, deferring more technical conversations directly to the NIIF management team. This process has proven effective in establishing contacts with SWFs in particular. In addition, NIIF initiates contacts with many SWFs, pension funds, and institutional investors directly.

NIIF's clear commercial orientation, professional management, and the fact that the government does not have majority control and cannot skew investments away from the commercial goals are also very important aspects. According to NIIF management, ADIA's investment in the Master Fund, while kick-started by the memorandum of understanding, was ultimately driven by commercial considerations. Target portfolio company returns discussed with ADIA are in line with the typical equity return expectations for infrastructure projects. ADIA's infrastructure investment team analyzed the opportunity as any other commercial investment in ADIA's portfolio and decided to pursue it on the basis of risk/return considerations. The more recent commitments of AustralianSuper and Ontario Teachers further demonstrate the perceived strength of NIIF's governance, value added, and attraction as a local manager and partner for international capital.

NIIF has offered investors in the Master Fund a board seat in NIIF Limited, the fund management company. The bar for investors to obtain a board seat is set at 10 percent of the total target capital committed to the Master Fund, or just over US$200 million. Despite falling below the threshold, the four domestic investors also received, collectively, one board seat. See the governance subsection for more details on board composition.

INVESTMENT STRATEGY

By design, NIIF exclusively pursues investments offering a commercial, risk-adjusted return. Each of the three funds has a different investment strategy, detailed in the following.

Master Fund strategy

The Master Fund aims to build a sizable portfolio of brownfield infrastructure projects in specific infrastructure sectors, establishing investment platforms that act as sector consolidators (see figure 12.2). A platform is a company fully or partially owned by the fund that acquires a series of operating infrastructure assets in a certain sector in India. Partners in the platform may be infrastructure investors or operators with relevant sector expertise. The maximum exposure the Master Fund can take in an investment is 25 percent of the investible portion of the fund, as prescribed by AIF rules. The Master Fund aims for control positions in these platforms and, if it has to take a minority stake, seeks protection

FIGURE 12.2
NIIF's Master Fund structure

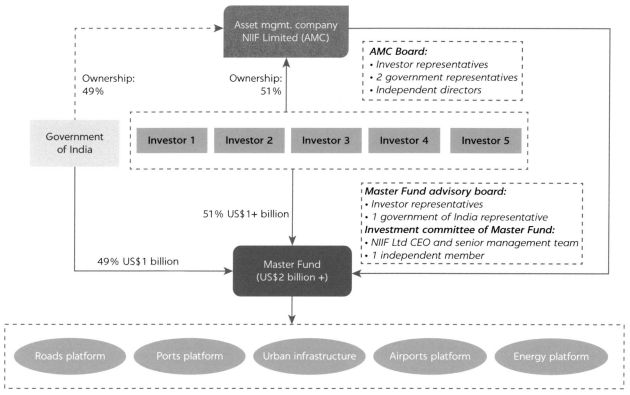

Co-investment pool 3:1 for existing Master Fund investors

Source: World Bank elaboration.
Note: AMC = asset management company; CEO = chief executive officer; mgmt. = management; NIIF = National Investment and Infrastructure Fund.

through board representation or contractual rights (for example, veto) over key decisions such as investments, capital expenditure, leverage, related-party transactions, dividend, corporate deals, and exit options. Some platforms may be newly incubated by the Master Fund. Platforms are meant not only to be a vehicle to channel international capital to India but also to build strong domestic expertise in infrastructure investment and development. A key part of the strategy is to generate co-investment opportunities for the investors as the platform companies grow. The expected holding period for a platform is 8–10 years. Exits may include sale to other investors (such as domestic or international insurance and pension funds), initial public offerings or listed trusts, and refinancing or buy-back by promoters. All platforms will operate on a commercial basis. The Master Fund will seek to diversify investments by vintage year.[5]

For example, in January 2018, the Master Fund established a platform with DP World, the Dubai-based port terminal owner and operator, to invest in ports, terminals, transportation, and logistics businesses in India. DP World controls the platform with a 65 percent stake and the Master Fund is a significant minority investor with the remaining 35 percent of the equity. The platform will invest up to US$3 billion of equity to acquire assets and develop projects in the sector. In March 2018, this platform made its first investment acquiring a 90 percent stake in Continental Warehousing, a terminal and logistics business previously controlled jointly by private equity firms Abraaj and Warburg Pincus, and the International Finance Corporation (IFC). The platform outbid PSA (the Singapore port operator) and Macquarie (the infrastructure fund) in a competitive tender. NIIF believes that the fresh ownership of Continental Warehousing and the willingness of the new investors to inject substantial capital will result in faster growth for Continental Warehousing. The port platform subsequently acquired other businesses. NIIF believes that providing efficient transport logistics on a countrywide scale will result in cost efficiencies for customers.

Additional platforms were established in 2019 to invest in road and renewable energy projects. In April 2019, the Master Fund launched a road platform together with ROADIS, a leading private investor and operator of transport infrastructure worldwide and a wholly owned subsidiary of the Public Sector Pension Investment Board, one of Canada's largest pension funds. The platform plans to invest up to US$2 billion of equity to target toll-operate-transfer models, acquisitions of existing road concessions, and other investment opportunities in the Indian road sector (NIIF 2019). In February 2019, NIIF announced an investment in Ayana Renewable Power, a renewable energy platform founded by CDC Group to develop utility-scale solar and wind generation projects across growth states in India (Everstone Capital 2019). At the time of writing, both platforms were in discussions to acquire assets.

Fund of Funds strategy

The Fund of Funds aims to provide anchor capital to fund managers with strong track records who are raising funds in infrastructure and allied sectors in India, including the following:

- *Green infrastructure, such as renewables, clean transport, water, and waste.* In April 2017, the Fund of Funds announced its first investment in this sector. The Fund of Funds and the UK Department for International Development provided £240 million in anchor capital (split 50/50) to the Green Growth Equity Fund, a newly established fund aiming to raise a total of £500 million to invest in power, distribution infrastructure, and energy services in India. The Green Growth Equity Fund is managed by EverSource, a joint-venture between Everstone, an Indian investment management firm, and Lightsource BP, a global renewable energy developer partially owned by oil major BP. The appointment of the fund manager was on a competitive basis. The fund is also set up as an alternative investment fund under SEBI regulations (Eversource Capital 2018).
- *Affordable housing.* In October 2018, the Fund of Funds committed to a US$100 million investment in a US$650 million new affordable housing fund launched by HDFC Capital, the investment arm of India's largest housing and mortgage finance company, Housing Development Finance Corporation.
- *Other core infrastructure verticals, social infrastructure sectors, such as primary and secondary health care, and digital infrastructure (for example, data centers).* At the time of this report, the Fund of Funds is looking for fund management partners for these sectors.

Strategic Opportunities Fund strategy

The Strategic Opportunities Fund seeks to invest in assets and businesses in the infrastructure and associated sectors that may require a longer investment horizon.

Investments made by the Strategic Opportunities Fund may include greenfield and higher-risk investments than those contemplated by the Master Fund.

INVESTMENT PROCESS

NIIF's investment process consists of three stages. During stage 1, the deal team working on the transaction analyzes preliminary information to assess the prospective investment and seeks approval from the Investment Committee to spend time undertaking a detailed internal appraisal and finalizing a term sheet. In stage 2, the investment committee approves the nonbinding term sheet and appointment of third-party due diligence advisers. The deal team discusses the due diligence findings with the Investment Committee and gets the committee's approval to execute the definitive documents in stage 3. Deals can be rejected for both financial and ESG-related reasons.

As far as risk management is concerned, all Category II AIFs regulated by SEBI must comply with regulatory exposure limits. In addition, each fund managed by NIIF Limited complies with additional exposure limits agreed on with investors.

ADDITIONALITY AND MULTIPLIER CONSIDERATIONS

Notwithstanding its commercial focus, NIIF aims to deliver additionality through several avenues.

- *Demonstration effect.* By investing on a commercial basis and crowding in commercial investors already at fund level, NIIF aims to demonstrate the feasibility and attractiveness of investing in Indian infrastructure. The initial focus on operating infrastructure, through the Master Fund, aims to maximize this demonstration effect by targeting lower-risk assets. As the demonstration effect plays out in operating assets, NIIF will move on to riskier, greenfield investments through the Strategic Opportunities Fund and, over time, through the Master Fund platform companies.
- *Demonstration effect for fund-of-funds investment.* Similarly, through the Fund of Funds NIIF aims to demonstrate the feasibility and attractiveness of indirect investing through a portfolio of third-party-managed funds. No fund of fund dedicated to Indian infrastructure exists at the time of writing.[6]
- *Local partner for foreign investors.* NIIF can provide a channel for international institutional investors and operators that often find it challenging to navigate the infrastructure sector in India. NIIF believes that, with its good governance and ESG practices, expert team, and high-quality shareholders, it provides investors with a credible, professional counterparty in India.
- *Access to local governments and networks.* NIIF can facilitate access to and dialogue with ministries and other government entities that are important stakeholders and counterparts in infrastructure projects.

NIIF expects to avoid crowding out other sources of private capital for the following reasons.

- *Minority government investment.* The government is, by design, a minority investor in each NIIF fund and a minority shareholder in NIIF Limited, with only two seats on the board. All other investors in the three funds and shareholders in NIIF Limited are commercial investors. This arrangement seeks to ensure that the government does not use NIIF to further its policy objectives, for instance, by causing NIIF funds to invest at nonmarket terms that would crowd out other commercial investors or in commercially unviable business opportunities.

- *Large uncovered infrastructure gap.* The opportunity for commercial investing in Indian infrastructure is considered by NIIF to be very large and still mostly untapped. NIIF aims to bring sizable capital to play, thanks to the government's commitment of US$3 billion, with about another US$3 billion to be brought by co-investors at fund level, and any other source of cofinance (equity or debt) that will materialize at the portfolio company level. As of 2018, the Ministry of Finance estimates India's infrastructure funding needs at US$200 billion per annum, of which US$110 billion is fulfilled—leaving a large gap of US$90 billion. In the past, foreign and private domestic investors have made significant investments in Indian infrastructure; however, aggressive underwriting of risks, excessive use of leverage, and poor regulation led to many project failures. For instance, in the 2007–12 period, many projects and companies benefiting from large investments at the beginning of that period fell into distress, leading to subsequent investor risk aversion and capital flight from the sector (Aiyar 2012).

NIIF does not have hard targets in terms of a private capital multiplier, but its very design ensures a high degree of mobilization and could lead to a multiplier estimated by NIIF at 15–20 times. In all funds, as previously discussed, commercial investors are involved directly at fund level, where they are to contribute 51 percent of the capital commitments. In addition, at the portfolio level,

- The Master Fund has the ability to set up platforms jointly with other equity co-investors. This was the case when the Master Fund took a 35 percent equity stake in the port platform, committing up to US$1 billion and attracting a 65 percent equity investment by DP World that could result in the mobilization of another US$2 billion equity. Such platform companies can also take equity co-investors in individual portfolio companies or take partial ownership of portfolio companies with existing company shareholders also remaining involved. This was the case for the port platform's first investment in Continental Warehousing, when the platform took a 90 percent equity stake and the company's founder remained involved with a 10 percent stake. Finally, individual investments can also be levered.
- The Fund of Funds can achieve similar mobilization ratios. The logic is the same; however, instead of taking equity stakes in platform companies, the Fund of Funds takes stakes in funds, always in conjunction with other co-investors. The underlying funds will then invest in several portfolio companies, take full or partial equity ownership, and leverage the business if appropriate. NIIF mentioned that one of the attractions of investing in the Fund of Funds for AIIB was the possibility of generating a high multiplier, because the subfunds of the Fund of Funds would invest in a large portfolio of companies.

GOVERNANCE

The government's investments in the three funds and its stake in NIIF Limited are overseen by the Department of Economic Affairs of the Ministry of Finance, with which NIIF Limited maintains an open line of communication. No separate ownership entity was established by the government to oversee its capital commitment to and investment in NIIF. A Governing Council, chaired by the Minister of Finance and including members of India's business, investment, and policy communities, meets annually to provide general guidance on NIIF's strategy.

NIIF Limited's board meets at least once every quarter to review NIIF's overall strategy and is responsible for appointing the Investment Committee for each fund. The board includes government representatives (in a minority position), any investor representing more than 10 percent of the Master Fund's capital (just over US$200 million), NIIF Limited's management, and independent members (figure 12.3 and table 12.2). The chair is selected at the beginning of each board meeting by board members. As new investors exceeding the 10 percent threshold commit capital to the Master Fund, the composition of the board will change accordingly. As of fall 2019, the board comprised eight members: two from the government (from the Department of Economic Affairs); one each from ADIA, AustralianSuper,[7] and Ontario Teachers; one collectively for the four domestic investors (the only exception to the 10 percent rule); the Managing Director and CEO of NIIF Limited; and one independent director.[8] Government representation on the board is limited to a minority by NIIF Limited's shareholder agreement. All directors have one vote each. At final close, NIIF Limited expects to have a board size of 11, with the government continuing to retain just two seats. No board member has a casting vote.

FIGURE 12.3

NIIF's governance structure

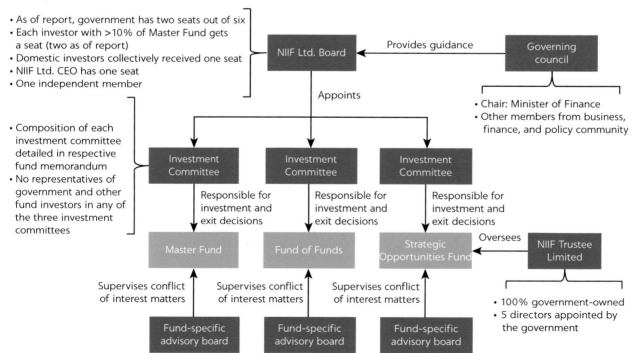

Source: World Bank elaboration.
Note: CEO = chief executive officer; NIIF = National Investment and Infrastructure Fund.

TABLE 12.2 **Summary of NIIF Limited's governance bodies**

BODY	COMPOSITION	FUNCTIONS
Governing Council	• Chaired by the Minister of Finance • At the time of writing also includes the Secretary of Department of Economic Affairs, Secretary of Department of Financial Services, and representatives from business and investment communities	• Meets annually and provides guidance on NIIF's strategy
Board	• At the time of writing, has 6 members: 2 from government, 1 from ADIA, 1 from a block of domestic investors in the Master Fund, NIIF Limited's Managing Director and CEO, and 1 independent • Allows a seat to every investor with more than 10% of the capital in the Master Fund • As of spring 2019, was looking to add 1 independent and 2–3 investor representatives, assuming the same number of large-ticket investors commit to the Master Fund	• Meets at least every quarter to establish and review NIIF's overall strategy • Appoints the Investment Committee • Approves annual budget
Investment Committees (one for each fund)	• Appointed by board • Include members from NIIF Limited management as key persons detailed in the private placement memorandum of each NIIF fund (with any changes triggering the filing of a memorandum amendment with SEBI) • Have no government representatives and other fund investors in any of the three committees • Do not have chairs • Master Fund: As of spring 2019, had 4 members—NIIF Limited's CEO, COO, Executive Director of Investments, and 1 independent member (none from government)	• Have sole power over investment decisions of the respective funds, based on the three-stage approval process previously described • Also decide on key portfolio action items and exits, and review investment performance on a periodic basis
Corporate Social Responsibility (CSR) Committee	• Includes CEO • Consists of 3 additional members of the board including the independent director	• Devises the CSR policy • Approves the expenditure to be made on CSR projects (with at least 2% of the average net profits of previous 3 years to be spent on CSR projects)
Nomination and Remuneration Committee	• Has one investor representative • Has one independent member • Has one government representative	• Devises compensation plans, policies, and succession plans for NIIF Limited's employees • Assists the board in matters regarding compensation of the directors and key managerial personnel
Audit and Risk Committee	• Has two investor representatives • Has one independent member • Has one government representative	• Ensures compliance with accounting, legal, and regulatory requirements • Ensures accuracy, integrity, and transparency of NIIF Limited's financial statements with adequate and timely disclosures • Evaluates matters pertaining to auditors' appointments and their report on the financial statements • Evaluates internal financial controls and risk management systems • Monitors adherence to the risk policy prescribed by board but does not involve itself in deal-specific risks
Advisory Boards (one for each fund)	• Provide only one government seat per fund (even if the government is the largest individual investor) • Master Fund: As of fall 2018, had 4 members representing ADIA, the domestic financial investor block, the government, and Temasek	• Provides oversight on the operations of the respective funds, with focus on conflicts of interest and related-party transactions, in case any such situations arise from time to time
Trustee (NIIF Trustee Limited, or NIIFTL)	• Is the trustee for the three funds managed by NIIF Limited • Is 100% owned by government of India • Has a board comprising 5 directors nominated by the government	• Oversees the operations of NIIF Limited at a high level under the Investment Management Agreement

Source: NIIF management.
Note: ADIA = Abu Dhabi Investment Authority; CEO = chief executive officer; COO = chief operating officer; NIIF = National Investment and Infrastructure Fund; SEBI = Securities and Exchange Board of India.

The board appoints the CEO and the Investment Committees of the three funds, which retain sole power over investment decisions. Government representatives and other fund investors are not represented on the Investment Committees, as contractually determined in fund documentation. The composition of the Investment Committee is detailed in the private placement memorandum of each fund, which is filed with SEBI. The Investment Committees do not have a chair. Although the board has the power to replace the Investment Committees, the need to modify the memorandum, refile with SEBI, and consider any consequence of the change of a key person in effect reduces the risk of discretional and unpredictable changes to the committees.

Each fund has an Advisory Board, including some investor representatives, consistent with global best practices. The Advisory Boards oversee the operations of the funds, with focus on conflicts of interest and related-party transactions. At the discretion of NIIF Limited, the four domestic financial institutions that invested in the Master Fund also received a seat on its Advisory Board.

STAFFING AND RECRUITMENT

At the time of writing, NIIF Limited's staff included 45 investment professionals with backgrounds in infrastructure—including domestic and international investing and operating experience. NIIF Limited plans to expand its current Mumbai office and establish a new office in Delhi with a higher staff capacity.[9] The team has worked with leading domestic and international institutions such as Actis, HDFC Equity, HSBC, IDFC, the IFC, Khazanah Nasional Berhad, KPMG, Macquarie, the State Bank of India, Tata Group, and others. Years of experience range from a minimum of 4 years typically for analysts, to more than 18 years for senior principals.

Remuneration includes a fixed and a variable element, the latter linked to market benchmarks. Although NIIF is not the highest payer in the market, the exposure and visibility of working for an important government-backed body have contributed to the attractiveness of working for NIIF.

ECONOMIC IMPACT AND ESG REPORTING

NIIF does not formally pursue a double bottom line, because of the belief that its entire strategy of supporting investments in India's infrastructure has development impact. Therefore, it does not formally track and report impact indicators.

NIIF Fund of Fund's ESG criteria align with those used by AIIB. Before AIIB's investment in the Fund of Funds, NIIF had not formalized its ESG policies. ESG management policy was a necessary condition for AIIB's involvement in the Fund of Funds, at which point NIIF developed and adopted (through a board decision) an ESG policy for all of NIIF funds. Screening for ESG risks and impacts of every investment is mandatory, from the early stages of the investment process. An Environmental and Social Action Plan must be included in the investment agreements signed with investment proponents and sponsors. After a deal closes, the plan, as agreed to with the investment proponent and as part of the investment agreement, is reviewed and monitored for compliance. In addition, depending upon the investment type, investment supervision is undertaken through desk review coupled with site visits.

NIIF maintains in-house ESG capacity at all times in the form of specialist resources and oversight from a member of the senior management team, with additional external resources available through as-needed or long-term contracting. Third-party fund managers of various subfunds in which the Fund of Funds has invested are required to formulate and institute an appropriate ESG organizational structure.

NIIF funds are not obliged to report to the public on the ESG compliance of their portfolio investments. NIIF Limited, however, ensures that portfolio subfunds managed by third-party fund managers under the Fund of Funds have in place a communication mechanism to address legitimate third-party enquiries on their own ESG processes and outcomes as well as ESG impacts and performance of their portfolio investments.

FINANCIAL DISCLOSURE

NIIF Limited produces quarterly fund reports for investors in its funds and for the board. It discusses the reports in follow-up calls. An independent evaluator conducts portfolio valuations every six months, based on market norms. Fund performance is not disclosed to the public. NIIF Limited's accounts are audited by Ernst & Young under Indian accounting standards.

NOTES

1. SEBI, which is also the regulator of AIFs, has classified AIFs into three categories: Category I (focused on sectors with positive spillover effects on the economy like venture capital, SME investing, social venture funds, and so on); Category III (funds having diverse investment strategies including high leverage, investment in listed securities and derivatives, and so on, similar to hedge funds) and Category II (funds not categorized as Category I or Category III). The regulation prescribes that Category II AIFs have a minimum tenure of three years.
2. Since the case study was written, the Master Fund achieved final close at $2.34 billion, higher than its target of $2.1 billion.
3. In addition, ADB invested US$100 million in the Fund of Funds after the case study write-up.
4. The Fund of Funds has adopted ADB environmental and social standards.
5. NIIF website (accessed September 2018).
6. Funds of funds exist in India, but are dedicated to other sectors, such as technology.
7. Appointment of AustralianSuper's board member pending at the time of writing.
8. Post case study write up, as of January 2021, the board has nine directors, with the addition of another independent director.
9. As of January 2021, NIIF's staff had increased to 75.

REFERENCES

AIIB (Asia Infrastructure Investment Bank). 2018. "AIIB Investment to Attract Private Capital, Help Indian Infrastructure Development." Press release, June 25, 2018. https://www.aiib .org/en/news-events/news/2018/AIIB-Investment-to-Attract-Private-Capital-Help -Indian-Infrastructure-Development.html.

Aiyar, S. A. 2012. "Infrastructure Crisis Endangers Future Growth." Times of India, September 30, 2012. https://timesofindia.indiatimes.com/blogs/Swaminomics/infrastructure -crisis-endangers-future-growth/.

Eversource Capital. 2018. "Lightsource BP and Everstone Group Form 'EverSource Capital' to Invest in Green Infrastructure in India." Press release, April 18, 2018. https://www .eversourcecapital.com/eversource_formation/.

Everstone Capital. 2019. "EverSource Capital and NIIF Announce Partnership with CDC to Invest in Its Renewable Energy Platform Ayana." Press release, February 28, 2019. https:// www.everstonecapital.com/2019/02/28/eversource-capital-and-niif-announce -partnership-with-cdc-to-invest-in-its-renewable-energy-platform-ayana/.

Monk, Ashby, Rajiv Sharma, and Duncan L. Sinclair. 2017. *Reframing Finance: New Models of Long-Term Investment Management.* Stanford, CA: Stanford University Press.

NIIF (National Investment and Infrastructure Fund). 2018a. "National Investment and Infrastructure Fund (NIIF) Secures Investments of up to USD 400 Million from Temasek." Press release, September 6, 2018. https://www.niifindia.in/uploads/media_releases /Press%20Release%20-%20National%20Investment%20and%20Infrastructure%20 Fund%20(NIIF)%20secures%20investments%20of%20up%20to%20USD%20400%20 million%20from%20Temasek-converted.pdf.

NIIF (National Investment and Infrastructure Fund). 2018b. "NIIF to Acquire IDFC Infrastructure Finance Limited from IDFC." Press release, October 31, 2018. https://www .niifindia.in/uploads/media_releases/Press%20Release%20-%20NIIF%20to%20 acquire%20IDFC%20Infrastructure%20Finance%20Limited%20from%20IDFC -converted.pdf.

NIIF (National Investment and Infrastructure Fund). 2019. "NIIF and ROADIS Partner to Create Platform for Investment in Road Sector." Press release, April 3, 2019. https://www .niifindia.in/uploads/media_releases/Press%20Release%20-%20NIIF%20and%20 ROADIS%20Partner%20to%20Create%20Platform%20for%20Investment%20in%20 Road%20Sector-converted.pdf.

PTI (Press Trust of India). 2019. "AustralianSuper and Ontario Teachers' Pension Plan to Invest up to USD 2 Billion through NIIF." *Times of India*, August 6, 2019. https://timesofindia .indiatimes.com/business/india-business/australia-canadian-funds-to-invest-up-to-usd-2 -bn-through-niif/articleshow/70551731.cms?utm_source=amp_slider&utm_medium =referral&utm_campaign=TOI&from=mdr.

13 Case Study—Nigeria Sovereign Investment Authority–Nigeria Infrastructure Fund*

BACKGROUND AND MISSION

The Nigeria Infrastructure Fund (NIF) is a fund established by the Nigeria Sovereign Investment Authority (NSIA), an investment entity set up at the federal level, to boost the development of the country's infrastructure, with the double bottom line goal of realizing a commercial return and investing in infrastructure that might otherwise not be financed and developed. NIF has a long-term investment horizon, exceeding 20 years, and acts exclusively as a provider of new funding, investing across the capital structure, from senior secured debt to equity. The fund size was US$650 million as of June 2018.

NSIA's mission is to play a leading role in driving sustained economic development for the benefit of all Nigerians by enhancing the development of Nigeria's infrastructure, building a savings base for future generations, and providing stabilization support in times of economic stress. This mandate is carried out via three separate funds: NIF, the Future Generations Fund, and the Stabilization Fund. This case study focuses on NIF.

NSIA is funded with hydrocarbon revenues in excess of Nigeria's budgetary requirements, allocated to central and local governments and then partially channeled to NSIA. Nigeria's federal constitution allocates oil revenues to central and subnational governments in predetermined ratios. In turn, these recipients allocate funds to NSIA according to the same ratios, which are reflected in their ownership stakes in NSIA. NSIA's ownership structure is as follows: federal government, 45.8 percent; state governments, 36.2 percent; local governments, 17.8 percent; and federal capital territory, 0.2 percent.

NSIA commenced operations in 2012 and began investment activities in the third quarter of 2013, with seed capital of US$1 billion. An additional US$250 million was committed by the National Executive Council in November 2015 and received in 2016. Another capital injection of US$250 million was approved in 2016 and received in 2017. Capital injections reflect oil prices: in years when the

---

*Research for this case study was completed between 2018 and 2019. The text reflects the circumstances at that time.

oil price is below budget breakeven levels, no contribution is made to NSIA, unless other sources can be identified (for example, some of the profits of the state-owned liquified natural gas producer can also be used to capitalize NSIA). Funds are deposited in a central bank account pertaining to NSIA and, at that point, only NSIA can authorize transfers.

NIF was initially allocated 40 percent of NSIA's fund, but this share subsequently increased to 50 percent following a five-year review by the NSIA board that was conducted in October 2017. Initially, NSIA allocated its capital in the following ratios: 40 percent each to NIF and the Future Generations Fund, and 20 percent to the Stabilization Fund. This resulted in total funding to NIF of US$600 million, which increased—as a result of realized returns of US$50 million—to US$650 million as of June 2018. At the October 2017 review, the NSIA board decided to allocate 50 percent of all future capital injections to NIF, 30 percent to the Future Generations Fund, and 20 percent to the Stabilization Fund.

In addition, in May 2018, Nigeria's president approved the establishment of a separate Presidential Infrastructure Development Fund (PIDF) to invest specifically in large road and power projects across the country (NSIA 2018a). Although separate from NIF, PIDF will be managed by the NIF team under the standard operating procedures of NSIA. Seed funding of US$650 million for PIDF will come from the Nigeria Liquified Natural Gas Dividend Account, as authorized by the National Economic Council. The investments will yield returns, which are expected to diversify revenues to federal states and improve Nigeria's fiscal sustainability profile. Potential projects include a large hydropower plant and four nationally strategic toll roads. PIDF will secure counterpart funds required for projects being codeveloped with China Exim Bank and China Development Bank, and mobilize any additional funding required from development partners. Up to US$300 million of the original NIF capital can be used for co-investments in PIDF projects. Taking into account both NIF and PIDF, NSIA's cumulative commitment to infrastructure investments is US$1.3 billion.

LEGAL STRUCTURE

NSIA was established by ad hoc parliamentary law—the Nigeria Sovereign Investment Authority (Establishment, etc.) Act, 2011, or NSIA Act 2011—in May 2011, as a body corporate. It is not a fund governed by securities law, nor is it a company in a strict sense, governed by corporate law. As a body corporate under the definition of the NSIA Act 2011 (1) it can sue and be sued; (2) it can acquire, hold, and sell assets necessary for the performance of its functions; and (3) it is "independent in the discharge of its functions and shall not be subject to the direction or control of any other person or authority."

NIF is a ring-fenced pool of capital managed by NSIA under its own distinct investment policy. It is a fund without a separate legal identity. The same is true of the Future Generations Fund and Stabilization Fund. For instance, as a fiscal stabilization mechanism, the Stabilization Fund is focused on capital preservation and invests primarily in short-term, low-risk investments. The Future Generations Fund is mandated to establish an intergenerational savings pool and, coherently, pursues long-term investments. Both funds invest in externally managed funds. In contrast, NIF pursues direct investments in Nigerian infrastructure.

Unlike private infrastructure funds, NIF does not have a fixed investment horizon and does not earn management fees or carried interest. NSIA must reinvest all proceeds of its investment activities (net of operating expenses) in existing or new assets of the fund. The only form of payout from NIF is through a dividend or distribution of profits to stakeholders. The NSIA Act 2011 states that that board can elect to make distributions after five years of consistent profitability in all three NSIA funds. Deal costs, which in a private fund would be covered by the management fee, are capped on a per-deal basis (annual budget approved by the board, against which amounts of more than US$80,000 must be approved by the board's Direct Investments Committee) and cumulative basis (up to 1.5 percent of NIF capital).

MANDATE FOR INVESTMENT

NIF invests in infrastructure projects in sectors with the potential to contribute to the growth and diversification of the Nigerian economy, create jobs, and—where possible—attract foreign investment.

NIF focuses on four core sectors—agriculture, health care, power, and motorways—but has the flexibility to also invest in other infrastructure and noninfrastructure sectors. These other sectors include free trade zones and industrial parks; retail and industrial real estate; refining; water resources; ports; mining and basic materials; gas pipeline, storage, and processing; aviation; waste and sewage; tourism; rail; and communication. These sectors as well as general guidelines to NIF's investment activities are described in a rolling five-year investment plan for NIF that, in accordance with the NSIA Act 2011, NSIA develops each year. The plan is a living document that is revised regularly throughout the year as government priorities and macroeconomic circumstances evolve. It is not intended as a detailed, prescriptive to-do list, but rather as general guidance for NIF's deal origination and investment strategy.

Some of the sectors within NIF's mandate would not be conventionally considered direct infrastructure investments, but are considered as such by NSIA because of their potential to support and enable the economic growth of the country. For instance, NIF has invested in private schools, cancer treatment and diagnostic centers, an infrastructure debt fund, and an infrastructure bond guarantee company. The development benefits of these projects are evident, but they are very different from the typical infrastructure concession projects, which are designed to earn regulated tariffs over a long concession period.

NIF targets for each investment a return in excess of US inflation and consistent with "reasonable expectations from a diversified portfolio of risk assets" (NSIA 2019). When NIF's investment strategy was defined in 2014, the premium over inflation was set at 5 percent, resulting in target average annual returns at the time of 6 percent[1] in US dollars. At the time of writing, the return target is US inflation plus 3 percent. Such a target reflects NSIA's overall objective to preserve and grow its long-term purchasing power in US dollar terms, to support Nigeria's population and its economic growth, and to maximize returns on behalf of the Nigerian people. NIF's actual return in 2017 was 6.2 percent, consistent with targets.[2]

In addition, up to 10 percent of the NIF capital available for investment in any fiscal year can be invested in social infrastructure projects that promote economic development in underserved sectors or regions of Nigeria and may present less favorable financial return potential ("Development Projects" in NSIA-NIF terminology). All potential Development Projects identified and supported by NSIA are submitted to a committee (set up for this purpose by the National Economic Council) that decides whether NSIA may invest in such Development Projects; this committee is not a standing one and its decision-making processes are not disclosed to NSIA. A comprehensive feasibility study is required to demonstrate how a prospective Development Project serves the public interest and has clear potential to provide economic and employment stimulus. Financially, NIF seeks to recover at least the total cost of operations during the life of the project (net of any government subsidies the project may receive).

The NSIA Act 2011 requires NSIA to review and analyze against the criteria of financial return (specified in the subsection on investment strategy) all written proposals submitted by the federal government and any state or local government. In order to be considered by NSIA, investment proposals have to be submitted in formal letters. Before being sent to NSIA, such written proposals are usually approved at a very senior level in the presidential office, ministries, or other government bodies—therefore ensuring that NSIA is not overloaded with requests of little strategic priority for the government. Once it receives a written proposal, NSIA is required to review it, regardless of the government entity submitting it. The investment decision-making process is the same as for any other investment considered by NSIA, as described in the governance subsection and figure 13.2 later in this case study: three levels of due diligence and screening by the investment team, Executive Committee, and Direct Investment Committee, followed (in the best scenario) by board approval. NSIA analyzes investment proposals received from government entities in complete independence and is free to reject transactions that do not meet its financial return requirements.

NSIA also aims to enable the government to realize its infrastructure and PPP development plan by offering, on an informal basis, capacity building services and advice. NSIA's staff comes predominantly from the international private financial services sector. Capacity building support includes enabling the government to attract broader investment participation in Nigerian infrastructure, catalyzing further international investment and project development and financing skills, developing the government's technical transaction skills, improving technical prequalification processes and concessioning of projects, and improving capacity of local project sponsors. More generally, when selecting investments, NSIA takes into account the demonstration effect and potential to encourage other parties to invest in Nigerian infrastructure.

INVESTMENT STRATEGY

NIF pursues three broad strategies for its commercial portfolio (in addition to the Development Projects pocket):

1. *Direct investments in infrastructure, with focus on four sectors: agriculture, health care, motorways, and power.* NIF uses portfolio diversification to achieve a balance between financial and investment objectives, risk tolerance, and need

for liquidity. The goal is twofold: first, ensure that no project or manager; regional, political, or economic events or circumstances; or infrastructure sector has a disproportionate impact on NIF's aggregate results; second, ensure a more even spread of the benefit of the investment capital available to NIF. NIF cannot commit more than 25 percent of total assets to one project or manager or more than 35 percent to one infrastructure subsector in Nigeria.

2. *Co-investments through funds managed by external managers, subject to a cap of 50 percent of total NIF assets.* Allocation to external managers is also subject to concentration limits: no more than 10 percent of NIF assets can be allocated to a single, externally managed fund and no more than 20 percent to a single external fund manager. When co-investing with, or investing in, a third-party fund, NIF evaluates that fund's expertise in the target sector, investment track record, and return potential.

3. *Creation of institutions and financial services companies* that fill the gap for infrastructure financing and other sectors of national importance in Nigeria.

NIF has a long-term investment horizon exceeding 20 years. This time frame allows it to navigate multiple economic and market cycles and focus on greenfield investments with a long gestation period. NSIA is willing to invest in projects that may not generate any cash flows and may require significant capital injections in the short term but produce attractive long-term returns.

Pending investments in long-term infrastructure opportunities, NIF can make short- and medium-term fixed-income investments with unspent funds. It can purchase only investment grade instruments with a maximum tenor of three years (board approval required for tenors of more than one year). These investments must be approved by the Investment Committee on the recommendation of the executive management.

NIF acts exclusively as a provider of new funding and invests across the capital structure, from senior secured debt down to equity. It does not buy out existing shareholders, refinance existing debt, or issue guarantees. Return expectations vary depending on the instrument invested. Except for investments categorized as Development Projects, however, all have to comply with the 6 percent floor discussed previously.

NIF can incur leverage at either NSIA or project level. Leverage decisions are made by the Direct Investment Committee on a project-by-project basis. Debt issued by NSIA does not enjoy any implicit or explicit government guarantees. NIF may seek government guarantees on major infrastructure projects, but they have to be negotiated and the government is under no obligation to provide them.

Internal investment procedures are standardized. Investment officers use a standard valuation model and valuation materials, reviewed periodically by the Investment Committee.

PORTFOLIO AND TRACK RECORD

NIF has committed and partially drawn down US$350 million for several direct and indirect investments in its target sectors, and has earmarked US$300 million of capital for co-investments in large PIDF projects. Table 13.1 summarizes NIF's current and expected future commitments as of the time of writing.

TABLE 13.1 **NIF current and expected future capital commitments**

DEAL	INVESTMENT SIZE (US$, MILLIONS)	SECTOR	RATIONALE
Direct investments			
Second Niger bridge	75 (deal in progress, financial close not yet reached at time of writing)	Transport	To ease burden on existing bridge, reduce heavy congestion, and promote regional links
Integrated mill	12.5	Agriculture	To support agricultural production
Ammonia production plant	Undisclosed commitment	Agriculture	To reduce Nigeria's reliance on fertilizer imports
Nigeria commodity exchange (in progress)	10	Agriculture	To develop Nigeria's commodity trading capabilities to promote agricultural trade, facilitate financial derivatives trading, and support robust warehouses (NIPC 2017)
Lagos University Teaching Hospital (LUTH) Center for Advanced Medical Care (Partnership with private equity firm Abraaj and LUTH)	15	Health care	To develop a modern radiation therapy center, to be run by an independent operator but integrated with the LUTH oncology unit
Two medical diagnostic centers	10	Health care	To develop two diagnostic centers housed at existing hospitals but operated independently as financially sustainable businesses
Presidential Infrastructure Development Fund	650	Transport	To invest in four strategic national road infrastructure projects as well as a power project
Babban Gona	5	Agriculture	To create an agriculture franchise for smallholder farmers
Ogun State Land Degradation Neutrality Project	Feasibility study phase	Agriculture	To transform 108,000 hectares of degraded land into arable green land, in partnership with Ogun state government and cement company Lafarge
Indirect investments			
Fund for Agriculture Finance in Nigeria (co-sponsored with German development agency KfW and the Nigerian Federal Ministry of Agriculture and Rural Development)	7.5	Agriculture	To provide tailored capital and technical assistance to commercially viable agricultural SMEs and intermediaries in Nigeria with US$100 million target investment fund
Nigeria Infrastructure Debt Fund	5	Infrastructure	To create first local currency infrastructure debt fund focused on Africa
NSIA-UFF Agriculture Fund (set up jointly with Old Mutual Investment Group of South Africa)	25	Agriculture	To invest in Nigeria's agricultural enterprises (initial commitment of US$25 million each from NSIA and Old Mutual, with total fundraising target of US$200 million)[a]
Middle Market Industrialization Fund	Yet to be launched	Industry	To promote middle-market industrialization in Nigeria
Real estate investment fund (with Old Mutual)	100[b]	Real estate	To diversify the Nigerian economy away from oil, in part, through investment in core sectors like real estate that will stimulate sustainable growth[c]

continued

TABLE 13.1 *continued*

DEAL	INVESTMENT SIZE (US$, MILLIONS)	SECTOR	RATIONALE
Creation of institutions			
Nigeria Mortgage Refinance Company[d]	10	Financial services	To address Nigeria's large housing deficit by facilitating financing solutions
Family Homes Funds[e]	—	Financial services	To support mass housing development and provide affordable homes and mortgages[f]
Infrastructure Credit Guarantee Company[g]	25[h]	Financial services	To provide local currency guarantees to enhance the credit quality of debt instruments issued by corporates, states, and governments to finance creditworthy infrastructure assets in Nigeria that conform with eligibility criteria
			To act as a sustainable framework for stimulating infrastructure investments in key sectors of the Nigerian economy (in particular by pension and insurance funds), and to foster the development of the Nigerian debt capital markets
Presidential Fertilizer Initiative[i]	100	Agriculture	To revive fertilizer blending plants in Nigeria and reduce the country's reliance on fertilizer imports
Development Projects			
Bridge International Academies[j]	5 (13% stake)	Education	To provide innovative, affordable schooling solutions

Source: NSIA presentation to the Governing Council at the National Economic Council Meeting, June 28, 2018; interviews with NSIA management and NSIA press releases.
Note: When a deal is in progress, deal size is an estimate provided by Nigeria Sovereign Investment Authority (NSIA). SME = small and medium enterprise; — = not available.
a. NSIA and Old Mutual Investment Group 2016.
b. NSIA and Old Mutual Investment Group 2016.
c. Launched in 2016, but no deals closed as of 2018 due to deterioration in Nigerian economy (Old Mutual 2016).
d. Launched in partnership with the Ministry of Finance; NSIA is the largest shareholder.
e. Flagship initiative of the Minister of Finance, which owns a 51% equity stake; NSIA advised ministry and owns the remaining 49% stake.
f. NSIA 2018b.
g. Joint initiative with GuarantCo, which is part of the Private Infrastructure Development Group. Incorporated as a private limited liability company based in Lagos, InfraCredit runs on a commercial basis. NSIA provided equity while GuarantCo provided second-loss contingent capital (NSIA 2017). First guarantee issued in 2017 allowed a power company to replace expensive short-term bank loans with a N10 billion 10-year bond subscribed by pension funds and insurance companies.
h. NSIA 2017.
i. NSIA owns the special purpose vehicle running the initiative. At the time of writing, NSIA's investment is being replaced by borrowings from Nigeria's Real Sector Support Fund.
j. Co-invested with International Finance Corporation.

ADDITIONALITY AND MULTIPLIER CONSIDERATIONS

NIF's investment policy mentions additionality as one of the fund's key performance indicators (KPIs). The board exercises its discretion in evaluating additionality, which is considered highly desirable but is not a necessary condition. The evaluation of additionality is conducted as part of the five-year rolling plans discussed earlier. Additionality is defined as the successful financing of projects that otherwise may not have happened without NSIA's involvement. The investment policy specifies that NIF has been established in part to address the poor track record of infrastructure projects through private or public-private partnership solutions. The evaluation is largely subjective and assessed case by case, based on whether NSIA's funding was required to attract other investors, underwrite certain phases (for example, construction), or perhaps complete the entire investment. Because additionality is not a necessary condition for NSIA to invest, the additionality evaluation is completed after the successful closing of an investment.

NSIA-NIF management representatives believe that NIF has several features that are conducive to additionality.

- *Focus on greenfield infrastructure development.* NIF aims to bring value added in getting new infrastructure projects off the ground, with hands-on involvement in project development. This focus differentiates NIF from commercial funds that seek operational, yield-producing projects. Of eight projects closed in the first half of 2018, half were sourced and developed by the NIF investment team; the rest were brought to NIF's attention by external sponsors.
- *Long-term investment horizon.* According to NIF, infrastructure financing in the Nigerian banking sector generally does not exceed 7 years, with rare exceptions of 12–15 years. Pension funds, which would normally seek long-term yielding instruments, are constrained by prudential rules and tend to focus on lower-risk investments such as sovereign debt. NIF, by accepting horizons of 20 years or more, provides tenors that are not supplied by the market.
- *Presence on the ground.* Unlike some of the international private equity funds, NSIA-NIF has full-time presence in Nigeria, a feature that it deems essential for a hands-on, upstream-focused fund.

NIF does not have any specific guidelines or targets with respect to capital multiplier.

GOVERNANCE

The Governing Council of NSIA, which mostly comprises federal and state government representatives, has only an advisory role and has no say in investment decisions. The council is chaired by the president of Nigeria and comprises a large number of central and local government representatives, reflecting Nigeria's federal structure; in addition, the president appoints some council members from the private sector, civil society, and academia. Table 13.2 summarizes the composition and powers of the Governing Council and other bodies of NSIA and NIF. Every 12 months, NSIA provides the Governing Council with a report of its assets, liabilities, investment, and divestment activity; performance by asset class; and significant trends affecting its activities. The council reviews

TABLE 13.2 **NSIA-NIF core governance bodies**

GOVERNANCE BODY	COMPOSITION AND APPOINTMENT CRITERIA
NSIA Governing Council	• Council provides advice and counsel to the NSIA board, while observing its independence. • Council is chaired by the President of Nigeria, who also appoints some of its members. • According to the NSIA Act 2011, the following government representatives have an automatic seat on the Council: President, 36 state governors, Attorney General, the Minister of Finance, minister in charge of the National Planning Commission, governor of the central bank, and chief economic adviser to the President. • In addition, the President appoints to the council four reputable representatives of the private sector, two representatives of civil society (such as NGOs or professional organizations focused on civil rights), two representatives of Nigerian youth, and four academics.
NSIA board	• Board is the main body responsible for the attainment of the objectives of NSIA, as established by the NSIA Act 2011. • Board operates via five subcommittees (all composed of nonexecutive board members): direct investment committee, externally managed investment committee, audit committee, finance and general purpose committee, and compensation and human resources committee. • It has nine members: three executive and six nonexecutive (with all nonexecutive directors coming from the private sector at the time of writing, although in principle they could also be drawn from the public sector, at the discretion of the Nominations Committee). • All board appointments are made by the President on recommendation of the Minister of Finance, who consults with the National Economic Council. The minister establishes an Executive Nomination Committee of five people (including the minister) with the qualifications and market experience to identify high-quality candidates. This committee coordinates with the National Economic Council and recommends candidates to the President. • Nonexecutive board members include the chairman of the board, one member who is a distinguished legal practitioner, and four other professionals. • Executive members of the board include the managing director of NSIA and, at the time of writing, the chief operating officer and chief investment officer. The President appoints the managing director. • With the exception of the board member who is a legal practitioner, the NSIA Act 2011 establishes that all members must hold a university degree in economics, finance, or similar subject and possess at least 10 years of financial or business experience at senior management level. • All members must have a clean legal record. • Terms of appointment for the executive members are as long as their employment with NSIA continues; for nonexecutives, appointments are four years for the chairman and five years for the others (all renewable for one more five-year term).
Direct Investment Committee	• This committee is specifically dedicated to assisting the board with regard to NIF investment decisions. • It is a committee of the NSIA board, comprising three members who should aim to serve a term of at least three years. • Responsibilities include, among others, setting NIF's investment policies and guidelines (to be ratified by the board); overseeing investment and reinvestment of funds into NIF portfolio; monitoring portfolio performance and compliance with investment policies, and reporting findings to the board; advising the head of NIF and managing director of NSIA; ensuring the development of local, internal investment management expertise; developing selection policies and criteria for solicited and unsolicited infrastructure-related proposals, and evaluating the investment management aspects of new proposals; considering various measures of investment portfolio risk, such as volatility and liquidity, and advising the board accordingly; and advising the board on setting risk thresholds that appropriately reflect the board's risk appetite. • Any member of the committee may be removed or replaced, for any reason at any time, by a majority vote of the board. • If authorized by the board, the committee can invite professionals with experience in infrastructure investing, who are not board members, to attend committee meetings. • The chairmen of the board's Audit Committee and Finance and General Purpose Committee may be invited to attend meetings in a nonvoting capacity. • It convenes at least four times a year, requires a quorum equal to the majority of its members, and decides by simple majority (albeit seeking consensus to the extent possible). It informs the board of significant actions taken or issues discussed. • The committee chair coordinates with the NSIA's managing director and chief investment officer to prepare an agenda and discussion materials ahead of a board meeting. • It can retain independent advisers to assist in the performance of its responsibilities or conduct investigations. • It performs a self-evaluation annually and reports findings to the board.

continued

TABLE 13.2 *continued*

GOVERNANCE BODY	COMPOSITION AND APPOINTMENT CRITERIA
Externally managed investment committee	• This committee is responsible for investment decisions of NSIA's Stabilization Fund and Future Generations Fund. • It is a committee of the NSIA board, with different composition and functions than the Direct Investment Committee.
Compensation and Human Resources Committee	• This committee comprises three nonexecutive members who should aim to serve a term of at least three years. • It assists the board in fulfilling its oversight responsibility for ensuring that the compensation structure for NSIA employees is consistent with NSIA's long-term objectives. • Any member of the committee may be removed or replaced, for any reason at any time, by a majority vote of the board. • It convenes at least two times a year, requires a quorum equal to the majority of its members, and decides by simple majority. • It can retain independent advisers to assist in the performance of its responsibilities or conduct investigations. • It performs a self-evaluation annually and reports findings to the board.
Audit Committee	• It is a committee of the NSIA board, comprising three board representatives, all selected from the nonexecutive directors and serving for a period of at least three years. • It assists the board in fulfilling its oversight responsibilities relating to NSIA's accounting and financial reporting policies and practices, compliance programs, internal controls, and general compliance with applicable laws and regulations. • The committee meets at least four times a year, requires a majority as quorum, and decides on a simple majority basis. • It meets at least annually with NSIA's chief financial officer and the external auditor. • It has the right to meet privately with any person it desires.
Finance and General Purpose Committee	• It comprises three nonexecutive directors. • It assists the board in exercising its oversight responsibility with respect to NSIA's material and strategic financial matters, including those related to funding, budgeting, expenditure, and general operation and financial structure.

Source: NSIA presentation to the Governing Council at the National Economic Council Meeting, June 28, 2018.

Note: NGO = nongovernmental organization; NIF = Nigeria Infrastructure Fund; NSIA = Nigeria Sovereign Investment Authority.

the report and has the opportunity to raise questions and give counsel. Any resolution of the council is passed by simple majority. More broadly, the council reviews mid- and long-term investment policies; modification of financial status, such as the increase or decrease of capital; entrustment of assets to NSIA; appointment or dismissal of executive officers; valuation of management's performance; and overall outlook of the fund.

The NSIA board is the main body responsible for the attainment of NSIA's objectives, as established by the NSIA Act 2011. It has nine members—three executive and six nonexecutive. All members are appointed by the President, on recommendation of a Nominations Committee led by the Minister of Finance, and must have relevant financial and private sector experience at senior management level. The three executive members are NSIA's managing director and two other NSIA executives, currently the chief operating officer and chief investment officer. At the time of writing, all nonexecutive directors come from the private sector, although in principle they could also be drawn from the public sector, at the discretion of the Nominations Committee. The board meets at least once a quarter, requires a quorum of seven representatives, and decides on a simple majority (the chair has a casting vote). The executive board members and other senior management representatives constitute the Executive Committee, a management-level (not board-level) committee in charge of day-to-day management of the organization.

The NSIA board is in charge of investment decisions, after the screening and preparatory deal work has been conducted by the Executive Committee and Direct Investment Committee (figures 13.1 and 13.2). The investment team, after conducting due diligence, presents opportunities for consideration to the Executive Committee. If the latter deems the project of interest and compliant with the mandate and requirements of NIF, the investment opportunity is presented to NIF's Direct Investment Committee.[3] This is a committee of the NSIA board, comprising three nonexecutive board members who decide on a majority

FIGURE 13.1

NIF investment decision responsibilities

Investment team	Executive Committee	Direct Investment Committee	NSIA board
• Conducts due diligence and analysis of investment opportunities • Presents deal to Executive Committee	• Screens deals based on compliance with NIF's mandate and return targets • Presents deal to Investment Committee	• Screens deals to be submitted to NSIA board for final decision • Majority-based decision (but consensus sought)	• Approves deal • Majority-based decision (but consensus sought)

Source: NIF management interviews.
Note: NIF = Nigeria Infrastructure Fund; NSIA = Nigeria Sovereign Investment Authority.

FIGURE 13.2

NIF investment process

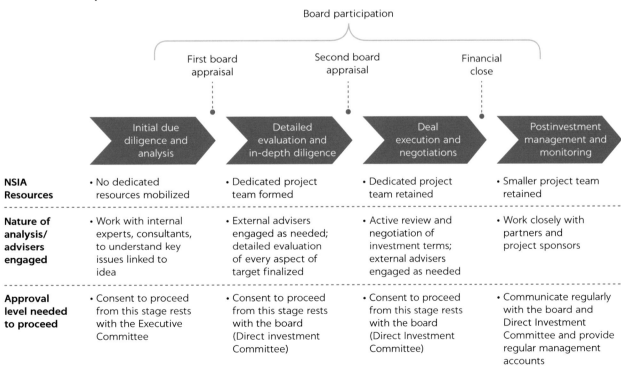

Source: NSIA presentation to the Governing Council at the National Economic Council Meeting, June 28, 2018.
Note: NIF = Nigeria Infrastructure Fund; NSIA = Nigeria Sovereign Investment Authority.

basis—although in practice unanimity is sought in most investment decisions.[4] Since the beginning of 2018, the Direct Investment Committee has also been entrusted to play the role of risk committee. This setup was deemed by the board as operationally more efficient than having separate investment and risk committees. If the project passes the screening of the Direct Investment Committee, it moves up to board level, where the ultimate investment decision is made— again on a majority basis but with an effort to reach broad consensus; the chair of the Direct Investment Committee presents projects for board approval, after a positive deliberation by the Direct Investment Committee.

Conflict of interest procedures are in place to ensure that board members have no interest in matters considered by the board. Members must disclose the nature of their interest in advance of board consideration, cannot seek to influence a decision relating to that matter, and have to leave the meeting during the discussion of that matter. In addition, no board member or other NSIA executive can be involved in a personal capacity, directly or indirectly, in the purchase of assets of or by NSIA.

The Compensation Committee of the NSIA board annually reviews and approves the compensation structure of NSIA's staff and senior management. This committee also comprises three nonexecutive board members, ideally serving a term of at least three years and deciding on a majority basis. It reviews and approves staff and senior management compensation in light of market dynamics and NSIA's long-term objectives. See the subsection on staffing and recruitment for more detail on staff compensation and incentives.

The Audit Committee's role is to assist the board in fulfilling its oversight responsibilities relating to NSIA's accounting and financial reporting policies and practices, compliance programs, internal controls, and general compliance with applicable laws and regulations. Among other functions, the Audit Committee reviews the financial reports, internal control and audit systems, and compliance with applicable laws; selects, reviews, and recommends the appointment of external auditors; and ensures disclosure of related-party transactions and conflicts of interest. The committee consists of three nonexecutive board members, who decide on a simple majority basis.

STAFFING AND RECRUITMENT

Despite offering lower remuneration than equivalent private sector funds, NIF has managed to hire a qualified team of investment professionals with international academic and professional backgrounds, including a secondee from the IFC. The NIF investment team has 12 members, including a director (IFC secondee), 2 senior vice-presidents, a vice-president, and 6 associates. This team is part of a broader NSIA team of 30 investment professionals. At the time of writing, NSIA is still hiring and sometimes competes with private equity funds for candidates. NIF staff members come primarily from investment banks, infrastructure-focused private equity funds, industry sectors (for example, construction and power), consulting firms with infrastructure and project finance implementation expertise, and public policy. NIF's skill set combines technical and financial expertise. Years of experience are a minimum of 2 for junior hires to more than 20 for senior hires.

Compensation is largely fixed, with a 10 percent element that is performance based. The Compensation Committee can commission surveys to assess market compensation levels and trends. Senior management compensation reflects market conditions, peer group practices, and performance, among other variables. The board strives to maintain compensation levels in the top quartile of the benchmark peer group. Performance assessment is conducted by NSIA's managing director and is reviewed and approved by the Compensation Committee. The committee also reviews management development and succession plans.

ECONOMIC IMPACT AND ESG REPORTING

NSIA highlights the transparency of its operations and compliance with ESG best practices. It is a signatory of the Santiago Principles and often co-invests with funds or development institutions that require compliance with rigorous ESG criteria. In addition, when selecting Development Projects for NIF, it applies indicators developed by the Global Impact Investing Network and recorded in its framework Impact Reporting and Investment Standards.

NIF evaluates all its direct investments against a list of KPIs, but investments in externally managed funds are not evaluated against these KPIs. Table 13.3 summarizes the KPIs, the body in charge of their evaluation, and the evaluation time horizon. Some KPIs are assessed before investment, and compliance with them—particularly the return KPI—is a necessary condition to investment approval. Other KPIs are evaluated ex post, through risk, compliance, and project monitoring reports submitted at quarterly board meetings.

NSIA presents quarterly to the board a development impact report with key evidence of its achievements at portfolio and select deal levels. The report includes the number of deals, recent deal activity, number of beneficiaries reached, job creation, amount of additional investment attracted, and vulnerable groups benefited (for example, women). The development impact report is not disclosed to the public, other than references to it made in the annual report. At the time of writing, NSIA was also considering producing a separate impact report for public disclosure.

NSIA is refining the impact monitoring and evaluation framework for NIF according to four steps:

1. *Develop project-specific development impact frameworks.* Outline the expected development impact for all NIF projects, including a road map and NSIA's involvement to achieve the impact goals, and set performance metrics.
2. *Monitor.* Actively work with NIF's portfolio companies, project sponsors, development finance institutions, co-investors, and other stakeholders to measure impact.
3. *Report.* Incorporate development impact in NSIA's annual report and external communications, and update the board on development impact.
4. *Build in-house capacity.* Provide training, develop impact investment tools, and work with partners to enhance development impact outcomes.

FINANCIAL DISCLOSURE AND RISK POLICIES

Because NIF is a subfund operating under the NSIA umbrella structure, it does not have separate financial statements. Rather, its financial performance is

TABLE 13.3 NIF Investment Policy Statement: Impact and financial KPIs

KPI	DESCRIPTION	PURPOSE	BODY IN CHARGE OF EVALUATION	TIME FRAME OF EVALUATION
Long-term return benchmark	Long-term return target, on a project basis, of US CPI + 5%, excluding Development Projects, uncommitted funds, and returns from pending investment	This is the core measure of NIF's long-term success in growing purchasing power. Compliance with this KPI is a necessary condition for investment approval.	Board	Periods of at least 10 years, but preferably 15 or more due to the long-term nature of infrastructure
Allocation	NIF's chosen allocation between different infrastructure sectors	Purpose is to support the diversification of risk and contribution toward the development of a number of different infrastructure sectors.	Direct Investment Committee	Rolling five-year periods to reflect the objectives of NSIA's five-year plan
Project development	The successful development and operation of projects in which NSIA is invested	This KPI determines NSIA's success in achieving both its investment objectives and its policy objectives.	Direct Investment Committee	Periods of at least five years to accommodate the long development lead time typical in infrastructure
Project development milestones	Ideally, realistic milestones for NSIA's development of projects	The board occasionally reviews subsequent contributions to NIF, which may be increased or decreased depending on the available pipeline of projects and their potential deployment timetable. By spreading development activity over time, NIF aims to mitigate risk, and more efficiently use the resources at its disposal.	Board	Aim of achieving full investment of NIF within 10 years, provided that the appropriate investment opportunities exist
Additionality	The successful financing of projects that may have otherwise not occurred without NSIA's involvement	The track record of infrastructure projects through private or PPP solutions has been poor in Nigeria. NIF was established, in part, to address this issue. Additionality is not a necessary condition for investment approval.	Board	Five-year rolling periods, updated annually
Development Projects	Investment of up to 10% of NIF's capital in social infrastructure projects.	Purpose is to invest in social infrastructure projects that promote economic development in underserved sectors or regions of Nigeria and may present less favorable financial return potential.	Direct Investment Committee	Ten years or the date upon which NIF has been at least 80% invested, whichever is earlier
Liquidity	Return of capital investment within a reasonable time frame, with a guideline target of 10 years where possible	This is good investment practice and requires particular focus in the infrastructure sector.	Board	Ten years is the goal, with extension possible on a case-by-case basis given the long-term nature of infrastructure investment

Source: NSIA 2019.

Note: CPI = Consumer Price Index; KPI = key performance indicator; NIF = Nigeria Infrastructure Fund; NSIA = Nigeria Sovereign Investment Authority; PPP = public–private partnership.

disclosed in the segment reporting section of NSIA's financial statements. NSIA, as a body corporate, publishes an annual report with consolidated financial statements, audited by PricewaterhouseCoopers under International Financial Reporting Standards. NIF investments are recorded as assets on NSIA's balance sheet, together with assets held by the Future Generations Fund and the Stabilization Fund. NIF assets are illiquid and recorded at cost on NSIA's balance sheet, consistent with International Financial Reporting Standards criteria. NSIA does not publish a marked-to-market valuation of the NIF portfolio or its individual investments, or NIF performance updates. Monthly NIF performance reports and quarterly portfolio monitoring reports are generated for internal monitoring and reporting purposes.

The Direct Investment Committee is accountable for assessing the risks of investment projects brought before it, undertaking a holistic risk-benefit analysis during its deliberations. Risk assessment is performed in the project due diligence phase, and results are included in a specific section of the investment memo provided to the Executive Committee, the Direct Investment Committee, and the board for decision-making (see the governance subsection for a description of the investment decision process and bodies). The risk assessment process is meant to be managed by a head of infrastructure risk reporting directly to the managing director. This role was vacant at the time of writing, but recruitment was in progress.[5]

NSIA has developed a bespoke tool for ex ante risk assessment of all infrastructure projects. The tool takes into account several factors including a project's fit with NIF's mandate, integrity checks of project counterparts, and any technical, commercial, and financial risks. The infrastructure investment team is responsible for conducting the analysis, which is reviewed and approved by the head of infrastructure risk. Factors that are deemed as medium or high risk are included in the investment memo for approval along with proposed actionable mitigants.

In addition to assessing investment-specific risks, NIF must comply with portfolio concentration limits, which are regularly monitored by the compliance team. As of December 2018, limits included commitments to one project or one manager capped at 25 percent of total NIF assets; commitments to any one infrastructure sector in Nigeria capped at 35 percent of total NIF assets; a ban on providing guarantees to any infrastructure project, other than wholly owned subsidiaries or affiliates of NSIA; commitments to external fund managers or intermediaries capped at 50 percent of total NIF assets; exposure to a single external fund manager capped at 20 percent of total NIF assets; and exposure to a single external fund capped at 10 percent of total NIF assets.[6]

NOTES

1. See the "Fund Mandates" page on the NSIA website (http://nsia.com.ng/about-us/fund-mandates).
2. NSIA presentation to the Governing Council at the National Economic Council Meeting, June 28, 2018.
3. So called to distinguish it from a separate Externally Managed Investment Committee in charge of both the Future Generations and Stabilization funds.
4. Executive board members can attend Direct Investment Committee meetings but are not allowed to vote.

5. Although this role is vacant, the head of compliance performs this function.
6. According to an unpublished December 2018 Infrastructure Fund Investment Compliance Report provided by NIF management.

REFERENCES

NIPC (Nigerian Investment Promotion Commission). 2017. "NSIA Outlines Strategic Investment Plans for Nigeria Commodity Exchange." https://www.nipc.gov.ng/2017/01/13 /nsia-outlines-strategic-investment-plans-nigerian-commodity-exchange/.

NSIA (Nigeria Sovereign Investment Authority). 2017. "NSIA & GuarantCo Establish the Infrastructure Credit Enhancement Facility (InfraCredit)." Press release, January 17, 2017.

NSIA (Nigeria Sovereign Investment Authority). 2018a. "NEC Approves $650M Seed Funding as FG Establishes Presidential Infrastructure Development Fund." Press release, May 17, 2018. https://nsia.com.ng/~nsia/sites/default/files/press-release/NEC%20Approves%20 Press%20Release.pdf.

NSIA (Nigeria Sovereign Investment Authority). 2018b. "NSIA Announces Audited Financial Results for 2017 Financial Year." Press release, June 8, 2018. https://nsia.com.ng/~nsia/sites /default/files/press-release/Press%20Release%20-%202017%20Financial%20Statement _Updated_08062018_Final%20Version.pdf.

NSIA (Nigeria Sovereign Investment Authority). 2019. "Infrastructure Fund Investment Policy Statement as Approved on April 6, 2019." NSIA, Abuja. https://nsia.com.ng/~nsia/sites /default/files/downloads/Nigeria%20Infrastructure%20Fund%20Investment%20 Policy%20Statement%20-%20April%2016%202018_0.pdf.

NSIA (Nigeria Sovereign Investment Authority) and Old Mutual Investment Group. 2016. "NSIA and Old Mutual Investment Group Announce Partnership Agreement for Investments in Real Estate and Agriculture." Press release, August 12, 2016. https://nsia.com.ng/~nsia /sites/default/files/press-release/Press-Release-NSIA-Announces-Partnership-with -OMIG.pdf.

Old Mutual. 2016. "Old Mutual Partners with Nigeria's Sovereign Wealth Fund." Press release, September 2016. http://ww2.oldmutual.co.za/old-mutual-partners-with-nigeria -s-sovereign-wealth-fund.

Thematic Reviews

THEMATIC REVIEW 1. SIFS' STRATEGIES TO ATTRACT DOMESTIC INSTITUTIONAL CAPITAL TO INFRASTRUCTURE FINANCE: THE EXAMPLE OF INFRACREDIT IN NIGERIA*

This topical review examines an interesting example of how strategic investment funds (SIFs), in partnership with development institutions, can attract domestic institutional capital to infrastructure finance and, at the same time, contribute to a country's capital market development.

In 2017, the Nigeria Sovereign Investment Authority's Nigeria Infrastructure Fund (NSIA-NIF) partnered with GuarantCo to launch InfraCredit, an independent, for-profit guarantor of long-term, local currency bonds issued to finance infrastructure projects in Nigeria. NSIA-NIF—described in detail in the NSIA-NIF case study in appendix A—is a US$650 million infrastructure SIF wholly capitalized by the Nigerian state. GuarantCo is the credit enhancement unit of the Private Infrastructure Development Group (PIDG), an infrastructure development and finance organization funded by several bilateral and multilateral institutions. GuarantCo provides local currency contingent credit solutions, including guarantees to banks and bond investors. It received US$310 million in funding from PIDG backers and, as of the end of 2017, had US$886 million in total outstanding commitments.[1] Unlike other providers of credit guarantees, GuarantCo expressly aims to run out of business by enabling developing countries to set up and operate their own local, independent guarantee providers. By doing so, it aims to promote local capital market development.

NSIA and GuarantCo's initiative responded to a double objective:

1. *Expanding the supply of debt for Nigerian infrastructure projects.* Banks are the main providers of credit to the Nigerian economy. Loans, however, are generally short-dated and therefore unsuitable to finance infrastructure projects, which require tenors of 10 years or more. The local currency corporate bond market, which in developed economies contributes to filling the gap for long-term infrastructure finance, was in its infancy at the time of InfraCredit's launch.

---

* This thematic review was completed in 2020 on the basis of information collected from 2018 to 2019. It reflects the situation at that time.

2. *Tapping into a large and growing domestic institutional capital pool and promoting capital market development.* At the time of writing, GuarantCo estimated the pool of pension fund capital in Nigeria at US$20 billion. This amount is expected to grow fast, in line with Nigeria's economic development and also as a result of the introduction of automatic pension fund enrollment schemes. Institutional investors in Nigeria primarily invest in domestic sovereign bonds. They are eager to find additional avenues to deploy their capital—particularly in long-dated, local-currency bonds—but have limited understanding and track records of investing in corporate bonds.

The two partners started analyzing the opportunity in 2014. Conversations were facilitated by GuarantCo's prior knowledge of the Nigerian market and NSIA's realization that, alone, it did not have the expertise to start a guarantee company from scratch. GuarantCo had started investigating direct guarantee opportunities in the country in 2009, providing its first local currency guarantee in 2011 for a bond issued by an aluminum producer. In that context, it provided training to Nigerian pension funds on the credit analysis of infrastructure bonds.

In January 2017, NSIA and GuarantCo announced the launch of InfraCredit, capitalizing it with equity and second-loss contingent capital, respectively. InfraCredit is set up as a private limited liability company under Nigerian corporate law. NSIA provided the first US$25 million of equity capital. Although other potential investors (including development finance institutions, DFIs) were initially approached, NSIA was the only one willing to invest in what was then an unproven business model. In December 2018, another US$25 million in equity was provided by the Africa Finance Corporation, a pan-African DFI set up in 2007 to bridge's Africa's infrastructure finance gap. GuarantCo provided US$50 million in second-loss contingent capital, bringing the total balance sheet to US$100 million. NSIA and GuarantCo plan to double the balance sheet to US$200 million by sourcing another US$50 million in equity and US$50 million in contingent capital. GuarantCo will act as lead arranger for the additional contingent capital, which it expects to come from international DFIs with high investment grade ratings (NSIA 2017).

In order to secure a AAA credit rating from Nigerian rating agencies, which is essential to its standing as a guarantor, InfraCredit agreed to limit its underwriting commitments to a maximum notional of five times its total capital, or US$1 billion once the capital-raising plan is fully executed.

The backing from a well-known guarantee provider such as GuarantCo, with a high investment grade rating of AA–/A1, was also critical to obtain a AAA rating at the inception of the operations and before InfraCredit's having underwritten any deals. With the start of underwriting activities, the quality and diversification of InfraCredit's portfolio, diversification of its sources of capital, and quality of the management team are crucial to maintaining a AAA rating.

InfraCredit is the only provider of local currency guarantees focused on the Nigerian infrastructure sector and has an explicit, for-profit mandate. Although other local currency guarantee providers exist, they focus on different sectors, such as small and medium enterprise lending and mortgages.

InfraCredit prices its guarantees at commercial levels, on the basis of project-specific credit risk assessments. It guarantees long-dated bonds, allowing for financing tenors beyond those of commercial bank loans but with comparable interest rates. It issued its first guarantee in 2017, for a N10 billion (about US$28 million)[2] bond issued by Viathan, a power generation company in Lagos state. As of late 2018, it expected its pipeline to increase by another N25 billion (on two deals) that year and targeted additional guarantees of N60 billion in 2019. Although its guarantees are priced commercially, nothing prevents InfraCredit from being involved in deals that may have a concessional component, such as a technical assistance facility or other layers of the capital structure that are concessional (for example, a concessional loan from a development bank in addition to the commercial bond guaranteed by InfraCredit).

As its main business challenge, InfraCredit mentioned sourcing of a pipeline of deals that suit its underwriting criteria. Part of the challenge stems from InfraCredit's exclusive focus on brownfield infrastructure and unwillingness to take greenfield risk.

InfraCredit operates in full independence from NSIA. This independence was also essential to securing a AAA rating, mitigating the rating agencies' concerns over potential political interference on underwriting decisions. InfraCredit's independence manifests itself in several ways.

- NSIA acts as a passive shareholder, and its relationship with InfraCredit is on an arm's-length basis. NSIA holds two out of six seats on InfraCredit's board. Two more seats are allocated to Africa Finance Corporation representatives, one seat to a GuarantCo representative, and one seat to InfraCredit's chief executive officer. At the time of writing, InfraCredit's credit committee, responsible for all underwriting decisions, comprised two NSIA representatives, one GuarantCo representative, and one independent member; its composition, however, was expected to change with the entry of new equity investors, diluting NSIA's representation.
- Clear conflict of interest procedures exist. InfraCredit has, in principle, the ability to guarantee deals in which NSIA is involved as an investor (although it had not done so at the time of writing). Should such circumstance arise, NSIA representatives on InfraCredit's credit committee would not be allowed to participate in the underwriting decision.
- InfraCredit is fully responsible for deal origination and has the staffing and capacity to execute this task. Of InfraCredit's 13 staff members, 5 are exclusively devoted to deal sourcing. InfraCredit can leverage NSIA's network to originate deals, but all underwriting decisions are made on an arm's-length basis. InfraCredit also receives solicitations from banks looking to refinance their exposures to infrastructure projects.
- Because InfraCredit is a for-profit entity, its shareholders are focused on value creation and may look to exit their investment in the future. Although still in the early stages, InfraCredit's management mentioned an initial public offering as a possible future strategic direction.

In addition to contingent capital, GuarantCo provided InfraCredit with technical assistance and capacity-building support, in line with its objective to enable InfraCredit to become an independent provider of guarantees in Nigeria. GuarantCo's support—costing approximately US$1 million and funded through PIDG's Technical Assistance Facility—included

- Funding the production of a feasibility study and business plan for InfraCredit, before its launch;
- Funding some of InfraCredit's setup costs;
- Appointing GuarantCo's chief credit officer on InfraCredit's credit committee;

- Training of and knowledge exchange with InfraCredit's staff, including sharing GuarantCo's best underwriting practices and visits to GuarantCo's offices; and
- Sharing best practices with regard to governance, reporting, and environmental, social, and governance (ESG) standards.

In addition, with the objective of promoting local capital market development, GuarantCo and InfraCredit have been actively involved in training Nigerian pension funds on all aspects of investing in infrastructure bonds. Capacity building included not just deal evaluation but also compliance with ESG standards. InfraCredit believes an ongoing investment will be required to continue these market promotion activities and may seek additional technical assistance funding from donors.

GuarantCo believes the InfraCredit model is replicable, with necessary variations in other emerging market and developing countries, and is evaluating opportunities to launch similar initiatives.

THEMATIC REVIEW 2. COOPERATING WITH SIFS: THE PERSPECTIVE OF INFRASTRUCTURE PRIVATE EQUITY FUNDS*

This topical review discusses the value added of cooperating with a SIF, from the perspective of an infrastructure private equity fund that invests directly at the project level. This topic is relevant in light of one of the key objectives of SIFs, namely mobilizing additional private capital. The following discussion is based on feedback from Meridiam, a global infrastructure fund manager headquartered in Paris. Meridiam has €6.2 billion of assets under management across seven funds, targeting Africa, Europe, and North America. Its Africa fund has €205 million in assets under management and invests in infrastructure projects that facilitate access to essential, affordable services in the energy, water, waste, and transport sectors.[3]

As part of its strategy, Meridiam partners with local public investors, including SIFs, in many of the countries where it invests. In Africa, Meridiam entered into partnership agreements with SIFs in Gabon (Fonds Gabonais d'Investissements Strategiques), Ghana (Ghana Infrastructure Investment Fund), and Senegal (Fonds Souverain d'Investissements Stratégiques [FONSIS]).[4] The relationship with FONSIS started as a joint development agreement on a specific transaction (the solar power project Senergy) but evolved into a broad partnership agreement under which the two parties openly share pipeline opportunities while retaining full discretion over investment decisions. Meridiam also partners with public investors in high-income economies, such as the state-controlled financial institution Caisse des Dépôts et Consignations in France, and a public pension fund in the US state of Texas.

Meridiam believes that cooperating with SIFs can bring several advantages to infrastructure funds, especially in developing countries.

- *Sharing project pipeline.* Especially in countries where they have not invested before, infrastructure funds can benefit from pipeline sharing agreements

---

* This thematic review was completed in 2020 on the basis of information collected from 2018 to 2019. It reflects the situation at that time.

with SIFs. Meridiam had identified Senegal as a priority market for its Africa fund but had no prior experience investing there. Its partnership agreement with FONSIS calls for both parties to share pipeline transparently, potentially opening new investment opportunities; the agreement does not include any obligation to co-invest, leaving flexibility to both parties.

- *Increasing the probability of success of early-stage development projects.* From the perspective of a fund such as Meridiam, governments' infrastructure agendas in developing countries are good at identifying the infrastructure needs of a country. The pathway from agenda to project execution, however, is often lengthy and unpredictable. Because of their access to government decision-makers, SIFs can increase the probability of projects being kick-started, and shorten the time required to go from concept to execution. Transaction costs may also decrease to some extent as a result of shorter project timelines—although infrastructure funds will still want to go through thorough project preparation and incur the associated transaction costs (due diligence, legal, and so on). In addition, better prospects of deal execution will act as an incentive for infrastructure funds to get involved.

- *Building trust in the infrastructure fund.* A partnership with a SIF can highlight the infrastructure fund's long-term commitment to the country and sector, and solidify the private fund's standing as a serious counterpart (for instance, when it comes to negotiating offtake agreements with utilities). This effect will play out if the SIF itself is perceived as a player trusted and empowered by the government. A positive investment track record in the country and strong management team will further enhance the private infrastructure fund's credibility.

- *Facilitating the dialogue with government decision-makers and navigating political change in the long term, when the infrastructure asset is operational.* Political risk is ever present in infrastructure projects in developing countries. Governments, especially newly appointed ones, may want to revisit the commercial terms of an infrastructure concession. Although cooperating with SIFs is no substitute for contractual protection (for example, political risk insurance), Meridiam believes it helps to have open communication with the government, especially at times of leadership change. As a long-term investor, sometimes for up to 25 years, Meridiam values a stable partner that can help it navigate this political change. A SIF co-investor, for instance, can provide to the government all the evidence needed to show that existing concession terms are fair to both the private investor and infrastructure users.

- *Participating in project codevelopment.* Meridiam and similar infrastructure funds typically play the role of lead project developers. A SIF co-investor, even in a minority position, is expected to be actively involved and supportive in all project phases, from due diligence and design to negotiation and financial close. For instance, in energy infrastructure projects a SIF can support negotiations of power offtake agreements with national utilities. A SIF co-investor also has an inherent interest in being actively involved, because the design and financial structure of a project affect the potential returns of the private fund and SIF alike.

- *Making introductions to local banks and DFIs.* SIFs can help infrastructure funds source deal funding from local capital providers, such as domestic commercial banks or national DFIs. Although such sourcing may not be necessary in all deals, greater funding flexibility is usually appreciated by infrastructure funds.

Compared with the preceding advantages, the size of a SIF co-investment in a deal is less crucial, in Meridiam's view. In practice, SIFs in many developing countries have limited financial resources and are able to participate only with small tickets in deals. Meridiam, however, still values the cooperation with a SIF, regardless of co-investment ticket size, because of the qualitative factors described above.

Meridiam believes that, in order to effectively bridge the gap between infrastructure funds and governments, SIFs should be staffed with a balanced mix of international investment professionals and local professionals. The international staff, often coming from the diaspora and from sectors such as investment banking or fund management, can bring global technical expertise and best practices. Domestic staff, especially if from a civil servant background, will be best positioned to foster an open dialogue with government stakeholders.

Infrastructure funds, for their part, can also benefit SIFs by sharing international best practices. In the partnership approach, Meridiam emphasized the importance of the infrastructure fund's proactive sharing of information with SIFs, involvement in decision-making, and support of the learning process.

THEMATIC REVIEW 3. MEASURING DEVELOPMENT IMPACT FROM THE DOUBLE BOTTOM LINE: THE EXAMPLE OF IFC'S ANTICIPATED IMPACT MEASUREMENT AND MONITORING FRAMEWORK*

One of the key distinguishing factors of a SIF is the economic or development component of the double bottom line. Therefore, the measurement of this economic impact is critical to assessing the success of the SIF. Most SIFs, however, focus on measuring financial returns rather than measuring the less easily quantifiable socioeconomic impact of their investments.

This thematic review covers how the International Finance Corporation (IFC) measures the development impact of its investments through its Anticipated Impact Measurement and Monitoring (AIMM) framework. The AIMM system is a tool for IFC to demonstrate its development impact to shareholders that want more clarity on the development agenda and, internally, to adjust or rebalance the portfolio accordingly. The AIMM framework provides a structure to identify and measure a project's relevant impact components ex ante during the investment decision-making process before the project is submitted for board approval. The AIMM system complies with the Operating Principles for Impact Management, adopted by nearly 100 public and private asset owners and managers.[5]

The crux of the framework is an AIMM rating that delivers an ex ante score from 10 to 100. This AIMM score signals a project's potential contribution to development and provides a link between ex ante impact claims and the realization of those claims in supervision.

---

* This thematic review was completed in 2020 on the basis of information collected from 2018 to 2019. It reflects the situation at that time.

The AIMM rating achieves multiple purposes:

- It drives project selection and design ex ante, thus deepening IFC's ability to maximize impact.
- It provides an operational framework for setting impact ambitions.
- It strengthens IFC's capacity to deliver the appropriate mix of projects that generate impact alongside adequate financial returns.
- It gives the World Bank Group board more visibility on the development intentions of IFC projects.

The AIMM rating process is managed by IFC's Sector Economics and Development Impact department, which has over 50 results measurement specialists, who work with IFC investment teams. The process is as follows:

1. IFC investment teams identify new potential projects and engage with an AIMM team assigned to each project during the concept stage to form a development impact thesis for IFC's intervention.
2. The AIMM team advises the deal team on the development potential of a project, including how impact potential could be maximized with changes in project design.
3. During the appraisal stage, the investment team works with the potential investee on the terms of the investment and targets to be achieved upon exit, and collects data for further analysis.
4. The investment team then provides the AIMM team with baseline data from the prospective investee or borrower for each of the AIMM indicators that will be tracked, as well as target metrics established for the prospective investee to meet.[6]
5. The AIMM team establishes an AIMM score by weighing the data from the potential project against benchmarks established from project-, sector-, and country-specific data sets (see box A.1 on the composition of the score).[7]
6. The AIMM team submits its initial score to a Sector Economics and Development Impact industry manager for validation, after which a final score is assigned to the potential project. Projects proposing "strong" market potential are validated instead by an AIMM Panel comprising senior-level IFC staff and expert consultants.
7. The AIMM score (and other documentation) is presented at an Investment Review in which IFC senior management judges each potential project holistically (that is, not just development impact) and determines whether to send it to IFC's board for approval.
8. If the project clears that stage, then it is submitted to the IFC board for final approval and subsequent investment/disbursal.

A "low" or "satisfactory" (as opposed to "good" or "excellent") AIMM score is not always a bad result, because the IFC board must take a portfolio approach to balance its development mission with its requirement to maintain financial sustainability. AIMM scores are audited every year by an external auditor, and an aggregate summary of impact for all projects is given in IFC's annual report.

Key components of the AIMM score

The International Finance Corporation's (IFC's) Anticipated Impact Measurement and Monitoring (AIMM) score is composed of project potential and market potential, which consider the magnitude of the project's effects:

- *Project potential (or project outcomes).* Project outcomes include effects on stakeholders (for example, customers and suppliers), the economy (for example, jobs created, value added multipliers, and economic rate of return), and the environment (for example, emissions reduction).
- *Market potential (or market outcomes).* Market outcomes deal with effects that extend beyond the project and result in changes to the structure and functioning of markets, such as introducing new technology, promoting private sector participation in a state-dominated sector, expanding geographic coverage to un-/underserved areas, spreading replicable business models, and others. The objective of market potential is to recognize systemic changes in markets' competitiveness, integration, inclusiveness, resilience, and sustainability.

The AIMM score also takes into consideration the likelihood that the project will achieve these claims (see figure BA.1.1). Low, medium, or high likelihood of the occurrence of expected impacts is estimated using criteria derived from the available data on the macro-economy, sector trends, and other sources or reports.[a] Once the AIMM team adjusts for likelihood, the resulting AIMM score provides a risk-adjusted assessment of the potential development impact of a given intervention.

FIGURE BA.1.1

AIMM rating methodology

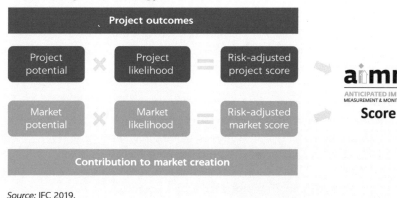

Source: IFC 2019.

a. The relevant data are validated by separate groups in IFC's Economics and Private Sector Development vice presidency unit: the Global Macro, Market, and Portfolio Research Group as well as Sector Economics colleagues in the relevant field offices.

THEMATIC REVIEW 4. FORMALIZING A SIF'S RISK MANAGEMENT PROCESS: THE EXAMPLE OF CDP EQUITY*

This thematic review examines how CDP Equity has formalized its risk assessment and monitoring processes. CDP Equity is a holding company 100 percent owned by the Italian national promotional institution Cassa Depositi e Prestiti Group.

---

* This thematic review was completed in 2020 on the basis of information collected from 2018 to 2019. It reflects the situation at that time.

What is distinctive about CDP Equity is its proprietary risk rating model, which assigns a risk profile to each investment and the portfolio (on an aggregate basis). This model is seen as a good tool to discipline both the investment evaluation and supervision phases.

Background on CDP Equity

CDP Equity is a holding company fully owned by Cassa Depositi e Prestiti Group (the parent company), a joint-stock company majority controlled by the Italian Ministry of Economy and Finance and Italy's national promotional institution.[8] Established in 1850 as a deposit-taking bank, Cassa Depositi e Prestiti Group evolved into a key player in Italy's industrial policy, receiving in 2015 from the Italian government and the European Union the designation of national promotional institution (CDP 2018). As such, Cassa Depositi e Prestiti Group is in charge of implementing the European Commission's Investment Plan for Europe (known as the "Juncker Plan"),[9] whose aim is to foster the European Union's economic recovery by removing obstacles to investment, providing technical assistance and visibility to investment projects, and making smarter use of public and private financial resources.[10]

CDP Equity has approximately €3.5 billion in capital and is mandated to invest in Italian companies of "major national interest," as defined in government decrees of 2011 and 2014. It provides patient equity capital to listed companies or nonlisted companies aiming to list in the medium term, acquiring mainly minority stakes in businesses with sound finances and prospects. Investments in unlisted companies represent the majority of the portfolio. As of February 2019, CDP Equity had invested approximately €2.5 billion in 11 companies. Approximately two-thirds of the portfolio was allocated to unlisted companies. The main listed holding is a 12.5 percent stake in Saipem, an oil services company in which CDP Equity invested €903 million in 2015.[11] CDP Equity has an active management approach, implemented through governance (for example, representation on a portfolio company's board) and proactive engagement with portfolio companies' main shareholders and management teams.

CDP Equity is structured as a holding company dedicated to investing equity to support the Italian economy with a long-term perspective. In line with its mandate to be a patient investor in primarily unlisted businesses, CDP Equity's investment team has mostly a private equity investment background and applies due diligence and investment practices typical of that sector.

CDP Equity's risk management setup

CDP Equity's risk appetite and risk framework are detailed in a risk policy document approved by the CDP Equity board and regularly reviewed. The risk policy describes the risks CDP Equity is exposed to, as well as the way in which risks are measured and managed. Roles and responsibilities are identified along with the risk management process and the detailed methodology to assess the risk profile of a single investment, the portfolio as a whole, and operational risks for CDP Equity. The risk profile includes an assessment of ESG risks and reputational risks.

CDP Equity defines risk appetite in terms of risk limits and risk-return objectives, and therefore deems it crucial to define how to measure equity risk.

A risk team, independent from the investment team, is charged with evaluating the risk profile and advising CDP Equity's board—the body responsible for investment decisions—on all other risk matters. The chief risk officer has a staff of three and reports directly to CDP Equity's chief executive officer as well as to the parent company's chief risk officer. CDP Equity's board is in charge of all investment and divestment decisions, which it makes on the basis of the separate advice it receives from the investment and risk teams. During the investment evaluation phase, the risk team can challenge the investment thesis but has no formal veto on investment decisions. The risk team is involved from the early stages of due diligence and collaborates closely with the investment team and external deal advisers. Once an investment is made, the risk team regularly monitors compliance with CDP Equity's risk criteria, also through meetings or calls with the portfolio company's management.

As an additional risk control measure, the risk team has the ability to escalate certain decisions to the risk committee of the parent company's board. Escalation applies particularly to prospective investments that are larger than a certain threshold (defined in millions of euros), that present reputational risks for CDP Equity and the parent company, or that exceed CDP Equity's risk limits (described in the next subsection). Should the escalation process apply, the parent company provides a nonbinding opinion to CDP Equity's board before the approval of the investment.

CDP Equity's proprietary risk-rating model

CDP Equity's risk team evaluates the risk profile of each investment by assigning an equity risk rating derived according to a risk model developed in house. Results are then aggregated to derive a portfolio-level risk profile.

The equity risk rating is meant to evaluate the risk that a certain investment does not meet CDP Equity's internal rate of return target. To do so, CDP Equity's model scores each investment on 12 risk factors (based on quantitative and qualitative data) and then computes a weighted average, with the highest risk scores receiving the highest weight (so-called weakest link approach). Table A.1 summarizes the 12 risk factors. Such analysis is performed both for target companies, in the investment phase, and for portfolio companies, in the monitoring phase. On the basis of the equity risk scores, investments are grouped in nine rating classes (also with the support of a calibration approach to define the distribution of rating scores and identify percentile thresholds). The risk profile of the portfolio as a whole is calculated as the average of the individual risk scores (weighted by size of the investments), with some adjustments for concentration, liquidity, and counterparty risks.

On a quarterly basis the risk management team presents a risk report to CDP Equity's board, describing the risk profile of the portfolio. The risk report is also discussed internally at the equity investments committee.

The risk profile does not represent a hard threshold to investment approval but is seen as an effective tool to establish discipline in both the investment evaluation and the supervision phases. Specifically,

- In the evaluation phase, it forces the investment team and board to determine whether the prospective returns are commensurate with the assessed risk level.
- When the board decides to pursue an investment exceeding the maximum acceptable risk prescribed by the risk policy ("high risk" profile), it has to

TABLE A.1 **Twelve risk factors assessed in CDP Equity's equity risk model**

RISK FACTOR	DESCRIPTION
1. Liquidity risk (exit risk)	Assessment of potential exit strategy and its feasibility, also considering the company's valuation multiples at entry and governance rights negotiated by CDP Equity
2. Concentration risk	Assessment of company's concentration in terms of clients, suppliers, geographies, and products
3. Financial, credit, and refinancing risk	Company's credit risk profile including refinancing risk (also considering a headroom analysis) and compared with sector-specific levels
4. Interest rate risk	Exposure to interest rate risk including hedging strategies in place
5. Exchange rate risk	Exposure to exchange rate risk including hedging strategies in place
6. Business risk	Assessment of (1) the company's competitive position within reference markets, (2) barriers to entry, (3) expected growth rates, and (4) business cyclicality and seasonality; includes country risk assessment
7. Technology risk	Company's reliance on certain technologies and degree of predictability over potential changes in the technological environment
8. Margins and financial results risk	Assessment of earnings quality (for example, presence of one-off factors affecting earnings) and margins' volatility over time, also compared with peers
9. Operational, legal, and tax risks	Operational risks including legal and litigation risk and potential tax issues
10. Regulatory risk	Degree of predictability over potential changes in the regulatory environment affecting the company
11. Quality of management and business plan execution	Assessment of the quality of the management team, including its track record and potential key-men risk; assessment of business plan execution risk, including strategic objectives
12. ESG and reputational risks	ESG assessment usually performed with the support of independent ESG advisers. The reputational assessment is performed internally by CDP Equity's compliance team.

Source: World Bank.
Note: ESG = environmental, social, and governance.

provide an explanation as to why that decision was made. The board resolution should describe the strategic, financial, and economic reasons for such high-risk investments.

- In the investment monitoring phase, if the risk profile of the portfolio exceeds the risk limits, the investment team should identify management strategies and actions to reduce the risk profile. Investments exceeding certain risk ratings are nevertheless not automatically liquidated, also given the illiquidity of the portfolio. In some cases, parent company approval is also required to exceed risk ratings.

Other features of CDP Equity's risk management process

In line with private equity–style funds and other SIFs, CDP Equity must comply with a range of risk limits. Risk limits, laid out in the risk policy approved by the board, include (1) maximum investment size (also considering entry valuation multiples compared with peers); (2) cumulative exposure to one industry sector capped to 20 percent of total fund assets;[12] (3) as previously discussed, limits on the maximum acceptable risk profile for a new investment, also compared with expected returns; (4) prohibition to invest in distressed companies without positive economic and financial projections;[13] and (5) soft limits on liquidity of the holding company, to ensure it has enough liquid resources to cover its commitments (the holding company does not usually assume debt).

In addition to its formal risk policies, CDP Equity believes that its role as an active owner contributes to minimizing the investment risk at portfolio company level. In particular,

- As a minority investor, CDP Equity pays particular attention to the competence and integrity of majority co-investors when evaluating prospective deals.
- CDP Equity seeks to maximize its impact on portfolio companies' strategy and protect its downside through governance arrangements—particularly board representation as a precondition to almost any investment, and standard minority protection measures, such as veto rights on certain corporate decisions (for example, capital expenditure and assumption of new debt above certain thresholds, or payment of extraordinary dividends).
- CDP Equity monitors conflicts of interest and other compliance risks, and is available to support companies in the implementation of ESG standards.
- A dedicated team reporting to CDP Equity's chief financial officer supports the portfolio companies in their application of best practices in financial reporting, accounting, and information technology systems.
- In some cases, CDP Equity was able to agree with the majority shareholder of a portfolio company on a set of underperformance standards that trigger the right to replace the company's management. Such standards were related to the achievement of business plan goals (for example, earnings before interest, tax, depreciation, and amortization or underperformance versus plan).

NOTES

1. From the PIDG website (https://www.pidg.org/our-business/how-we-operate /credit-solutions/).
2. At the exchange rate of US$1.00 = N360.00 (Nigeria naira), as of mid-February 2019.
3. From Meridiam's website (https://www.meridiam.com).
4. FONSIS stands for Fonds Souverain d'Investissements Stratégiques (Sovereign Fund for Strategic Investments).
5. See the Operating Principles for Impact Management website (www.impactprinciples .org).
6. For example, at disbursement, the investee will have targets for volume and number of small and medium enterprise loans by a certain date. The indicators will vary by sector. Benchmarks established from the internal and external country- and sector-specific data help circumscribe AIMM rating judgments.
7. For benchmarking, the AIMM team uses data from completed projects, IFC beneficiary surveys, World Bank Enterprise Survey, Global Findex, World Development Indicators, International Monetary Fund country profiles, and other data sets specific to the relevant sector (for example, climate, housing, and so on). IFC beneficiary surveys are in-house, proprietary surveys of the customers of IFC investees or borrowers. The World Bank Enterprise Survey is a firm-level survey of a representative sample of an economy's private sector (https://www.enterprisesurveys.org/en/enterprisesurveys). The Global Findex database tracks financial inclusion (https://globalfindex.worldbank.org). The World Development Indicators are compiled from international sources and present global development data (https://datacatalog.worldbank.org/search/dataset/0037712).
8. National promotional banks and institutions are "legal entities carrying out financial activities on a professional basis which are given a mandate by a member state or a member state's entity at central, regional or local level, to carry out development or promotional activities." See https://institutdelors.eu/wp-content/uploads/2018/07/TheRoleofNPBI sintheEUBudget-Rubio-July2018-2.pdf.

9. The Investment Plan for Europe was approved under Jean-Claude Juncker's presidency of the European Commission in November 2014.

10. See the European Commission's website (https://ec.europa.eu/commission/priorities /jobs-growth-and-investment/investment-plan-europe-juncker-plan/what-investment -plan-europe_en).

11. See the "Portfolio" page on the CDP Equity website (https://en.cdpequity.it/Portfolio /Investments/Saipem.kl).

12. See the "About Us" page on the CDP Equity website (https://en.cdpequity.it/about-us /regulatory-framework.kl).

13. See the "About Us" page on the CDP Equity website (https://en.cdpequity.it/about-us /regulatory-framework.kl).

REFERENCES

CDP (Cassa Depositi e Prestiti Group). 2018. "Half-Yearly Financial Report at 30 June 2018." CDP, Rome. https://www.cdp.it/resources/cms/documents/RFS062018_ENG_P4_CP_1 .pdf.

IFC (International Finance Corporation). 2019. "IFC's Anticipated Impact Measuring and Monitoring (AIMM) System: Project Assessment and Scoring Guidance Note." IFC, Washington, DC. https://www.ifc.org/wps/wcm/connect/15565802 1b1c 4697 a4cf -45d675dd5640/AIMM-General-Guidance-Note-Consultation.pdf?MOD=AJPERES &CVID=mDqGyqA.

NSIA (Nigeria Sovereign Investment Authority). 2017. "NSIA & GuarantCo Establish the Infrastructure Credit Enhancement Facility (InfraCredit)." Press release, January 17, 2017.

APPENDIX B

Illustrative List of Global Strategic Investment Funds

TABLE B.1 National strategic investment funds

ECONOMY	NAME	YEAR	SIZE (US$, MILLIONS)	MANDATE	PRIMARY TARGET REGION	TARGET SECTORS	FUND MANAGER	PREFERRED INVESTMENTS
Angola	Fundo Soberano de Angola (FSDEA; Alternative Investment Portfolio)	2008	5,000	To invest with a long-term vision and to maximize profits. Part of the FSDEA portfolio is focused on investments that generate economic growth and have a positive social impact for a large part of the Angolan population.	Sub-Saharar Africa	Diversified	Internal	Private equity and other asset classes
Bahrain	Bahrain Mumtalakat Holding Company (Bahrain Portfolio)	2006	16,800	To create a thriving economy diversified from oil and gas, focused on securing sustainable returns and generating wealth for future generations. Key sectors include infrastructure, financial services, telecommunications, real estate, transportation, and aluminum production.	Bahrain/global	Diversified	Internal	Equity, fund of funds
China	Silk Road Fund	2014	56,000	To invest in sectors such as infrastructure and resource and energy development in geographies affiliated with the Belt & Road Initiative.	China, emerging markets	Infrastructure	Internal	Primarily equity
Egypt, Arab Rep.	The Sovereign Fund of Egypt	2018	280	To contribute to sustainable economic development domestically through investing in domestic and international opportunities.	Middle East and North Africa	Diversified	—	Flexible
Gabon	Fonds Gabonais d'Investissements Stratégiques	2012	—	To invest in key sectors aligned to Gabon's economic transformation, such as renewable energy and water management infrastructure, SMEs, land and urban projects, health, and education. The fund's mandate is aligned with the government's Plan d'Accélération de la Transformation, which prioritizes projects that improve living conditions for Gabon's population.	Gabon/Africa	Diversified	Internal	Flexible

continued

TABLE B.1 *continued*

ECONOMY	NAME	YEAR	SIZE (US$, MILLIONS)	MANDATE	PRIMARY TARGET REGION	TARGET SECTORS	FUND MANAGER	PREFERRED INVESTMENTS
Georgia	Partnership Fund	2011	2,500	To implement Georgia's development agenda through private equity investments in areas such as energy, real estate, agriculture, and manufacturing. To manage a portfolio of national infrastructure companies.	Georgia	Diversified	Internal	Equity, debt
Ghana	Ghana Infrastructure Investment Fund	2014	—	To develop and invest in a diversified portfolio of infrastructure projects in Ghana that support national development.	Ghana	Infrastructure	Internal	Equity, debt
India	National Investment and Infrastructure Fund	2014	3,000 (Government of India commitment)	To catalyze foreign institutional equity capital for the Indian infrastructure sector and related businesses: • Master Fund is focused on creating scalable sectoral platforms in core infrastructure and in collaboration with strong and reputed operating and financial partners. • Fund of Funds is focused on anchoring and investing in credible and reputed third-party managers with a strong track record across diversified sectors within infrastructure services and allied sectors. • Strategic Opportunities Fund is focused on investing in strategic assets and projects with longer-term horizons across various stages of development.	India	Infrastructure	Internal (dedicated fund manager)	Equity, fund of funds

continued

TABLE B.1 *continued*

ECONOMY	NAME	YEAR	SIZE (US$, MILLIONS)	MANDATE	PRIMARY TARGET REGION	TARGET SECTORS	FUND MANAGER	PREFERRED INVESTMENTS
Iran, Islamic Rep.	National Development Fund of Iran	2011	68,000	To use part of the proceeds from the sale of oil, gas, and condensate to generate wealth and contribute to future generations through investments in line with economic development objectives. To insulate the government's budget against oil revenue fluctuations.	Iran, Islamic Rep.	Diversified	Internal and external	Equity, debt
Ireland	Ireland Strategic Investment Fund (Irish Portfolio)	2014	8,800	To promote the Irish economy, create jobs, and attract foreign investments. All transactions are required to generate both risk-adjusted commercial returns and an economic impact in Ireland.	Ireland	Diversified	Internal	Equity, debt, fund of funds
Kazakhstan	JSC Samruk-Kazyna	2008	75,700	To enhance the national welfare of Kazakhstan, and to support the modernization of its economy.	Kazakhstan	Diversified	Internal	Equity
Malaysia	Khazanah Nasional Berhad	1993	37,600	To increase the country's long-term wealth and contribute to Malaysia's economic development through investments via a Commercial Fund and a Strategic Fund. Khazanah's Strategic Fund is development-focused and holds a portfolio of national assets.	Global	Diversified	Internal	Equity, debt, fund of funds
Malta	National Development and Social Fund	2015	477	To support nationally important large projects and initiatives that help develop the economy and public services, and focus on the interests of present and future generations.	Malta/global	Diversified	—	—

continued

TABLE B.1 *continued*

ECONOMY	NAME	YEAR	SIZE (US$, MILLIONS)	MANDATE	PRIMARY TARGET REGION	TARGET SECTORS	FUND MANAGER	PREFERRED INVESTMENTS
Morocco	Ithmar Capital	2011	1,800	To support the implementation of Morocco's Vision 2020 strategic plan for tourism (initial mandate). In 2016, Ithmar's mandate was expanded from tourism to cover broader areas of the economy, with a geographic focus on both Morocco and the African continent. Ithmar is capitalized two-thirds by state funds and one-third by the Hassan II Fund, an entity wholly owned by the state.	Morocco	Diversified	Internal	Equity, fund of funds
Nigeria	Nigeria Sovereign Investment Authority (Nigeria Infrastructure Fund, NIF)	2012	650	To boost the development of the country's infrastructure, with the double bottom line goal of realizing a commercial return and investing in infrastructure that might otherwise not be financed and developed. NIF has a long-term investment horizon, exceeding 20 years, and acts exclusively as a provider of new funding, investing across the capital structure, from senior secured debt down to equity.	Nigeria	Infrastructure	Internal	Equity, debt, fund of funds

continued

TABLE B.1 *continued*

ECONOMY	NAME	YEAR	SIZE (US$, MILLIONS)	MANDATE	PRIMARY TARGET REGION	TARGET SECTORS	FUND MANAGER	PREFERRED INVESTMENTS
Oman	Oman Investment Fund[a]	2006	7,100	To build a diversified portfolio in the production and services sectors, projects, and other related fields, which does not contradict the objectives of other government funds of Oman. Oman Investment Fund is fully funded by the Ministry of Finance, Oman.	Oman	Diversified	—	—
Oman	Oman State General Reserve Fund (Local Initiatives Portfolio)[b]	1980	34,400	To target areas of economic and social value for the people of Oman and the economy as a whole.	Oman/global	Diversified	Internal and external	Equity, debt, fund of funds
Russian Federation	Russian Direct Investment Fund	2011	10,000	To make equity investments in strategic sectors within the Russian economy on a commercial basis by co-investing with large international investors in an effort to attract long-term direct investment capital. Every transaction is mandated to be co-invested with an international investor. Investment is predominately into Russia, with up to 20% allowed to be deployed outside of Russia.	Russia/global	Diversified	Internal	Equity
Rwanda	Agaciro Development Fund	2012	55	To build up public savings to achieve self-reliance, maintain stability in times of shocks to the national economy, and accelerate Rwanda's socioeconomic development goals.	Rwanda/global	Diversified	—	Equity, debt

continued

TABLE B.1 *continued*

ECONOMY	NAME	YEAR	SIZE (US$, MILLIONS)	MANDATE	PRIMARY TARGET REGION	TARGET SECTORS	FUND MANAGER	PREFERRED INVESTMENTS
Saudi Arabia	Public Investment Fund	1971	350,000	To contribute to the development and diversity of Saudi Arabia's economy, drive the diversification of the government's sources of income, launch new sectors in the local economy, and localize technology, knowledge, and innovation. To complement, enable, and partner with the private sector, by creating new opportunities through its investments.	Saudi Arabia	Diversified	Internal	Equity
Saudi Arabia	Saudi Arabian Industrial Investment Company (Dussur)	2014	156	To advance industrialization and diversification away from oil through the creation of profitable companies that might not be developed by the private sector alone. The company focuses on investments in Saudi Arabia through joint venture partnerships with global industry leaders, with each investment designed to be sustainable and active. To accelerate industrial development in Saudi Arabia by actively investing in or creating profitable entities in strategic industrial sectors leading to increased competitiveness of the sectors and increased private sector participation.	Saudi Arabia	Industrials	Internal	Equity

continued

TABLE B.1 *continued*

ECONOMY	NAME	YEAR	SIZE (US$, MILLIONS)	MANDATE	PRIMARY TARGET REGION	TARGET SECTORS	FUND MANAGER	PREFERRED INVESTMENTS
Senegal	Fonds Souverain d'Investissements Stratégiques S.A. (FONSIS)	2012	17	To invest or co-invest (with national and international partners) in strategic projects that generate financial and economic returns predominantly via equity or quasi equity. To support Senegalese SMEs through different vehicles including dedicated subfunds. To hold and manage equity stakes in SOEs and other assets on behalf of the state. To maintain and invest some financial reserves for the benefit of future generations.	Senegal	Diversified	Internal	Equity, quasi equity, fund of funds
Turkey	Turkey Wealth Fund	2016	40,000	To generate long-term and low-cost finance for strategic, large-scale investments contributing to Turkey's economic development. The fund was established with initial capital of TRY 50 million, although the state aims for growth up to TRY 722 billion (US$200 billion).	Turkey	Diversified	Internal	Equity
United Arab Emirates (Abu Dhabi)	Mubadala Investment Company	2002	225,000	To diversify the economy of Abu Dhabi, focusing on long-term investments that provide substantial financial returns, as well as social benefits to Abu Dhabi and the surrounding United Arab Emirates.	Abu Dhabi/global	Diversified	Internal	Equity
United Arab Emirates (Dubai)	Investment Corporation of Dubai	2006	230,000	To enhance Dubai's position as a global, competitive economy by investing in opportunities to protect and grow its wealth, and secure a prosperous future for its people.	Dubai/global	Diversified	Internal	—

continued

TABLE B.1 *continued*

ECONOMY	NAME	YEAR	SIZE (US$, MILLIONS)	MANDATE	PRIMARY TARGET REGION	TARGET SECTORS	FUND MANAGER	PREFERRED INVESTMENTS
Vietnam	State Capital Investment Corporation	2005	3,100	To monitor and invest capital on the basis of market mechanisms. To promote strategies to support market development, jobs, and economic growth in Vietnam; to reduce government ownership in domestic companies. To facilitate corporate restructuring and promote SOE reforms.	Vietnam	Diversified	Internal	Equity
West Bank and Gaza	Palestine Investment Fund	2003	760	To strengthen the local economy through strategic investments in underserved sectors, while maximizing long-run returns for the fund's ultimate shareholder—the people of West Bank and Gaza. The fund aims to do so by encouraging growth in the private sector by investing in socially responsible projects in vital economic sectors in West Bank and Gaza. Specificallly, it looks to promote job creation as a means to spur economic growth.	West Bank and Gaza/global	Diversified	Internal	Equity, debt

continued

TABLE B.1 *continued*

ECONOMY	NAME	YEAR	SIZE (US$, MILLIONS)	MANDATE	PRIMARY TARGET REGION	TARGET SECTORS	FUND MANAGER	PREFERRED INVESTMENTS
Zimbabwe	Zimbabwe Sovereign Wealth Fund	2014	—	To make secure investments for the benefit of future generations of Zimbabweans. To support the development objectives of the government, including its long-term economic and social development. To support fiscal or macroeconomic stabilization. To contribute to the revenues of Zimbabwe from the net returns on its investments.	Zimbabwe/global	Diversified	Internal	—

Sources: Strategic investment fund websites and World Bank.

Note: Table compiled with data collected between 2018 and 2019. Fund sizes and other details may have changed by the time of publication. — = not available; SME = small and medium enterprise; SOE = state-owned enterprise; TRY = Turkish lira.

a. In June 2020, the Oman Investment Fund merged with the Oman State General Reserve Fund to establish the Oman Investment Authority.

b. In June 2020, the Oman State General Reserve Fund merged with the Oman Investment Fund to establish the Oman Investment Authority.

TABLE B.2 Multinational strategic investment funds

ORIGINATOR	NAME	YEAR	SIZE (US$, MILLIONS)	MANDATE	PRIMARY TARGET REGION	TARGET SECTORS	FUND MANAGER	PREFERRED INVESTMENTS
Asian Development Bank (ADB)	Asia Climate Partners (ACP)	2014	450	To offer the largest, full-fledged private equity investment platform for environmental finance in emerging Asia. ACP partners with established environmental businesses, with sound operating fundamentals and strong growth potential that benefit from the rapid macroeconomic and environmental dynamics in the target regions.	Asia	Renewables and other green sectors	External	Equity
ADB, Algemene Pensioen Groep, Government Service Insurance System, and Macquarie	Philippine Investment Alliance for Infrastructure (PINAI)	2012	625	To invest in core infrastructure assets in the Philippines. PINAI is a 10-year private equity fund.	Philippines	Infrastructure	External	Equity, quasi equity, mezzanine
ADB, Belgian Investment Company for Developing Countries, Calvert, Deutsche Investitions- und Entwicklungsgesellschaft (DEG), FMO, Green Energy Efficiency and Renewable Energy Fund, and Overseas Private Investment Corporation (OPIC)	Renewable Energy Asia Fund (REAF I)	2009	100	To invest in small hydro, wind, geothermal, solar, landfill gas, and biomass projects in Asian developing markets, with a primary focus on India and the Philippines. It is fully invested.	Emerging Asia	Renewables and other green	External	Equity
African Development Bank (AfDB), through the Sustainable Energy Fund for Africa and the Climate Technology Fund	Africa Renewable Energy Fund	2014	200	To invest in small hydro, wind, geothermal, solar, and biomass projects across Sub-Saharan Africa, excluding South Africa.	Sub-Saharan (excluding South Africa)	Renewables and other green	External	Equity

continued

TABLE B.2 *continued*

ORIGINATOR	NAME	YEAR	SIZE (US$, MILLIONS)	MANDATE	PRIMARY TARGET REGION	TARGET SECTORS	FUND MANAGER	PREFERRED INVESTMENTS
AfDB and Central Bank of the States of West Africa	Africa50	2012	800	To help address the most pressing impediments to infrastructure provision on the continent. Africa50 helps develop a pipeline of bankable projects to mobilize public and private sector funding, and accelerate private investment into African infrastructure.	Africa	Infrastructure	Internal	Equity, quasi equity
AfDB, Development Bank of Southern Africa, and South Africa Government Employees Pension Fund	Pan-African Infrastructure Development Fund (PAIDF)	2007	625	To carry out diverse investments in all regions of Africa in infrastructure projects as well as investments in securities of companies that own, control, operate, or manage infrastructure and infrastructure-related assets, and also may participate in joint ventures with corporate and governmental partners. In addition to financial return objectives, PAIDF invests only in infrastructure projects with a favorable economic and social impact on the population and that respect good governance and transparency standards.	Africa	Infrastructure	External	Equity
Asian Infrastructure Investment Bank (AIIB)	Asia Investment Fund	2019	575	To mobilize private capital for infrastructure and other productive sectors by investing in noncontrolling equity stakes in companies in AIIB members via a fund.	Asia	Infrastructure and other sectors	External	Equity

continued

TABLE B.2 *continued*

ORIGINATOR	NAME	YEAR	SIZE (US$, MILLIONS)	MANDATE	PRIMARY TARGET REGION	TARGET SECTORS	FUND MANAGER	PREFERRED INVESTMENTS
Austria, Czech Republic, Hungary, Slovak Republic, and Slovenia, along with the European Investment Fund and International Investment Bank	Central Europe Fund of Funds	2017	97	To boost equity investments into SMEs and small mid-caps across the region, establishing a sound market-based risk financing infrastructure, implementing the best market standards for equity investments in businesses, and attracting institutional investors and investment managers to Central Europe.	Central European countries	SMEs and mid-caps	Internal	Equity, fund of funds
BGK Bank Poland, European Investment Bank (EIB), CDP France, CDP Italy, Instituto de Credito Oficial Spain, KfW Development Bank (KfW), and private Investors	Marguerite II	2017	855	To act as a catalyst for greenfield and brownfield infrastructure investments in renewables, energy, transport, and digital infrastructure, implementing key EU policies in the areas of climate change, energy security, digital agenda, and trans-European networks.	EU and accession countries	Infrastructure	External	Equity, quasi equity, mezzanine
CDP France, CDP Italy, EIB, Instituto de Credito Oficial Spain, KfW, and PKO Bank Polski	Marguerite I	2010	809	To make capital-intensive infrastructure investments within the EU. The first fund managed by Marguerite, the 2020 European Fund for Energy, Climate Change and Infrastructure (Marguerite I), was established in 2010 with the backing of six major European public financial institutions and the European Commission, with €710 million of commitments.	EU and accession countries	Infrastructure	External	Equity, quasi equity, mezzanine

continued

TABLE B.2 *continued*

ORIGINATOR	NAME	YEAR	SIZE (US$, MILLIONS)	MANDATE	PRIMARY TARGET REGION	TARGET SECTORS	FUND MANAGER	PREFERRED INVESTMENTS
China	China–Africa Development Fund (CADFund)	2007	5,000	To encourage and support Chinese enterprises to invest in Africa. CADFund focuses on solving the three bottlenecks (inadequate infrastructure, lack of professional and skilled personnel, and funding shortage) that Africa faces in its course of development. It supports the acceleration of the industrialization and agricultural modernization in Africa, and helps Africa to realize sustainable development on its own.	Africa and China	Diversified	Internal	Equity, quasi equity, fund of funds
China	China–Latin America Cooperation Fund	2016	10,000	To promote investment and economic and trade cooperation between China and Latin American and Caribbean countries, and actively participate in the development of their respective economies. To implement China's Belt and Road initiative. By providing financial and intellectual support, the fund actively assists and guides Chinese enterprises to "go global" and implement the 3x3 model of China-Latin production capacity cooperation.	Latin America and the Caribbean	Diversified	External	Equity
DEG, FMO, International Finance Corporation, Lereko, and South Africa PIC	Lereko Metier Sustainable Capital Fund	2013	120	To target investment in energy efficiency, renewables, and water and waste management businesses and projects supporting Africa's development objectives and environmental commitments.	Africa	Renewables and other green	Internal	Equity

continued

TABLE B.2 *continued*

ORIGINATOR	NAME	YEAR	SIZE (US$, MILLIONS)	MANDATE	PRIMARY TARGET REGION	TARGET SECTORS	FUND MANAGER	PREFERRED INVESTMENTS
European Union, Germany, Norway, and private investors	Green Energy Efficiency and Renewable Energy Fund (GEEREF)	2008	253	To invest public and private sector risk capital in specialist renewable energy and energy efficiency private equity funds developing small and medium-sized projects in emerging markets. Private investors contributed €110 million; the EU, Germany, and Norway €112 million.	Global emerging markets	Renewables and other green	Internal	Fund of funds
German Federal Ministry for Economic Cooperation and Development, Allianz Global Investors, DEG, and KfW	AfricaGrow Fund	2019	400	To be a fund of funds for African venture capital funds, with KfW providing a first-loss tranche to encourage additional investors on behalf of the German Federal Ministry of Economic Co-operation and Development. The network is meant to facilitate market entry of German small businesses and the expansion of businesses in African growth markets by informing European companies on investment opportunities in Africa and support instruments by the German government.	12 African states form part of the G20 Compact with Africa initiative: Benin; Burkina Faso; Côte d'Ivoire; Egypt, Arab Rep.; Ethiopia; Ghana; Guinea; Morocco; Rwanda; Senegal; Togo; and Tunisia.	Diversified	External	Fund of funds
Green Energy Efficiency and Renewable Energy Fund (GEEREF)	Renewable Energy Asia Fund (REAF II)	2016	200	To invest in small hydro, wind, geothermal, solar, and biomass projects in Asian developing markets, with a primary focus to date in India, Indonesia, and the Philippines.	Emerging Asia	Renewables and other green	External	Equity

continued

TABLE B.2 *continued*

ORIGINATOR	NAME	YEAR	SIZE (US$, MILLIONS)	MANDATE	PRIMARY TARGET REGION	TARGET SECTORS	FUND MANAGER	PREFERRED INVESTMENTS
Inter-American Development Bank and OPIC	Fund Mujer	2018	200	To narrow the gender financing gap in Latin America and the Caribbean by supporting investment strategies focused on women-owned businesses, female entrepreneurs, and firms that generate jobs or consumer products for women.	Latin America and the Caribbean	Diversified	Internal	Equity, debt
International Finance Corporation (IFC)	IFC Africa Capitalization Fund	2010	182	To make equity and equity-related investments in banking institutions throughout Africa.	Africa	Financial institutions	External	Equity, quasi equity
IFC	IFC Africa, Latin American and Caribbean Fund	2010	1,000	To make equity and equity-related investments in companies across Sub-Saharan Africa and Latin America and the Caribbean.	Africa and Latin America and the Caribbean	Diversified	External	Equity, quasi equity
IFC	IFC Capitalization (Equity) Fund	2009	1,275	To make equity and equity-related investments in systemic banks in developing countries.	Global emerging markets	Financial institutions	External	Equity, quasi equity
IFC	IFC Catalyst Fund	2012	418	To invest in private equity funds, platform companies, and co-investments focused on providing capital to renewable energy projects and to companies that develop resource-efficient, low-carbon products and services in emerging markets.	Global emerging markets	Renewables and other green	External	Fund of funds
IFC	IFC China-Mexico Fund	2014	1,200	To make equity, equity-related, and mezzanine investments in privately held companies in Mexico.	Latin America and the Caribbean	Diversified	External	Equity, quasi equity, mezzanine
IFC	IFC Emerging Asia Fund	2016	693	To make equity, equity-related, and mezzanine investments across all sectors in the emerging markets of Asia.	Asia (emerging)	Diversified	External	Equity, quasi equity, mezzanine

continued

TABLE B.2 *continued*

ORIGINATOR	NAME	YEAR	SIZE (US$, MILLIONS)	MANDATE	PRIMARY TARGET REGION	TARGET SECTORS	FUND MANAGER	PREFERRED INVESTMENTS
IFC	IFC Financial Institutions Growth Fund	2015	515	To invest in financial institutions (commercial banks, insurance companies, and other nonbank financial institutions) across global emerging markets.	Global emerging markets	Financial institutions	External	Equity
IFC	IFC Global Emerging Markets Fund of Funds	2015	800	To invest in private equity funds, secondaries, and co-investments in emerging markets.	Global emerging markets	Diversified	External	Fund of funds
IFC	IFC Global Infrastructure Fund	2013	1,200	To make equity and equity-related infrastructure investments in companies focused on power, transportation, water, telecommunications, oil, and gas sectors.	Global emerging markets	Infrastructure	External	Equity, quasi equity
IFC	IFC Middle East and North Africa Fund	2015	162	To make equity and equity-related investments in companies across the MENA region.	MENA	Diversified	External	Equity, quasi equity
Macquarie	Macquarie Mexican Infrastructure Fund (MMIF)	2010	550	To provide Mexican and international institutions with a vehicle to invest in a domestic infrastructure portfolio and contribute to the nation-building goals set out in the government's infrastructure plan. MMIF is Macquarie's first managed fund in Latin America, and is the first peso-denominated fund solely focused on investment opportunities in Mexican infrastructure projects.	Mexico	Infrastructure	External	Equity, quasi equity

continued

ORIGINATOR	NAME	YEAR	SIZE (US$, MILLIONS)	MANDATE	PRIMARY TARGET REGION	TARGET SECTORS	FUND MANAGER	PREFERRED INVESTMENTS
Private Infrastructure Development Group (PIDG) and funded by UK Foreign, Commonwealth & Development Office; Netherlands Directorate-General for International Cooperation (DGIS); and Switzerland State Secretariat for Economic Affairs (SECO)	Infraco Africa	2004	171	To provide funding and expertise to projects at their earliest stage, enabling them to grow from an initial concept to a bankable investment opportunity. Infraco Africa works with projects directly where they already have an experienced lead developer, or it can provide on-the-ground project development expertise through its own developer teams. It can also provide equity to fund the construction of pioneering projects or for innovative infrastructure businesses that need to scale up and demonstrate commercial viability to attract further investment.	Sub-Saharan Africa	Infrastructure	Internal	Equity
PIDG and funded by Australia's Department of Foreign Affairs and Trade, DGIS, SECO, UK Aid, and others	Infraco Asia	2009	130	To fund high-risk infrastructure development activities by taking an equity stake with a focus on socially responsible and commercially viable infrastructure projects that contribute to economic growth, social development, and poverty reduction.	South and Southeast Asia	Infrastructure	Internal	Equity, mezzanine

Sources: Strategic investment fund websites and World Bank.
Note: Table compiled with data collected between 2018 and 2019. Fund sizes and other details may have changed by the time of publication. MENA = Middle East and North Africa; SMEs = small and medium enterprises.

List of Interviewees

STRATEGIC INVESTMENT FUNDS

Interviews were conducted primarily between 2018 and 2019. Since then, interviewees may have left the organization or changed title or role. Several people in the following list were interviewed more than once.

Asia Climate Partners

Duarte da Silva, Managing Director, Southeast Asia

Shoji Misawa, Managing Director, Head of Operations

Rajat Narula, Associate

Fleur Parkinson, ESG [Environmental, Social, and Governance] Manager

Cilia Sze, Director, Head of Finance and Operations

CDP Equity

Angelo Cortese, Head, Equity Risk Management and Chief Risk Officer

Fonds Souverain d'Investissements Stratégiques (Sovereign Fund for Strategic Investments) (FONSIS)

Serigne Dame Diakhoumpa, Executive Director, Fundraising and Chief Financial Officer

Papa Demba Diallo, Chief Executive Officer (At the time of the interview, Mr. Diallo was the Executive Director for Information and Communication Technology and Services at FONSIS; as of this writing, he is the Chief Executive Officer of FONSIS.)

Ndèye Diago Dieye, Investment Manager

Ibrahima Kane, (former) Chief Executive Officer

Mamadou Mbaye, Executive Director, Energy and Mines

Ireland Strategic Investment Fund

Kieran Bristow, Senior Investment Director

Joanne Conlon, Legal Counsel

Aoife Gibson, Senior Legal Advisor, National Treasury Management Agency

Alison Hodge, Senior Legal Advisor

Evelyn Leen, Senior Investment Manager

Eugene O'Callaghan, Director

Adrian O'Donovan, Secretary, National Treasury Management Agency

Susan O'Halloran, Legal Counsel

Khazanah Nasional Berhad

Tengku Dato' Sri Azmil, Deputy Managing Director and Head of Investments

Nicholas Khaw Hock-Lu, Senior Vice President, Investment Strategy

Ahmad Zulqarnain Onn, Deputy Managing Director

Hafriz Abdul Rahman, Vice President, Risk Management

Dato' Mohamed Nasri Sallehuddin, Chief Legal Officer

Suhana Dewi Selamat, Head, Governance, Risk, and Compliance

Marguerite Investment Management SA

David Harrison, Managing Partner and Chief Financial Officer

Nicolas Merigó, Managing Partner and Chief Executive Officer

Adrian Pawelec, Partner and Legal Counsel

National Investment and Infrastructure Fund

Sujoy Bose, Chief Executive Officer

Rajiv Dhar, Chief Operating Officer and Executive Committee

Saloni Jhaveri, Head, Investor Relations

Prakash Rao, Executive Director

Nigeria Sovereign Investment Authority–Nigeria Infrastructure Fund

Hanspeter Ackermann, Chief Investment Officer and Executive Director

Richard Eckrich, Head, Nigeria Infrastructure Fund

Stella Ojekwe-Onyejeli, Executive Director and Chief Operating Officer

Ezinwa Okoroafor, Legal Counsel

Uche Orji, Chief Executive Officer

Palestine Investment Fund

Abed Al-Abwah, Chief Audit Executive

OTHER ORGANIZATIONS

Interviews were conducted primarily between 2018 and 2019. Since then, interviewees may have left the organization or changed title or role. Several people in the following list were interviewed more than once.

Africa50

Raza Hasnani, Head of Project Finance

Asian Development Bank

Janette Hall, Director, Investment Funds and Special Initiatives

European Investment Bank

Barbara Boos, Head, Equity Funds

GuarantCo

Lasitha Perera, Chief Executive Officer

Hunton Andrews Kurth

James Comyn, Partner

InfraCredit

Chinua Azubike, Chief Executive Officer

International Finance Corporation

Johanna Klein, Principal, IFC Asset Management Company Catalyst Fund

Maria Kozloski, IFC Private Equity Funds

Nicholas Vickery, IFC Private Equity Funds

K&L Gates

Margaret Niles, Partner

Charles Purcell, Partner

Meridiam

Joe Aiello, Partner and Board Member (retired)

Mathieu Peller, Chief Operating Officer, Africa Group

Mountain Pacific Group

Leo de Bever, Senior Advisor

Ropes & Gray

Timothy Diggins, Partner

Daniel Kolb, Partner

Rothschild Global Advisory

Solomon Adegbie-Quaynor, Senior Advisor, Emerging Markets

UDO Udoma & Belo-Asagie

Nicholas Okafor, Partner

World Bank

Richard Claudet, Senior Financial Sector Specialist

Henri Fortin, Lead Financial Management Specialist

Don Purka, Senior Infrastructure Finance Specialist

Bibliography

ACP (Asia Climate Partners). 2018. "Strategic Investment Funds—ACP Case Study." Presentation shared by ACP team, ACP, Hong Kong SAR, China.

ADB (Asian Development Bank). 2003. "Gender and Development." Policy Paper, ADB, Manila. https://www.adb.org/sites/default/files/institutional-document/32035/gender-policy.pdf.

ADB (Asian Development Bank). 2009. "Safeguard Policy Statement." Policy Paper, ADB, Manila.

ADB (Asian Development Bank). 2016. "Development Impact Report to Asia Climate Partners Limited Partners." ADB, Manila.

Ambachtsheer, Keith. 2011. "How Should Pension Funds Pay Their Own People?" *Rotman International Journal of Pension Management* 4 (1): 18–25.

Ashbaugh, Hollis, Daniel W. Collins, and Ryan LaFond. 2004. "Corporate Governance and the Cost of Equity Capital." http://w4.stern.nyu.edu/accounting/docs/speaker_papers/fall 2004/Hollis_Ashbaugh_10-20-04-nyu-emory.pdf.

Auerbach, A. J., and K. A. Hassett. 2003. "On the Marginal Source of Investment Funds." *Journal of Public Economics* 87 (1): 205–32.

Benton, Gary. 2017. "Arbitrating Private Investment Disputes: Private Equity, Venture Capital and other Private Placements." College of Commercial Arbitrators. https://www.ccarbitrators .org/wp-content/uploads/2021/05/Private-Investment-Disputes.pdf.

Bernstein, Shai, Josh Lerner, and Antoinette Shoar. 2009. "The Investment Strategies of Sovereign Wealth Funds." NBER Working Paper 14861, National Bureau of Economic Research, Cambridge, MA.

Bertram, R., and B. Zvan. 2009. "Pension Funds and Incentive Compensation: A Story Based on the Ontario Teachers' Experience." *Rotman International Journal of Pension Management* 2 (1): 30–33.

Blundell-Wignall, A., Y. Hu, and J. Yermo. 2008. "Sovereign Wealth and Pension Fund Issues." OECD Working Papers on Insurance and Private Pensions, No. 14, Organization for Economic Co-operation and Development, Paris. http://www.oecd.org/finance /private-pensions/40345767.pdf.

Buchanan, Christine, and Shruti Shah. 2017. "Safeguarding Private Equity Firms: Six Key Risk Management Strategies to Head Off Trouble." KPMG. https://assets.kpmg/content/dam /kpmg/us/pdf/2017/03/us-private-equity-safeguarding-private-equity-firms.pdf.

BVCA (British Venture Capital Association). 2002. "Limited Partnership Agreement: Explanatory Notes." BVCA, London. https://www.bvca.co.uk/Portals/0/library/Files /StandardIndustryDocuments/LPAgreement.pdf?ver=2013-06-14-113435-360.

BVCA (British Venture Capital Association). 2010. "A Guide to Private Equity." BVCA, London. https://www.bvca.co.uk/Portals/0/library/Files/Website%20files/2012_0001_guide_to _private_equity.pdf.

Cambridge Associates. 2014. "Sector-Focused Private Equity Funds Often Outperform Generalists and Should Be Considered When Building Portfolios, Says Cambridge Associates Report." Press release, November 12, 2014. https://www.cambridgeassociates.com /press-releases/sector-focused-private-equity-funds-often-outperform-generalists-and -should-be-considered-when-building-portfolios-says-cambridge-associates-report/.

Chow, Eric. 2019. "Mergers and Acquisitions: Overview of a Transaction." DLA Piper LLP. https://www.dlapiperaccelerate.com/knowledge/2017/mergers-and-acquisitions-overview -of-a-transaction.html.

Divakaran, Shanthi, Johanna Klein, Anthony Njoroge, and Andrea Onate. Forthcoming. "Are Government Set-Up SME Funds Doomed to Fail?"

EMPEA (Emerging Markets Private Equity Association). 2012. "EMPEA Guidelines: Key Elements of Legal and Tax Regimes Optimal for the Development of Private Equity." EMPEA. https://www.empea.org/empea-guidelines/.

EVCA (European Venture Capital Association). 2012. "EVCA Handbook: Professional Standards for the Private Equity and Venture Capital Industry." EVCA. https://www.investeurope.eu /uploadedFiles/Home/Toolbox/Industry_Standards/FINAL%20EVCA%20 Handbook%20of%20Professional%20Standards%20180112.pdf.

Fang, Lily, Victoria Ivashina, and Josh Lerner. 2015. "The Disintermediation of Financial Markets: Direct Investing in Private Equity." *Journal of Financial Economics* 116 (1): 160–78.

Gelb, Alan, Silvana Tordo, and Håvard Halland. 2014. "Sovereign Wealth Funds and Domestic Investment in Resource-Rich Countries: Love Me, or Love Me Not?" *World Bank – Economic Premise*, Issue 133.

Green Investment Group. 2017. "Annual Report and Financial Statements 2016–17." Green Investment Group. http://greeninvestmentgroup.com/media/185901/gib-annual-report -2016-17-final.pdf.

Green Investment Group. 2017. "Green Purposes Company Statement on GIB Sale." Green Investment Group. http://greeninvestmentgroup.com/news-and-insights/2017/green -purposes-company-statement-on-gib-sale/.

Haberly, Daniel. 2011. "Strategic Sovereign Wealth Fund Investment and the New Alliance Capitalism: A Network Mapping Investigation." *Environment and Planning A: Economy and Space* 43 (8): 1833–52.

Hamilton, Ron, and Alexander Berg. 2008. "Corporate Governance of SOEs in Zambia." Unpublished.

Hsu, Po-Hsuan, Hao Liang, and Pedro Matos. 2018. "Leviathan Inc. and Corporate Environmental Engagement." Darden Business School Working Paper No. 2960832; ECGI – Finance Working Paper No. 526/2017. https://ssrn.com/abstract=2960832.

IDFC (International Development Finance Club). 2015. "IDFC Green Finance Mapping For 2014." IDFC, Frankfurt.

IFSWF (International Forum of Sovereign Wealth Funds). 2011. "IFSWF Members' Experiences in the Application of the Santiago Principles." Report prepared by IFSWF Sub-Committee 1 and the Secretariat in collaboration with the Members of the IFSWF.

IMF (International Monetary Fund). 2008. "The Statistical Work on Sovereign Wealth Funds." Twenty-First Meeting of the IMF Committee on Balance of Payments Statistics BOPCOM-08/19, IMF, Washington, DC.

IMF (International Monetary Fund). 2013. "Sovereign Wealth Funds: Aspects of Governance Structures and Investment Management." IMF Working Paper 13/231, IMF, Washington, DC.

J.P. Morgan Asset Management. 2018. "Portfolio Insights. Investing in Private Equity." J.P. Morgan.

McCahery, Joseph, and F. Alexander de Roode. 2017. "Co-investments of Sovereign Wealth Funds in Private Equity." In *The Oxford Handbook of Sovereign Wealth Funds*, edited by Douglas Cumming, Geoffrey Wood, Igor Filatotchev, and Juliane Reinecke. Oxford: Oxford University Press.

Metrick, Andrew, and Ayako Yasuda. 2010. "The Economics of Private Equity Funds." *Review of Financial Studies* 23 (6): 2303–41.

Myers, Stewart C. 1984. "The Capital Structure Puzzle." *Journal of Finance* 39 (3): 574–92.

Natural Resource Governance Institute. 2015. "Legal Framework Navigating the Web of Laws and Contracts Governing Extractive Industries." *NRGI Reader,* March 2015. https://resourcegovernance.org/sites/default/files/nrgi_Legal-Framework.pdf.

NBIM (Norges Bank Investment Management). 2011. "Compensation Principles for Norges Bank Investment Management Employees." NBIM. https://www.nbim.no/en/organisation/governance-model/executive-board-documents/compensation-principles-for-norges-bank-investment-management-employees/.

NSIA (Nigeria Sovereign Investment Authority). 2013. "Audit Committee Charter." NSIA, Abuja.

NSIA (Nigeria Sovereign Investment Authority). 2013. "Compensation Committee Charter." NSIA, Abuja.http://nsia.com.ng/~nsia/sites/default/files/downloads/6.%20Compensation%20Committee%20Charter.pdf.

NSIA (Nigeria Sovereign Investment Authority). 2013. "Direct Investment Committee Charter." NSIA, Abuja. http://nsia.com.ng/sites/default/files/downloads/3.%20Direct%20Investment%20Committee%20Charter.pdf.

NSIA (Nigeria Sovereign Investment Authority). 2017. Consolidated and Separate Financial Statements for the Year Ended 31 December 2017. NSIA, Abuja. http://www.nsia.com.ng/~nsia/sites/default/files/annual-reports/2017%20Audited%20Financial%20Statement_0.pdf.

NSIA (Nigeria Sovereign Investment Authority). 2017. "Infrastructure Fund Investment Policy Statement." NSIA, Abuja. http://nsia.com.ng/~nsia/sites/default/files/downloads/Nigeria%20Infrastructure%20Fund%20Investment%20Policy%20Statement%20-%20April%2016%202018_0.pdf.

NSIA (Nigeria Sovereign Investment Authority). 2018. "Infrastructure Fund Investment Compliance Report December 2018." NSIA, Abuja.

NTMA (National Treasury Management Agency). 2017. "Audit and Risk Committee Terms of Reference." NTMA, Dublin, February.

NTMA (National Treasury Management Agency). 2017). "Remuneration Committee Terms of Reference." NTMA, Dublin, March.

NTMA (National Treasury Management Agency). 2017). "Investment Committee Terms of Reference." NTMA, Dublin, November.

OECD (Organisation for Economic Co-operation and Development). 2011. "Competitive Neutrality and State-Owned Enterprises: Challenges and Policy Options." Corporate Governance Working Paper 1, OECD Publishing, Paris.

OECD (Organisation for Economic Co-operation and Development). 2016. G20/OECD Support Note on Diversification of Financial Instruments for Infrastructure. OECD, Paris. https://www.oecd.org/finance/private-pensions/G20-OECD-Support-Note-on-Diversification-of-Financial-Instruments-for-Infrastructure.pdf.

OECD (Organisation for Economic Co-operation and Development). 2018. *Making Blended Finance Work for the Sustainable Development Goals.* Paris: OECD Publishing.

Pham, Peter Kien, Jo-Ann Suchard, and Jason Zein. 2012. "Corporate Governance, Cost of Capital and Performance: Evidence from Australian Firms." *Journal of Applied Corporate Finance* 24 (3): 84–93.

Pouget, Sophie. 2013. "Arbitrating and Mediating Disputes: Benchmarking Arbitration and Mediation Regimes for Commercial Disputes Related to Foreign Direct Investment." Policy Research Working Paper 6632, World Bank, Washington, DC.

Preqin. 2018a. *Preqin Global Infrastructure Report—Sample Pages.* Preqin. https://docs.preqin.com/reports/2018-Preqin-Global-Infrastructure-Report-Sample-Pages.pdf.

Preqin. 2018b. *The 2018 Preqin Sovereign Wealth Fund Review—Sample Pages.* Preqin. https://docs.preqin.com/reports/The-2018-Preqin-Sovereign-Wealth-Fund-Review-Sample-Pages.pdf.

Preqin. 2018c. "Preqin Special Report: Sovereign Wealth Funds." Preqin, August. https://docs.preqin.com/reports/Preqin-Special-Report-Sovereign-Wealth-Funds-August-2018.pdf.

Preqin. 2018d. "Private Equity Industry Grows to More Than \$3tn in Assets." Press release, July 24, 2019. https://docs.preqin.com/press/PE-Assets-Jul-18.pdf.

Preqin. 2019. "Preqin Quarterly Update: Infrastructure. Q1 2019." Preqin. https://docs.preqin .com/quarterly/inf/Preqin-Quarterly-Update-Infrastructure-Q1-2019.pdf.

Preqin. 2019. "Preqin Quarterly Update: Private Equity & Venture Capital. Q1 2019." Preqin. https://docs.preqin.com/quarterly/pe/Preqin-Quarterly-Update-Private-Equity-Q1 -2019.pdf.

Preqin. 2019. "Private Debt Industry Keeps Up Its Momentum." Press release, February 21, 2019. https://docs.preqin.com/press/GPDR-Launch-2019.pdf.

PwC. 2016. "Sovereign Investors 2020: A Growing Force." PwC. https://www.pwc.com/gx/en /sovereign-wealth-investment-funds/publications/assets/sovereign-investors-2020.pdf.

Rearick, Andrew C., and David P. Iozzi. 2012. "The Many Shades of Co-Investing," Debevoise and Plimpton, Summer/Fall 2012, Vol. 13, Number 1. https://www.debevoise.com/insights /publications/2014/02/the-many-shades-of-coinvesting.

Republic of Senegal. 2014. "Plan Sénégal Emergent." https://www.economie.gouv.sn/en /dossiers-publications/publications/pse.

Robbins, Adam. 2014. "Sovereign Wealth Fund Governance: A Statistical and Cluster Analysis." Unpublished.

Rozenberg, Julie, and Marianne Fay, eds. 2019. *Beyond the Gap. How Countries Can Afford the Infrastructure They Need while Protecting the Planet.* Washington, DC: World Bank Group.

Stone, Sarah E., and Edwin M. Truman. 2016. "Uneven Progress on Sovereign Wealth Fund Transparency and Accountability." Policy Bulletin 16-18, Peterson Institute for International Economics, Washington, DC.

Wells, Peter. 2016. "Temasek Brings in Top European Advisers." *Financial Times*, January 20, 2016. https://www.ft.com/content/7addbded-0422-340f-9229-c3d7a9bc57a8.

World Bank. 2004. *Corporate Governance of State-Owned Enterprises: A Toolkit.* Washington, DC: World Bank. https://openknowledge.worldbank.org/bitstream/handle /10986/20390/9781464802225.pdf?sequence=1&isAllowed=y.

World Bank and FIRST Initiative. 2015. "Principles for Public Credit Guarantee Schemes for SMEs." World Bank, Washington, DC. http://documents.worldbank.org/curated /en/576961468197998372/pdf/101769-REVISED-ENGLISH-Principles-CGS-for-SMEs.pdf.

World Bank Group and International Monetary Fund. 2018. "G20 Note: Improving Public Debt Recording, Monitoring, and Reporting Capacity in Low and Lower-Middle-Income Countries: Proposed Reforms." World Bank Group and International Monetary Fund, Washington, DC. https://documents1.worldbank.org/curated/en/645621532695126092 /pdf/128723-repo-For-VP-IMPROVING-PUBLIC-DEBT-RECORDING-clean.pdf.

Zhu, Feifei. 2009. "Cost of Capital and Corporate Governance: International Evidence." University of Wisconsin, Milwaukee. https://www.researchgate.net/publication /228775167_Cost_of_Capital_and_Corporate_Governance_International_Evidence.